Stephen King Films
FAQ

Series Editor: Robert Rodriguez

Stephen King Films FAQ

Everything Left to Know About the King of Horror on Film

Scott Von Doviak

APPLAUSE
THEATRE & CINEMA BOOKS
An Imprint of Hal Leonard Corporation

Published in 2014 by Applause Theatre & Cinema Books

An Imprint of Hal Leonard Corporation
7777 West Bluemound Road
Milwaukee, WI 53213

Trade Book Division Editorial Offices
33 Plymouth St., Montclair, NJ 07042

The FAQ series was conceived by Robert Rodriguez and developed with Stuart Shea.

All images are from the author's collection.

Printed in the United States of America

Book design by Snow Creative Services

Library of Congress Cataloging-in-Publication Data

Von Doviak, Scott, 1967–
   Stephen King films FAQ : all that's left to know about the king of horror on film / Scott Von Doviak.
     pages cm
   Includes bibliographical references and index.
   ISBN 978-1-4803-5551-4 (pbk.)
1. King, Stephen, 1947—Film adaptations. 2. American fiction—20th century—Film adaptations. 3. Horror films—History and criticism. I. Title.
   PS3561.I483Z913 2014
   791.43'6164—dc23
                                                              2013041907

www.applausebooks.com

This one's dedicated to that old gang of mine from the haunted halls of Charlesgate, our very own Overlook Hotel.

Contents

Skeleton Crew: Short Subjects

Creepshows: Miniseries, TV Series, and TV-Movies

Sometimes They Come Back: Sequels and Remakes

Rock-Bottom Remainders: Oddities and Ephemera

Acknowledgments

Writing this book proved to be a far more massive undertaking than I had originally envisioned, and it could not have been done without the help of the following individuals:

Mike Edison, who edited my previous book for Hal Leonard, *If You Like The Terminator*, and then immediately asked, "What else you got?" Mike helped shepherd this book through its early stages, and it probably would not exist without him.

Marybeth Keating, my editor on this project, and FAQ series editor Robert Rodriguez. Marybeth was not only invaluable in helping me shape this book into its current form, but displayed infinite patience in answering all my questions along the way. Rob was also quick to respond to any of my questions about the FAQ series.

Desirée Butterfield-Nagy, archivist and special collections librarian at the Raymond H. Fogler Library at the University of Maine in Orono. Desirée helped me secure permission to sift through the Stephen Edwin King Special Collection and arranged for my requested items to be retrieved from storage.

Marsha DeFilippo, personal assistant to Stephen King, who granted permission for me to access the Special Collection.

Filmmakers Shawn S. Lealos, John Campopiano, and Justin White for submitting to interviews.

Hayden Childs and William Ham, cofounders of pop culture webzine *The High Hat* (http://www.thehighhat.com/), for which I wrote the column "The Bottom Shelf." Portions of my column on the subject of Stephen King movies (issue 9's "Maine Attractions") have been repurposed for this volume.

In addition to the books listed in the bibliography, I need to make special mention of several invaluable resources. Back issues of *Cinefantastique* and *Fangoria*, particularly from the eighties and nineties, are jam-packed with in-depth reports on the making of many King films. Several issues of the long-defunct Stephen King newsletter *Castle Rock*, which I happened to find in the closet of my old bedroom in the house I grew up in, also came in handy. A number of online fan sites proved useful, none more so than Lilja's Library (http://www.liljas-library.com/), a treasure trove of interviews and useful links. And I'm lucky enough to live in a city (Austin, Texas) that's still home to several thriving video stores, notably Vulcan Video and I Luv Video. Many of the more obscure items covered in this book were found on their shelves.

Special thanks to Shasta Blaustein, Ernie Cline, Jennifer Hill-Robenalt, Jaime Nelson, Leonard Pierce, and Davey Schmitt-Schrenker.

Introduction
The Maine Attraction

In the summer of 1980, a few weeks before my 13th birthday, I saw my first R-rated movie in a theater. I tagged along with my friend Paul and his family to the Maine Coast Cinemas in Ellsworth for a matinee show of *The Shining*. I wasn't sure what to expect, but the TV ads had been enough to terrify me, so I approached the movie with the sort of trepidation reserved for particularly daunting roller coasters. And indeed, I did watch portions of Stanley Kubrick's film with fingers poised over my eyes, ready to block out anything that might prove too nightmarish for my adolescent sensibilities.

As it turned out, however, the film affected me in ways I couldn't have predicted beforehand. The scares were primarily psychological and difficult to pin down. Why were those two little girls standing at the end of the hallway so unnerving? Why was a thick stack of paper consisting of one sentence typed over and over again one of the most horrifying images I'd ever seen? What was the deal with that guy in the bear suit? I needed to know more, so as soon as the movie ended, I popped into Mr. Paperback and emerged seconds later with a paperback copy of *The Shining*, a novel by Stephen King. I began reading it in the car on the way home from the movie and continued deep into the night, long after everyone else in my house had gone to bed. Did I sleep with the light on that night? There's a pretty good chance I did.

I didn't know much about King at the time, but I was at least aware he was a Maine author who lived not so far from that well-lit bedroom where I devoured *The Shining*. In truth, the book wasn't much help in shedding light on Kubrick's film. They were completely different entities (as will be discussed in detail within these pages), and I loved them both for different reasons. King wasn't a tenth the stylist Kubrick was, but he had narrative gifts to burn. His version of the Overlook cast its own sort of spell over me, and I could hardly turn the pages fast enough.

Over the course of that summer and into the fall, I made my way through all the Stephen King works available at the time: *Carrie*, *'Salem's Lot*, *Night Shift*, *The Stand*, and *The Dead Zone*. I reread *The Shining* several times, and when *Firestarter* became available through the book-of-the-month club, I ordered it and read that, too. And then something happened that seems hilarious and unimaginable now: There was no more Stephen King to read! When *Cujo* was published in the fall of 1981, I despaired of waiting a full year for the paperback, but that Christmas, I found the hardcover waiting under the tree for me. It was the beginning of a tradition that would last nearly thirty years, as my mother, who had enjoyed reading through my stack of King paperbacks as well, made sure that each Christmas morning would bring me the latest from the master of horror.

Of course, that initial obsessive period passed, as I moved on to other interests, but it was always reassuring to know—whether I was attending college in Boston, struggling to find a foothold in the movie industry in Los Angeles, or establishing my writing career in Austin—that each Christmas would bring me back to the house I grew up in on the coast of Maine, where a new King volume awaited under the tree. I can't say I read them all immediately (or at all in some cases), but every now and then one of them would grab me in the same way that initial batch of paperbacks had when I was thirteen, and I'd find myself turning the pages late into the night in my old bedroom, as the winter wind howled outside.

I'm back in that bedroom right now, except this time instead of reading a Stephen King book, I'm writing one. It's the week between Christmas and the New Year, and I'm home for a few days. My mother passed away in January 2011, less than a month after one final Christmas with King under the tree (the novella collection *Full Dark, No Stars*), so it's just me and Dad in the house right now. A nor'easter is blowing outside, rattling the windowpanes, and that familiar old wind is whistling through the rafters. We've already lost the power once today, and the sun is setting early, as it does this time of year. It's perfect Stephen King weather, I think you'd have to agree.

But this is not a book about the novels of Stephen King (although, of course, those are touched on in passing), nor is it a biography of the author (although biographical details are included when warranted). This is a book about movies. In a way, it's been more than three decades in the making, dating back to that summer afternoon when I first saw *The Shining*. The first VCR was introduced into our household in the early eighties, just in time for the boom of Stephen King movies around that time. Between August 1983 and May 1984, five King adaptations were released in theaters, a glut that led to a string of "King-movie-of-the-month" jokes from critics and talk show comics. All of these movies reached video store shelves within a few months of each other, and I distinctly remember a late-night marathon of *Cujo*, *The Dead Zone*, and *Christine* courtesy of my local mom-and-pop rental emporium.

Go to Stephen King's page on the Internet Movie Database today, and you'll find over 160 movies, miniseries, and TV shows credited to the master of horror. It's no exaggeration to say that "Stephen King" has become a genre unto itself, and like any movie genre, it's one worthy of study. No one could make the claim that all of these films are worth seeing and keep a straight face; quite a few of them are terrible, and King himself would be the first to agree (and has, on many occasions). But sift through the filmography and you'll find a handful of acknowledged classics, a few underappreciated gems, some entertaining failures, and even an overrated white elephant or two.

Among other things, this is a book about adaptation. What does it mean for a film to be faithful to its source? How can a movie stick closely to the plot, dialogue, and characterizations of the novel on which it's based and still fail to convey the book's spirit or the voice of its author? Is fidelity to the source really that important, or should the filmmakers feel free to use the written work as a jumping-off point to create a unique work of art? Why is the one movie that's both written and directed by Stephen King actually one of the least satisfying King adaptations of all? And why is the greatest of all King adaptations so dissatisfying to the author himself?

In writing this book, one of my primary objectives is to synthesize as much information about the subject as possible into one self-contained volume: That is, after all, what the *FAQ* series is all about. This is not the first book on the subject of Stephen King movies, but I am quite confident that it is the most comprehensive (so far, anyway; time marches on, and the tide of King adaptations shows no sign of slowing). In these pages, you'll find all of the theatrical releases, television productions, and straight-to-video cheapo sequels made to date. You'll also find chapters on the "Dollar Babies" (student shorts sanctioned by King for the price of a buck), the films that never were, and those yet to come. But that's not all! You'll also find a thumbnail history of the horror genre, with a special focus on those films that most influenced the young Stephen King. We'll explore King's works in other media, including comic books, radio plays, and the ill-fated *Carrie* musical. Many chapters will feature special "Bloodlines" sections, offering a selection of non-King movies for further study, as well as "Deep Cuts" segments delving deep into trivia related to these productions.

Because I don't want this book to read like a series of Wikipedia entries, you'll also find my critical reaction and analysis of all the adaptations discussed in these pages. My approach will be irreverent and (I hope) humorous where warranted, but above all honest: I don't see any point in pretending all (or even most of) the works discussed herein would be best served by a dry, academic approach. Some King-related books have followed that path, to their detriment, I think. For the most part, we're dealing with popcorn movies here; in another time, they'd best be seen at a drive-in on a hot night, with a cold six-pack on hand. That said, my opinions don't always line up with the critical consensus or the majority of King fans. If I prefer *The Mist* to *The Shawshank Redemption*—and, spoiler alert, I do—I'm going to say so.

You don't have to read this book in order; hell, it wasn't *written* in order. Feel free to dip into the chapters that most interest you first and skip over those that don't grab you. But if you *do* read it in order, I think you'll find a narrative thread of some interest, about a Hollywood outsider who seized more control as his clout within that weird, insular world grew more powerful. This is my third published book, and in many ways, it was the hardest to write. The sheer volume of material became overwhelming at times. But it all stems from a place of affection; no matter how critical or snarky I may be within these pages, it's really the story of a three decade-plus relationship between an extraordinarily prolific creative force and one of his millions of admirers.

Whatever you may think of his work, King has a remarkable talent for connecting with what he calls his "constant readers." Our paths have crossed—at a stoplight in Brewer, Maine; at a matinee show of *Stand by Me* in Bangor; at the movie memorabilia store in Harvard Square I managed for a year after college—but I'd be lying if I said I know Stephen King. Yet I can't help but feel like I do, and if you're reading this book, you probably do, too. For me, it all dates back to that summer afternoon in 1980 when I saw *The Shining*—when the magic of the movies took hold of me and carried me on a journey that led me back to this bedroom I grew up in on the coast of Maine. It's pitch-black outside and the snow is falling. There's not a car on the road outside my window, and not a creature is stirring inside. It's Stephen King time.

Apt Pupil

Precursors and Influences

Abominations

Birth of a Genre

The Silent Scream

It always seems to start with Georges Méliès. The French stage magician turned silent film pioneer directed what is generally regarded as the first science fiction film, 1902's *A Trip to the Moon*. But six years before that groundbreaking piece of cinema, Méliès made a three-minute short called *Le manoir du diable*, literally translated as "Manor of the Devil" but also known by the English title *The Haunted Castle*. With its ghosts in sheets, creepy skeletons, and bat that transforms into a demonic figure (played by Méliès himself), it's certainly no stretch to call *Le manoir du diable* the first horror film.

There's no reason to believe Stephen King was especially familiar with the works of Méliès when he began writing horror stories in the early 1960s—indeed, he's often made it clear that his taste in movies ran toward drive-in fare like *Them!* and *Creature from the Black Lagoon*. But for our purposes, it hardly matters whether King was directly influenced by the earliest horror films. This book is about movies, after all, and the dozens of filmmakers who have tackled King's material over the years all owe a substantial debt to what has come before. What follows is not intended as any kind of comprehensive history of the horror movie genre; there are a number of fine volumes you can seek out for further study, if so inclined. Instead, these first few chapters offer a thumbnail sketch of the genre's evolution from the earliest days of cinema to the arrival of Stephen King as a dominating force in the horror field.

What's most striking about the dawn of horror movies, at least for the uninitiated, is how early on some of the most enduring icons of the genre made their film debuts. Most of us would agree on the original Big Three of literary horror: Mary Shelley's *Frankenstein*, Bram Stoker's *Dracula*, and Robert Louis Stevenson's *Dr. Jekyll and Mr. Hyde*. (In fact, an omnibus edition of all three novels was published in 1978, featuring an introduction penned by—you guessed it—Stephen King.) Of the three, *Frankenstein* made its way to the screen first, in a 1910 short produced by the Edison Manufacturing Company. As directed by J. Searle Dawley, this twelve-minute take on the Shelley classic is almost comically skimpy on exposition (after opening with a short scene of Frankenstein heading off to college, a title card reading "TWO YEARS LATER FRANKENSTEIN HAS

DISCOVERED THE MYSTERY OF LIFE" appears), but it's easy to imagine audiences being genuinely frightened by some of the film's effects. The creature's emergence from Frankenstein's vat of chemicals is obscured—we could be looking at the flaming skeleton of some enormous insect or reptile—and when the abomination is finally revealed, it looks more like a rotting Alice Cooper than the classic Frankenstein's monster to come. Grotesque makeup, it seems, has been a staple of the horror film since the beginning.

By 1920, Stevenson's *Dr. Jekyll and Mr. Hyde* had been adapted for the screen no less than five times. Like so many early silents, the 1908 version is lost to history, but those made in 1912 and 1913 persist, and can be found easily on YouTube. (Of the two, the 1912 take features the more impressive transformations, while the tedious 1913 attempt visualizes Mr. Hyde by way of Moe Howard.) A forty-minute 1920 adaptation was largely overshadowed by the feature-length version starring John Barrymore (grandfather of *Firestarter* and *Cat's Eye* star Drew Barrymore) released the same year. Barrymore eschewed elaborate makeup in his depiction of the fearsome Mr. Hyde; aside from the prosthetics used to give Hyde tendril-like fingers, the actor relied on facial contortions to convey Dr. Jekyll's transformation into his darker self.

That leaves Dracula, who would not reach the screen under that name until the 1931 release of the beloved Bela Lugosi adaptation that kicked off the Universal Pictures monster cycle. But Bram Stoker's vampire did appear under an alias in one of the great motion pictures of all time—one made in Germany as part of a film movement that would cast a shadow over the horror genre for decades to come.

Nosferatu and German Expressionism

A darkness gripped Germany in the years following the First World War. The country was economically devastated and forced to pay billions in reparations, the Weimar Republic government struggled to maintain order, and food shortages resulted in death by starvation for hundreds of thousands. But as so often happens during dark times, when people yearn for some escape from or meaningful reflection of an unpleasant reality, the arts thrived. Postwar Berlin was a cultural hotbed, home to the Bauhaus school, the Brecht collective, and Expressionism, a new strain of cinema drawing not only on art movements of the time such as Cubism and Fauvism, but on the collective fears and lingering nightmares of the German people.

One of the earliest German Expressionist films, and perhaps the most extreme of them all, was 1920's *The Cabinet of Dr. Caligari*, produced by Erich Pommer and directed by Robert Wiene. The story concerns a carnival barker, the titular Caligari (Werner Krauss), and his star attraction, the somnambulist Cesare (Conrad Veidt). Cesare, Caligari claims, has slept for twenty-three years with no interruption, but will now awake to answer questions about the future. One audience member unwisely asks, "How long will I live?" The answer, "Until dawn tomorrow," proves prophetic, as the man is murdered in his bed by a shadowy figure.

The dead man's friends Francis and Jane investigate the killing, uncovering evidence that Caligari and Cesare have been involved in a string of homicides. Inspired by a monk who had used a somnambulist to carry out murders in the early eighteenth century, Caligari has been hypnotizing Cesare to do his dirty work. But in a twist ending that feels very modern, it is revealed that Francis and Jane are actually inmates in a madhouse, of which Caligari is the director.

The story of *Dr. Caligari* is secondary to its highly exaggerated and deeply influential visual style. The backgrounds are painted canvas flats depicting buildings, walls, and staircases at skewed angles. The sets are crooked alleys and hallways offering bizarre perspectives, sparsely decorated with oddball furniture. Shadows and light patterns are painted directly onto the walls and floors. The acting is over-the-top even by silent movie standards, emphasizing the heightening of emotion that gave Expressionism its name. It looked like nothing that had come before, and while few of the Expressionist films that followed would go to the same extremes, the concept of conveying psychological terror through visual means became a bedrock of the movement. Paul Wegener's *The Golem*, Fritz Lang's *Dr. Mabuse the Gambler*, and Robert Wiene's *The Hands of Orlac* are all striking examples of the form, but the masterpiece of the genre is undoubtedly F. W. Murnau's 1922 vampire film *Nosferatu*.

Murnau was an art student at the University of Heidelberg when he was discovered by theatre impresario Max Reinhardt. Murnau's career as a stage actor was cut short by World War I, but after returning from his Air Force service (during which he survived seven plane crashes), Murnau formed his own film production company. One of his early directorial efforts, *The Janus Head*, was a thinly veiled retelling of *Dr. Jekyll and Mr. Hyde*, made without the permission of Robert Louis Stevenson's estate. That film is now lost to history, but the director's next unauthorized adaptation of a horror classic would endure through the ages.

Unable to obtain the rights to Bram Stoker's *Dracula*, Murnau and his screenwriter, Henrik Galeen, proceeded to adapt the novel anyway, changing the names of the major characters and a few other details along the way. Jonathan Harker becomes Thomas Hutter, Renfield is called Knock, and Dracula himself is now Count Orlok. As in Stoker's book, Hutter is dispatched to Transylvania to meet with the mysterious count about a real estate purchase. "It will take a bit of effort," Knock tells him. "A bit of sweat and perhaps a bit of blood." Along the way, Hutter stops for supper at an inn, where his passing mention of Orlok freaks out the locals. His carriage driver refuses to take him beyond a particular bridge. But Hutter, who apparently can't take a hint, continues on to Orlok's castle.

Upon arrival, Hutter is greeted by the count, a gaunt, shriveled wraith with bat-like ears, rat-like teeth, and long talons for fingernails. When Hutter accidentally cuts himself during dinner, Orlok grabs for his hand and begins sucking the blood from his finger. Even finding the count asleep in a coffin isn't enough to spur Hutter to take action, and soon it is too late; Orlok has left on a sea voyage back to Hutter's hometown. *Nosferatu* deviates from Stoker's novel in the end, as Orlok meets his demise when the first rays of the morning sun catch him still feeding on Hutter's wife, Ellen.

As with *The Cabinet of Dr. Caligari*, it's the Expressionist style that elevates *Nosferatu* to the first rank of horror movies. But unlike *Caligari*, Murnau's film is no stagebound exercise in artifice. In a rarity for those days, the demanding director took his cast and crew on location, shooting first in the German port of Wismar, then in the mountains of northern Slovakia. Murnau's footage of the "Transylvanian" exteriors is perhaps even more eerie today than in 1922: The experience of watching *Nosferatu* can be like peering through a murky portal in time. Yet the film is hardly stodgy or old-fashioned. Its fearsome images are as

German filmmaker Werner Herzog paid homage to one of the earliest horror classics with his remake of *Nosferatu* starring Klaus Kinski.

potent as any in all of cinema: Orlok rising, stiff as a board, from his coffin; his oversized, sharply angled shadow sweeping across a wall; the shadow of his hand closing over his victim's heart.

Murnau must share the credit for Orlok's indelibly macabre presence with the actor who brought him to life (or at least undeath): Max Schreck. Schreck's appearance and performance were so striking and enduring that producer Richard Kobritz and director Tobe Hooper would replicate the Orlok makeup some five decades later for the vampire Barlow in their television production of Stephen King's *Salem's Lot*. King himself was never a fan of this choice, telling interviewer Paul R. Gagne, "This is the third time that particular makeup concept has been used, and I think they could have been more original."

Lon Chaney: The First Horror Star

The silent era of horror in Hollywood had a face; in fact, it had a thousand of them. Lon Chaney Sr. was born to deaf parents in Colorado Springs, Colorado, in 1883. Out of necessity, young Chaney developed the ability to communicate extensively with hand gestures and facial expressions while growing up. This proved to be a marketable skill when he turned his attention to show business, first as a stage actor and dancer with a comedy troupe, then as an extra and minor character actor in the nascent film industry. Chaney's facility with makeup and prosthetics, developed during his time on the stage, eventually earned him the nickname "The Man of a Thousand Faces." He played a Chinese servant, an armless knife-thrower, and even a vampire in the long-lost *London After Midnight*, one of ten films he made with director Tod Browning. But he is still best known for two films considered to be essential forerunners of the horror genre: *The Hunchback of Notre Dame* and *The Phantom of the Opera*.

Carl Laemmle's 1923 production was not the first film based on Victor Hugo's classic novel, and it was far from the last, but Chaney's interpretation of Quasimodo remains the most iconic. The makeup is immediately arresting, of course: In addition to the famous hump, Chaney's bell ringer boasts bulging cheekbones, sharp fangs, and ragged Rolling Stones hair, with one eye popping and the other squinted shut. His appearance is that of a caveman, but he moves like an acrobat, swinging from his bell to the spires and nooks of Notre Dame Cathedral with incongruous grace. But it's his demeanor that's most surprising, particularly for those accustomed to the sentimentalized (and Disneyfied) Quasimodo of more recent vintage. This Quasi is a snotty punk—jeering, sticking out his tongue, spitting on the Parisian revelers below, and gleefully tolling the death knell. He's like a fifteenth-century Johnny Rotten, which is particularly startling given that the film is now over ninety years old.

The Phantom of the Opera is a different matter. Again Chaney fashioned a makeup that has endured as one of the most striking visages in all of cinema. As the organist haunting the Paris Opera House, he contorts his face into a living skull, using dark makeup around his eyes to create a sunken impression, wearing jagged false teeth, and, most famously, using hidden wires to pull his nose back into a snout. But Chaney is absent for much of the movie, and when he first appears over thirty minutes in, his face is covered with a mask, rendering his gift for pantomime moot. When it comes, the unmasking scene is undeniably effective, but much of the film (which suffered from a weirdly disjointed production) is poorly paced and uninvolving.

How Chaney's theatrical style might have translated into the sound era is anybody's guess, as the actor succumbed to complications from lung cancer after completing work on *The Unholy Three*, a remake of an earlier Chaney film and his only talkie. Chaney's legacy is not limited to his own performances, however, as his son would carry on the family tradition for the next generation of horror films.

Bloodlines: *Nosferatu* Revisited

Throughout his career, maverick German filmmaker Werner Herzog has gone his own way, following his idiosyncratic muse to the Peruvian rainforest (for *Aguirre, the Wrath of God*), the burning oil fields of Kuwait (*Lessons of Darkness*), and the most remote outpost in the frozen Antarctic (*Encounters at the End of the World*). He's the last person you'd imagine remaking an established classic—which may be exactly why he decided to tackle a new version of *Nosferatu* in 1979.

Herzog felt it was important to connect the New German Cinema filmmakers (which included Rainer Werner Fassbinder, Wim Wenders, and Volker Schlöndorff, in addition to himself) to the work of an earlier generation. "As a German filmmaker, we had no real fathers to learn from and no points of reference," says Herzog on his *Nosferatu* DVD commentary. "We were a generation of orphans. And you can't work without having some sort of reference to your own culture . . . It was our grandfathers—Murnau, Fritz Lang, Pabst, and others who were our teachers. And for me, Murnau's film *Nosferatu* is the very best German film ever."

Herzog's version serves as both homage to Murnau and a continuation of his own New German aesthetic, exploring such recurring themes as insanity, obsession, and mankind pitted against (super)natural forces he cannot comprehend. But *Nosferatu* is also an outlier of sorts in the Herzog filmography, as it is one of his rare attempts at working within the framework of a genre picture. "The images found in vampire films have a quality beyond our usual experiences in the cinema," Herzog told interviewer Paul Cronin. "For me genre means an intensive, almost dreamlike, stylization on screen, and I feel the vampire genre is one of the richest and most fertile cinema has to offer."

Freed of the copyright restrictions that bedeviled Murnau, Herzog reverted to the original names from Bram Stoker's novel, so that Knock was once again Renfield, Hutter reverted to Harker, and most importantly, Count Orlok was restored to Count Dracula. For anyone familiar with Herzog's career, the casting of Klaus Kinski as the vampire must have come as something of a surprise. In their only previous collaboration, 1972's *Aguirre, the Wrath of God*, Herzog and Kinski clashed so violently, it was rumored that the director pulled a gun on his star to convince him to finish his performance. (Herzog has always denied this, although he admits to threatening to shoot Kinski with a rifle if he attempted to walk off the set.) But Herzog insists that Kinski was patient and in good humor on the set of *Nosferatu*, mainly because the extensive application of makeup sapped all the fight out of him. "He was more contained. It was like a harness," Herzog told interviewer Lyall Bush. "You see, if he threw a tantrum and beat the ground with his fists, the make-up would be ruined and he would be another four hours."

Indeed, Kinski (who had previously played Renfield in Jess Franco's adaptation of *Dracula*) gives a remarkably restrained performance, lending an unexpected poignancy to the Count's repressed existence—one punctuated by sudden bursts of violence and fury. Herzog pays tribute to the signature images from Murnau's original, even using some of the same locations in northern Germany as his predecessor. But from the opening shots of actual mummies from a Guanajuato, Mexico, museum, Herzog puts his own stamp on the material. The early scenes vividly capture the strangeness of a man out of his element in the wilds of Eastern Europe, amid gypsies, wolves, and mist-shrouded castles. The striking image of a wooden raft piled high with black coffins inevitably recalls *Aguirre* and its bizarre signature shot of a raft overrun with monkeys. And it wouldn't be a Herzog movie without a behind-the-scenes story to rival the on-screen madness. In his DVD commentary, Herzog delights in telling of the day he and his crew released thousands of rats onto the streets of Delft, Holland. Herzog had the go-ahead from the city council because he had an airtight plan to keep them from escaping (involving nets, movable walls, and sealed side streets and alleys), but the townspeople were nervous because of an earlier rat infestation in the city. According to Herzog, however, every rat was recovered at the end of the day. Even Murnau might be impressed.

In 2000, director E. Elias Merhige (*Begotten*) paid a very different sort of homage to Murnau and *Nosferatu* with *Shadow of the Vampire*. A docudrama with a twist, Merhige's film told the story of the making of *Nosferatu*, with John Malkovich as a particularly megalomaniacal F. W. Murnau. *Shadow* deviates ever so slightly from the historical record when it becomes clear that Max Schreck, the mysterious actor hired to play Count Orlok, is himself a vampire. Willem Dafoe was nominated for an Oscar for his richly imagined performance as Schreck, which married a note-perfect impersonation of Orlok's feral physicality to a puckish but volatile persona. (When he announces "I don't think we need the writer anymore," it's an even more ominous threat than usual.)

Yet in Merhige's telling, Murnau is as much a monster as the vampire, if not more. There's even a touch of Herzog in Malkovich's portrayal of a filmmaker who will stop at nothing, not even the murder of his entire cast, to put his vision on the screen. *Shadow of the Vampire* isn't for everyone, but for hardcore movie buffs, it's a fascinating funhouse reflection of horror's silent era.

House of Frankenstein

The Universal Monsters and the Hammer Revival

Dracula: The First Hollywood Horror

In spite of the silent-era films discussed in the previous chapter, many motion picture historians pinpoint the 1931 release of Tod Browning's *Dracula* as the beginning of the horror genre. According to one school of thought, the sound of screaming is so integral to the horror film that no movie made before the advent of talkies can truly be considered part of the genre. (How anyone who has ever seen *Nosferatu* can subscribe to this point of view is a real head-scratcher.) But let's not quibble. By any measure, *Dracula* is one of the most important films in the history of horror: it launched the entire line of Universal monster movies and by extension, the modern horror film as we know it. It's just a shame it isn't a better movie.

A theatrical production of *Dracula* made its debut on the London stage in 1924 before arriving on Broadway in 1927. Adapted from the Bram Stoker novel by Hamilton Deane, the British production starred Raymond Huntley as Count Dracula, but by the time the show debuted on the Great White Way, Bela Lugosi had taken over the role, his first English-speaking part. The success of the play did not go unnoticed in Hollywood, particularly at Universal Pictures, where production chief Carl Laemmle Jr. hoped to reunite director Tod Browning with his longtime star Lon Chaney. But although Chaney seemed a natural fit for Dracula's cape, the actor died of cancer before production could begin.

Universal wanted nothing to do with the relatively unknown Lugosi in the title role, but when none of their other casting possibilities panned out, the nearly forty-year-old Hungarian actor won the part after all. The film's screenplay by Garrett Fort relied heavily on the stage adaptation, which differed from the Stoker novel and other screen versions of the story in several respects. For one thing, the role of Jonathan Harker was greatly reduced in favor of the bug-eating Renfield, played to hammy, sniveling perfection by Dwight Frye. It is Renfield who journeys to Transylvania to meet with the Count, although the suspense-building travel sequence is omitted—the first sign that we're dealing with a very stagebound adaptation indeed.

The enormous set constructed for Dracula's castle is easily the film's most impressive visual: it's all towering columns, massive crumbling staircases, and gigantic cobwebs, infested with rats and some very lost armadillos. But Browning does little to invest this setting with mystery and dread; in fact, the entire movie is visually flat and poorly paced, punctuated with long, inexplicable silences. According to David J. Skal's book *The Monster Show: A Cultural History of Horror* (an invaluable resource for anyone looking for a more in-depth exploration of the early days of horror), Browning may not have had very much to do with the picture at all. David Manners, who played the wimpy nonentity Harker, insisted that it was actually cinematographer Karl Freund who set up the shots and worked with the actors, while Browning hovered on the periphery.

As for the film's most famous performance, well, there's a reason Lugosi's Dracula has been parodied so often over the years: it was practically parody to begin with. Yes, such lines as "Listen to them: the children of the night . . . what music they make!" and "I never drink . . . wine" have long since embedded themselves in the cultural consciousness. But there's absolutely nothing frightening about Lugosi's performance, especially when compared to the nightmare fuel that was Max Schreck in *Nosferatu*. His signature move, a spotlit close-up of his "hypnotic" eyes, becomes laughable with repetition. To compare his screen presence with that of Christopher Lee in the later Hammer *Dracula* films is to compare a lightning bug with lightning. Heck, Ed Wood got better performances out of Lugosi than Browning or Freund or whoever actually directed *Dracula*. Yet it cannot be denied that it is Lugosi's vampire that has endured through the decades, and his portrayal must have worked on audiences of the time, as the movie was a big hit at the box office. It has been theorized that Depression-era filmgoers were desperate to escape into some kind of artificial horror, and that may be the case, although such attempts to explain the appeal of scary movies inevitably reek of psychobabble.

For many horror buffs, the Spanish version of *Dracula*, shot concurrently and on the same sets as the Lugosi version, but with a different cast and director, is the real deal. But one thing is certain: However dimly we might view it today, Browning's *Dracula* served as the launchpad for Hollywood's ongoing obsession with the horror genre . . . along with another adaptation of a literary classic released later the same year.

Frankenstein and Friends

Once he saw that *Dracula* was a moneymaker, Carl Laemmle didn't hesitate to snap up the movie rights to another Hamilton Deane–produced play based on a classic horror tale, Mary Shelley's 1818 novel *Frankenstein; or The Modern Prometheus*. It was generally assumed that Bela Lugosi would take on the role of Dr. Frankenstein's creation, and indeed, an early promotional poster for the film promised "Bela Lugosi (Dracula himself) . . . as the leading spine-chiller." Lugosi turned down the part, however, when he learned that the creature would have no dialogue. As legend has it, director James Whale spotted Boris Karloff having lunch in the Universal commissary and knew he'd found his monster.

Film historians will forever debate who was more responsible for the most recognizable movie makeup of all time: Whale, who sketched a preliminary design of Karloff as the creature, or Jack Pierce, the revered Universal makeup artist who actually applied the flattop and neck bolts to Karloff's head. But film is always a collaborative process, so suffice it to say that Whale, Pierce, and Karloff combined to bring one of the signature icons in American pop culture history to life. (Although Karloff, who was listed only as "?" in the opening credits, was kept under wraps until the last minute.)

Unlike *Dracula*, *Frankenstein* lives up to its reputation as a classic of horror cinema. The sets are even more spectacular than those featured in Browning's film, and Whale brings a spooky Gothic sensibility, drawing heavily on the shadowy work of the German Expressionists, to the proceedings. Karloff lends a distinct core of melancholy to the stitched-together abomination, making it very clear that the casting of Lugosi as the creature would have been disastrous. Like all great horror films, *Frankenstein* transgressed the dominant morality of its time. Local censorship boards trimmed the crucial scene in which the creature innocently tosses a small girl into a lake, never realizing that she'll drown until it's too late. In doing so, they unwittingly allowed audience members to imagine that the creature had actually done much worse.

That scene has long since been restored (along with Dr. Frankenstein's controversial line, "Now I know what it feels like to be God"), and *Frankenstein* has taken its rightful place on the Mt. Rushmore of horror cinema. But Whale's film also has to carry the burden of being among the first to kick off Hollywood's ongoing obsession with sequel mania. The irony, of course, is that *Frankenstein* is one of the few films (along with *The Godfather*) that many would argue was surpassed by its sequel in quality. Not that the follow-up was easy in coming: Although Universal commissioned *The Return of Frankenstein* shortly after the success of the original picture, four years would pass before the sequel materialized, during which time several more Universal monsters made their debut.

Karloff took on the title role in 1932's *The Mummy*. Despite the popular image of a fully wrapped mummy, Karloff only appeared in bandages briefly during the initial unveiling of his well-preserved Imhotep. After being restored to life, Imhotep appears as a modern-day Egyptian, and the resulting film is not particularly scary or exciting. Lugosi appeared in three films loosely based on the works of Edgar Allan Poe (*Murders in the Rue Morgue*, *The Black Cat*, and *The Raven*), joined by Karloff in the latter two. (These are not the "Poepictures" King discusses in *On Writing*, although we'll get to those a bit later.) Claude Rains took on the unenviable task of playing *The Invisible Man* in 1933 and somehow managed to frighten audiences without ever being seen until the film's last minute.

And Frankenstein finally made his return in 1935, the high-water mark of the Universal monsters series.

For *Bride of Frankenstein* (the eventual title of the sequel), Whale retained the German Expressionist–influenced look of the original while bringing new layers of subtext, pathos, and comedy to the story of Dr. Frankenstein's efforts to construct a mate for his creature. Now a star, albeit a typecast one, Karloff saw his role expanded to include dialogue and his name finally in lights above the title in the opening credits. Elsa Lanchester took on a dual role, first as the creature's true creator, Mary Shelley, in a somewhat silly prologue, and then as the bride herself, a visual as indelible as her would-be mate in her electrified shock of white-streaked hair. In the context of *Bride*, "We belong dead" are among the most romantic words in Hollywood history.

Bride was a modest hit for Universal, but the studio was in upheaval following a string of flops. Their first attempt at a wolfman picture, 1935's *Werewolf of London*, featured a meandering story line, inferior makeup, and a tedious variety of "comic relief" courtesy of its working-class British supporting characters, and failed to connect with audiences. A string of flops forced the Laemmles out of Universal and put an end to the first cycle of monster movies in 1936. But as always proved true in the pictures, Dracula, Frankenstein, and company refused to stay dead.

The Second Wave

Universal reissued the first wave of monster movies in the late 1930s, to surprising box office success. It didn't take long for the new executives in charge to realize that reviving the classic creatures might be the best way to reestablish Universal as an industry force. So it was that 1939 saw the release of *Son of Frankenstein*, marking Boris Karloff's third and final appearance as the monster. Basil Rathbone, best known as Sherlock Holmes, starred as Wolf von Frankenstein, the titular heir to the original mad scientist. Bela Lugosi gave perhaps his most compelling performance in a Universal creature feature as Ygor, Dr. Frankenstein's hunchbacked assistant. (Contrary to popular belief, the hunchback in the first Frankenstein film, played by Dwight Frye, was not Igor but Fritz.) Director Rowland V. Lee drew even more heavily on German Expressionism than had James Whale to create a stylized, weirdly angled house of Frankenstein, draped in oversized shadows. But the compelling visuals weren't enough to distract from the fact that the series was already running dangerously low on new ideas.

In 1941, Universal rebooted the werewolf movie with *The Wolf Man*, starring Lon Chaney Jr. as Larry Talbot. Although a verse repeated throughout the film insists that "even a man who is pure in heart and says his prayers by night may become a wolf when the wolfbane blooms and the autumn moon is bright," Talbot seems anything but pure. In fact, he's a peeping Tom, a stalker, and a sexual harassment lawsuit waiting to happen—at least from a modern perspective. In the context of the times, however, Talbot is portrayed as an innocent schlub who falls victim to the bite of a gypsy werewolf. Much of the werewolf mythology that endures to this day, including silver bullets and the passing of the curse through biting, derives from this film (although the "full moon" aspect wasn't solidified until the sequel).

Throughout the 1940s, Universal continued to churn out sequels, mixing and matching their monsters and actors in ways that would mystify anyone who regards Marvel's *Avengers* as a groundbreaking exercise in cinematic cross-pollination. In *Ghost of Frankenstein*, the role of the creature was taken over by Lon Chaney Jr., who also played the vampire "Count Alucard" to utterly unterrifying effect in *Son of Dracula*. But Chaney returned to his Larry Talbot role in *Frankenstein Meets the Wolf Man*, in which Bela Lugosi finally found himself in the creature makeup he'd so disdained when turning down the role of the monster in the original *Frankenstein*. Boris Karloff returned to the series for *House of Frankenstein*, but in an entirely different role as a new mad scientist (accompanied, naturally, by yet another hunchbacked assistant: Daniel, played by J. Carrol Naish). *House* also featured Dracula (this time played by John Carradine), abruptly dispatched halfway through the film, and the Wolfman, again played by Chaney. This "monster rally" concept (utilized again in 1945's *House of Dracula*) had potential, but the movies themselves reeked of creative desperation.

The monster cycle had long since deteriorated into self-parody by the time Abbott and Costello made it official in 1948. In *Abbott and Costello Meet Frankenstein*, the "Who's on first?" comedy duo star as a pair of baggage handlers tasked with delivering some oversized boxes to a "house of horrors." As it turns out, the boxes contain the not-quite-dead bodies of Count Dracula (Lugosi, returning to the role for the first time since the original *Dracula*) and Frankenstein's monster (Glenn Strange). Despite the attempts of Larry Talbot (Chaney yet again) to prevent the delivery, the Universal monsters are soon awake once more. Visually and story-wise, the film is almost indistinguishable from the other monster mash-ups, but in practice, it's an initially amusing and eventually rather tedious farce. (Here is the movie's one joke: Costello sees Dracula and Frankenstein and gets scared. Abbott doesn't believe him and yells at him. Repeat for ninety minutes.) Still, audiences ate it up, and Abbott and Costello went on to meet the Invisible Man, the Mummy, and Dr. Jekyll and Mr. Hyde before the Universal monsters were finally put to rest. Or were they?

Hammer Time: The Brits Get Bloody

Less than a decade after being forced into retirement by Universal, Frankenstein and his monster returned to the screen, albeit in very different form. A British film production company that had been around since the 1930s, Hammer Films scored a surprise hit in 1955 with the sci-fi/horror flick *The Quatermass Xperiment*, adapted from a BBC television serial. Convinced that the market for horror could be lucrative indeed, Hammer head James Carreras announced plans for a new adaptation of Mary Shelley's *Frankenstein* in 1956.

Universal wasn't happy to hear this and made it very clear that the studio's distinctive makeup design for the creature was protected by copyright, along with any and all story elements added to Shelley's original by the Universal screenwriters. Hammer would have to return to the book and start from scratch, or face possible legal action. This proved to be more of a blessing than a curse, as Hammer was able to carve out a distinctive house style for its long line of horror films right from the start.

In November 1956, Hammer began production on *The Curse of Frankenstein*, with Terence Fisher directing Peter Cushing and Christopher Lee, the two stars who would become synonymous with Hammer Films over the next decade and more. There was no danger of anyone confusing Hammer's creature with the classic Universal flattop-and-bolts look: Lee's monster was a pale, malformed oaf with a poorly stitched-together face and blotchy, bubbly skin. He was hideous to behold and, unlike Karloff's creature, did little to elicit the viewer's sympathy. But the real monster here, and the true star of the film and its sequels to come, was Cushing's Baron Frankenstein. This was no mad scientist in the cackling Universal mode, but rather a cold, cruel, and sadistic man of science . . . who happened to have a jar of eyeballs in his office.

Perhaps the most important visual difference between the Hammer *Frankenstein* and its Universal predecessors was the simplest: In lieu of Gothic, shadowy black-and-white derived from German Expressionism, Fisher's film splashed across movie screens in vivid color. Outraged critics reacted as if the predominant shade on offer was bloodred, but although *Curse of Frankenstein* was considered incredibly gory at the time, it actually makes sparing but effective use of its organs and bodily fluids. The flashes of grue and violence (not to mention Lee's hideous appearance) work especially well in contrast with the simple elegance of the period design and the stiff-upper-lip Victorian characterizations. Audiences certainly responded, as the film broke box office records in Britain and, importantly for Hammer's future, became a smash hit in the United States as well.

The logical follow-up was, of course, *Dracula*. This time, however, Hammer reached an agreement with Universal, allowing them to remake the Bela Lugosi original without fear of reprisal. Once again, Christopher Lee and Peter Cushing were enlisted, with Lee taking on the title role and Cushing costarring as the vampire's nemesis, Van Helsing. Stephen King, for one, approved of Lee's casting. In the Turner Classic Movies special *The Horrors of Stephen King*, the author speaks of his inability to take Lugosi's "whacked-out concert pianist" seriously. "Lee was much more sinister, much more magnetic." Indeed, the tall, dark, and handsome Lee was much more in keeping with Bram Stoker's creation: the sexual predator Lugosi could never be.

Released as *Horror of Dracula* in the States, the film was another Hammer success on both sides of the pond. And like Universal before it, the British studio could not resist making franchise characters of both the vampire and the

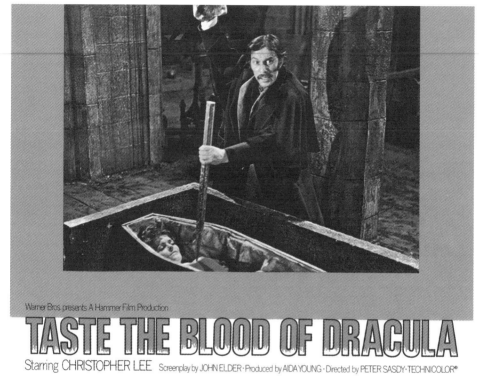

Warner Bros. presents A Hammer Film Production

TASTE THE BLOOD OF DRACULA

Starring CHRISTOPHER LEE   Screenplay by JOHN ELDER · Produced by AIDA YOUNG · Directed by PETER SASDY · TECHNICOLOR®

Hammer Films revived the classic Universal monsters in vivid, bloody color in films such as *Taste the Blood of Dracula.*

monster-maker. First up was 1958's *The Revenge of Frankenstein*, which featured the return of Cushing as Baron Frankenstein but not Lee as his original creation. Instead, the good doctor transplants the brain of his hunchbacked assistant Karl into a new body, with the usual disastrous results.

Unlike Peter Cushing, who was happy to reprise his *Frankenstein* role, Christopher Lee was reluctant to don Dracula's cape again for fear of being typecast. That proved no hindrance to Hammer, which went ahead with 1960's *Brides of Dracula*, in which Cushing reprised the role of Van Helsing, but neither Lee nor the character of Dracula appeared. Lee's typecasting worries didn't prevent him from taking on the title role in 1959's *The Mummy*, however, even though playing an ancient Egyptian wrapped in bandages and caked with dirt would appear to be a much less glamorous assignment than the suave Transylvanian. Neither Lee nor Cushing appeared in 1961's *Curse of the Werewolf,* as Hammer sought out a new star to don the fur and fangs; thus, Oliver Reed found his first leading role.

Hammer horror was not limited to reboots from the Universal catalogue; other titles included the *Psycho* riff *Paranoiac*, the Greek mythology–inspired *The Gorgon*, and Christopher Lee as *Rasputin, the Mad Monk.* Still, Frankenstein and Dracula remained the studio's bread and butter throughout the sixties and early seventies. In 1964's *The Evil of Frankenstein*, Hammer took advantage of its agreement with Universal to design a creature much more in keeping with the classic Karloff look. Martin Scorsese, asked to name his guilty pleasures in a 1998 issue of *Film Comment*, cited 1967's *Frankenstein Created Woman*. "I like all Hammer films," Scorsese said. "If I singled this one out, it's not because I like it the best—it's a sadistic film, very difficult to watch—but because, here, they actually isolate the soul: a bright blue shining translucent ball. The implied metaphysic is close to something sublime." The series wheezed on until 1974, when *Frankenstein and the Monster from Hell* completely failed to live up to its wonderfully pulpy title: The monster from Hell turned out to be a cross between Sasquatch and a shirtless Ernest Borgnine.

Lee was finally persuaded back into the cape for *Dracula, Prince of Darkness* in 1966, though he so detested the script, he refused to speak any of its dialogue. Despite his increasing disdain for the series, he kept returning, although his appearances grew increasingly fleeting in such entries as *Dracula Has Risen from the Grave* and *Taste the Blood of Dracula*. The appeal of the later sequels was often limited to seeing what creative method the writers concocted to revive the count after his most recent demise, but even these became repetitive over time. The series should have gotten a jolt from *Dracula A.D. 1972*, which sprung the eternal vampire from the Victorian era to the Swinging London of the then-present day. But the movie does absolutely nothing with this premise: If Lee's Dracula gives any notice that his surroundings have changed in the past hundred years, he keeps it to himself. Hammer stuck with the modern-day conceit for 1974's *The Satanic Rites of Dracula*, but to no avail. The franchise had been staked for good.

The demise of Hammer was probably inevitable once indie filmmakers like George Romero and Wes Craven began pushing the genre boundaries and Hollywood started turning out its A-list horrors like *The Exorcist* (more on those later), but the declining quality of its two signature series didn't help. Of the studio's later efforts, 1968's *The Devil Rides Out* is probably the most highly regarded. Scripted by Richard Matheson (one of Stephen King's favorite authors), the Terence Fisher film stars Christopher Lee as the heroic but humorless Duc de Richleau, who takes on a Satanic cult led by the menacing Mocata (Charles Gray). It's well crafted and boasts several adroit scare sequences, but compare it to 1968's similarly themed *Rosemary's Baby*, a prestige studio production overseen by a genuine auteur, Roman Polanski, and it looks a bit quaint. As the seventies progressed, Hammer releases became increasingly rare, finally coming to a halt following the flop remake of *The Lady Vanishes* in 1979. As happened so many times in Hammer films, however, death proved a temporary condition. In 2007, Hammer was purchased by John De Mol, a Dutch producer best known for the *Big Brother* reality series. The revived Hammer has released five films to date, but only 2010's *Let Me In* (a remake of the Swedish vampire film *Let the Right One In*, produced in conjunction with two other companies) has made much of an impact.

Bloodlines: Dracula and Frankenstein Through the Decades

Even beyond their many outings in the Universal and Hammer films, the Frankenstein and Dracula characters have appeared in dozens of movies over the years, rivaling such other public-domain characters as Tarzan and Sherlock Holmes for the most screen appearances of all time. Here are ten more worthy, notable, or just plain weird films featuring these famous monsters of filmland.

Count Dracula (1970)—Christopher Lee took a rare non-Hammer turn as Dracula is this adaptation by Spanish cult director Jess Franco (*Venus in Furs*). Here Lee's Count is a gray-haired, mustachioed gentleman who grows younger as he feeds on his victims. *Count Dracula* plays up the gore and eroticism a bit more than earlier versions, but it's still surprisingly tame. Franco manages some eerie effects, but his zoom-happy direction becomes laughable (particularly in a scene in which the vampire hunters get freaked out by a roomful of stuffed animals), and the movie overall is repetitive and lethargic. (It also features some of the worst day-for-night shots ever committed to celluloid.) Klaus Kinski would seem to be a perfect fit for the role of Renfield, but either he or Franco made the odd decision to portray the bug eater as a near-catatonic rather than a raving madman—a choice emblematic of the movie as a whole.

Dracula vs. Frankenstein (1971)—Anyone with a taste for the incredibly strange bad movies of Ed Wood (*Plan 9 from Outer Space*) and Ray Dennis Steckler (*Rat Pfink a Boo Boo*) will find a feast of folly in schlockmeister Al Adamson's bumble of a monster rumble. J. Carrol Naish stars as Dr. Duryea, proprietor of an amusement park sideshow who is in reality the last descendant of Dr. Frankenstein. His mentally challenged assistant is played by Lon Chaney Jr. in what would sadly prove to be his final screen appearance. The deliriously incoherent story includes decadent hippies, vengeful bikers, a petulant dwarf, a desultory Las Vegas production number, plentiful dismemberments and beheadings, and an acid trip straight out of Otto Preminger's *Skidoo*. Adamson added the titular monsters after much of the film had already been shot under the title *The Blood Seekers*, and it shows. Zander Vorkov looks like he should be starring in a seventies porn version of *Dracula*, while Frankenstein's monster has a face like an angry marshmallow. Their climactic fight scene won't make anyone forget Clay vs. Liston, but rarely has low-budget incompetence been this entertaining from start to finish.

Blacula (1972)—This blaxploitation take on the vampire legend isn't a spoof, exactly, although there's certainly some humor to be mined from the spectacle of an eighteenth-century African prince-turned-vampire on the loose in early seventies Los Angeles. William H. Marshall stars as Mamuwalde, who is turned by Dracula himself in 1780 and spends nearly two centuries in his coffin before being awakened by a pair of swishy interior decorators who have acquired Dracula's effects in an estate sale. The cultured vamp is soon making the scene in LA's finer discos (the Hues Corporation, who would later have a hit with "Rock the Boat," perform several funky numbers), romancing a woman he believes to be his reincarnated bride, and biting a few necks along the way. This mildly diverting time capsule was followed by a sequel, *Scream Blacula Scream.*

Andy Warhol's Frankenstein (1973)—Also known as *Flesh for Frankenstein,* this campy take on the legend written and directed by Paul Morrissey has enough gore, nudity, and softcore sex to make the Hammer films look like elementary school productions. Udo Kier stars as the most perverse version of Baron Frankenstein yet: His ethos is summed up by the line, "To know death, Otto, you have to fuck life in the gall bladder." And that he does, vigorously thrusting into the open, oozing orifices of his stitched-together creations (in 3D, no less—at least in the film's initial theatrical release). With its buckets of viscera, stew of impenetrable accents (Joe Dallesandro's Brooklyn honk clashes hilariously with the Teutonic tones of his castmates), and general air of depravity, this is not a *Frankenstein* for the faint of heart, but Kier's hilariously deranged performance is worth a look.

Young Frankenstein (1974)—The rare parody that nearly transcends its source material, this affectionate send-up of the Universal *Frankenstein* series is also the funniest movie Mel Brooks ever made. Cowritten by Brooks and Gene Wilder, who conceived the story and stars as the great-grandson of the original Baron Frankenstein, the film expertly replicates the black-and-white Gothic look of its Universal forebears, right down to the original lab equipment created by Kenneth Strickfaden. The script is endlessly quotable ("Put . . . the candle . . . back!"), and the cast, including Marty Feldman, Cloris Leachman, Teri Garr, and Peter Boyle (who achieves a poignant slapstick grace as the creature), is first-rate. Brooks went back to the well for 1995's *Dracula: Dead and Loving It,* but by then, he was a shadow of his former self.

The Bride (1985)—Touted as a feminist take on *The Bride of Frankenstein* at the time of its release, this incredibly silly reimagining is actually something of a bait and switch. As it begins, Baron Frankenstein (Sting) has already completed his first creature (Clancy Brown) and is putting the finishing touches on its mate, Eva (Jennifer Beals). As in the original *Bride,* the creature destroys Frankenstein's lab after a bad first date, but the resemblance pretty much ends there. Despite the title, much of the film (written by Lloyd Fonvielle and directed by Franc Roddam) concerns the creature (who comes to be called Viktor) and his unlikely friendship with circus dwarf Rinaldo (David Rappaport). This is understandable, since most of the scenes between the Baron and Eva are dead on the screen. Beals justifiably won a Razzie Award for Worst Actress, but Sting is equally terrible. This one is for connoisseurs of eighties trash only.

Frankenstein Unbound (1990)—Roger Corman returned to the director's chair for the first time in nearly two decades (and the last time to date) for this time-tripping riff on the Mary Shelley tale. Shelley herself is a character in the film, which blasts a scientist from the year 2031 (John Hurt) back in time, where he encounters both of the Frankenstein monster's creators—the not-yet-author of the novel (Bridget Fonda) and a real-life Dr. Frankenstein (Raul Julia)—as well as the creature itself (which resembles a Klingon on steroids). Although he's working with a more distinguished cast than usual, Corman's B-movie instincts prevail, with generally entertaining results.

Bram Stoker's Dracula (1992)—Francis Ford Coppola liked to claim that his revamp of the Dracula legend was the most faithful of all adaptations, but his "erotic nightmare" about the Count wooing the reincarnation of his long-lost love actually owes as much to *Blacula* as it does to Stoker's novel. For an hour or so, the movie gets by with its hypnotic visuals (Coppola eschewed digital effects in favor of old-fashioned in-camera trickery, with striking results) and hammy turns by Gary Oldman (doing a hilariously corny Lugosi accent) as Dracula and Tom Waits as Renfield. But the second hour bogs down into turgid melodrama, and the performances by Winona Ryder and Keanu Reeves are positively bloodless.

Gods and Monsters (1998)—Based on the 1995 novel *Father of Frankenstein* by Christopher Bram, this fictionalized biopic written and directed by Bill Condon (who won an Oscar for his screenplay) tells a what-if story about the final days of *Frankenstein* and *Bride of Frankenstein* director James Whale (Ian McKellen). Years after making those pictures, Whale is adrift in his memories of an impoverished childhood, a horrific stint in the trenches of World War I, and the creation of his monsters on the Universal soundstage. Whale forms a tentative friendship with his yard man, Clayton Boone (Brendan Fraser), but neither man can be what the other is seeking: in Boone's case, a father figure, and in Whale's, the young, virile embodiment of his glory days as a gay filmmaker in Hollywood. *Gods and Monsters* is a bit too melodramatic at times, but *Frankenstein* buffs will appreciate the cameos by lookalikes Jack Betts and Rosalind Ayres as Boris Karloff and Elsa Lanchester, as well as fantasy sequences featuring Fraser as both the mad scientist and his creation.

Dracula: Pages from a Virgin's Diary (2002)—Leave it to the eccentric, independent Canadian filmmaker Guy Maddin (*The Saddest Music in the World*) to direct what is easily the most unusual adaptation of the Dracula story to date. Maddin was tasked with filming the Royal Winnipeg Ballet's 2002 production of *Dracula*, adapted and choreographed by Mark Godden. But with Maddin at the helm, the finished product is anything but a straightforward performance film. The director augments the dance sequences with silent-era gimmickry, non-sequitur intertitles, brisk montages, and jokey asides, playing up the sexual metaphor of the vampire mythos at every turn (as when a blood-transfusion sequence turns into a raunchy bit of slapstick). Most interesting, especially for those overfamiliar with Stoker's story, is the way *Pages from a Virgin's Diary* marginalizes the menfolk, shifting the focus to Lucy and Mina. From a narrative standpoint it may not be the most compelling adaptation, but as a mood piece, it's one of a kind.

Creature Features

Horror at the Drive-In

Teenage Kicks

They always existed, of course, but as a social and economic force, the "teenager" was truly born in the 1950s. The postwar boom led to an expanding middle class, and the era of "children should be seen and not heard" melted away as young people with disposable cash and no pressing responsibilities began to reshape the culture in their image. The decade ushered in the birth of rock 'n' roll, hot rods, milkshakes at the diner, and that whole *American Graffiti/Happy Days* scene that has been mythologized to death by now. It also brought a new wave of horror movies and new ways of watching them.

The first drive-in theaters opened in the 1930s, after a New Jersey chemical plant owner patented the process, testing his own invention in his driveway with a screen nailed to trees and a projector on the hood of his car. But outdoor theaters really took off in the fifties, for two reasons: The entire family could pile in the car for a cheap night of entertainment, or a teen boy with a driver's license could take his girl for an evening that probably wouldn't be spent in rapt attention to whatever was playing on the screen. Most likely, that would have been a B picture in either the horror or sci-fi genre, as drive-ins generally weren't able to book A-list material.

Like the drive-in, the 3-D movie had been introduced decades earlier but failed to gain any traction until the 1950s. And like the drive-in, the gimmick, which required the wearing of flimsy cardboard glasses with different-colored lenses, was an attempt by the film industry to combat the encroaching menace of television. The first color feature released in 3-D was 1952's *Bwana Devil*, a story of railway workers in Africa under siege by man-eating lions. Although several 3-D westerns and musicals were made, the process found its most natural match with the horror movie. Among the most popular 3-D horror films—and the first movie Stephen King recalls seeing in a theater (a drive-in, of course)— was *The Creature from the Black Lagoon*.

Universal had exhausted its stable of monsters. The Frankenstein and Dracula movies hadn't made their way to television yet, and 1950s audiences no longer hungered for Gothic-flavored terrors set in remote European villages. Producer William Alland had heard a legend about a half-man, half-fish

The original *Creature from the Black Lagoon* is the first movie Stephen King recalls seeing at the drive-in (in 3-D, of course).

living on the Amazon River, and after several years of development his idea was fleshed out into a screenplay by Harry Essex and Arthur Ross. Jack Arnold, who had just made *It Came from Outer Space* in 3-D for Universal, was hired to direct. The creature, known as "the Gill-Man," was designed by artist Millicent Patrick, although makeup man Hamilton "Bud" Westmore tried to claim full credit for the creature.

Most of the film was shot on the Universal lot in California, but the underwater footage (captured with a lightweight 3-D camera rig designed by Scotty Welbourne) was filmed in Florida. As a consequence, two men actually portrayed the Gill-Man: Ben Chapman in the studio footage and Ricou Browning in the underwater shots. Universal released *Creature from the Black Lagoon* on March 4, 1954, and it was clear right away that this was a different kind of monster movie. Dark castles had given way to an exotic Amazon setting (studio-bound though it may have been), and repressed Victorian characters had been replaced by attractive young people in bathing suits. The picture was aimed squarely at the youth market, and the audience responded.

But if the trimmings were fresh, the meat of *Black Lagoon* was squarely in the monster-movie tradition, not too far removed from *King Kong.* After a fossil of a previously unknown species is discovered, an expedition sets out on the Amazon in search of the missing link between man and fish. The crew is at odds about what to do with this creature if it's found: Dr. David Reed (Richard Carlson) feels they should collect whatever evidence they can and leave the creature in its natural habitat, while Dr. Mark Williams (Richard Denning) wants to kill it and bring it back to America for further study. The debate is short-circuited when the Gill-Man falls for Reed's girlfriend, Kay (Julie Adams), and kidnaps her. Once again, 'twas beauty killed the beast, as the creature goes down in a hail of bullets.

Jack Arnold and his crew concocted some eerie underwater effects: the creature swimming upside down underneath a blissfully unaware Kay; his scaly hand reaching out of the depths for her leg, just missing it several times. It's clear that Spielberg had *Black Lagoon* in mind while making *Jaws*, particularly in the opening scene of the lone female swimmer and the unseen beast below. If the rest of the picture is rather rote and undistinguished, audiences didn't seem to mind: *Black Lagoon* spawned two sequels (1955's *Revenge of the Creature* and 1956's *The Creature Walks Among Us*) and remains one of the iconic horror films of its period.

As the fifties went on, Hollywood courted the teenage market even more brazenly with movies like 1957's *I Was a Teenage Werewolf*, in which Michael Landon's adolescent body undergoes some strange changes, and 1958's *The Blob*, with its group of youngsters (including Steve McQueen in his first leading role) battling a gelatinous creature from outer space. Monster movies continued to flourish throughout this period, but the fifties creature feature tended to be rooted in some very modern fears.

Terrors of the Atomic Age

As the Cold War and the threat of nuclear annihilation became an entrenched reality, the horror film incorporated this new normal into an unlikely form of escapism for moviegoers. Now the monsters were not only rediscovered prehistoric creatures and blobs from outer space but creatures born of radiation and atomic fallout. Children in schools were being taught to "duck and cover" under their desks in case of nuclear attack, but surely no child's desk or fallout shelter could protect us from the terrors of giant ants, lizards, and spiders that would arise in the aftermath of an atomic war.

Them!, released by Warner Bros. in 1954, typified this new strain of nuke-fueled anxiety. A series of deaths and disappearances goes unexplained in the New Mexico desert until a strange footprint leads the authorities to the culprits: giant-sized ants. Entomologist Harold Medford (Edmund Gwenn) determines the cause: mutation due to radiation from the atomic blast tests conducted nearby. In the end, the queen and her nest are destroyed with flamethrowers, but the damage is done. As Medford notes, "When man entered the atomic age, he opened the door to a new world. What we may eventually find in that new world, no one can predict."

Japan experienced the terrors of the atomic age firsthand in the blasts at Hiroshima and Nagasaki. Less than a decade later, Japanese cinema transformed those very real horrors into a high-rise lizard rampaging through Tokyo. Ishiro Honda directed 1954's *Gojira*, in which this atomic fire-breathing creature born of a nuclear explosion wreaks havoc on modern-day Japan. Two years later, a reedited version of the film premiered in the United States. Now called *Godzilla: King of the Monsters*, the American version contained newly shot footage featuring Raymond Burr as foreign correspondent Steve Martin. Despite the primitive special effects—the monster was clearly an actor in a rubber suit—the movie was a hit in both its versions, spawning a nearly endless series of sequels and spin-offs, including *King Kong vs. Godzilla, Destroy All Monsters, Rodan*, and *Godzilla vs. Mechagodzilla.*

But the effects of radiation were not limited to its power to create enormous beasts. Quite the opposite result is on display in *The Incredible Shrinking Man*, written by Richard Matheson, one of Stephen King's heroes and strongest influences. Like many fifties genre pictures, *Shrinking Man* straddles the line between science fiction and horror. Adapted by Matheson from his own book and directed by *Black Lagoon*'s Jack Arnold, this 1957 film considers the plight of Scott Carey (Grant Williams), an everyman exposed to a mysterious radioactive mist. When Scott notices he's losing weight, he visits his doctor, who determines he's also losing height. All the tests confirm that Scott is actually living up to the movie's title: He's growing smaller and smaller with each passing day.

Made for $700,000, *Shrinking Man* gets plenty of bang for its buck. The special effects may be primitive, but more often than not, they work surprisingly well. Arnold employed oversized props, rear-screen projection, and forced perspective shots to track Scott's journey from boy-sized to doll-sized and finally to miniature flyspeck who lives in a matchbox. On the most surface level, the movie can be appreciated for its suspenseful qualities: the race against time to find a cure; Scott's battles with a housecat and a spider; his struggle to survive the flooding basement.

But the movie's most fascinating journey is Scott's internal one. The story can be read as a metaphor for male inadequacy, with Scott growing increasingly embittered toward his wife, Louise (Randy Stuart), as his shortcomings become more apparent. But a remarkable thing happens once Scott is presumed dead in the cat attack. Taking refuge in the basement, too small to mount the stairs or for his voice to be heard, his resolve and ingenuity only grow larger. He is able to overcome his existential crisis and become the master of his world; a hatpin becomes a sword, a kitchen match serves as a flamethrower, and a spool of thread offers a limitless supply of rope. In the end, his fear of shrinking into nothingness gives way to a serene sense of connection to the cosmos: He may disappear from this world, but a whole new "infinitesimal" universe awaits on the other side. It's a moment of transcendence few B movies ever attempt, and Scott's final words, "I still exist," are as poignant as any in cinema.

For our purposes, *The Incredible Shrinking Man* is especially notable as a forebear of many of the Stephen King films to be discussed in this book. Taking an ordinary suburban man, subjecting him to some fantastic or horrific occurrence, and working through all the possible implications of that twist of fate is the sort of storytelling King thrives on, and he's never made a secret of his debt to Matheson. King's book *Thinner*, filmed in 1996, is clearly his variation on *Shrinking Man*; he returned the favor by blurbing a new edition of Matheson's book, calling it "a horror story if ever there was one . . . one of that select handful I have given to people, envying them the experience of the first reading."

Fifties Fearmongers

The 1950s were not an auteurist era in horror cinema in quite the way the 1970s would turn out to be, but the decade did give rise to a number of filmmakers who thrived in the horror milieu. Most of them, like Bert I. Gordon, the director of such low-budget endeavors as *The Amazing Colossal Man* and *Attack of the Puppet People*, were unabashed schlock merchants. A few transcended that status, if not through talent then through personality . . . and if not through personality, through outright gimmickry.

Whatever else you want to say about Edward D. Wood Jr., he was certainly a personality: a World War II veteran injured in combat, a cross-dresser with an angora fetish, and a filmmaker widely derided as the Worst Director of All Time. That last designation is debatable, but there's certainly no mistaking a Wood film for the work of anyone else. Best known for *Plan 9 from Outer Space*, Wood also gave Bela Lugosi his last major speaking role in 1955's *Bride of the Monster*, in which the one-time Dracula unleashes an unhinged speech about perfecting his own "race of atomic supermen which will conquer the world!" (Lugosi also appeared in *Plan 9*, but famously died during production and was replaced by a chiropractor holding a cape over his face.) Filled with unspeakable dialogue, cardboard sets and tinfoil special effects, and bizarre casts of characters (including Swedish wrestler Tor Johnson, unreliable psychic Criswell, and late-night TV host Vampira), Wood's films have become cult classics more fondly remembered today than many of the A-list pictures of the time.

The films of William Castle are far less celebrated than the gimmicks he employed to fill the seats with paying customers. Castle directed countless programmers for Columbia Pictures before striking out on his own with 1958's *Macabre*. (In his horror survey *Danse Macabre*, Stephen King recalls this as the "gotta-see" movie of his childhood, although most of his friends mangled the pronunciation as "McBare.") Castle mortgaged his house to finance the low-budget suspense story about a father's race against time to find his daughter, who has been buried alive by a madman. The movie doesn't amount to much more than a handful of people with shovels wandering around a graveyard, with the occasional cutaway to a literal ticking clock, but Castle was able to sell it on the strength of a unique promotional tactic: Each paying customer was insured

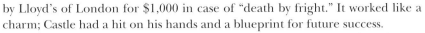

by Lloyd's of London for $1,000 in case of "death by fright." It worked like a charm; Castle had a hit on his hands and a blueprint for future success.

Castle followed *Macabre* with *The House on Haunted Hill* starring Vincent Price. This time the gimmick was "Emergo," which only meant that, at a certain point near the end of the movie, a glow-in-the-dark skeleton would be sent out on a wire to hover over the audience. Another success meant more and more promotional stunts: *13 Ghosts*, for which viewers were given a "ghost viewer" (a piece of cardboard with strips of red and blue cellophane; red made the ghosts appear, blue made them disappear); *Mr. Sardonicus*, the ending of which was determined by an audience poll (legend has it that viewers always voted for the vlllain's death); and *Homicidal*, featuring a "fright break" allowing audiences to leave and get their money back before the real terror began.

But Castle's masterpiece of gimmickry had to be 1959's *The Tingler*, also starring Price. As with most of his movies, it featured a forgettable story, this one about a parasite that latches onto the human spine and feeds on fear. In select theaters, *The Tingler* was presented in "Percepto," which meant that a few of the seats were rigged with electrical buzzers. At a point in the film when the Tingler escapes into a movie theater, the film would "break," the screen would go dark, and the buzzers would buzz as the voice of Vincent Price announced that the Tingler was loose in *this very theater*. The only solution? "Scream! Scream for your lives!"

Another prolific horror director and producer of this period was known less for his promotional tactics than for his thrifty and expedient method of cranking out drive-in fare. Between 1955 and 1960, Roger Corman directed more than 25 features in every genre, shooting many of them in as little as a week's time. Corman's horror titles included *Attack of the Crab Monsters*, *A Bucket of Blood*, and *The Little Shop of Horrors*, famously filmed in only two days. Most of the movies he churned out during the fifties were instantly forgettable exploitation jobs, made on the cheap in black and white, but in 1960 Corman would alter the course of his career with a relatively lavish, full-color adaptation of a story by a legendary writer considered to be the father of the horror genre: Edgar Allan Poe.

The "Poepictures"

Roger Corman's Buckets of Blood

Corman in Color

In his manual-turned-memoir *On Writing*, Stephen King writes about the movies he loved in his adolescence, in particular those he used to see with his friend Chris Chesley in Lewiston, Maine. "Chris and I liked just about any horror movie, but our faves were the string of American-International films, most directed by Roger Corman, with titles cribbed from Edgar Allan Poe. I wouldn't say *based upon* the works of Edgar Allan Poe, because there is little in any of them which has anything to do with Poe's actual stories and poems . . . And yet the best of them—*The Haunted Palace, The Conqueror Worm, The Masque of the Red Death*—achieved a hallucinatory eeriness that made them special. Chris and I had our own name for these films . . . Poepictures."

Roger Corman had been making black-and-white horror pictures on the cheap for AIP in the late fifties, sometimes shooting two features back-to-back in twenty days for $100,000 apiece. Corman had grown restless with this process and disappointed that the resulting films came and went with little notice. In 1959, AIP's Sam Arkoff and James Nicholson met with Corman to propose more of the same, but Corman had a counterproposal. "What I'd really like to do," Corman recalls telling Arkoff and Nicholson in his memoir *How I Made a Hundred Movies in Hollywood and Never Lost a Dime*, "is *one* horror film in color, maybe even Cinemascope, double the budget to $200,000, and go to a three-week schedule. I'd like to do a classic, Poe's 'The Fall of the House of Usher.'"

Arkoff and Nicholson didn't think much of the idea at first. They weren't convinced that teenagers were quite as into Poe as Corman seemed to believe, and besides, Arkoff noted, "There's no monster in this movie!" Corman assured him that the house *was* the monster and made a convincing enough case that AIP agreed to fund a fifteen-day shoot on a budget of $270,000, $50,000 of which went to Corman's star of choice, Vincent Price. Price had done horror films before, notably *The Fly* and William Castle's *The Tingler*, and he had the "cultural refinement" Corman needed for the role of Roderick Usher.

Richard Matheson wrote a screenplay loosely based on Poe's tale, inventing a romance for Mark Damon's Philip Winthrop and Myrna Fahey's Madeline Usher. In Corman's film, Winthrop arrives at the House of Usher with plans of taking his fiancée, Madeline, with him when he leaves. Roderick urges him to go, explaining his sister is unable to leave the house due a condition the siblings share: an acute sensitivity to light, sound, touch, taste, and smell. Despite Roderick's insistence that he and Madeline will soon both be dead, Winthrop won't take no for an answer. Before they can leave, however, Madeline suddenly dies—or so Winthrop is told. Actually, she suffers from catalepsy, a condition that simulates death, and has been buried alive. Madeline escapes her coffin and has her vengeance on her brother, bringing down the House of Usher in the process.

As usual, Corman's timing was perfect. By the time production began on *House of Usher*, the Hammer horror films from Britain were already crowding the cheap black-and-white American creature features out of the marketplace. With their rich production values, better class of actors, and full-color imagery, including splashes of blood and gore, the Hammer pictures forced Corman to raise his game. His talent for stretching a dollar was never more tested, and he proved up to the challenge. His art director, Dan Haller, bought huge stock sets from Universal for $2,500. (For subsequent Poe films, Haller would simply add onto the sets he'd already purchased, resulting in ever more lush production design for pennies on the dollar.) For the shots of the House of Usher in flames, Corman gave the owner of a barn scheduled for demolition fifty dollars to burn it down instead. He also took advantage of a forest fire in the Hollywood Hills to grab the shots of a horse and carriage riding through burnt-out terrain.

House of Usher still bore some relation to the Corman cheapies of old, particularly in its cheesy matte shots of the Usher mansion, but with its dreamy pacing, well-appointed Gothic atmosphere, and florid Vincent Price performance, it represented a big step up from *Attack of the Crab Monsters* and *She Gods of Shark Reef*. Still, even Corman and the AIP brass were taken aback by the film's success, as *Usher* brought in over $1 million in rentals. A follow-up was inevitable, though nobody involved knew at the time that they'd kicked off a long-running Poe cycle. "When the first film was a hit, they still didn't consider doing a Poe series," Matheson told Ed Naha, author of *The Films of Roger Corman: Brilliance on a Budget.* "They just wanted another movie with a Poe title affixed to it . . . It went on and on like that for years. It was like making shoes or something."

From the Pit to the Palace

Corman's follow-up to *Usher, The Pit and the Pendulum*, played much like a remake of its predecessor with a few plot details tweaked. Once again a horse and carriage bearing an unwanted guest arrives at a looming Gothic locale: This time, rather than a mansion in a burnt-out forest, it's a castle on a hill above the seashore. The visitor, Francis Barnard (John Kerr), is looking for his sister Elizabeth (Barbara Steele), but Elizabeth's husband, Nicholas Medina (Price again), informs him that she's dead. Medina, whose father was a member of the Spanish Inquisition, has a torture chamber containing not only the titular implement (a swinging blade that is lowered onto its victim), but an Iron Maiden in which

As a child growing up in Maine, Stephen King loved the "Poepictures": Roger Corman's loose adaptations of Edgar Allan Poe stories, including *The Pit and the Pendulum.*

Elizabeth supposedly met her end. It turns out, however, that Medina is being gaslighted by a still-living Elizabeth and her lover, Dr. Leon (Antony Carbone). In the end, Medina snaps and, believing himself to be his father, straps Francis to the table beneath the pendulum. After a narrow escape during which Medina falls into the pit, it is revealed that he has trapped Elizabeth in the Iron Maiden after all.

Most of these plot details again came courtesy of screenwriter Matheson, as Poe's story is concerned solely with the efforts of an unnamed prisoner to escape the pit and the pendulum. Despite its similarities to *House of Usher*, however, Corman's second Poe effort improves on its predecessor in nearly every respect. The production is even more lush, Price's performance even more excessive (which, in the context of some rather stiff acting by the rest of the cast, counts as a plus), and Corman's direction even more assured. Where *Usher* was sometimes stodgy, *Pendulum* takes a number of wild turns, from the "lava lamp" opening credits to the tinted and distorted dream sequences to the genuinely riveting grand finale. The torture chamber set, augmented by a still-impressive matte painting in long shots, is one of the most visually arresting in the Poe series. The final "gotcha" shot of Elizabeth in the Iron Maiden remains one of the more effective stingers in all of horror cinema. (The film was also a huge influence on the teenage Stephen King, who wrote his own eight-page "novelization" of

The Pit and the Pendulum and sold copies of it at school until the principal caught on. Still, as King noted in *On Writing*, it was his first best seller.)

Audiences ate it up, as *Pendulum* reaped nearly twice the box office receipts as *House of Usher*. Corman took notice, deciding he was due a bigger cut of the proceeds than Nicholson and Arkoff were willing to offer. Corman decided he didn't need them, after all: He was well within his rights to make his own Poe movie, and he soon reached an agreement with the new distribution arm of Pathé, the lab that did the print work for AIP and other production companies. The only problem was that Vincent Price was under exclusive contract to AIP, so Corman hired Ray Milland to star in *The Premature Burial*. Just as he began shooting, however, Nicholson and Arkoff showed up on the set to welcome Corman back to the AIP family: They'd acquired the distribution rights to the film from Pathé. (Corman has long suspected that his once and future producers strong-armed the company by threatening to pull all of their lab work.)

Price may have been gone, but the formula remained the same. By now, fans could tick off the elements in their sleep: the arrival by carriage at a foreboding, exotic locale; the rude welcoming of the guest; the thick Gothic atmosphere; the near-psychedelic dream sequence; the "buried alive" plot twist (this time given away in the title); the loved one's betrayal; and the inevitable shock ending. The only thing missing was the stock footage of burning rafters falling from the ceiling, a staple of nearly every other Poe picture.

But if fans were tired of these tropes, the box office didn't reflect it. Corman enjoyed the success but felt a bit constrained by the formula. With his next entry, *Tales of Terror*, he shook things up a bit by crafting an anthology film based on four Poe short stories: "Morella," "The Black Cat" and "The Cask of Amontillado" (which were combined into one segment in rather ingenious fashion), and "The Facts in the Case of M. Valdemar." Corman particularly enjoyed the middle segment, with its more comedic tone and hammy interplay between Price and Peter Lorre. He took this a step further with his follow-up, *The Raven*, which reunited Price and Lorre (along with Boris Karloff) for a scenery-chewing competition that has rarely been topped. Although Price reads from Poe's titular poem over the opening credits, the movie's tone could hardly bear less resemblance to the author's gloomy, lovelorn verse: It was a full-blown comedy and essentially worked as a parody of the Poe series to date. (Corman then topped himself by filming the bulk of another movie with Karloff, *The Terror*, in three days on sets left over from *The Raven*.)

The sixth Poe film took the disconnect from its source material to new heights of absurdity. Although the title card reads *Edgar Allan Poe's The Haunted Palace*, the movie is actually based on the novella *The Case of Charles Dexter Ward* by H. P. Lovecraft. The mentions of Cthulhu, Yog-Sothoth, and the Necronomicon throughout the film are a dead giveaway, but, apropos of nothing, Price does recite a couple of lines from Poe's poem "The Haunted Palace" on a voice-over track. Despite its origins, however, the movie is very much in keeping with the rest of the Poe series, as Price plays both a Satanic warlock and the great-grandson who comes to claim his ancestor's property (another Gothic castle looming on a hill, natch) many years later. By the time the film ends with yet another conflagration, you can practically sense Corman growing restless behind the camera. His run of Poe pictures was nearly at an end.

Nevermore

Corman had originally hoped to film *Masque of the Red Death* as his follow-up to *House of Usher* but ended up doing *The Pit and the Pendulum* instead. By 1964, however, he was ready to tackle Poe's tale of Prince Prospero and his efforts to evade a deadly plague sweeping the land. But Corman was equally influenced by Ingmar Bergman's *The Seventh Seal*, with its personification of Death as a dark-cloaked figure. The screenplay by Charles Beaumont and R. Wright Campbell would also incorporate elements from other Poe stories, notably the vengeful dwarf jester from "Hop-Frog."

Masque would become the most lavish production in the entire Poe oeuvre. Corman shot the film in England on an unprecedented (for AIP) five-week schedule, using opulent sets left over from *Becket*. His cinematographer was Nicolas Roeg, the remarkable visual stylist who would go on to direct *Walkabout* and *The Man Who Fell to Earth*. Price starred once again, playing Prospero as a maniacal Satan worshipper who believes his deal with the devil will spare him from the plague wiping out the peasants he disdains. Certainly Corman's artiest effort in the series (the scene in which Prospero removes the Red Death's mask to reveal Price's face is one of the more laughably heavy-handed touches), *Masque* is also one of the most enjoyable, and a visual treat from start to finish.

Corman ended his Poe cycle with *The Tomb of Ligeia*, scripted by Robert Towne, who would go on to write *Chinatown*. Price returned again, this time as a tormented widower haunted by his late wife. *Ligeia* marked something of a departure from the earlier films, as it was shot on location, often in broad daylight, but in terms of its content, it was far from a fresh start. "I was repeating myself," he wrote in his memoir, "taking ideas, images, themes, and techniques from my own earlier work." Corman was done with Poe, but AIP didn't find it quite as easy to move on. As late as 1968, Nicholson and Arkoff were trying to keep the series alive, releasing a British production called *Witchfinder General* in American under the title *The Conqueror Worm* and adding a few seconds of Price reading Poe's poem in voice-over to justify the change. But although it stars Price and is set in the 1600s, it doesn't bear much resemblance to Corman's Poe work. The Gothic artifice has been scraped away in favor of a more modern approach: natural light, handheld camera, a grittier production design, and far more graphic violence. The horror movie was changing rapidly, and a new generation of filmmakers was about to make the Poe pictures look very quaint indeed.

Dark Visions

Night of the Living Dead, The Exorcist, and the Rise of Modern Horror

Innocence Lost

In the 1960s, the horror movie, like American society itself, divided and developed along two parallel tracks. The traditionalists continued to churn out drive-in fodder: exploitation pictures with no agenda aside from drawing a few quick bucks from the teenage crowd. But a revolution was brewing within the industry, as both established auteurs and young, hungry mavericks saw the potential for a more ambitious and sophisticated breed of horror film, and the studios saw dollar signs in a formerly disreputable genre.

Alfred Hitchcock was among the first of the old guard to pick up on the changing times. To the surprise of many, including executives at his home studio, Paramount, he decided to follow up a string of lavish, star-laden productions like *North by Northwest* and *Vertigo* with a disturbing thriller inspired by a gruesome series of real-life murders in Wisconsin. When Paramount executives balked at financing such an endeavor at Hitchcock's usual budget, the director decided to make a down-and-dirty version with the crew from his television series *Alfred Hitchcock Presents*. The film, based on Robert Bloch's novel and scripted by Joseph Stefano, was, of course, *Psycho*.

Hitchcock's 1960 film broke the rules in several ways. Its ostensible lead character, Marion Crane (Janet Leigh), was killed off roughly forty-five minutes into the film, at which point a disturbed, cross-dressing multiple murderer becomes our protagonist. The famous shower scene pushed the boundaries of on-screen violence, despite the fact that the knife is never seen penetrating Crane's body. The movie's overall aesthetic—low-budget, black and white, grittier in content than the director's usual fare—had much in common with the drive-in offerings of the day, but the level of craft and sophistication elevated it to the realm of a classic.

Not that everyone felt that way at first. *New York Times* critic Bosley Crowther did not find "an abundance of subtlety" in *Psycho* and cluelessly bemoaned its lack of "significant and colorful scenery." But audiences flipped for it, forming lines around the block and giving Hitchcock his biggest box office hit of all. The director would further push the boundaries of acceptable standards of violence with *The Birds* and *Frenzy*, and *Psycho* would prove influential on two fronts. Exploitation filmmakers seized on the slasher element, leading to the "splatter" films of, among others, Herschell Gordon Lewis. And Hollywood looked past the disreputable B-movie reputation of the genre to see the earning potential of a more refined breed of horror film.

Among those who rushed to copy the success of *Psycho* was, of course, Roger Corman. After making *The Young Racers* in Europe, the always thrifty producer decided to finance a second picture while he still had a crew and equipment. His second assistant director and sound man, Francis Ford Coppola, was eager to direct. He suggested a low-budget psychological thriller about an axe murderer, and Corman agreed to finance it for $20,000. Upon arriving in Ireland, where he was to make the picture, Coppola was able to secure an additional $20,000 from a local producer in exchange for the British distribution rights. Coppola wrote the screenplay in three days, filled the cast with friends from UCLA and local members of a theater troupe, and spent nine days shooting the film at Ardmore Studios in Dublin.

The film Coppola shot, eventually titled *Dementia-13*, didn't exactly match Corman's expectations of "*Psycho* with an axe," despite the director's assurances that the picture would contain plenty of sex and violence. The producer hired another one of his protégés, Jack Hill, to write and direct an additional axe murder scene along with voice-over to clarify what he felt was a murky, disjointed story. The resulting film still doesn't achieve much in the way of coherence; although it boasts several eerie sequences, it would be fair to say that its director went on to better things in the future.

While the independents looked to *Psycho* for inspiration, Hollywood turned to the classics for a pair of well-regarded Gothic horror pictures of the early sixties. In 1961, 20th Century-Fox released *The Innocents*, based on *The Turn of the Screw* by Henry James. Directed by Jack Clayton and adapted by William Archibald and Truman Capote, the film concerned a governess (Deborah Kerr) who takes a job caring for the orphaned niece and nephew of a wealthy man. The children's odd behavior leads her to believe they are possessed by two previous inhabitants of her employer's country estate. As Miles and Flora, Martin Stephens and Pamela Franklin are the archetypal "creepy kids" of cinema, ancestors of many King characters to come (most notably in *The Shining*). Holding up less well over time is Robert Wise's 1963 *The Haunting*, adapted from Shirley Jackson's *The Haunting of Hill House*. Wise's direction is atmospheric, but although audiences were frightened at the time, the movie's "things that go bump in the night" conceit invokes more tedium than terror. But the Hollywood horror movie was about to undergo a seismic change, thanks to a couple of young-turk directors prepared to show the audience no mercy.

The Devil Inside

In 1967, Random House published Ira Levin's novel *Rosemary's Baby* and saw it become one of the top-selling books of the decade. William Castle, the master huckster himself, bought the rights the novel while it was still in galleys. While one shudders to think what gimmick Castle might have hatched had he directed the film himself (Diaper-Vision, perhaps?), we'll never know. Robert Evans of Paramount Pictures wanted to make the movie, but he didn't want Castle to direct. Reluctantly, Castle agreed to produce the movie and go with Evans's choice of director: Roman Polanski.

Polanski had made a name for himself with edgy imports like *Knife in the Water* and *Repulsion,* and had his eye on making the skiing picture *Downhill Racer* as his Hollywood debut. Instead, after Evans handed him the galleys, Polanski stayed up all night reading *Rosemary's Baby* and agreed to direct it.

Mia Farrow starred in Roman Polanski's *Rosemary's Baby,* one of the New Hollywood's horror highlights.

Evans and Polanski clashed over casting: The director wanted Tuesday Weld to play Rosemary, but Evans eventually sold him on Mia Farrow, a bigger name thanks to her work on *Peyton Place* and her marriage to Frank Sinatra. Evans also wanted Robert Redford to play Rosemary's husband, Guy, but Redford turned down the role. Jack Nicholson was considered, but Polanski decided on John Cassavetes, certainly a darker, more intense presence than Redford would have been. Polanski filled the supporting cast with Old Hollywood types: Ralph Bellamy, Elisha Cook Jr., Patsy Kelly, and Ruth Gordon, who would go on to win an Oscar for her performance as chatty neighbor and secret coven member Minnie Castevet.

Another important casting decision was suggested by production designer Richard Sylbert, who recommended the Dakota, the apartment building on the Upper West Side where John Lennon later lived and was killed, as the Bramford, new home of Guy and Rosemary Woodhouse. (The fact that struggling actor Guy could afford an apartment in the Dakota should have been Rosemary's first clue that he was in league with the devil.) Filming took place in the fall of 1967 and was plagued with difficulties; most notably, when shooting ran over schedule, Frank Sinatra insisted his wife leave the production in time to costar with him in *The Detective*. When she refused, he had Farrow served with divorce papers on the set.

Released on June 12, 1968, *Rosemary's Baby* was an enormous box office hit (taking in over $33 million on a $2.3 budget) and cultural milestone. Its all-consuming aura of paranoia and encroaching evil made it the ideal cracked reflection of one of the most turbulent times in American history. By design (and by the filmmakers' own admission), it begins like one of the harmless Doris Day movies of the early sixties, with Guy and Rosemary moving into their new apartment and establishing a cozy domesticity. But like the decade itself, the movie only grows stranger and more uncertain as it goes along. A dream sequence incorporates elements of reality, but the line between them is blurred. Perfectly normal moments take on an air of menace through simple camera placement, as in the scene where Guy is partially blocked by a doorway while taking a phone call (a moment that famously had audiences craning their necks, as if they could peer around the obstruction).

For most of the movie Polanski straddles the line, allowing us to believe that Rosemary is either imagining her troubles or that her husband has really fallen in with a Satanic cult with nefarious designs on her unborn child. (A case in point is William Castle's cameo appearance: We first see him from behind, blocking Rosemary's exit from a telephone booth but unnoticed by her. We assume he's with the coven, as does she when she spots him, but when he turns around, he's just a friendly, cigar-chomping man who needs to use the phone.) Not until the end is it revealed that everything she (and we) inferred is truth: When Rosemary stumbles upon the coven, the sight of these Old Hollywood relics chanting "Hail, Satan!" is somehow far more disturbing than a Manson-type cult would have been.

Speaking of which, the movie would take on a new and sinister resonance the following year when members of Charles Manson's cult murdered Polanski's pregnant wife Sharon Tate and four others at the director's Cielo Drive home. Castle would come to believe that the movie was cursed after that incident and several others, including the untimely death of composer Krzysztof Komeda and his own ill health following the production . . . unless, of course, all of his "curse" talk was simply the old huckster's last hurrah at hyping a movie through unconventional means.

A few years later, another demonic best seller would reach the screen, directed by another Hollywood *enfant terrible*. William Friedkin wasn't a newcomer by any means—he'd won an Oscar for 1971's *The French Connection*—but he already had a reputation for clashing with studio executives when he was hired to direct an adaptation of William Peter Blatty's *The Exorcist* for Warner Bros. (Arthur Penn, Mike Nichols, Peter Bogdanovich, and Stanley Kubrick had all reportedly turned down the job.) Like Polanski with *Rosemary's Baby*, Friedkin says he stayed up all night reading *The Exorcist*, and like Polanski, he butted heads with the studio over casting. "The studio wanted Audrey Hepburn, Jane Fonda or Anne Bancroft—all very good actresses—to play the actress whose daughter becomes possessed in the film," Friedkin wrote in a 2013 *Hollywood Reporter* remembrance about the film. For various reasons, none were available. Friedkin wanted Ellen Burstyn, and despite the protests of Warners exec Ted Ashley, she got the part.

Max von Sydow had the gravitas Friedkin wanted for Father Merrin, the exorcist, and Jason Miller, then best known as the playwright behind *That Championship Season*, was his unconventional choice for the doubting Father Karras. Thirteen-year-old Linda Blair, a relative unknown, beat out over six hundred other young actresses who tested for the role of Regan MacNeil. Production began in August 1972, with location filming taking place in Iraq, Washington, D.C., and Georgetown, and the interior of the MacNeil home built on a set in New York. As with *Rosemary's Baby*, several members of the cast and crew came to be convinced there was a curse on the production: A fire destroyed part of the set, Miller's son was injured during shooting, and a priest was supposedly brought in to exorcise the set. (Of course, there just may have been some publicity value in that last claim. William Castle would approve.)

If *Rosemary's Baby* made a splash at the box office, *The Exorcist* emptied the pool. It took in over $66 million in its first release, making it the second-biggest movie of 1973 behind *The Sting*. (Subsequent rereleases would bring its total to over $200 million.) Tonally, *The Exorcist* had little in common with *Rosemary*; Friedkin had no use for Polanski's ironies, instead playing absolutely straight (to the point of complete humorlessness) Blatty's tale of a young girl possessed by a demon and the two priests who help free her. Friedkin's movie is as much about Damien Karras, the priest struggling with his belief, as it is Regan's story, and although it can be seen as a metaphor for any number of things (the helplessness of seeing a close family member struggling with a debilitating illness, for example, or a *Carrie* precursor in exploring the turbulence of adolescence through supernatural means), it is ultimately an exploration of the nature of faith. Many of the characters in the film doubt that Regan is actually possessed, but the movie is quite certain about it, and Friedkin never plays it coy. But although the director claims he never thought of *The Exorcist* as a horror movie, his firm grounding of the picture in mundane reality makes its leaps into the supernatural that much more terrifying.

Despite the impressive success of *Rosemary's Baby* and *The Exorcist*, however, it wasn't long before the era of the "Easy Riders, Raging Bulls" generation passed in Hollywood. Polanski went into European exile, and Friedkin fell off the A-list after 1977's *Sorcerer*, which was crushed at the box office by *Star Wars*, signaling the dawn of the blockbuster era. By then, the horror film's evolution was no longer being shepherded by the studios: It was in the hands of a few independent visionaries, making their names with some of the most chilling movies ever made.

The American Nightmare

After graduating from Pittsburgh's Carnegie Mellon University, George Romero spent much of the sixties making commercials and industrial films. The work was steady but dull, and Romero and friends itched to make a feature capitalizing on the public fascination with horror. Forming a production company called Image Ten, Romero and company began with a budget of only $6,000, but that figure would balloon to over $100,000 in the course of production. Romero hatched the story, inspired by Richard Matheson's *I Am Legend* (and in particular, the first filmed adaptation of that novel, *The Last Man on Earth*), and he and cohort John Russo cowrote the screenplay.

The movie, which would come to be titled *Night of the Living Dead*, was filmed between July and December 1967 in rural areas surrounding Pittsburgh. Romero shot in black and white in a near-documentary style, using a cast of unknowns. In a highly unusual move at the time, Romero cast Duane Jones, an African American actor, in the role of the heroic male lead, Ben. Although Romero has been quoted as saying Jones simply gave the best audition, his race ended up lending the film a resonance it might not otherwise have had.

The film's graphic violence and uncompromising ending made finding a distribution deal difficult. Eventually the Walter Reade Organization picked it up, and *Night of the Living Dead* premiered on October 1, 1968 in Pittsburgh. A wider release followed, to the consternation of many: The MPAA rating system had not yet gone into effect, so many theaters were admitting children to the shows. Although the movie would eventually garner a reputation as one of the greatest of all horror films, the initial reviews were largely negative. But audiences turned out in droves, keeping *Night of the Living Dead* in theaters for months or even years in the case of midnight screenings.

That the movie was a reflection of its times is undeniable, although over the years, critics and historians have disagreed about exactly what *Night of the Living Dead* was reflecting. J. Hoberman, longtime *Village Voice* critic and coauthor of the book *Midnight Movies*, wrote that Romero's film "could only be understood as a movie about the Vietnam War." Others saw echoes of the civil rights movement in the movie's lynch mobs, redneck sheriffs, and especially its bleak finale, in which Ben is mistaken for one of the living dead, shot through the head, and dragged away by meathooks. In the 2000 documentary *The American Nightmare*, Romero simply notes that "what's happening in the world creeps into any work."

Made on a shoestring budget during a hot Texas summer, Tobe Hooper's *The Texas Chain Saw Massacre* remains one of the most terrifying films ever made.

But while the specifics may be up for debate, it's clear that *Night of the Living Dead* is a landmark work of horror cinema that kicked off a wave of low-budget, independently made films far more outrageous, relevant, and downright terrifying than the cheapie exploitation pictures that preceded it. From its opening moments, when a brother and sister paying a visit to their mother's grave are stalked by a seemingly harmless bum who turns out to be a flesh-eating ghoul, to that shocker of a closing scene, *Night of the Living Dead* is an unrelenting nightmare come to life. Taboos were of no concern to Romero and company, up to and including the indelible image of a little girl zombie sinking her teeth into her dead father's intestines. Yet the film also taps a vein of pitch-black humor, as when the redneck sheriff tells a reporter, "Yeah, they're dead. They're all messed up."

Romero would later work with Stephen King on *Creepshow* and *The Dark Half*, along with at least a half-dozen unrealized projects (most notably, a feature film version of *The Stand*). That's something he had in common with several of the young independent filmmakers who would follow in his footsteps. One notable exception was Wes Craven, a refugee from academia who made his directorial debut with 1972's *The Last House on the Left*. Using Ingmar Bergman's *The Virgin Spring* as his model, Craven's attempt to expose the rotten underbelly of the sixties counterculture concerns two young women who are raped and murdered by a gang of criminals, who are in turn tortured and murdered by the parents of one of the women. Extraordinarily grisly, unpleasant, and difficult to watch, *Last House* received largely hostile reviews, although Roger Ebert gave it three and a half stars, calling it "a powerful narrative, told so directly and strongly that the audience (mostly in the mood for just another good old exploitation film) was rocked back on its psychic heels."

In the summer of 1973, Austin native Tobe Hooper, who had studied filmmaking at the University of Texas, gathered a cast and crew to shoot what is still *the* masterpiece of low-budget independent horror. With a minimum of gore but no shortage of creative ferocity and cinematic ingenuity, *The Texas Chain Saw Massacre* repurposed the Ed Gein legend that served as the basis for *Psycho* into something far more primal and dangerous. Hooper's film (cowritten with Kim Henkel) set the template for many a backwoods horror movie to come (a van full of young people, a suspicious old man at the gas station, a family of freaks with a taste for weird meat), but none would ever equal its grimy authenticity or depraved energy.

In 1977, Romero followed up *Night of the Living Dead* with another zombie opus channeling the zeitgeist of its times: *Dawn of the Dead* with its biting satire of Me Decade consumerism. In 1978, USC graduate John Carpenter would birth the slasher movie, a horror subgenre that would dominate the next decade, with the nerve-shattering *Halloween*. By now, a new name had begun to dominate the world of horror fiction, and like Romero, Hooper and Carpenter would have a hand in aiding and abetting Stephen King's transition from bookstores to the silver screen.

1976 to 1983

Becoming a Brand Name

The Boogeyman

Carrie and *Salem's Lot* Introduce America's New Horror King

From Trash to Treasure

When Tabitha King fished the manuscript of her husband's novel-in-progress *Carrie* out of the trashcan and urged him to complete it, she set off a chain reaction that would have far-reaching ramifications for the couple, not to mention American pop culture. Selling the completed manuscript to Doubleday for $2,500 in March of 1973 was the breakthrough Stephen King had been working toward for years, but it was a drop in the bucket compared to what would follow. Only two months later, Doubleday sold the paperback rights to the novel to New American Library for $400,000, half of which went to King. For a struggling married couple raising two children in a trailer in Hermon, Maine, it was truly life-changing money.

Although the hardcover edition of *Carrie* was not a best seller, the cinematic potential of its story of a tormented teenage girl with telekinetic powers was readily apparent. King and his publisher hoped to score another big payday by auctioning off the movie rights, but although the book drew some interest from Hollywood, most of the offers were underwhelming. In August 1974, a one-year option was purchased for $45,000 by Paul Monash, producer of *Butch Cassidy and the Sundance Kid* and screenwriter of the excellent Boston crime drama *The Friends of Eddie Coyle*, which King particularly admired. "We didn't do wonderfully well," King noted, "but I got a piece of the action, so the money end of it was all right." As it turned out, however, the film version of *Carrie* would have an incalculable effect on King's career, far beyond the "all right" money end of it.

The novel presented several challenges for Monash and his cowriter Lawrence D. Cohen as they set about adapting it for the screen. It's hard to believe, given the thousand-page behemoths King would routinely turn out over the years, but the author's original draft of *Carrie* barely qualified as a novella. In order to pad it out to novel length, King added mock newspaper articles, journal entries, and transcripts from a "White Commission Report" on the events of the story. Initially, Monash and Cohen tried to incorporate these elements into the screenplay using a flashback structure, with Carrie's story unfolding through the testimony of surviving high school student Sue Snell. Cohen retained this device for the script's second draft (credited to him alone), but eventually this pseudo-documentary technique was abandoned altogether.

With a workable script in hand, Monash made the rounds of the Hollywood studios. "I think he went to Twentieth Century first," King recalled, "then Paramount, and finally got this deal with United Artists." Now *Carrie* needed a director . . . and as it turned out, a director needed *Carrie*, too.

De Palma's Date with *Carrie*

Once he'd sold the movie rights to *Carrie*, Stephen King had no say over any aspect of the production, including the script, casting, and choice of director. Nonetheless, when asked who he would pick to direct it if he could get anyone at all, King replied, "There's this guy named Brian De Palma who did a film called *Sisters*. It was a scary monster." As it happened, a writer friend of De Palma's had given him a copy of *Carrie* shortly after it was published. The director loved the book and immediately set his sights on turning it into a movie.

A contemporary of the "New Hollywood" filmmakers such as Francis Ford Coppola, Martin Scorsese, and George Lucas, De Palma had begun his directing career in the 1960s, collaborating with a young Robert De Niro on the experimental comedies *Greetings* and *Hi, Mom!* His fixation on the films of Alfred Hitchcock, in particular *Psycho*, became apparent in the early 1970s, with such visually striking psychological thrillers as *Obsession* and the aforementioned *Sisters*. It's easy to see why De Palma was attracted to King's novel, which offered the opportunity to showcase his bag of tricks for a wider audience.

As De Palma recalled in a 1977 interview with *Cinefantastique*, Monash was not convinced he was the man to direct *Carrie*, but United Artists executives Mike Medavoy and Eric Pleskow "were emphatic that they wanted me to direct the film. They didn't think it should be made by anyone else . . . it was only because of pressure brought about by the studio people that [Monash] came around to thinking that maybe I was the right person for his film." De Palma was hired and given a tight budget of $1.8 million to bring *Carrie* to the screen.

Intent on finding fresh faces to portray the high school characters in the film, De Palma joined fellow filmmaker George Lucas for an auspicious joint casting session. "George and I were both looking for unknowns," De Palma noted in the DVD documentary *Acting Carrie*, "so we sat together and literally went through hundreds of boys and girls looking for the cast for *Carrie* and *Star Wars*." William Katt was considered for the role of Luke Skywalker, and Lucas had his eye on Amy Irving for Princess Leia, but in the end, both wound up in De Palma's cast. (The actress who *did* play Princess Leia, Carrie Fisher, has denied a long-standing rumor that she lost the title role in *Carrie* because she refused to do nudity.)

For the role of Carrie's fanatical mother, De Palma managed to lure Piper Laurie, who had not appeared on the big screen since 1961's *The Hustler*, out of retirement. Betty Buckley, Nancy Allen (who would later marry De Palma), and John Travolta (already a television star on *Welcome Back, Kotter*) rounded out the supporting cast. The lead role proved the toughest to crack. Linda Blair, Melanie Griffith, and Glenn Close all auditioned for the part, but Sissy Spacek, who was married to *Carrie*'s art director, Jack Fisk, and had worked as a set dresser on De Palma's *Phantom of the Paradise*, was intent on landing the role.

As Spacek recalls in her memoir *My Extraordinary Ordinary Life*, "I wanted this part so badly I could taste it . . . I got ready for the test by not showering and smearing Vaseline in my hair. I rummaged through my trunks and found a pale blue sailor dress that my mother had someone make for me in the seventh grade. I looked like a total dork, and that was the point." Spacek's unique preparation had the desired effect, and the star-making role of Carrie White was hers.

Production on the film began in February 1976 and continued for fifty shooting days at various locations around Southern California. (Like most of King's novels, *Carrie* is set in Maine, but De Palma's version seems to take place in Anytown, USA.) The final shooting script stuck closely to King's core story of a teenage outcast with extraordinary powers. Raised in a strictly religious household by her fanatical mother, Carrie White is the black sheep among her classmates at Bates High School (cheekily named, in typical De Palma fashion, for Hitchcock's psycho Norman Bates). When school heartthrob Tommy Ross invites her to the prom, under pressure from his girlfriend, Sue, to show the poor girl some pity, popular kids Chris Hargensen (described in the script as "sexual dynamite," and as portrayed by Nancy Allen, living up to the billing), and Billy Nolan (a meaner variation on *Kotter*'s Barbarino) plot a final humiliation: rigging the vote for prom king and queen in Carrie's favor, then dousing her with pig's blood during her moment of triumph. The plot backfires when a mortified Carrie unleashes her telekinetic abilities, laying waste to her tormentors and innocents alike.

Although relatively unknown at the time, Sissy Spacek beat out Linda Blair, Melanie Griffith, and Glenn Close for the title role in Brian De Palma's *Carrie*.

De Palma establishes Carrie's place in the high school hierarchy immediately and efficiently, with an opening volleyball scene that makes clear (without ever stating it) that Carrie was picked last. One of the film's signature sequences follows, as the director takes us into the girls' locker room-as-*Penthouse Forum* letter: steam, slow motion, delicate piano and strings, towel snapping, and ample nubile nudity. Carrie is in the shower—it sometimes seems as though De Palma has spent half his career coming up with variations on *Psycho*'s shower scene—when the movie's tone turns on a dime (not for the last time).

Blood trickles down her leg as she gets her period for the first time. She has no idea what's happening. Terrified, she staggers out into the locker room, where her sympathetic and understanding classmates pelt her with tampons while chanting, "Plug it up!" (It's fitting that Stephen King's first published novel, as well as the first film made from his work, is based in high school—for many of us, our first taste of true horror.) De Palma hints at Carrie's power when a light blows out, accompanied by the first two notes from Bernard Herrmann's famous *Psycho* score. (We hear the same two notes a bit later, when Carrie uses her powers to knock over a kid circling her on his bike and taunting her.)

Despite these early signals that *Carrie* is just another *Psycho* pastiche, however, De Palma's film carves out its own territory, and would go on to become as influential on a new generation as Hitchcock's work had been on its. The whole "Dead Teenager" genre, from *Halloween* to *Friday the 13th* to *A Nightmare on Elm Street*, owes a debt to De Palma's *Psycho*-meets-*American Graffiti* template.

Still, echoes of *Psycho* reverberate in the scenes of Carrie's home life with her deeply disturbed mother, played to larger-than-life perfection by Piper Laurie. The Gothic atmosphere of the White residence inevitably recalls the Bates mansion and any number of haunted houses from Hollywood past, but its dark recesses, oppressive religious decor, and hundreds, perhaps thousands, of burning candles make for a uniquely oppressive, unwelcoming environment. That Margaret White's notion of cozy domesticity is serving the family dinner under a wall-sized mural of the Last Supper tells us all we need to know about her.

In marked contrast to these bleak domestic vignettes, the scenes revolving around Carrie's "cool kid" classmates have a comic, lightly parodic tone that anticipates high school comedies of the eighties, such as *Fast Times at Ridgemont High*. The girls' detention workouts under the supervision of Miss Collins are accompanied by wheezing synthesizer bleats 180 degrees removed from composer Pino Donaggio's neo-Herrmann orchestration. When a throwaway sequence in which Tommy and his friends try on tuxedos runs a little long for De Palma's liking, he simply hits the fast-forward button, a prescient nod to the short attention spans of the home video generation to come.

De Palma's movie-movie sensibility reaches its apotheosis with the prom sequence, still probably his crowning achievement as a filmmaker. The artifice of the setting is perfectly matched to the unreality of the situation that confronts Carrie: Tommy has asked her to the prom under duress from his guilt-ridden girlfriend, Sue. When she asks him why he chose her, he responds, "maybe because you liked my poem"—a poem he didn't write in the first place. Unbeknownst to either of them, the voting for prom king and queen has been rigged in their favor. When their names are announced as the winners, the victory is as phony as the tinfoil stars hanging overhead. Yet Tommy embraces the scene, and experiences a rush of emotion for Carrie, perhaps *because* none of this is real: it's just a moment suspended in time, and no one can suspend it quite like De Palma.

The director uses every visual tool in his kit for the ten-minute sequence that begins with Tommy and Carrie being announced as prom king and queen. Time becomes elastic, multiple points-of-view are tracked, and suspense is stretched to its absolute breaking point. The camera stalks the happy couple to the stage, under which Chris and Billy are giggling, holding a rope we track up to the rafters, where the bucket of pig's blood awaits its role in an entire town's fate. As in the shower scene earlier, there is a split-second tipping point, from Carrie's Cinderella moment of bliss to her sheer mortification as the blood drenches her and her mother's words, "They're all gonna laugh at you," prove prophetic.

De Palma's visual pyrotechnics would amount to little more than empty technique if not for Spacek's transformative performance. Until now, Carrie has been the picture of childlike innocence: naive, bashful, yearning to be part of a world that has rejected her. At the very instant of wish fulfillment, the rug is yanked out from under her, and all of her defenses come crashing down. De Palma switches to split screen, holding tight on Spacek's wide-eyed, Halloween-mask expression while the effects of her telekinetic rampage play out in stereo.

Carrie takes its most notable liberties with its source material in its last twenty minutes. One alteration was strictly budgetary: In the book, Carrie destroys much of her hometown following the prom, but that simply wasn't financially feasible for De Palma and company. (Carrie's rampage is reduced to flipping a car containing an escaping Chris and Billy, a stunt depicted in a camera-spinning shot that may be the movie's cheesiest moment.) Another major change involves the death of Carrie's mother. King had Carrie use her powers to stop Margaret White's heart, a turn of events that worked well enough on the page but wasn't nearly cinematic enough for De Palma's tastes. His solution took its cue from the grisly St. Sebastian statue seen earlier in the Whites' closet shrine, as Carrie mentally flings an entire cutlery set into her mother, who responds with ecstatic rapture.

The grand finale, in which Carrie destroys the house by raining stones down upon it, was never photographed convincingly enough for De Palma's liking. (Rocks can be glimpsed falling through the ceiling in the interior shots, but the exteriors simply show the house collapsing and bursting into flames.) But the director did manage to one-up the book's author with the addition of a dream-like coda in which Sue Snell visits Carrie's grave. The shocker that made movie audiences leap as one from their seats—Carrie's hand emerging from the earth to grab hold of Sue—riffed on a similar dream sequence at the end of *Deliverance*.

This vintage *Carrie* lobby card reveals the twist ending that made Stephen King himself jump out of his seat.

But it proved to be a game-changer for the genre, as nearly every horror film that followed included a similar stinger in the end.

Carrie was a hit with critics and audiences alike, taking in more than $33 million at the U.S. box office—not a bad return on an investment of under $2 million. More surprisingly—in fact, nearly unprecedented for a genre movie—it earned two major Academy Award nominations, for Sissy Spacek (Best Actress) and Piper Laurie (Supporting Actress). It was the hit Brian De Palma needed to establish himself as one of the key filmmakers of the era, and would eventually spawn a sequel, two remakes, and an ill-fated Broadway musical (all of which will be discussed later in this book). Over the years, it has garnered a deserved reputation as a modern classic of the horror genre.

Most importantly for our purposes, it established Stephen King as more than just the author of an "unassuming potboiler," as Pauline Kael called *Carrie* in her review of the film. The paperback edition of King's first novel had sold about a million copies in its initial run, but when a movie tie-in edition was released in 1976, sales more than tripled. King wasn't quite a household name yet, but he was now a known commodity in Hollywood. As King told the *New York Times* in 1979, "The movie made the book and the book made me."

Bloodlines: Five Brian De Palma Suspense/Horror Films

The career of Brian De Palma is one of the all-time great argument-starters among film buffs. For every fan who agrees with Pauline Kael's assessment of him as a peerless pop artist on par with early seventies Altman and Coppola, there's a detractor who finds his work derivative, overheated, or just plain silly. Judge for yourself with these five case studies in the suspense/horror vein.

Sisters (1973)—The first of De Palma's Hitchcockian thrillers rips entire pages out of the Master of Suspense's playbook, drawing most heavily on *Psycho* for its effects. Margot Kidder stars as Danielle, a model suffering a psychological breakdown after being separated from her conjoined twin Dominique (also Kidder). Jennifer Salt is the nosy neighbor who insists she's seen a murder take place in Danielle's apartment. As in Hitchcock's 1960 classic, the ostensible lead character is killed off roughly thirty minutes into the film and the killer eventually revealed to be a manifestation of another character's split personality. De Palma even lured Hitchcock's longtime composer, Bernard Herrmann, out of retirement to compose the *Psycho*-esque score. But unlike De Palma's lethargic *Vertigo* riff *Obsession*, *Sisters* exerts a voyeuristic fascination of its own, aided by some of the director's earliest experiments with split screen as a suspense-building technique.

Phantom of the Paradise (1974)—Destined to become a cult object from the moment of its release, this horror-musical-comedy veers sharply away from Hitchcock, into glam-rock phantasmagoria. Beating Ken Russell's adaptation of *Tommy* to the punch, De Palma's rock opera concerns a music mogul named Swan (played by ubiquitous seventies presence Paul Williams) who steals a modern adaptation of *Faust* from aspiring musician Winslow Leach (William Finley). Clad in a mask and cape, Leach returns to haunt the Paradise Theater and uncover the secret of Swan's pact with the devil. It's a rollicking departure for the director, although he still manages to squeeze in another homage to *Psycho*'s shower scene—this time with a toilet plunger instead of a knife.

The Fury (1978)—De Palma's follow-up to *Carrie* treads some of the same ground, but Stephen King fans will recognize story elements that turned up in a later King work, *Firestarter*. This time Amy Irving is the girl with telekinetic powers, which make her a person of interest to a shadowy government agency intent on using her abilities as a weapon. There are flashes of originality here, as when De Palma visualizes Irving inside her own psychic visions (now a common technique), but *The Fury* is mostly reheated leftovers. Still, no one who's seen it will ever forget the explosive finale in which John Cassavetes chews the scenery, then becomes part of it.

Dressed to Kill **(1980)**—The culmination of De Palma's *Psycho* obsession, from its opening shower scene to the early murder of its ostensible lead character to its climactic revelation of a transvestite serial killer with a split personality, *Dressed to Kill* finds the director attempting to top himself at every turn, and often succeeding. It's a stylistic tour de force—a wordless, endless cat-and-mouse sequence in a museum straddles the thin line between hypnotic and hysterical—but so derivative it even cops *Psycho*'s worst bit: the psychiatrist's mumbo-jumbo explanation of the movie we've just seen.

Raising Cain **(1992)**—De Palma took a hiatus from suspense thrillers for a while, dabbling in gangster pictures (*Scarface, The Untouchables*), war movies (*Casualties of War*), and box office calamities (*Bonfire of the Vanities*). But he returned with a vengeance, deploying every gimmick in his playbook for this nutty tale of a child psychologist with multiple personalities. Dreams, flashbacks, hallucinations, hallucinations within flashbacks within dreams, John Lithgow hamming it up in at least three different Lithgow-ian ways, shot-for-shot Hitchcock rips, gauzy lighting, Herrmann-esque music, slow motion . . . it's *exhausting*, but even the most stonehearted De Palma agnostic has to admire its unbridled kinetic lunacy.

The Long Road to *Salem's Lot*

Given the success of *Carrie*, it's hard to believe three years would pass before another Stephen King work reached the screen. In fact, Warner Bros. had purchased the rights to King's second novel, *'Salem's Lot,* even before De Palma's film had been released. When *Carrie* turned out to be a hit, Warner Bros. tried to strike while the iron was hot, hiring Stirling Silliphant (*In the Heat of the Night, The Towering Inferno*) to script a big-screen version of King's tale of vampires in a small New England town.

Silliphant's screenplay didn't work. (King called it "dead on the page," presumably with no pun intended.) Neither did follow-up attempts by Robert Getchell (*Bound for Glory*) or Larry Cohen (the cult writer-director behind *It's Alive* and *God Told Me To*, not to be confused with the Lawrence Cohen who scripted *Carrie*). The problem was one that many a would-be King adapter would face in years to come: Unlike the trim, focused *Carrie, 'Salem's Lot* is a sprawling, multicharacter novel, with numerous intersecting story lines. Fitting it all into a coherent, two-hour film proved to be a challenge none of the screenwriters could crack. By 1978, with Stanley Kubrick's adaptation of *The Shining* already in the pipeline, the theatrical arm of Warner Bros. gave up on *'Salem's Lot*, passing it on to the TV division.

Warner Bros. Television executive Richard Kobritz took charge of the project, making the decision to turn *'Salem's Lot* into a four-hour miniseries. (Or, more accurately, a 183-minute film, airing over two nights, accompanied by 57 minutes worth of commercials.) Finding nothing usable in the existing scripts, Kobritz hired Paul Monash, the producer of *Carrie*, to write the teleplay—a decision the book's author supported. "His screenplay I like quite a lot," King told *Cinefantastique*. "Monash has succeeded in combining the characters a lot, and it works." The hands-on Kobritz also cast many of the major roles even before hiring a director. (King was somewhat more muted in his praise of Kobritz's choice for the lead role of writer Ben Mears: "I think the casting of David Soul is fine. I have no problem with that at all.")

Kobritz screened a number of then-recent horror films in his search for a director, but his eventual choice must have unsettled the Warners brass (not to mention the suits at CBS, the network that had agreed to cofinance and broadcast the miniseries). Kobritz hired Tobe Hooper on the strength of *The Texas Chain Saw Massacre*, indisputably one of the most terrifying motion pictures ever made but not one that would ever suggest its maker was suited to the strictures of network television. Remember, this was the 1970s, the era of *Happy Days*, *The Love Boat*, and *Little House on the Prairie*. Leatherface had no place on the prime-time schedule between *The Waltons* and *Barnaby Jones*.

It's fun to think about what the Tobe Hooper of *Chain Saw* might have done with *Salem's Lot*; it's less fun to sit through the heavily compromised version that originally aired on CBS on November 17th and 24th, 1979. Hanging too much of the blame on Hooper would be misguided, however. Throughout its history, and certainly in the seventies, television has generally been a writer- and producer-driven medium, and *Salem's Lot* was no exception. Kobritz made many of the creative decisions before Hooper had even been hired, and by his own admission was a constant presence on the set, hovering over his director's shoulder. (This same dynamic would come back to haunt Hooper later in his career, when he was hired to direct the Steven Spielberg–produced *Poltergeist*.) In addition, television standards and practices were much stricter in those days, particularly on "the Tiffany network." Stephen King had often expressed his doubts about network television's ability to handle the horror genre, and in *Salem's Lot*, those fears were largely borne out.

Today, CBS is home to *CSI* and its spin-offs, where blood trails, decapitations, and misplaced bodily organs signify just another day at the office. In 1979, however, even the suggestion of a child in peril was beyond the pale. Given that the plot of *Salem's Lot* involved an ancient vampire arriving in a small Maine town and draining its residents, including several children, of their blood, this posed a problem for the production. Still, a watered-down approach to horror was hardly the only problem with the miniseries. The general lameness of the era's television aesthetics proved to be too big a hurdle for Hooper to overcome.

Decades before the advent of widescreen HD plasma screens, the cinematic style we now associate with such shows as *The Sopranos*, *Lost*, and *Breaking Bad* was rarely even attempted on the tube. The flat, enervated, shapeless quality of *Salem's Lot* may have seemed acceptable at the time, but it's torture today. Nearly an hour passes before the first hints of supernatural activity occur, which would be fine if the early scenes had worked to establish a believable community and involve us emotionally in its residents. But despite the best efforts of an eclectic supporting cast, including Fred Willard, Elisha Cook Jr., Geoffrey Lewis, and George Dzundza, there's never any sense that these characters share the same streets. They all seem to occupy their own little pockets in the narrative, and there's no life around the edges. When you consider that the premiere of *Twin Peaks* was only a little over a decade away, the complete failure of *Salem's Lot* to sketch the contours of a distinctive, lived-in small town is particularly disheartening.

Stephen King may have had "no problem" with the casting of David "Hutch" Soul, but there's a reason he wasn't particularly excited about it, either. As writer Ben Mears, who has returned to his boyhood hometown because of his enduring obsession with the "evil" Marsten House, Soul is initially a creepy, off-putting presence. Eventually he settles into a blandly dour mode, striking no sparks with Bonnie Bedelia as the local girl who falls for him. Lance Kerwin (*James at 15*) seems to have been cast as Mark Petrie, the kid who teams up with Mears to battle the vampires, mainly for his physical resemblance to Soul.

Still, isolated moments from the miniseries stand out amid the murk. The Marsten House that becomes the home of antiques dealer Straker (James Mason, giving an enjoyable mustache-twirler of a performance) and his mysterious employer Barlow (Reginald Nadler) is an appropriately malignant presence, sprawling and weather-beaten. Looming over the town from atop a hill, it looks like it belongs in the Maine village of Salem's Lot, although the film's exteriors were shot in the northern California town of Ferndale. The images of vampire children emerging from the fog to scratch on bedroom windows were terrifying by the prime-time standards of the time, and still hold up to this day. Likewise the first appearance of Barlow, the *Nosferatu*-influenced vampire, his ghastly, blue-tinged, rotting head bursting into frame to startling effect. (King disliked Barlow's throwback look, which didn't jibe with the debonair Euro-vamp from his book, but Hooper's sparing use of the hideous creature works well enough on the screen.) That Mark Petrie is a horror buff who uses his knowledge of movie vampires to save himself is a canny twist, predating the age of meta-horror movies like *Scream* by many years.

Despite some misgivings (in addition to describing the Barlow makeup as "a failure of imagination," King quite rightly noted that it rarely turns out well when actors attempt Maine accents), the creator of *'Salem's Lot* pronounced himself largely satisfied with the adaptation, which proved to be a ratings success. King's concerns about the viability of the horror genre on network television remained, however, and more than a decade would pass before another of his novels was adapted for the small screen.

Bloodlines: Vampires on Television

It's not surprising to learn that CBS seriously considered green-lighting a proposed weekly version of *Salem's Lot* picking up after the events of the miniseries. If anything, it's a surprise that such a series has never materialized, especially given the recent onslaught of vampire-related television. But of course, there *was* a TV series about a vampire bringing his ancient evil to a contemporary small Maine town—one that might have been loitering in Stephen King's subconscious when he created *'Salem's Lot.*

In June 1966, a new daytime serial from producer Dan Curtis debuted on ABC television. The story of a young woman who travels to the town of Collinsport, Maine, to take a job as a boy's governess, *Dark Shadows* was not initially a supernatural-themed show—nor was it initially a ratings hit. That changed beginning with the 210th episode, in which a would-be grave robber unwittingly awoke Barnabas Collins, the vampire who would turn actor Jonathan Frid into a most unlikely sex symbol. Audiences, particularly young viewers catching the show after school, went crazy for Barnabas, making *Dark Shadows* a cult favorite.

That's not to say the show was particularly *good*. Like most soap operas, it mastered the art of turning two minutes of plot into a week's worth of episodes, and its rapid-fire production resulted in all manner of gaffes and few nuanced performances. But give the show credit for its willingness to push daytime television into some bizarre new realms: By the time *Dark Shadows* went off the air in 1971, its story lines had encompassed not only vampires and ghosts, but werewolves, zombies, time travel, and alternate universes. Barnabas remained its signature character to the end, though, as Tim Burton demonstrated (as part of his ongoing effort to exhume every piece of pop culture from the sixties and seventies) by casting Johnny Depp as his childhood idol in the big-screen remake of *Dark Shadows.*

Dan Curtis went on to produce *The Night Stalker,* one of the best made-for-television movies of the seventies, in which reporter Carl Kolchak (Darren McGavin) investigates a series of vampire attacks in Las Vegas. But the vampire did not become a staple of prime-time television again until 1997, when Joss Whedon made what seemed at the time to be an ill-advised decision to bring his flop movie *Buffy the Vampire Slayer* to the small screen. The resulting series about a suburban high school student (Sarah Michelle Gellar) chosen to battle vampires and other demons went on to become one of the most acclaimed TV shows of the nineties, thanks to its witty scripts, charismatic cast (including Alyson Hannigan as Buffy's nerdy friend Willow and Anthony Stewart Head as her droll "watcher" Giles), and innovative serial storytelling. Its spin-off series, *Angel,* transplanted *Buffy*'s main vampire character (played by David Boreanaz) into a noir-ish context, making him a Los Angeles private detective specializing in demonic crimes.

The success of *Buffy* opened the floodgates (or bloodgates, perhaps) for a vampire takeover of pop culture in general (see the *Twilight* series of novels and films) and television in particular. In 2008, *Six Feet Under* producer Alan Ball brought his adaptation of Charlaine Harris's Sookie Stackhouse novels to HBO. With its liberal dosage of blood, nudity, and outrageous plot twists, *True Blood* proved to be the network's biggest hit since *The Sopranos* cut to black. Its debt to

Buffy was clear in its central love triangle (a superpowered blonde hottie and two vampires, one brooding brunette and one blonde bad boy), but as the seasons went on, *True Blood* began to mimic the scattershot supernatural approach of *Dark Shadows*, with increasingly incoherent results.

Not every attempt at small-screen vampirism has achieved ratings success, as the producers of ABC's short-lived *The Gates* could tell you. But with *The Vampire Diaries* carrying on the *Buffy* tradition of blending teenage romanticism and Gothic horror, and *Being Human* (about a vampire rooming with a werewolf and a ghost) succeeding in both British and American incarnations, don't be surprised if that *Salem's Lot* series eventually sees the light of day after all.

Deep Cuts

- In a 1983 *Playboy* interview, King mentioned that *Carrie* was "derived to a considerable extent from a terrible B-grade movie called *Brain from Planet Arous*." King has made this connection several times since, while admitting he's unclear on exactly how this 1957 sci-fi flick influenced his novel. Directed by Nathan Juran (under the alias Nathan Hertz, which he also used for *Attack of the 50 Foot Woman*), the low-budget *Arous* concerns a giant floating brain with eyeballs taking over the body of an ordinary man (John Agar) in order to conquer the earth. It's an amusing piece of fifties schlock, but aside from a scene in which the brain-possessed Agar uses his enhanced mental abilities to destroy a town built for nuclear testing, there's not much here to suggest a precursor to *Carrie*.

- They're uncredited in the film, but the band playing at the prom in *Carrie* is Vance or Towers. Consisting of vocalist/guitarist Michael Towers, vocalist/keyboardist Glen Vance, bassist Dan Protheroe, and drummer Jim Said, the band released only one album, the eponymous *Vance or Towers*, in 1975. A&M Records did little to promote the record, which quickly sank into obscurity and has never been released on CD. It's a shame, because *Vance or Towers* contains some terrifically catchy seventies power pop tunes (some of which can be found on YouTube), including "Education Blues," the Cheap Trick-esque rocker they play in *Carrie*.

- One reason *Carrie*'s concluding dream sequence is particularly eerie is that it's played in reverse (a technique David Lynch would later employ to legendary effect on *Twin Peaks*). When we see Amy Irving walking toward Carrie's final resting place, she was actually walking backwards away from it. Pay attention to the background action and you'll see a car traveling in reverse behind Irving. The hand emerging from the grave was actually Sissy Spacek's. De Palma didn't think this was necessary, but Spacek insisted on it.

- What happened to the apostrophe in *Salem's Lot*? King had planned to call his novel *Jerusalem's Lot*, which is the full name of the town in the book. His publisher wanted something shorter and less religious-sounding, so he changed it to *'Salem's Lot*, the abbreviation many of the book's characters use.

In the reality of the TV miniseries, however, the town's name had long ago been officially shortened to Salem's Lot, hence the vanishing apostrophe.

- A 112-minute theatrical version of *Salem's Lot*, with several alternate scenes, was edited for release in European markets. It is this cut that was released on VHS, under the title *Salem's Lot: The Movie*, in 1987. The full-length miniseries is now available on DVD.

- The casting of Elisha Cook Jr. and Marie Windsor was something of an inside joke on the part of producer Richard Kobritz. Cook and Windsor had played a married couple in Stanley Kubrick's 1956 heist picture *The Killing*, and Kobritz decided to pay homage by casting them as former lovers. Coincidentally or not, Kubrick was at that very moment working on his own Stephen King adaptation: *The Shining*.

Forever . . . and Ever . . .

The Enduring Mysteries of *The Shining*

Ghosts of the Overlook

Stephen King's third novel was inspired by a visit to the Stanley Hotel in Estes Park, Colorado. King and his wife Tabitha were the only guests, as the hotel was shutting down for the winter, and wandering its empty corridors late at night put the author in a suitably spooky mood. He'd been working on a story about a telepathic child, and now he had the setting: The Stanley would become the Overlook, and the novel tentatively titled *Darkshine* became *The Shining*.

The book was published in 1977, and King sold the movie rights to the Producer's Circle, a production company founded by Martin Richards and Johnson & Johnson heiress Mary Lea Johnson. "With that one, under contract, I had a screenplay and a rewrite," King told interviewer David Chute. "I did a screenplay for it, and while I was working on it, Producer's Circle just turned around and sold the book to Warner Brothers . . . What Producer's Circle did, in effect, was serve as an agent; they took a commission by reselling the book at a profit. At that point, my rights lapsed."

(King did complete a draft of the screenplay, which is now part of the Fogler Library's special collection at the University of Maine at Orono. King's version opens with a shotgun blast over a black screen, followed by a scream and a voice praying for forgiveness, and ends on an upbeat note, with Overlook chef Dick Hallorann still very much alive and fishing with Danny Torrance while his mother Wendy looks on. In between, King delves much more into the history of the Overlook than the eventual film would.)

Stanley Kubrick, the mercurial director of *Dr. Strangelove* and *2001: A Space Odyssey*, had a multipicture deal with Warner Bros. and was known to be interested in making "the world's scariest movie." Warners executives were constantly sending Kubrick material in hopes of getting his creative juices flowing, but as the years went on, the filmmaker's working methods became more and more deliberate and his choice of projects extremely selective. Warners even offered him *Exorcist II: The Heretic*, but Kubrick wisely passed.

Stanley Kubrick, the masterful director of *Dr. Strangelove* and *2001: A Space Odyssey,* surprised many (including Stephen King) when he decided to adapt *The Shining* for the screen.

One day, so the legend goes, Kubrick was going through the latest batch of material sent by Warners executive John Calley. His secretary would hear a "thump" every fifteen minutes or so, as Kubrick tossed another inadequate book against the wall. Suddenly the thumping ceased, and after some time had passed, the concerned secretary went in to check on her boss. She found him immersed in the Stephen King novel *The Shining*: Stanley Kubrick had found his new project.

The legend may be a little too good to be true, but Kubrick did indeed agree to direct *The Shining* for Warner Bros. "I thought it was one of the most ingenious and exciting stories of the genre I had read," Kubrick later told Michel Ciment. "It seemed to strike an extraordinary balance between the psychological and the supernatural in such a way as to lead you to think that the supernatural would eventually be explained by the psychological . . . The novel is by no means a serious literary work, but the plot is for the most part extremely well worked out, and for a film that is often all that really matters."

For that reason, Kubrick wanted no part of King's screenplay and had no interest in working with the author on a new one. He did call King for an impromptu preproduction consultation, a story the author has recounted many times over the years. As King tells it, he was shaving one morning, battling a hangover, when he heard his wife screaming that Stanley Kubrick was on the phone, startling King so badly that he cut himself. Dispensing quickly with the pleasantries, Kubrick said, "I think all ghost stories are inherently optimistic, don't you?" When King replied that he wasn't sure what Kubrick meant, the director said that ghost stories presuppose life continuing after death, which was an optimistic notion. "But what about Hell?" King asked. After a long pause, Kubrick responded, "I don't believe in Hell."

Instead of working with King, Kubrick approached novelist Diane Johnson, whose book *The Shadow Knows* he had admired. Johnson agreed to come to London to collaborate with Kubrick on the screenplay. They worked together for eleven weeks, breaking down the book into component scenes that would work well for a movie and making a number of changes to King's story. Most notably, Kubrick and Johnson eliminated the hedge animals that come to life in the novel, both because they would be difficult if not impossible to create in those pre-CGI days and because they didn't fit the filmmaker's conception of the story. They substituted a hedge maze, a motif much more in keeping with the psychological puzzle Kubrick wanted to construct. Kubrick also hated the novel's ending, in which the Overlook boiler explodes and the hotel burns to the ground. It took him some time to come up with an alternative, at one point asking King what he thought of the Torrance family appearing in the last scene as ghosts looking on as the new caretaker is hired. King felt this would be cheating the audience, and Kubrick ended up discarding the idea in favor of the maze chase that ends the film.

King expressed doubt early on about Kubrick's casting choices. The director wanted no one else but Jack Nicholson, then one of the biggest stars in Hollywood. King thought Nicholson would seem too crazy from the outset, and preferred a "regular guy" type like Michael Moriarty or Martin Sheen. For the wife, who was a fairly strong character in the book, Kubrick likewise had only one choice in mind: Shelley Duvall, who had appeared in a string of Robert Altman films. King, in one of his more blunt, unkind assessments, called this "an example of absolutely grotesque casting," but Kubrick felt Jack's wife, Wendy, had to be something of doormat, or else she'd never have stayed with him so long.

For the role of Hallorann, the Overlook chef, Kubrick initially wanted his Dr. Strangelove star Slim Pickens, but Pickens wanted nothing more to do with the director after their first working experience. On Nicholson's recommendation, Kubrick instead selected Scatman Crothers, a jazz singer and character actor who had worked with Nicholson several times before. A massive casting call was conducted in three American cities—Denver, Chicago, and Cincinnati—in order to find the Torrances' young son Danny. The part went to Danny Lloyd, five years old at the time, with no acting experience.

The final major casting decision concerned the Overlook Hotel itself. Although Kubrick considered returning to the United States for the first time in nearly two decades to make the film, he eventually decided to shoot it on the soundstages and lots of Elstree Studios in Borehamwood, England. For the exterior shots of the hotel, Kubrick selected the Timberline Lodge on Mount

Hood in Oregon. Those shots, along with the eerie helicopter footage taken in Glacier National Park, Montana, were filmed by a second-unit crew headed by Greg MacGillivray. Kubrick sent production designer Roy Walker to photograph luxury hotels all over the United States, and selected his designs for the various Overlook rooms from those photos (which helps explain some of the wild seventies carpeting in the film).

The Overlook set constructed at Elstree was massive, particularly since Kubrick wanted many of the rooms and corridors to connect. That was because he was planning to employ a new piece of equipment on the picture: the Steadicam. Kubrick had seen a test reel for this stabilized moving camera several years earlier and been very impressed with its gliding, controlled images. He brought in the Steadicam's inventor, Garrett Brown, to operate his creation throughout the shoot.

Production began in May 1978 on what was scheduled to be a seventeen-week shoot. Kubrick's methodical approach, which sometimes called for up to eighty takes on a single shot, ensured that schedule would never be kept. Although a noted control freak, Kubrick wasn't the sort of director who planned everything out on storyboards before shooting. He came up with his shots on the day, taking his time to work within a given space until the best visual approach presented itself. As he was shooting *The Shining*, his daughter Vivian was directing a making-of documentary (included on the DVD release), which gives rare insight into Kubrick's working methods. While Nicholson was happy to do things the director's way, Shelley Duvall found the experience much more traumatic. Kubrick was very hard on her, hoping to push her to the state of hysteria he wanted from the Wendy character.

The production schedule doubled, then tripled, stretching on into 1979. Temperatures on the set reached triple digits, thanks to the banks of lights erected to create the illusion of natural winter light pouring through the Overlook windows. *The Empire Strikes Back*, booked to shoot at Elstree, was forced to relocate as *The Shining* continued to occupy the stages. Finally, in April 1979, production wrapped just in time for *Raiders of the Lost Ark* to take over the studio.

Warner Bros. set the film for a summer 1980 release, and Kubrick took every bit of available time to edit the footage. *The Shining* premiered in New York and Los Angeles on May 23, 1980; five days later, Kubrick sent an editor to every theater exhibiting the movie with orders to excise an epilogue in which hotel manager Stuart Ullman (Barry Nelson) visits Wendy and Danny Torrance in the hospital. Although script pages of this scene have recently surfaced online, the footage has never been seen again; only those who saw the movie in its first five days of release ever saw the epilogue.

Initial critical reaction to the film was mixed to negative: Reviews suggested it was too slow, too cold, and not scary enough, with *Variety* going so far as to say "Kubrick has teamed with jumpy Jack Nicholson to destroy all that was so terrifying about Stephen King's bestseller." But the public disagreed; in only ten theaters on its opening weekend, *The Shining* grossed over $600,000. When the movie went into wide release, it became one of the summer's biggest hits, eventually grossing more than $44 million. It was far behind the likes of *The Empire Strikes Back*, of course, but given its estimated $19 million budget, it was a success for Warner Bros.

Over the years, the initial critical reception has been turned inside-out, and *The Shining* is routinely regarded as a masterpiece of the horror genre. Its following is worldwide, massive, and tends toward the obsessive. But one man has always been ambivalent at best and extremely critical at worst toward the movie, and that is Stephen King.

Inside Kubrick's Maze

King had never shied away from his opinion that Kubrick and Nicholson were a bad fit for his story, even before he'd seen the film. He made one set visit during the production, but otherwise was not at all involved; when he finally saw *The Shining*, it was as an outsider. Shortly after seeing the film, he told interviewer David Chute, "I think that the movie is brilliant. And at the same time, I wanted *more* . . . basically, it's a film by a man who thinks too much." In his 1981 survey of the horror genre, *Danse Macabre*, however, King lists Kubrick's film as one of his top 100 horror movies, marking it with an asterisk as one of his personal favorites. "Kubrick is a director who shows an almost exquisite sensitivity to the nuances of light and shadow," he writes. In a 1986 interview with *American Film*, King continues to praise Kubrick's technical mastery, but not his narrative sense. "There's a lot to like about it. But it's a great big beautiful Cadillac, with no motor inside . . . The real problem is that Kubrick set out to make a horror picture with no apparent understanding of the genre."

As he'd predicted before seeing the movie, King found Nicholson's performance problematic. "He's too dark right from the outset of the film," he told Paul R. Gagne in 1980. "The horror in the novel comes from the fact that Jack Torrance is a nice guy, not someone who's just flown out from the cuckoo's nest." By 1986, King was openly badmouthing the film, telling interviewer Jessie Horsting, "I like most of the adaptations pretty well. The only two real exceptions to that are *The Shining* and *Children of the Corn*." He talked about someday writing and directing his own version of the movie. "I would do everything different." King would eventually get the chance to make *The Shining* his way, although Kubrick, tired of King's complaints, attached a gag order as part of his agreement to allow the remake. That vow of silence apparently expired with Kubrick in 1999: In King's commentary on the ABC miniseries of *The Shining*, he allows that he's finally made his peace with the 1980 version.

But all of King's complaints about the film essentially boil down to one thing: it's Kubrick's vision, not his own. In that regard, the author has a point; fidelity to the source material is certainly not one of the movie's strong suits. But it's possible for two things to be true at the same time: that Kubrick's film is not a very good adaptation of Stephen King's novel but that's it a great movie

King wasn't crazy about the casting of either Jack Nicholson or Shelley Duvall, and hasn't been shy about expressing his dissatisfaction with Kubrick's film.

nonetheless. The best pure adaptations discussed in these pages are the ones in which the filmmaker's sensibility fuses with the essence of the source material in a way that makes for exciting cinema without losing the voice of the author. (*Carrie* and *Stand by Me* are two notable examples.) In the case of *The Shining*, Kubrick couldn't care less about the voice of the author, only the blueprint his novel provides for constructing a wholly original work.

Kubrick strips away much of King's narrative detail, such as the history of the Overlook and the specifics of Jack's battle with the bottle, but the building blocks of the story remain. Jack Torrance is a former teacher with a history of alcoholism and child abuse (the latter accidental, at least in his mind) who takes a job as the winter caretaker of the Overlook Hotel in the remote Colorado Rockies. He brings his wife Wendy and six-year-old son Danny, who has a psychic gift known as "the shining," with him to spend the winter. Once they are all snowbound, madness sets in and the ghosts of the Overlook come alive.

The Shining establishes its eerie, unsettling mood from its opening helicopter shots, unnaturally smooth as the camera glides along the mountain roads to find Jack's VW making its way to the hotel. The accompanying music, an electronic version of Hector Berlioz's "Dies Arae" performed by Wendy Carlos and Rachel Elkind, adds to the uncanny effect with its ominous progression and spirit-world trills. The visual of the tiny car against the majestic, foreboding backdrop prefigures the central condition of the movie: three people trapped together in the massive Overlook. This will be a domestic tragedy on an operatic scale.

Jack's job interview with Ullman is boring to some, but it's crucial in the development of the movie's rhythms. In the novel, you know exactly what Jack is thinking: that Ullman is an "officious little prick." In Kubrick's film, the dialogue is so banal as to tell you nothing (at least until Ullman gets to the part about "the tragedy" that happened a few years earlier), but between the lines, the dynamic between the characters is fascinating. The hint of madness to come may dance in Jack's eyes, but here he's clearly keeping a lid on it with charm and small talk. Ullman's motives remain obscure. Might he be an agent of whatever evil forces inhabit the Overlook? Does he hire Jack precisely *because* of that mad gleam in his eyes? Or is he simply the bureaucratic functionary he seems? (For one thing, it's not clear the Overlook even *needs* a winter caretaker; we certainly never see Jack doing any work in the movie, although Wendy at one point takes some dial readings from the boiler that plays a much bigger part in the novel.)

Those who say Jack seems crazy from the beginning are doing a disservice to Nicholson's modulated, exquisitely calibrated performance. Indeed, Kubrick's Jack is not the nice, normal guy of King's novel, but that's by design: The director chooses instead to take three characters already on edge and put them in a situation guaranteed to push them over the brink. That's especially true in Jack's case, as it's clear from the family ride to the Overlook on closing day that his patience with his family is already hanging by a thread . . . but it is, indeed, still hanging.

After the family's arrival and tour of the hotel, and Hallorann's conversation with Danny about "shining," a title card reads "ONE MONTH LATER," suggesting that the Torrance family's time at the Overlook passed in relative harmony as long as the roads were still open. Again, Kubrick's conception is more "cabin fever" than "haunted hotel"; he uses the Steadicam not as a new toy but as a crucial component of the movie's entrancing mood. As the camera follows Danny's big wheel around and around the hotel, it's as if a hypnotic spell is cast, and the Overlook becomes a sort of shared dream-space for both characters and audience.

That sense of shared hypnosis is essential, as Kubrick's horror effects tend toward the psychological rather than traditional haunted house fare (at least until all hell breaks loose toward the end). Who knew a camera gliding down an empty hallway could be so unnerving? Or that two little girls standing at the end of the hall could provoke more terror than the flashes of those same girls as bloodied corpses? Or that page after page covered with typescript reading "All work and no play makes Jack a dull boy" could be a more indelible image of madness than a crazed axe murderer burying his weapon in another man's chest?

Nicholson's performance is part and parcel of the film's mesmerizing effect: It's simply impossible to take your eyes off him as he escalates from thinly veiled contempt to barely controlled fury to all-out bullgoose lunacy, punctuated by moments of disturbing catatonia. As often funny as he is terrifying, but without descending into the self-caricature that would mark much of his later work,

Nicholson is larger than life in the best possible way; it's one of the all-time-great movie performances of its type.

It's safe to say that Duvall's turn as Wendy is somewhat less beloved by the film's fans and detractors alike, but her performance is an impressively sustained act of hysteria (aided and abetted by Kubrick's less-than-compassionate methods). Lloyd projects a precocious intelligence and instinct for physical action; for example, he reportedly came up with the idea for his finger movements when talking to his imaginary friend Tony. (After only one more screen role, as young G. Gordon Liddy in a TV-movie adaptation of the Watergate criminal's autobiography, Lloyd gave up acting entirely. He is now a college professor in the Midwest who wants nothing to do with *The Shining* or his contributions to its legacy, although he did make a rare horror convention appearance for charity in 2009.)

One of King's frequent complaints about the film is that Kubrick appears indifferent to the conventions of the horror film. As far as the author is concerned, the director doesn't even understand the genre. But when has Kubrick ever cared about genre conventions? Certainly not when he made *2001: A Space Odyssey*, which reinvented the science fiction film, or *Full Metal Jacket*, with its unique bifurcated structure. Kubrick spoke of his desire to "explode the traditional narrative structure," and *The Shining* may be his ultimate expression of that aesthetic. Emptied of King's specifics, *The Shining* becomes a cinematic Rorschach test, its baroque visuals, haunting music, and entrancing rhythms forcing the audience into active participation. It's certainly possible to view it as a straightforward horror story about alcoholism or family dysfunction or even writer's block, but its style invites obsessive scrutiny, and its seductive expression of madness makes it an inviting target for a particular strain of cinephilic insanity.

Room 237

In January 2012, a most unusual documentary premiered at the Sundance Film Festival. Subtitled "Being an inquiry into *The Shining* in nine parts," director Rodney Ascher's *Room 237* explores some of the most prominent theories about Kubrick's film that have surfaced over the past three decades. Comprised of clips from *The Shining* and other movies (mostly, but not all, by Kubrick), often manipulated and repurposed, and voice-only interviews with five obsessive *Shining* fans, *Room 237* imagines the movie as, among other things: an allegory for the genocide of the American Indian; a secret history of the Holocaust; an exercise in subliminal imagery inspired by Madison Avenue; and, most outrageously, Kubrick's apology for faking the moon landing.

Ascher's film takes its name from the room Halloran tells Danny to avoid in the Overlook Hotel; it's a room Danny is continually drawn to, and later, the room in which his father encounters a beautiful woman who turns into a decaying hag. It's one of *The Shining*'s open-ended mysteries: We don't really know what happened there, or why that room in particular is singled out when the entire hotel appears to brimming with evil. In the context of Ascher's documentary, "Room 237" represents that aspect of *The Shining* that allows our imaginations to run wild. And over the years, Kubrick's film has attracted more than its share of wild interpretations.

The first such theory to gain widespread notoriety was ABC news reporter Bill Blakemore's analysis of the film as allegory for the Native American genocide. In 1987, around the time of *Full Metal Jacket*'s release, Blakemore wrote an article for the *San Francisco Chronicle* called "The Family of Man." In it, he argued that the film's many American Indian motifs, including the cans of Calumet baking powder seen in the pantry and the suggestion that the Overlook was built on "an old Indian burial ground," are signifiers of the real story Kubrick is telling. "It is about the murder of a race—the race of Native Americans—and the consequences of that murder," Blakemore writes.

"AN AMAZING DOCUMENTARY ABOUT STANLEY KUBRICK'S 'THE SHINING.' IT'S A VERITABLE KUBRICKIAN DA VINCI CODE."
—OWEN GLEIBERMAN, ENTERTAINMENT WEEKLY

ROOM 237

OFFICIAL SELECTION SUNDANCE FILM FESTIVAL · OFFICIAL SELECTION CANNES FILM FESTIVAL · OFFICIAL SELECTION NEW YORK FILM FESTIVAL · WINNER BEST DIRECTOR FANTASTIC FEST

MANY WAYS IN, NO WAY OUT.

IFC MIDNIGHT & HIGHLAND PARK CLASSICS PRESENT "ROOM 237" FEATURING INTERVIEWS WITH: BILL BLAKEMORE, GEOFFREY COCKS, JULI KEARNS, JOHN FELL RYAN AND JAY WEIDNER MUSIC JONATHAN SNIPES & WILLIAM HUTSON AND THE CARETAKER SOUND EDITOR IAN HERZON HPC ☐ EDITOR ANDREW HERWITZ PRODUCER P. DAVID EBERSOLE TODD HUGHES DIRECTOR OF PHOTOGRAPHY TIM KIRK DIRECTED BY RODNEY ASCHER IFC

Fans of Kubrick's *The Shining* tend to be obsessive, as this unique documentary exploring some of the wildest theories about the film proves.

Geoffrey Cocks disagrees. A professor at Albion College and the author of *The Wolf at the Door: Stanley Kubrick, History, and the Holocaust*, Cocks believes Kubrick was stymied in his attempts at taking on the Holocaust directly and therefore chose to make *The Shining* as his oblique commentary on the subject. He points to the German-made typewriter, the music selections, and the frequent use of the number 42 as evidence of his assertions. Then there are those, including conspiracy theorist Jay Weidner, who believe Kubrick staged the Apollo 11 moon landing footage for NASA in 1969, and was so consumed with guilt that he made *The Shining* as his veiled confession.

Others tumble down the rabbit hole of frame-by-frame analysis, creating elaborate maps of the Overlook's impossible architecture or finding hidden meanings in the patterns that appear when the film is simultaneously projected forward and backward. Continuity errors (a chair disappearing from the background of one shot) take on totemic significance, and scrutiny of the smallest details becomes the basis of ever more wild theorizing. (Just who is the enigmatic Bill Watson who sits in on Jack's job interview? And why is Jack reading a *Playgirl* magazine in the waiting room?)

In some quarters, *Room 237* has been mistaken for an endorsement of the views it presents, while others find it to be a condescending mockery of same. But in its form as well as its content, Ascher's film is a fascinating exploration of the power of pure cinema and, more specifically, the Kubrick mystique. Ascher's collage approach allows us to experience familiar, iconic images in a new way, and his interview subjects form an entertaining gallery of case studies on the vastly different ways we process art. Their observations run the gamut from the downright silly (such as the freeze-frame in which the In-box on Stuart Ullman's desk resembles an erect penis emerging from his pants) to the thought-provoking (the notion that, contrary to the popular belief that the only undeniably supernatural moment in the movie is when Jack is released from the pantry—presumably by Grady's ghost—there is a possible rational explanation: that Danny let him out).

Room 237 comes at its subject from seemingly every angle except one: as an adaptation of Stephen King's novel. In fact, one commenter believes Kubrick planted a clue revealing that his *Shining* is specifically *not* King's. In the novel, the Torrances' Volkswagen is red, but in the movie it's yellow. We do see a red VW, however, in one of the shots of Hallorann making his way to the Overlook in the Sno-Cat: There's an accident to the side of the road, and the car is crushed beneath an 18-wheeler. Was this Kubrick's kiss-off to Stephen King, or merely a coincidence?

The problem with some of these very specific interpretations is that they actually diminish *The Shining*. If Kubrick's film is really just a veiled statement on Indian genocide or the Holocaust, that closes off too many possibilities and makes it a much less interesting movie. *The Shining*'s open-endedness is part of its fascination: it's a puzzle that can never really be solved, and to try to concoct one grand unifying theory is to miss the point. For those who love *The Shining*, it's the enduring mysteries that draw us back time and time again to the Overlook Hotel.

8

Blaze

Cujo, The Dead Zone, and Christine Ignite the King Phenomenon

Bad Dog

By 1983, Stephen King had already been one of the best-selling authors on the planet for several years. He was famous, certainly, but there are degrees of fame, and it took the attention of Hollywood to turn a celebrity author into a worldwide pop culture phenomenon. In the realm of entertainment journalism, three of anything equals a trend, and 1983 saw three films based on King novels reach the screen within a five-month period. It was a burst of activity that made the likes of *People* magazine take notice.

First up was *Cujo,* based on a 1981 novel King barely remembers writing due to his heavy drinking at the time. Cujo is a good dog gone bad, a lovable St. Bernard driven mad by the bite of a rabid bat. When Donna Trenton and her young son Tad find themselves trapped in their broken-down car at a remote location with only Cujo for company, a siege of terror begins. It's one of King's darker, more claustrophobic and unrelenting tales, but as some reviewers of the time noted, it also reads a bit like a treatment for a motion picture.

King demurred in a 1981 *New York Times* interview, saying that he didn't think *Cujo* had the makings of a good movie. Nevertheless, he did sell the motion picture rights to Taft International, formerly known as Sunn Classic Pictures, distributor of family-oriented fare like *The Life and Times of Grizzly Adams* and schlock-umentaries such as *In Search of Noah's Ark.* In its Taft incarnation, however, the company had released a low-budget horror movie called *The Boogens,* which counted Stephen King among its admirers. (King called it "a wildly energetic monster movie" in a review published in the now-defunct *Twilight Zone* magazine.) Based on his somewhat inexplicable enthusiasm for that film, King felt Taft would do right by *Cujo*—and he already had a director in mind for the movie.

In 1980, the latest in a string of *Jaws* knockoffs (including the Joe Dante cult favorite *Piranha* and the Dino De Laurentiis–produced *Orca*) was released. It was called *Alligator,* and today it's probably best-known for the amusing fact

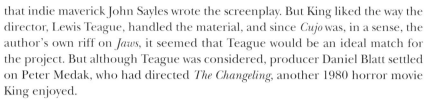

that indie maverick John Sayles wrote the screenplay. But King liked the way the director, Lewis Teague, handled the material, and since *Cujo* was, in a sense, the author's own riff on *Jaws*, it seemed that Teague would be an ideal match for the project. But although Teague was considered, producer Daniel Blatt settled on Peter Medak, who had directed *The Changeling*, another 1980 horror movie King enjoyed.

Not for the first or last time, King himself penned a screenplay for the film that wasn't used—or at least, not enough of it to convince the Writers Guild of America arbitrators that King should be credited as a cowriter of the final script. (He could have filed a grievance with the WGA, but he was busy promoting a novel in Europe and decided not to bother.) But King did make one crucial alteration to his original story that was retained in the final draft credited to Don Carlos Dunaway and Lauren Currier: Tad Trenton, the young boy who dies in the book, survives in the movie. "Films exist on a much more emotional level," King told *Cinefantastique* magazine. "It's all happening in front of you. So when Taft brought this up again, I said, 'Fine, let the kid live and see how that works."

With a $5 million budget and a distribution deal with Warner Bros. in place, *Cujo* went into production with Medak at the helm, Dee Wallace (*E.T.*) in the role of dissatisfied housewife Donna Trenton, and unknowns Daniel Hugh Kelly and Danny Pintauro as her husband Vic and son Tad, respectively. As it had in *Salem's Lot*, Northern California substituted for the Maine locations—specifically Mendocino, which was on the coast and had the sort of Cape Cod architecture necessary to pass for New England. After only one day of shooting, however, Medak departed the project (no doubt due to that eternal Hollywood bugaboo "creative differences"), and King's original choice, Lewis Teague, was given the reins on very short notice.

It was not an ideal situation, but Teague was delighted to get the gig and to this day considers *Cujo* his favorite of all the films he's directed. His biggest challenge, of course, was getting the dog to perform on cue. St. Bernards are not easily trained, it seems, and the production employed anywhere from five to ten dogs (no one who worked on the film can agree on the number) to perform different functions for the camera. But that wasn't all, as Teague explained in the documentary *Dog Days: The Making of Cujo*, included on the twenty-fifth anniversary DVD release. "We had a man in a dog suit, we had a mechanical dog head, and we had as a backup a dog suit we could put on a Labrador retriever, which we never actually used."

Teague apparently never heard the old W. C. Fields adage about never working with children or animals, because in addition to his kennel's worth of canine actors, he had a six-year-old novice in Danny Pintauro to deal with. Pintauro and Wallace spend nearly half the movie's running time trapped in a Ford Pinto together, and the challenge of filming these scenes was made even more difficult by uncooperative weather. Although the movie is set in the summer, and Donna

D'APRÈS LE ROMAN DE **STEPHEN KING**

CUJO

**MAINTENANT
LA TERREUR A UN NOM**

This French poster for *Cujo* suggests *Jaws* with a dog in place of a shark, which is what King had in mind when he wrote the novel.

and Tad are meant to be suffering from the suffocating heat, it was actually chilly and rainy much of the time their scenes in the car were shot. Still, by all accounts Pintauro was a trooper on the set, and a shoot that had begun in turmoil wrapped in relative harmony.

Released on August 12, 1983, *Cujo* opened to decent business and middling reviews. It went on to earn a little over $20 million at the domestic box office, a moderate success for a relatively low-budget film. As King adaptations go, *Cujo* is probably one of the most faithful to its source—which is not to say it's one of the best. To his credit, Teague does a solid job with the film's second half, in which Cujo terrorizes the Trentons trapped in the Pinto. The most effective scare comes when Teague (with the aid of cinematographer Jan de Bont, who would go on to direct *Speed* and *Twister*) tracks the camera at a low angle along the driver's-side door, suggesting Cujo's point of view . . . at which point the dog suddenly pounces on the passenger-side window. It's a bit of a cheat, but it works.

What really helps sell these scenes, however, is the acting by Pintauro and (especially) Wallace. As is often the case with very young performers, it's difficult to pinpoint exactly how much "craft" Pintauro bring to his role. Tad is certainly a shrill and irritating presence throughout the second half of the film (and some fans may not have been happy to see him live through the ordeal), but that's as it should be. Any terrified kid would behave exactly as Tad does in that situation, and his absolute inability to engage with the reality of their circumstances pushes Donna nearly over the edge. Wallace is ferocious in the moment Donna snaps at her child, shrieking, "All right, I'll get your daddy!" It may be the most believable scene in the movie.

Because St. Bernards are not easily trained, several different dogs were employed to perform different functions during the filming of *Cujo*.

Unfortunately, *Cujo* is already sunk by the time Donna and Tad arrive at the Cambers' garage. The domestic drama of the film's first half is woefully thin, as is the lightweight performance by Daniel Hugh Kelly. (He comes off as a soap opera actor, so it's no surprise to learn he spent three years on *Ryan's Hope*.) We aren't given enough reason to care about the Trentons' marital woes, so when the movie ends on a freeze-frame of the family reunited (after Donna has finally finished off Cujo), it doesn't feel like much of a triumph. Teague has said that his film is about overcoming irrational fears by confronting a very real threat, as if surviving a dog attack should put everything else in perspective and heal whatever rift had developed between Donna and Vic. That seems too simplistic, though, and the ending comes off as abrupt and unsatisfying.

King quite liked the adaptation, however, and has often stated that he felt Wallace should have been nominated for an Academy Award for her work in the film. "Dee Wallace gave the best performance I've ever seen in one of my movies," King said on the TCM special *The Horrors of Stephen King*. "It's a performance that grows, in my eye, every time that I see it." It's true that performances in genre pictures are too often overlooked by the Academy, but looking over the field of nominated actresses in 1983 (including Jane Alexander in *Testament* and Debra Winger and eventual winner Shirley MacLaine in *Terms of Endearment*), it's hard to find a slot for Wallace.

Cronenberg Enters the Dead Zone

"In order to be faithful to the book, you have to betray the book." So says David Cronenberg in the "making of" documentary included on the DVD of *The Dead Zone*, and while it might be a somewhat glib remark, there's a lot of truth in what he says. On one level, *Cujo* may be a more faithful adaptation than *The Dead Zone*, in that it more accurately replicates the content of its source material (with the notable exception of Tad's death). But like De Palma and Kubrick before him, Cronenberg found a way to connect his own unique obsessions and style to what King had written. In the process, he not only honored the book while staying true to himself, he crafted an outstanding genre film that can stand on its own merits.

Cronenberg might never have gotten the chance if not for a typically convoluted Hollywood development process. Screen rights to *The Dead Zone* were originally purchased by Lorimar, a television production company that had begun producing feature films in the mid-to-late seventies. One executive at the company had Cronenberg in mind from the start and actually offered the project to him, unaware that another exec had already hired Sydney Pollack to produce and Stanley Donen to direct. Donen, best known for codirecting *Singin' in the Rain* with Gene Kelly, had seen his recent work, including the period piece *Lucky Lady* and the sci-fi adventure *Saturn 3*, tank at the box office. Jeffrey Boam, a young screenwriter with only a cowriting credit on the Dustin Hoffman crime picture *Straight Time* to his name, was hired to write the script. Paul Monash, who had written the *Salem's Lot* screenplay, was later brought on to do another draft.

The project collapsed when the theatrical arm of Lorimar went belly-up, but independent producer Dino De Laurentiis acquired the rights in a liquidation sale. De Laurentiis was clearly eager to be in the Stephen King business, as he had earlier tried to pick up *Cujo* before Warner Bros. swooped in. Unhappy with Boam's script, De Laurentiis asked King himself to take a crack at it. He also hired Debra Hill, who had worked for him on the *Halloween* sequels, to oversee the production. By now Donen and Pollack were long gone, so Hill turned to Cronenberg, who had recently wrapped a taxing production in *Videodrome*. The director felt this might be the right time to take on an adaptation of someone else's story rather than start a new project from scratch, and agreed to take on the job.

On paper, King and Cronenberg might have seemed an ideal match. The director had cut his teeth on a series of low-budget Canadian horror movies, including *Shivers*, *Rabid*, and *The Brood*, and had a reputation for indulging in perverse themes and grotesque imagery. *The Dead Zone* was far more accessible material than his previous pictures (which inevitably led to cries of "sellout" in some quarters), and it wasn't really a horror story. In effect, the tale of a school-teacher gifted (or cursed) with second sight was a departure for both King and Cronenberg, but the director didn't exactly see it as a mainstream crowd-pleaser. He was drawn to the darkness of the novel—its vision of post-Watergate America in decay and its main character, an everyman transformed into a bogeyman by forces beyond his control.

While Cronenberg may have liked the book, his goodwill did not extend to the author's screenplay for *The Dead Zone*. "Stephen King's own script was terrible," he told interviewer Chris Rodley for the book *Cronenberg on Cronenberg*. "It was not only bad as a script, it was the kind of script that his fans would have torn me apart for doing; they would have seen me as the one who destroyed his work. It was basically a really ugly, unpleasant slasher script." Cronenberg wasn't alone in disliking the screenplay; De Laurentiis also rejected it, and Jeffrey Boam told interviewer Tim Lucas, "I think he missed the point of his own book."

That's probably overstating the case. More likely, King simply lacked the tools and the screenwriting savvy necessary to extract what was important in his novel and distill it into the screenplay format. Of course, no one knew the novel better than King himself, and he certainly must have understood the point of his book, but that doesn't mean he was the best man for the job. It doesn't mean he was the *worst* man for the job, either: That turned out to be Russian filmmaker Andrei Konchalovsky (*Siberiade*), who De Laurentiis hired to write another draft of *The Dead Zone* for reasons that no one has ever been able to adequately explain. Cronenberg didn't even bother to read Konchalovsky's script (which had to be translated from Russian to English, and then from English to Italian so De Laurentiis could read it); instead, he huddled with Hill and Boam for three days to hammer out a workable version of the screenplay Lorimar had commissioned in the first place.

Production began in January 1983, with Ontario locations (most notably Niagara-on-the-Lake) filling in for New England this time around. Geographically, as well as spiritually, this was closer to King Country than any previous adaptation had come. With a budget of $10 million and a Paramount distribution deal in place, *The Dead Zone* was by far the biggest film Cronenberg had yet helmed, but with the money came De Laurentiis's insistence on casting well-known American actors in lieu of the more obscure Canadian talent the director had worked with in his independent films. So while Cronenberg had considered Nicholas Campbell, who had starred in *The Brood*, for the lead role of Johnny Smith, it was Christopher Walken who eventually won the part. (Campbell took on the supporting role of Frank Dodd, the Castle Rock Killer.) Brooke Adams was cast as Johnny's lost love Sarah and Martin Sheen as political candidate Greg Stillson, with Tom Skerrit, Herbert Lom, and Colleen Dewhurst all taking supporting roles.

The novel had parallel story lines tracking the lives of two characters up to their climactic confrontation: Johnny Smith, who wakes from a five-year coma following a car accident to find he can see into the future, and Greg Stillson, a Bible salesman-turned-populist demagogue who launches a rabble-rousing campaign for the U.S. Senate. In an effort to streamline the narrative, Cronenberg chose to shift the focus to Johnny as sole lead character and introduce Stillson much later in the film. The director also decided that Johnny

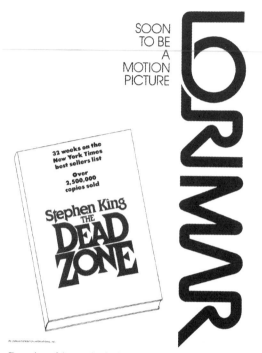

SOON
TO BE
A
MOTION
PICTURE

32 weeks on the New York Times best sellers list

Over 2,500,000 copies sold

Stephen King
THE
DEAD
ZONE

Despite this optimistic trade ad, the Lorimar Pictures version of *The Dead Zone* never materialized. Instead, the film became the first of many King adaptations to be produced by Dino de Laurentiis.

should appear within his visions (as De Palma had done with Amy Irving in *The Fury*), and that the visions should grow longer and more powerful as the film progressed, weakening Johnny in the process. In the finished version, however, Johnny only appears within a couple of his visions, most notably in the burning bedroom of his nurse's daughter. (This effect was achieved, in those predigital times, by having Walken stick his head and arms up through hidden holes in the bed, while a prosthetic torso burned in front of him.)

Cronenberg shot and discarded both a prologue (showing Johnny as a child, injuring his head during a hockey game) and an epilogue (a life-goes-on coda for Sarah following Johnny's death). When De Laurentiis could not come to financial terms with the director's usual composer, Howard Shore, Michael Kamen was brought in to contribute an appropriately somber score. Paramount decided on a late October release date for the film, which must have made sense at the time: King plus Cronenberg equals Halloween, after all. But *The Dead Zone* was never intended as the pure horror experience that combination of talent suggested, and although it opened respectably enough for the time (in second place behind *Never Say Never Again*, with a $4.5 million weekend), it ended up grossing about the same amount as *Cujo* on twice the budget.

With most critics, however, the film was a hit, and rightfully so. One knock on Cronenberg has always been the perception that he's too cold and clinical, but given the film's wintry climate (in both literal and psychological terms), his approach feels just right. The casting of Christopher Walken as everyman Johnny Smith may seem absurd from a twenty-first century perspective, given the rogues' gallery of warped characters he's portrayed over the past three decades, but with his goofy bowl haircut, thick glasses, and quick grin, he easily passes for normal in the early going.

Johnny is only a regular guy for a few scenes, anyway. After his horrific car accident (which inevitably calls to mind the *Annie Hall* scene in which Walken's character confides that he sometimes has the urge to steer into oncoming traffic) and the five-year coma that follows, he is transformed into a haunted, brooding lost soul. It's at this point that Walken makes the movie his own. With his hair now upswept; his waxen countenance and sunken eyes often framed by the black collar of his peacoat, upturned like bat-wings; and his gimpy, cane-aided stagger, he now resembles some lonely, broken creature wandered in from the bleak, frozen landscape. Only in fleeting moments—a brief reunion with his

Martin Sheen proved to be an inspired choice for the role of politician Greg Stillson, the central figure in Johnny Smith's apocalyptic vision.

lost love Sarah, a breakthrough with a withdrawn student he is tutoring—does Johnny's humanity emerge. He is the outcast, cursed by terrible visions, and Walken calibrates his torment with a piano tuner's precision, from a baseline of quiet desperation to crescendos of sudden fury ("The ice is gonna BREAK!").

The screenplay by Jeffrey Boam (with an assist from Cronenberg and Hill) is a model of economical storytelling. When a screenwriter is presented with a novel to adapt, it's almost as if he's a sculptor given a slab of marble that can be chiseled into any number of shapes. The story you want to tell is in there somewhere, and it's what you remove that reveals it. While Stephen King sculpted more of a slasher movie in his attempt (according to Cronenberg, at least), Boam and his collaborators uncovered a character-based dramatic thriller, one that takes exactly what it needs from the novel and not a sentence more.

Perhaps the movie's most overtly "Cronenbergian" moment comes after Johnny has identified the Castle Rock killer as the deputy Frank Dodd. As Johnny and the sheriff are closing in on him, Dodd performs a ritualistic suicide, propping up the scissors he has used to commit his crimes and lowering his mouth down onto them. We don't see the moment of penetration, only the bloody aftermath, but it sure as hell *feels* like we've seen it. More subtle is the way Cronenberg weaves his own "body horror" obsessions into Johnny's predicament: As his powers of the mind grow stronger, his body weakens, and each new vision brings him closer to death. Cronenberg also subverts the then-popular slasher movie trope we might call "Have Sex and Die." In the *Friday the 13th* movies and their ilk, sexually active teenagers are inevitably punished, but Johnny Smith crashes and burns immediately after deciding *not* to have sex with his fiancée. It's a sly twist on convention, especially given Cronenberg's own recurring themes of sexual revulsion.

The Dead Zone takes on political overtones in its second half, after Johnny shakes the hand of candidate Stillson and realizes that this man will one day be a president who triggers World War III. Martin Sheen's portrayal of Stillson is balanced on the edge of caricature, but given some of the cartoon characters who have run for higher office in recent years, it's hard to make the case that Sheen crosses the line. Stillson's third-party platform is deliberately vague, but we've seen this sort of man-of-the-people appeal to the baser emotions before, both in film and in real life. The climax of the movie is tricky, as even Cronenberg admits it can be seen as a justification for political assassination. It's a clever variation on the old "Would you kill Hitler if you had the chance?" conundrum (which Stephen King would explore again in his time-travel novel about the Kennedy assassination, *11/22/63*), but it works because Boam and Cronenberg have kept such a tight focus on Johnny throughout. By the time he shows up at the Stillson rally with a rifle, we're absolutely certain he's right about what he's seen, even if to all outward appearances he's another lone gunman nut. (The only real flaw resulting from the compression of the story for film is that it's never clear why Brooke Adams' sunny, intelligent, and nurturing Sarah would fall for Stillson's appeal to anger to the extent that she would become one of his most ardent campaign workers.)

Stephen King has cited *The Dead Zone* as one of the best films adapted from his work, praising Cronenberg's surprisingly human touch with the material, given his generally more cerebral approach to filmmaking. For his part, Jeffrey Boam complained in a 1989 interview that "that jerk Stephen King" refused to give him any credit for the movie's success. Boam, who went to write *Indiana Jones and the Last Crusade* and *Lethal Weapon 2*, died of a rare lung disease in 2000.

Bloodlines: Five Mind-Warping Cronenberg Horrors

Prior to *The Dead Zone*, David Cronenberg made his name with a series of low-budget bio-horror (or "body horror') movies produced in Canada. Cronenberg's major theme—that our own bodies will eventually betray us—is hard to argue with, but it's the

Christopher Walken spent much of his career typecast in weirdo roles, but he makes for a believable everyman in *The Dead Zone*.

graphic, often bizarre imagery he employed to explore that theme that had critics describing his early films as repulsive and depraved. Here are five of his most vivid excursions into horror, none suitable for the squeamish.

Rabid (1977)—Cronenberg's second feature film (following *Shivers*) concerns a young woman (seventies porn star Marilyn Chambers) who is badly injured in a motorcycle accident and brought to an experimental plastic surgery facility for treatment. For reasons that never quite become clear, the procedure causes her to sprout a vampiric armpit orifice, from which emerges a phallic protuberance used to drain victims of their blood while infecting them with a fatal strain of rabies. Chambers (who finally gets to do the penetrating in one of her films) thus becomes a modern Typhoid Mary, spreading vampirism throughout the Montreal metropolitan area. Chambers isn't bad, but she really isn't given a character to play, and the film's repetitive dramatic structure leaves something to be desired. (Cronenberg had wanted to cast Sissy Spacek in the role, but his producer, Ivan Reitman, insisted that Chambers's *Behind the Green Door* fame would carry more weight with foreign distributors. *Carrie* was released and became a big hit while *Rabid* was in production, and Cronenberg included a shot of Chambers walking past a *Carrie* poster of Spacek in the film.)

The Brood (1979)—Cronenberg has described this alternately dull and disturbing outing as his *Kramer vs. Kramer*, which sounds like a bad joke until you realize he's not joking. Oliver Reed stars as unconventional therapist Hal Raglan, whose "psychoplasmics" technique causes his patients to manifest their mental illnesses through physiological means. For some, this means childhood traumas emerge as sores on the skin; for Nola Carveth (Samantha Eggar), they emerge as murderous dwarf children hatched from womb-like sacs on her body. That Cronenberg views the film as a metaphor for his failed marriage is more interesting than much of *The Brood* itself, but the movie does build to a genuinely jaw-dropping (and repulsive) climax.

Scanners (1981)—Even if you've never seen *Scanners*, you're probably familiar with its signature "exploding head" scene, which has long since become one of the most popular animated gifs on the web. That particular image may have lost some of its power to shock over the years, but there's plenty more where that came from in Cronenberg's thriller about a defense company's attempts to control psychic mutants with powerful abilities. The movie has a generally low-key, unsettling vibe (epitomized by Stephen Lack's creepy, affectless performance), but when it does cut loose, as in the climactic telekinetic battle between Lack and Michael Ironsides, Cronenberg doesn't stint on the stomach-churning gore.

Videodrome (1983)—Cronenberg conducted a self-critique of sorts with this bizarre thriller about a small-time TV executive obsessed with violent, sexual imagery. James Woods is at his smarmy, fast-talking best as Max Renn, president of Toronto's Channel 83, who discovers a pirate signal seemingly emanating from a depraved sex dungeon. Reality and illusion begin to blur, as does the line between flesh and technology, as Renn is drawn deeper into a possible conspiracy. Perhaps too conceptual to be completely understood, even by Cronenberg himself, *Videodrome* nevertheless maintains an eerie, dislocating mood and boasts some of the director's most original (and gooey) visuals.

The Fly (1986)—If *The Dead Zone* marked the beginning of Cronenberg's brief "mainstream" period, then his remake of *The Fly* represented its full flowering (as well as its end point, as the filmmaker would soon return to alienating audiences with *Dead Ringers* and his peculiar adaptation of William S. Burroughs's *Naked Lunch*). And yet, in its melding of a fifties B-movie plot and the director's long-standing obsessions, *The Fly* is anything but a sellout; in fact, it's probably Cronenberg's finest hour (and a half). Casting real-life couples often backfires, but not in the case of Jeff Goldblum (as mad scientist Seth Brundle) and Geena Davis (as reporter Veronica Quaife), a perfectly matched pair of gangly, twitchy, hyperverbal misfits. Their undeniable chemistry is largely responsible for making this Cronenberg's most engaging and accessible work, but that's not to say it's all warm and fuzzy. This is, after all, a love story in which one of the

Before making *The Dead Zone*, David Cronenberg was known for disturbing and innovative low-budget thrillers like *Scanners*.

protagonists is slowly deteriorating into an unrecognizable monster, a condition that has been interpreted as a metaphor for AIDS, cancer, or garden-variety domestic dysfunction. Whatever the case, *The Fly* remains Cronenberg's most heartrending horror.

Christine: Behind the Wheel

By the end of 1983, it seemed that the increasingly prolific Stephen King could barely churn out new material fast enough for Hollywood's liking. While a number of King productions have become mired in development hell over the years, *Christine* set a new land-speed record for the shortest time elapsed between a book's publication and the release of the movie based upon it.

Christine came together so quickly because King had enjoyed his experience working with producer Richard Kobritz on *Salem's Lot* and had gotten in the habit of sending Kobritz his prepublication manuscripts. Kobritz passed on *Cujo*, but *Christine*, the story of a haunted car and its malignant influence on its nerdy teenage owner, struck his fancy. He quickly formed a new production company called Polar Films and purchased the rights to the novel before its publication.

Kobritz had a director in mind for the project: John Carpenter, who had directed one of the seminal horror films of the seventies, *Halloween,* as well as the Kobritz-produced TV-movie *Someone's Watching Me.* Coincidentally, Carpenter had been in preproduction on another King adaptation, *Firestarter*, at Universal, but that project collapsed due to budgeting woes and concerns over the box office failure of Carpenter's remake of *The Thing* in 1982. Carpenter agreed to take on the project and brought along screenwriter Bill Phillips, who had done a rewrite on the *Firestarter* script for him. Kobritz had a fortuitous lunch meeting with a Columbia Pictures executive who asked if he knew who owned the rights to the new Stephen King novel. Indeed, Kobritz did, and a distribution deal was made.

With a $10 million budget, big-name actors weren't an option. Kobritz and Carpenter opted for relative unknowns to play the teenage triangle at the center of the story. Kevin Bacon was an early contender for the lead role of Arnie Cunningham, but he opted to make *Footloose* instead. Keith Gordon, who had played Angie Dickinson's teenage son in De Palma's *Dressed to Kill*, impressed Kobritz and Carpenter at a New York reading and won the role. John Stockwell was cast as Arnie's best friend, the jock Dennis, and future *Baywatch* babe Alexandra Paul as the new girl in town, Leigh.

Perhaps the most arduous piece of casting, however, involved the title character, a red 1958 Plymouth Fury. After placing ads all over Southern California, the production rounded up twenty-four of the cars in various states of disrepair, out of which they were able to assemble seventeen complete Furies. As with the numerous dogs cast as Cujo, each car was designated for a particular function in the film: Some were built to run fast, some to withstand heavy damage, and some simply to be destroyed.

Filming began in April 1983, within days of the novel's hardcover publication, in Southern California. (King's novel had been set in Pennsylvania, but the location was shifted to the fictional Rockbridge, California, for the movie.) By all accounts, it was a loose, easygoing shoot, with most of the challenges coming courtesy of the four-wheeled diva star. A scene in which Christine regenerates herself after being trashed by Arnie's hoodlum tormentors wasn't completed until after principal photography wrapped; special effects supervisor Roy Arbogast used hydraulics to collapse the car in on itself while Carpenter shot a "poor man's reverse" with the camera upside-down. The film was then flipped to give the impression that the car was restoring itself to pristine condition.

Released on December 9, 1983, *Christine* performed on par with *The Dead Zone*, opening with a fourth-place, $3.4 million weekend and finishing with a $21 million total gross. While it received some positive notices—*Time* magazine's Richard Corliss called it Carpenter's best since *Halloween*—Carpenter himself never felt a strong connection to the film. He expressed regret about the streamlining of King's story, specifically the removal of the Roland LeBay character. In both book and movie, LeBay is Christine's original owner, who killed himself in the car; however, in the book, the rotting ghost of LeBay continues to haunt Christine and Arnie. Phillips had excised this supernatural element, which seemed a little too close to the recent hit *An American Werewolf in London*, in which Griffin Dunne's decomposing ghost haunts David Naughton.

Without the presence of LeBay to help explain the car's evil nature, the movie's *Christine* is simply born bad, a conceit expertly conveyed in the film's standout opening sequence. As George Thorogood's "Bad to the Bone" cranks on the soundtrack, we witness the birth of Christine on the Detroit assembly line in 1957. Carpenter and director of photography Donald Morgan (who does a stellar job throughout) used Fujifilm to give the fifties setting a softer, more nostalgic look than the rest of the film (set in 1978). As the cars roll along the line, Carpenter lingers over the tailfins and gleaming chrome of the Plymouth Furies, all of them white except one. The red car draws our eye, especially after its hood slams down on the hand of a mechanic. Later, another worker climbs behind the wheel and tunes the radio to Buddy Holly's "Not Fade Away." He drops cigar ash on the seat. Minutes later, he chokes to death.

The rest of the movie never lives up to this opening, although it's watchable enough. In his prime, Carpenter was the consummate genre craftsman; that may sound like a backhanded compliment, but it's not intended to be. *Escape from New York*, *The Thing*, and *They Live* remain among the most dependably entertaining science fiction films of the 1980s, and *Halloween* is still the apex of the slasher pictures. *Christine* isn't in the same rank as those movies, but it's a solid outing, with a handful of high points and a few notable flaws.

First the good: Carpenter cast veteran character actors Harry Dean Stanton, Roberts Blossom, and Robert Prosky in supporting roles, and each contributed his particular brand of crusty charm to the piece. Several set pieces, notably the sequence in which a flaming Christine pursues Arnie's nemesis Buddy Repperton (played by William Ostrander as a sort of Evil Barbarino) from an exploding gas station, and the grand finale in which Dennis uses a bulldozer to obliterate the car, are executed with pleasingly old-school panache. (In this digital age, it's always a treat to see practical effects and daring stuntwork: When the bulldozer mounts Christine from behind and its treads dig into the Fury's roof and hood, you can feel the weight of the metal-on-metal carnage.) And Keith Gordon has fun with the old Jekyll-and-Hyde routine as the geeky Arnie transforms into a sneering villain.

The main problem is that Arnie's arc is your basic "revenge of the nerd" scenario: He's Carrie with a killer car instead of telekinetic powers, but we don't feel a fraction of the empathy for him that we did for Spacek's character. Dennis and Leigh are rather lightweight and generic, both in conception and performance, so the film lacks any strong center. (And it never really makes sense that Arnie and Dennis would be friends, as even Carpenter concedes in his DVD commentary.) Carpenter does get some comic mileage from the "boy meets car" love story, but it would be overstating matters to claim that *Christine* functions as some kind of brilliant satire of America's automobile fetish. It's a movie about a haunted car, and not a bad one, but taking it too seriously wouldn't be doing it any favors.

Director John Carpenter and his crew used seventeen different 1958 Plymouth Furies during the production of *Christine*, including this one that was crushed in the film's climax.

Deep Cuts

- The name Cujo has gone on to become a recurring pop culture gag (usually involving a tiny, completely unthreatening dog), but the name's origin has been the cause of some confusion. Some have theorized that it's derived from Stephen Vincent Benet's poem "John Brown's Body," which references a house servant named Cudjo, while others speculate it's a variation on an American Indian, South American, or African word. The most plausible explanation, given King's research into the Symbionese Liberation Army for an aborted novel, is that he plucked the name from a 1974 *People* magazine obituary for slain SLA member Willie Wolfe, mourned as "Cujo" by Patty Hearst.

- The novel *Cujo* functions as a semisequel to *The Dead Zone*. *Cujo* takes place in the town of Castle Rock, Maine, sometime after the serial killer Frank Dodd has taken his own life, and the novel hints (or at least, some readers and critics believe it hints) that Dodd's evil spirit has possessed the dog. There is no such hint in the movie of *Cujo*, however, especially since it preceded *The Dead Zone* in theaters. However, a draft of the screenplay credited to Barbara Turner (who used the pseudonym Lauren Currier for the finished film) is included in the Stephen Edwin King Papers special collection at the University of Maine's Fogler Library. This draft opens with a voice-over explaining the Frank Dodd connection.

- The character of Sheriff Bannerman does appear in both *Cujo* and *The Dead Zone*, but there is no continuity between the two films—nor could there be, since Bannerman was killed by Cujo in the movie. Sandy Ward played Bannerman in *Cujo*, while Tom Skerritt took on the role in *The Dead Zone*. When *The Dead Zone* was later made into a television series, the character of Bannerman was combined with Sarah's new husband Walt into, you guessed it, Walt Bannerman (played by Chris Bruno).

- In addition to performing "Bad to the Bone," used in *Christine*'s opening sequence, George Thorogood was cast in a cameo role, along with screenwriter Bill Phillips. Thorogood and Phillips played the junkyard workers who crush Christine into a cube, but by Phillips's own admission, both were lousy actors, and their scene was scrapped from the finished film.

1984 to 1989

Overdrive

9

The Waste Lands

Children of the Corn, Firestarter, and Silver Bullet

Behind the Rows: *Children of the Corn*

By 1984, a Stephen King backlash was probably inevitable. A more calculating public figure might have fretted about the perils of overexposure, but King was simply too blue-collar at heart to ever give such considerations a second thought. In 1983, he'd published the hardcover edition of *Christine*, movie tie-in paperbacks of *Cujo* and *The Dead Zone*, and by the end of the year, both a regular paperback and a movie-tie version of *Christine*. But the backlash, when it came, had less to do with his literary output than with the cinematic product bearing his name.

The home video explosion of the early 1980s had a lot to do with this. The three King adaptations that had been released in theaters in 1983 had all made their way to video store shelves by mid-1984. This coincided with the boom in VCR sales at around the same time. By the end of 1983, eight million U.S. households owned VCRs, a number than would nearly double a year later. The mom-and-pop video store became a regular stop on an American family's shopping trip into town, but in those early years, the available product was a hodgepodge of classic films, recent theatrical releases, and whatever schlock could be cheaply obtained and stuffed into eye-catching boxes. Stephen King was already a brand name in bookstores, but he now became a genre unto himself in the video rental realm, as shops stocked the product made from his work together on shelves labeled with his name.

King became an easy target for late-night comedians—in a mid-eighties *Saturday Night Live* sketch, Jon Lovitz portrayed the author as having a terrifying bout of writer's block that lasts all of three seconds—but his books continued to be generally well received. The movies based on them were another matter. The sheer glut of King material at the multiplex and video store might have been enough to spark a backlash regardless of its quality, but beginning with the March 1984 release of *Children of the Corn*—the fourth King movie in a span of seven months—the quality took a precipitous dive. Even projects begun in good faith, with promising talent attached, were ground into sausage by the time they reached theaters. In several cases, the films had no harsher critic than Stephen King himself.

Children of the Corn, which had its origins in a short story from King's *Night Shift* collection, was a case in point. King had written a script based on the story in the late seventies, more or less as an exercise to hone his screenwriting skills. At around that time, King was approached by Harry Wiland and David Hoffman, partners in a Maine-based documentary production company called Varied Directions, who were interested in working with him on a low-budget project. King had long wanted to see one of his films shot in rural Maine, where the influx of money could provide a real boost to the economy, so he sold them the rights to *Corn* for "a song." When this grassroots version of the movie failed to materialize, the partners split up, agreeing that each would have a year to try to bring the project to fruition. Hoffman moved on, but Wiland sought deeper pockets and found them. The film was to be jointly financed by 20th Century-Fox and HBO, but the former backed out at the last minute, leaving the project in limbo.

Next in line was Hal Roach Studios, which acquired the rights and immediately hired George Goldsmith (*Force: Five*) to rewrite King's script. Goldsmith's draft caught the eye of Donald Borchers, an executive at New World Pictures, which had been founded (and by this point sold) by Roger Corman. New World struck a deal with Hal Roach in August 1983 and moved quickly to put the film in production. Cameras had to be rolling by September in order to accommodate the movie's star: corn. An appropriate field of dreams was located in Iowa,

Linda Hamilton is sacrificed to He Who Walks Behind the Rows in *Children of the Corn*, one of the worst King adaptations ever.

and under the auspices of first-time director Fritz Kiersch, the twenty-seven-day shoot got underway in time to wrap up before the harvest.

Before the film's release, the question of screenwriting credit had to be resolved. In the initial publicity for *Children of the Corn*, King was listed as coscreenwriter with Goldsmith, but the author wasn't so sure he wanted this honor. When Goldsmith petitioned the WGA for sole screenwriting credit, King decided to pass on the opportunity to protest. Although New World had sent him a copy of the screenplay purporting to be the final shooting script, King simply didn't trust them: He felt they were trying to trick him into leaving his name on something that bore little resemblance to what he'd actually written. His fears were borne out, but that didn't stop New World from plastering his name atop the posters when *Stephen King's Children of the Corn* hit theaters on March 9, 1984.

Audiences stayed away in droves on opening weekend, which brought in only a little over $2 million at the box office. The final gross of $14.5 million was far from disastrous, given the movie's $3 million budget (the lowest for a King movie to date), but the reviews were savage, and rightly so. As it turns out, corn isn't particularly frightening, and in this case, at least, neither are its children.

While earlier King adaptations had to contend with the thorny prospect of condensing the author's oft-mammoth novels, *Children of the Corn*, as the first feature made from a King short story, had the opposite problem: How do you turn a thirty-page story into a ninety-minute movie? It's a question screenwriter Goldsmith and director Kiersch never answer in any satisfactory way. The *Night Shift* story concerned squabbling couple Burt and Vicky, making a last-ditch effort to save their marriage by taking a road trip to California. While driving through Nebraska, Burt hits and apparently kills a young boy, although upon further inspection, it turns out that the kid's throat had already been slit. The couple drive the body to the nearby town of Gatlin, which proves to be deserted except for a pagan cult of children who worship a corn god known as "He Who Walks Behind the Rows." At this point, things go very badly for Burt and Vicky.

Goldsmith's script opens in Gatlin, with the children of the town massacring their elders in a diner. Cut to three years later: Bickering Burt and Vicky have become a young, unmarried couple en route to Seattle where Burt has accepted his first job in medical practice. (Burt and Vicky are played by then-unknowns Peter Horton, who would go on to star in TV's *thirtysomething*, and Linda Hamilton, who would play Sarah Connor in *The Terminator* later that same year.) Vicky is ready to get married, but Burt fears commitment, as we learn over and over while they spend the first thirty minutes of the movie driving around in circles. (Ah, so *that's* how you stretch a short story out to feature length!) This road trip to nowhere is broken up by a brief visit to a dilapidated gas station, where it becomes evident that Burt and Vicky have forgotten the first rule of horror movies: The old man at the gas station is always in on it. Whatever *it* is.

Burt runs over the kid with the slit throat and brings his body to Gatlin, where we find that none of the children from the first scene have aged in the intervening three years. This isn't due to any supernatural cause, as it is established that Gatlin's children are sacrificed to He Who Walks Behind the Rows upon reaching age nineteen; it's simply a product of the sloppy, hurried filmmaking that typifies the film. Kiersch invests the proceedings with all the terror and mounting dread of a deodorant commercial, which is the sort of thing he'd been directing before *Children of the Corn*.

It's easy to blame the low budget for the overall shoddiness of the production, but since some of the scariest movies of all time have been made for far less money, that seems misguided. The script is definitely no help. King doesn't always have the greatest ear for dialogue, but you can bet he didn't write lines like "Question me not, Malachai!" or "Outlander, we have your woman!" Even Vincent Price would have trouble making such dialogue sound menacing, so it's not like the poor kids cast as the corn children had much of a chance. Still, aside from Courtney Gains as Malachai, none of the child actors are particularly creepy; as embodied by John Franklin in his movie debut, supposedly terrifying cult leader Isaac is a pipsqueak with a voice like the Mayor of Munchkinland.

Horton and Hamilton are attractive ciphers, and there's never much sense that they're in danger. Burt and Vicky are both killed in the short story, but apparently that was never an option for screenwriter Goldsmith. "It's OK sometimes if the protagonist dies at the end," he told Paul Gagne in 1984, "but it's not often that the film succeeds commercially." Goldsmith also failed to provide a description of He Who Walks Behind the Rows, leaving it Kiersch to suggest the presence of the corn god without ever actually showing him. That can be an effective technique, as the early scenes in *Jaws* prove, but here the presence of the frightful demon is indicated only by swaying cornstalks and a shot of something burrowing under the ground like, in King's words, "a gopher from hell."

In a 2006 *Oklahoma Gazette* profile of Kiersch, who is now the chairman of Oklahoma City University's Moving Image Arts Program, it is suggested that the movie's perceived failings were actually intentional on the director's part. Kiersch, writes Rod Lott, made "a conscious decision to let the acting be stiff, the characters cardboard, the threats obvious and the monster intangible." So it was terrible on purpose? How convenient! Still, despite its monumental flaws, the movie attracted a cult following of its own through its home video release and endless airings on cable television throughout the eighties. A sequel followed, and another, and another, to the point where *Children of the Corn* has become a prolific horror franchise on par with *Friday the 13th* and *Halloween* (albeit a lower profile, straight-to-video one). That, however, is a story for later.

King certainly didn't mince words when asked his opinion of the movie in a 1985 *USA Today* interview. Drawing an analogy between selling his stories to Hollywood and sending his daughter off to college, he said, "You hope she'll do well. You hope she won't fall in with the wrong people. You hope she won't be raped at a fraternity party, which is pretty well what happened to *Children of the Corn*." In an article for the *Castle Rock* newsletter that same year, King wrote about the ten worst movies of all time, including *Blood Feast* and *Plan 9 from Outer Space*. Number six on his list was *Children of the Corn*.

Firestarter Fizzles

Before the hardcover edition of *Firestarter* had even been published in 1980, Stephen King sold the movie rights for $1 million to Dodi Fayed, a wealthy Egyptian film producer now best known for dying in a 1997 Paris car wreck along with his girlfriend, Princess Diana. Unable to get the project off the ground, Fayed sold the rights to Dino De Laurentiis, who was then in the process of snapping up every King property he could get his hands on. De Laurentiis set the picture up at Universal and hired John Carpenter, who had recently completed work on *The Thing*, to direct.

After commissioning a treatment from *Thing* screenwriter Bill Lancaster, Carpenter brought in Bill Phillips to write the screenplay. Phillips took great liberties with the source material, and very expensive liberties at that. When the proposed budget ballooned to upwards of $20 million, Universal got cold feet—a condition compounded by *The Thing*'s critical and commercial failure. (Although now considered a horror classic, Carpenter's remake of the 1951 Howard Hawks/Christian Nyby original was widely derided at the time

Dino de Laurentiis was convinced that Drew Barrymore was the next Shirley Temple. Her career sputtered after *Firestarter*, but she eventually achieved the stardom de Laurentiis had envisioned.

as a gratuitously gory exercise.) *Firestarter* was put on hold, and Carpenter and Phillips left the project to tackle another King adaptation, *Christine.*

De Laurentiis next set his sights on a less experienced (and less expensive) director in Mark L. Lester, whose *Class of 1984* had caught the producer's eye. Lester had helmed a number of low-budget exploitation films, including *Truck Stop Women* and *Roller Boogie,* but nothing on the proposed scale of *Firestarter.* Lester's first priority was to dump the Bill Phillips screenplay and bring on Stanley Mann (*Eye of the Needle*) to pen a draft that was not only far more faithful to the novel, but doable on the $15 million budget Universal was willing to provide.

For a while, at least, everyone was all smiles. King raved about the Mann screenplay in interviews, calling it the best that had ever been written from one of his works. De Laurentiis brought in big-name, Oscar-winning talent like George C. Scott, Louise Fletcher, Art Carney, and Burt Lancaster to fill out the supporting cast. When Lancaster had to drop out of the project for health reasons, Martin Sheen was brought in for his second role in a King movie in as many years (following *The Dead Zone*). For the lead role of Charlie McGee, the young girl who can start fires with her mind, De Laurentiis selected the eight-year-old he thought would be the Shirley Temple of the eighties, *E.T.* costar Drew Barrymore.

Production began in the fall of 1983 in Wilmington, North Carolina. Wilmington was chosen partly because it was home to an antebellum mansion

George C. Scott was absurdly miscast as the Native American assassin Rainbird, but *Firestarter*'s problems went deeper than that.

that could serve as a key location, but mainly because North Carolina was a right-to-work state, allowing De Laurentiis to keep his purse-strings tight by employing a nonunion crew. In fact, the producer was so taken with the Wilmington area and its cost-saving advantages that he immediately began work on establishing it as his new base of operations. Soundstages built for *Firestarter* would become the basis for DEG Studios, where many De Laurentiis productions (including several more King adaptations) would film in the coming years.

The biggest challenge Lester and his crew faced was realizing the many pyro-technic effects required to bring the screenplay to life. As in King's novel, the story concerned a father and daughter on the run from a government agency known as The Shop. Years earlier, Andy McGee (David Keith) had participated in a drug-testing program administered by The Shop, during which he'd met his wife-to-be Vicky (Heather Locklear). The experimental drug had given Andy psychic and telekinetic abilities, a form of which he passed on to his daughter Charlie (Barrymore). Now a preadolescent, Charlie can start fires with her mind, a power The Shop would like to harness and weaponize. After their capture, Charlie is befriended by a kindly orderly (George C. Scott), who is in reality a psychotic assassin on The Shop's payroll. After Andy is killed, Charlie unleashes her full fury on The Shop's compound, which is where the film's major fire effects come in.

Pyrotechnic specialists Jeff Jarvis and Mike Wood created all the fire effects on the set, working with stunt coordinator Glenn Randall Jr. to ensure safety during the grand finale. For Charlie's final firestorm, a replica of the Orton Plantation mansion that had been used as Shop headquarters was built on the premises and then burned to the ground (with ten cameras rolling, as no second take was possible). Twelve stuntmen were slathered with protective gel, then lit up for the scene. Styrofoam balls covered in rubber cement were lit by torch and launched from catapults. Gas jets were employed to blow flames from windows and doorways. For days on end, the set was a pyromaniac's playground.

Despite these challenges and director Lester's lack of big studio experience, the sixty-seven-day shoot went smoothly, in part because De Laurentiis kept a firm hand on the production (and an eye on the bottom line). Universal slotted *Firestarter* for a May 1984 release, making it the fifth Stephen King adaptation to hit theaters within a calendar year. The critics' knives were sharpened, and the finished film provided them plenty of red meat, even beyond the "Stephen King movie-of-the-month" jokes so many of the reviews led with.

If fidelity to the source material were truly the most important aspect of translating fiction into film, *Firestarter* might be the best Stephen King adaptation ever. That it's actually one of the worst is yet more evidence that being faithful to a book is not the same thing as making a good movie from it. With John Carpenter behind the camera, perhaps *Firestarter* would have had a compelling point of view, or hit upon an appropriately doom-laden tone, or built dramati-cally to an emotional and cathartic climax. But either Lester didn't have those skills in his toolbox or De Laurentiis didn't give him the opportunity to use them (or, most likely, some combination of the two). Some of Lester's B movies, notably *Class of 1984*, have a certain crudely comic flair, and his follow-up to *Firestarter*, the Arnold Schwarzenegger vehicle *Commando*, is one of the most enjoyable action flicks of the eighties—a brash, cheesy, over-the-top comic book of a movie.

But the things Lester did well never came into play on *Firestarter*, which takes its source material too seriously to be fun, but not seriously enough to be genuinely suspenseful or frightening. It just plods along, and worse, insults the audience's intelligence by spoon-feeding us every step of the way. David Keith's character speaks almost entirely in exposition: Even when he's alone, he says whatever he's thinking aloud just in case we're confused about the plot that's already been spelled out five times. Whenever Charlie tries to shut down her firepower (like the Hulk, you wouldn't like her when she's angry), she says "Back off! Back off!" out loud, just to be sure we get the point of those close-ups of ice blocks and water buckets suddenly beginning to steam. And as King himself has pointed out several times, there's no reason Charlie's hair should start to blow like she's in a wind tunnel every time she uses her powers, or that Andy should have to clutch the sides of his head in order to use his own. These are just obvious visual cues designed to make sure the slowest person in the theater understands that something freaky is happening.

Despite the presence of Oscar winners, the cast is problematic as well. Even Lester admits that Keith was the "fifteenth choice" for the role of Andy, but the fact that George C. Scott was even the 15,000th choice for the role of psycho killer Rainbird is baffling. It's a clear case of casting a name actor with no regard for his suitability for the role. And while things have certainly worked out for Drew Barrymore in the years since *Firestarter*, her range at age eight had only two settings: "adorable moppet" and "shrieking brat." That might have been a problem for any age-appropriate actress, however—Shirley Temple of our time or not.

The only laughs in the movie are of the unintentional variety. No matter how well executed the fire effects can be, there's just something about a man in a suit howling as his arm bursts into flame that induces the giggles. At one point, Andy uses his powers to convince two Shop agents that they're blind, but judging from the way they writhe around on the lawn afterward, you have to assume he also took away the use of their legs and made them soil their trousers while he was at it. The icing on this sad little cake is the horrendous synth-pop score by Tangerine Dream, which carbon dates the movie to the exact second of its release.

Of all the King movies to that point, *Firestarter* was the first outright flop. Although it grossed only a few million less than the likes of *Cujo* and *Christine*, its higher budget ensured its status as a box office loser. As with *Children of the Corn* before it, some of the most savage reviews came from King himself, sparking a war of word between the author and the film's director. Although he'd praised Stanley Mann's script, King called *Firestarter* "one of the worst of the bunch" and "flavorless . . . like cafeteria mashed potatoes." His comments incensed Lester, who claimed King had loved the movie after an early screening. "I guess he takes his evilness from his characters, his book," Lester told Gary Wood in 1991. "After the movie came out, I was appalled at some of the things he said . . . He's got a sick side, I guess. I've wanted to say this for years because he's attacked me so many times in print."

In a rebuttal published in *Cinefantastique*, King brushed off the criticism, insisting that he'd only seen "part of an early rough cut" at the screening with Lester. And he reserved most of his blame for the picture's failings for its producer, calling Lester "just another director who ended up with his scalp dangling from a pole outside the lodge of Chief Dino De Laurentiis." But King came around to that view of De Laurentiis rather late in the game. Unfortunately for the author and his fans, the failure of *Firestarter* did nothing to cool the producer's ardor for making Stephen King movies.

Off-Target: *Silver Bullet*

Silver Bullet opens with a title card reading "Dino De Laurentiis Presents." At this point, that reads more like a threat than a promise. Taking the long view, it's clear that loyalty has played an important role in the arc of Stephen King's side career in motion pictures. When King finds a comfort level with a given producer, director, or company, be it George Romero and Laurel Films, Rob Reiner and his Castle Rock Entertainment, or Mick Garris and ABC television, he generally sticks with them through thick and (too often) thin. Dino De Laurentiis certainly fits the bill. It's true that King had little or no say over De Laurentiis's acquisition of properties like *The Dead Zone* and *Firestarter*, which the producer picked up secondhand after they'd already been sold. But soon enough, King was working with the Italian minimogul of his own free will.

Their association began in earnest when King penned the screenplay for *Cat's Eye*, a 1985 anthology film based on several of the author's short stories (and discussed later in this book). Determined to milk King's name recognition for all it was worth, De Laurentiis continued to snap up the screen rights to everything short of the author's grocery list. That's only a slight

Quality control was not a priority for Dino de Laurentiis, who produced the abysmal werewolf movie *Silver Bullet*.

exaggeration when you consider that one of these works, *Cycle of the Werewolf*, started off as a wall calendar.

In 1979, a publisher of special editions approached King at a fan convention with an idea for a calendar that would feature text by the author and illustrations by comic book artist Berni Wrightson. King, who had already worked with Wrightson on the comic book adaptation of *Creepshow*, agreed. He even came up with an idea perfectly suited to the month-by-month format: a werewolf story in which the antagonist attacks by the light of each full moon in a calendar year. All parties concerned were probably a shade too optimistic, however, in believing the author of *The Stand* and *It* would be able to confine his text to the size of a calendar page. Instead, *Cycle of the Werewolf* became an illustrated "novelette," issued first in a limited edition and later as a trade paperback.

Whatever the format, Dino wanted it, and he wanted the author himself to adapt it for the screen. King jumped at the opportunity to flesh out the story by tightening its focus on wheelchair-bound ten-year-old Marty Coslaw and his rocky relationship with his sister Jane. Budgeting the picture at $7 million, De Laurentiis hired Don Coscarelli (*Phantasm*) to direct. Production would once again take place in the Wilmington, North Carolina, studios, as well as nearby Burgaw, doubling for the fictional small town of Tarker's Mills. There would be no all-star cast this time around; the most recognizable face belonged to Gary Busey, aptly cast as wild, drunken Uncle Red. Corey Haim and Megan Follows were chosen to play brother and sister Marty and Jane, with Everett McGill (now best known as Big Ed on *Twin Peaks*) as preacher with a secret Reverend Lowe.

Carlo Rambaldi, the *E.T.* puppeteer who had also built an animatronic troll for *Cat's Eye*, was brought in to design the werewolf. The 1981 release of *An American Werewolf in London* had upped the ante for such effects. No longer could a self-respecting wolfman movie get away with pasting fur all over an actor's face, Lon Chaney style. De Laurentiis and Rambaldi clashed over the look of the werewolf, and their disagreement dragged on long enough that Coscarelli was forced to begin shooting without the creature in place. After filming several non-werewolf scenes, Coscarelli departed the project, to be replaced by first-time director Daniel Attias, who had worked as first assistant director on *Firestarter*. (Attias would go on to direct episodes of *The Sopranos* and *The Wire*.)

In order to allow the production to continue, De Laurentiis finally gave his blessing to Rambaldi's version of the werewolf, despite the fact that it looked more like a bear than anything else. Shooting wrapped in late 1984, and the film was in theaters in time for Halloween the following year. Despite the fact that it had virtually no competition for the horror movie dollar, *Silver Bullet* followed the same lukewarm pattern as the other recent King releases, opening in third place (well behind Mark Lester's *Commando*, which may have given the *Firestarter* director a smile) and sinking quickly from view.

Maybe audiences were lycanthroped out following *American Werewolf in London*, *The Howling*, and *The Company of Wolves*, among others. Or maybe they'd just gotten wise to the Dino De Laurentiis seal of quality. Certainly *Silver Bullet* did nothing to change the impression that the producer was churning out King product as quickly as he could purchase and process it. The author must share some of the blame here, as his fictional town of Tarker's Mills is populated almost entirely with crude hick stereotypes, from the abusive, beer-guzzling wrasslin' fan to the deadbeat dad to the bat-wielding bartender. (Although Tarker's Mills is presumably located in Maine, as it was in *Cycle of the Werewolf*, everyone in town boasts a different accent; it's a melting pot of Southern drawls, Texas twangs, New England-isms, and Brooklynese.) The villain is one of King's least developed creations; although we find out about halfway through the movie that Reverend Lowe has a beast within, his backstory is never revealed and he doesn't seem to struggle much with his curse.

The central relationship between Marty and Jane is fairly standard-issue, and the movie goes into *Afterschool Special* mode in scenes dealing with Marty's disability, all of which are glazed with a treacly score courtesy of Jay Chattaway. Busey provides some juice as Uncle Red—it's certainly a role he was born to play, and he was encouraged to improvise on the set—and a dream sequence in which Lowe's congregation turns into a wolfpack is reasonably effective. But the movie's *Jaws*-like arc is too predictable, and it's doubtful that the transformation scenes gave Rick Baker many sleepless nights.

Given its kid-centric focus, it's likely *Silver Bullet*'s fortunes were damaged by its R rating. The final product may have been too violent for young viewers, but it didn't have much to offer older ones, either. Still, Dino De Laurentiis was undeterred; in fact, he was ready to double down. If Stephen King's name above the title was not enough to guarantee box office success, perhaps his name on the director's chair would seal the deal.

Bloodlines: Five Cult Classic Horror Movies of the Eighties

In addition to Stephen King adaptations, eighties horror cinema was dominated by the slasher movie. The decade is littered with endless sequels to *Halloween*, *Friday the 13th*, *A Nightmare on Elm Street*, and countless low-rent imitators, from *Slumber Party Massacre* to *Silent Night, Deadly Night*. But somewhere under this mountain of sleaze and gore, a few hidden gems sparkle. Some are well-known cult hits (*The Evil Dead*, *The Return of the Living Dead*), but here are five you may have missed.

Possession (1981)—For its first hour or so, this English-language film by Ukrainian-born director Andrzej Zulawksi is an intense, impressionistic, hyper-emotional portrait of a disintegrating marriage. Mark (Sam Neill) returns from a business trip to learn that his wife Anna (Isabelle Adjani) is having an affair, a revelation that sends him reeling to the brink of madness. But the real insanity begins when we learn Anna's secret lover is a tentacled demon (designed by our old friend Carlo Rambaldi) that has turned her into its murderous sex slave. Adjani gives a frighteningly unhinged performance—an extended seizure scene set in a subway tunnel is both excruciating and mesmerizing—and Zulawski pulls out all the stops to ensure the audience feels like we, too, are losing our minds.

Razorback (1984)—The late seventies and early eighties brought a wave of colorful and creative drive-in pictures from Down Under, a movement that would come to be known as "Ozsploitation." (For more on this phenomenon, check out the terrific documentary *Not Quite Hollywood*.) *Razorback*, directed by Russell Mulcahy, is one such film. Plotwise, the movie is little more than "*Jaws* in the Outback," with a giant boar substituted for the great white shark. Plot is a secondary consideration at best, however, when it comes to this supremely stylish film, part of the first wave of MTV-influenced movies. A brew of punk/new wave styles, western motifs, and post-*Road Warrior* junkyard aesthetics filtered through plenty of smoke machines, colored light gels, and fisheye lenses, it's certainly more stylistically adventurous than practically any contemporary American action/horror flick. Style trumps substance here, but there's no denying *Razorback* is a candy store for the eyes.

The Stuff (1985)—This consumerist satire-as-horror movie written and directed by Larry Cohen (who would go on to make *A Return to Salem's Lot* two years later) is not quite as heralded as similarly themed films like George Romero's *Dawn of the Dead* or John Carpenter's *They Live*, but it's worth a look. When miners discover a gooey, delicious substance bubbling up from underground, it's not long before the product is on grocery store shelves, packaged as "The Stuff." As it turns out, this goop is actually a living alien organism that takes over its hosts, first turning them into empty-headed advertisements for the Stuff, then bursting out of them in a variety of disgusting ways. Michael Moriarty turns in an enjoyably eccentric performance as a corporate saboteur in the employ of Big Ice Cream. Cohen's movie is very low-budget and ragged around the edges (it sometimes appears to have been edited with a machete), but stick with it and you'll find a witty, albeit gross, ode to the colorful, empty-calories eighties ethos.

Night of the Creeps (1986)—Fred Dekker's writing and directorial debut begins as an affectionate send-up of the black-and-white creature features of the fifties before turning into a free-for-all involving zombie teenagers, brain-sucking alien leeches, and gore and laughs in equal measure. Tom Atkins and his mustache star as a hardboiled detective investigating a series of brutal murders that remind him of the death of his ex-girlfriend more than twenty years earlier. "The good news is your dates are here. The bad news is they're dead," Atkin tells a houseful of sorority babes as a John Hughes prom night turns into a George Romero zombie massacre. Dekker's reverence for the horror genre (exemplified in his naming of characters after Romero, Sam Raimi, and John Carpenter, among others) lifts *Creeps* several notches above the average eighties dead-teenager movie.

Parents **(1989)**—Actor Bob Balaban made his feature-directing debut with this truly odd horror-comedy about suburban cannibalism. Randy Quaid and Mary Beth Hurt are the Laemles, a quintessentially square fifties married couple living a *Happy Days* existence with their young son Michael. Like most of us at one point or another during our childhoods, Michael suspects there's something very wrong with his parents. The difference is, Michael is right: The heaping platters of freshly grilled meat served at every meal in the Laemle household are, in fact, human flesh. What at first appears to be a lighthearted satire of childhood paranoia and suburban conformity turns nightmarish in a way that confirms all of Michael's fears. *Parents* might have been more powerful had it preserved its ambiguity to the end, but if any movie could turn a meat-lover into a vegan overnight, this is it.

Different Seasons

To Hell and Back with *Maximum Overdrive* and *Stand by Me*

But What I Really Want to Do Is Direct: *Maximum Overdrive*

The year 1986 is a pivotal one in the Stephen King filmography. Within a matter of weeks, the reputation of "the Stephen King movie" in the popular imagination completely bottomed out, only to be rescued by a film that did everything it could to disguise the fact that it was a Stephen King movie at all. One longtime association with a prominent producer came to an end, just as another, more creatively fruitful one was beginning. And a fledgling director who had never been a King fan proved far more adept at translating the author's voice to the screen than Stephen King himself could manage in his ill-fated directorial debut.

Maximum Overdrive holds a special place of infamy in the King filmography, but to look back at the circumstances of its production now is to wonder why it isn't even worse than it is. There was no grand design behind the film becoming Stephen King's directorial debut, and it certainly had never been the author's dream project. The rights to the story upon which it's based, "Trucks," had been sold and then resold along with a handful of other stories from the *Night Shift* collection, ending up in the hands of producer Milton Subotsky. Subotsky, best known for producing horror anthology films like *Tales from the Crypt* and *The House That Dripped Blood,* had been thwarted in several attempts at making similar films from the *Night Shift* stories.

Subotsky got no help from King himself, who wasn't a fan. (King had referred to him in interviews as "the Hubert Humphrey of horror" and someone who thinks "all horror pictures should somehow be uplifting.") The producer's first plan was to group together three revenge-themed stories—"Quitters Inc.," "The Ledge," and "Sometimes They Come Back"—in one film. He later sold these stories to Dino De Laurentiis, and got a coproducer credit on the very similarly conceived anthology film *Cat's Eye.* Subotsky's next plan was to group "Trucks" together with "The Lawnmower Man" and "The Mangler" for an anthology called *The Machines.* That project got as far as the scripting stage, with Edward and Valerie Abraham turning in a draft of the screenplay. But Subotsky was unable to secure funding for the project and, needing money to combat a lawsuit, again sold out to De Laurentiis.

By this point, De Laurentiis had done more to devalue the Stephen King brand at the box office than anyone else, including the author himself. The producer had basically turned King's published work into a strip-mining operation, focused only on churning out product with no regard for quality control. But King wasn't helping his reputation much by continuing to actively collaborate with the mogul of Wilmington, North Carolina. Just as he had done with *Cat's Eye* and *Silver Bullet* before it, King agreed to script a feature-length adaptation of "Trucks" for De Laurentiis.

Per his usual m.o., De Laurentiis planned to hire a relatively inexperienced (and relatively cheap) director for the project. But it wasn't until *Maximum Overdrive* was in preproduction that the identity of that director became clear. King had been thinking about directing for years, mentioning in interviews that he'd someday like to do *The Shining* his way, but the timing never seemed right. Having become quite accustomed to doing most of his work at home, King had no burning desire to leave his family behind for the months it would take to mount a feature film. By 1986, however, his children were grown enough that he felt comfortable stepping away for a bit, and when De Laurentiis offered him the chance to direct *Maximum Overdrive*, he decided it was time to step up to the plate.

"Dino is the sort of a guy who would take a chance on Jack the Ripper if he thought he could get a good picture out of him," King told *USA Today* before filming began. "I wanted to do it once because I thought I might be able to do a better job than some of the people who have done it." He certainly didn't do it for the money, as his reported $70,000 salary did not amount to a fraction of the reward a best-selling novel could net him. And the opportunity to sweat out the hot summer months in North Carolina wasn't much of a drawing card, either.

Still, it's easy to see what attracted King to the idea of directing the movie. It was Orson Welles who said that filmmaking was like "the biggest electric train set a boy ever had," and *Maximum Overdrive* would provide King with the opportunity to not only play with that train set but smash it to smithereens. The story "Trucks" was a tale of technology gone bad set at a truckstop under siege by 18-wheelers, bulldozers, and other oversized vehicles that have turned against their human creators. No explanation was ever given for this turn of events, and the story ended on an ambiguous note, with its narrator wondering if the trucks will eventually rust and fall apart, or if they have already taken over the assembly lines to churn out a new generation of killer machines.

For the screenplay, King expanded on the technology-run-amok theme to include jukeboxes, videogames, ATMs, electric knives, lawn mowers, soda machines, and any other gadgets with the potential to cause mayhem. At the studio's behest, he reluctantly included an explanation for the machines' behavior: Earth is passing through the tail of a comet, where it will remain for seven days. As usual with a De Laurentiis picture, production was set for

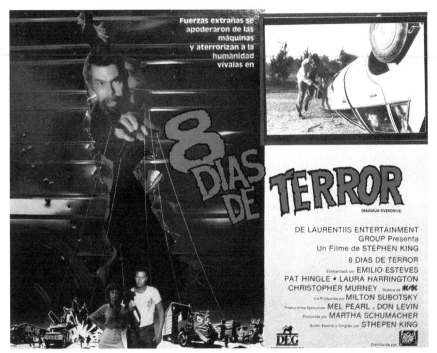

By any title in any language, *Maximum Overdrive* was a disappointing directorial debut for Stephen King.

Wilmington, North Carolina, and its surroundings—primarily ten miles west in Leland, where a full-scale Dixie Boy truck stop set was built. (The set proved convincing enough to fool many motorists, forcing the production to set up signs indicating that the Dixie Boy was fake.)

The project seemed primed for disaster from the first day of shooting in July 1985. After all, if you're going to hire a first-time director, why wouldn't you pair him with a cinematographer who speaks no English? That was the case with director of photography Armando Nannuzzi, who communicated with King through an interpreter during the shoot. Nannuzzi was a victim of life imitating art later in the production, when a remote-control lawn mower went haywire, striking a wooden block and sending splinters into his eye. (Nannuzzi lost the eye and later sued King for $18 million in damages, settling out of court.)

King made no secret of the fact that he didn't really know what he was doing and that, in effect, the production was his crash course in filmmaking. One story he has often told involves a series of insert shots designed to show a truck's mechanisms working without the aid of a driver. The clutch goes down, the gear shifts, the gas pedal goes down, and so on. One shot proved impossible to get from the angle at which they were shooting, so King suggested moving the camera to the passenger side. "Total silence," King told *American Film*. "I'd crossed the axis. It was like farting at the dinner party: Nobody wanted to say you've made a terrible mistake."

King struggled throughout the making of the film, finding the gig to be "one part on tour and two parts day labor and three parts detention hall monitor. I don't think it's the most glamorous job in the world." One reason he didn't enjoy it much was that he'd gone against the grain of his usual creative process. It's easy to rely on intuition when it's just you and your typewriter, but with a film crew waiting on his orders every day, and given his novice status, King felt he had to prepare like Hitchcock would have done, with extensive note cards and storyboards. (He's cited *The Birds* as a primary influence on *Maximum Overdrive.*) But as he would later admit to author Tony Magistrale, part of his preparation was decidedly un-Hitchcockian. "The problem with that film is that I was coked out of my mind all through its production, and I really didn't know what I was doing."

MGM had originally scheduled *Maximum Overdrive* for release in March 1986, but King felt that was a mistake. The studio agreed to move the film to summer if King would do a publicity tour for it. He did so, but his promotional technique demonstrated a firm grasp of the concept of lowering expectations. While the trailers for *Maximum Overdrive* featured the author-turned-director glowering with mock menace as he pointed at the camera and announced, "I'm gonna scare the hell out of you," King already knew he was going to do no such thing. "This is a moron movie," he told the Associated Press. "You check your brains at the box office and you come out 96 minutes later and pick them up again. People say 'How'd you like the movie?' and you can't say much."

Critics were in no mood to dispute that characterization when the movie opened on July 25, 1986. Most were only too happy to agree that King had made a moron movie, but they didn't intend that as a compliment. Ron Base of the *Toronto Star* called it "the year's silliest, most amateurish horror picture, a kind of crude camp classic of badness." The *Washington Post*'s Paul Attanasio noted, "It's hard to even imagine a movie so impeccably devoid of everything a movie ought to include." Both King and star Emilio Estevez were nominated for Razzie Awards, for Worst Director and Worst Actor, respectively. (Both lost to pop star Prince, who had made his own ill-fated directorial debut a few weeks before *Maximum Overdrive* with *Under the Cherry Moon.*)

The movie was a box office bomb as well, returning only about $7 million on its $10 million budget. But while it was fully deserving of its poor reception, *Maximum Overdrive* isn't quite as terrible as its reputation suggests. It's bad, of course, but there are better candidates for the title of Worst Stephen King Movie Ever Made. (And you've already read about some of them.) Under the right circumstances—at the drive-in on a hot night, with plenty of cold beer on hand—it's possible to imagine getting a kick out of it. There are a few chuckles to be had, as in King's early cameo as a bank customer who grows indignant when the ATM calls him an asshole. Some of the vehicular mayhem is effective, although the big opening sequence set on a drawbridge is overreliant on

Peckinpah-lite slow motion. (With its shots of watermelons crashing through windshields, the sequence plays a like a cross between an action movie and a Gallagher routine.) The soundtrack by AC/DC mostly consists of their greatest hits, which is never a bad thing.

Still, even the movie's modest pleasures are relentlessly juvenile. The low-brow aesthetic can be summed up in two scenes: one in which a delivery truck blows up and showers the Dixie Boy with thousands of rolls of toilet paper, and one set in a restroom, accompanied by some of the most grotesque farting noises in the history of cinema. About the kindest thing to be said about *Maximum Overdrive* is that it aims low and hits even lower.

That's the real disappointment for King fans, because it represents such a blown opportunity. For years, King had talked about watching bad horror movies and thinking he could do a better job, but after promising to scare the hell out of us, he didn't even really try. Instead, he made a comic, hyperviolent action movie that dozens of seasoned filmmakers could have done better. Again, it's easy to see why he did it: He wanted to play with all the big toys and make things go boom. And he reasoned that as an inexperienced director, he'd have an easier time working with mechanical stars than flesh-and-blood ones. (The irony is that this reasoning runs counter to the theme of the movie he was making.)

But even worse than not making a scary movie, King didn't even try to deliver on his stated goal of translating his sensibility from page to screen in a way that hadn't been done before. It's true that lowbrow humor and gross-out sequences have always been tools in his kit, but they represent a very thin sliver of what we think of as the Stephen King experience. His propulsive, absorbing storytelling; his relatable, all-too-human characters; his facility for building credible communities, particularly rural and working-class ones; and most of all, the reliable, down-to-earth voice that makes each reader feel as if King is telling the story to him or her alone . . . these are the qualities that typify the best of his written works, and they're nowhere to be found in *Maximum Overdrive*.

Even before he'd finished working on the film, King was telling interviewers he was in no hurry to direct again soon, if ever. And indeed, as of this writing, *Overdrive* remains his sole directorial credit. In his 2002 interview with Tony Magistrale, King mentioned that he "would like to try directing again some time. Maybe I'll direct *Gerald's Game*." It's an intriguing prospect, if only because that particular story is as close to the polar opposite of *Overdrive* as you'll find in the King oeuvre. Given that the novel unfolds as the interior monologue of a woman trapped in a room with her dead husband, *Gerald's Game* would be a challenge for any filmmaker, let alone one whose first and only directing experience came nearly three decades ago. But as a "do-over" experiment at bringing his sensibility to life on the screen, it would undoubtedly be a more worthy effort than his debut, whether it succeeded or not.

At least one thing can be said in *Maximum Overdrive*'s favor: It represented the end of King's working relationship with Dino De Laurentiis. The producer wasn't quite finished making Stephen King movies, as he still owned the rights to some stories, but the author would no longer actively collaborate with him. "I wish him nothing but the best," King told Gary Wood in 1991. "It got to the point where I said 'No more. Just absolutely no more.'" De Laurentiis didn't go quietly—he kept trying to acquire *Pet Sematary* even after King had sold it to Richard Rubinstein's Laurel Films—but King was finally able to resist his entreaties. When asked why he'd continued to work with De Laurentiis as long as he did, the author supplied a typically colorful answer. "It's like a girl who gets raped and says, 'Geez, I didn't like that very much. Why don't I turn over and you can stick it up my ass?'"

Bloodlines: Five Movies Directed by Novelists

Stephen King was neither the first nor last literary talent to try his hand at filmmaking. While most such authors have confined themselves to writing screenplays or taking a turn in front of the camera, here are five who have taken the plunge into directing, for better or worse.

Westworld (1973)—Michael Crichton had established himself as a popular writer of techno-thrillers (*The Andromeda Strain, The Terminal Man*) by the time he made his first feature as a director, but he chose to write an original script for his debut rather than adapting one of his existing novels. Like *Maximum Overdrive*, it's a cautionary tale of man's technology turning against him; in this case, in the context of an amusement park populated by robots programmed to help guests live out their fantasies of the Roman Empire, medieval times, and the wild, wild west. Unlike *Overdrive*, the film is a competent thriller with a solid concept, bolstered by a menacing turn by Yul Brynner as a black-hatted killing machine. Crichton would continue to direct films (*Looker, Runaway*), but had his biggest success as a novelist with what is essentially a reworking of *Westworld* with dinosaurs in place of robots: *Jurassic Park*.

92 in the Shade (1975)—Thomas McGuane (*The Sporting Club*) adapted his own novel for this rarity starring Peter Fonda, Warren Oates, Harry Dean Stanton, and Margot Kidder. A shaggy-dog tale about an aspiring fishing guide (Fonda) who draws the ire of an established local (Oates) in the Florida Keys, the movie was overshadowed at the time of its release by its swinging seventies offscreen drama, which saw McGuane bedding two of his actresses while Fonda carried on with his wife. Seen today, it's an amiable artifact of its times, although McGuane's direction is sketchy at best. The ending comes out of nowhere, and McGuane's penchant for shooting directly into the sun renders the title unintentionally ironic.

Tough Guys Don't Dance (1987)—In the late sixties and early seventies, Norman Mailer directed three experimental films, including *Maidstone*, best known for an all-too-real fight between the author and Rip Torn. (Torn attacked Mailer with a hammer, and in the ensuing scuffle, Mailer bit off part of Torn's ear.) But it was not until the director had passed his sixtieth birthday that he made his feature filmmaking debut, an adaptation of his own novel, *Tough Guys Don't Dance*. A work of unintentional camp, this nonsensical crime story stars a hapless Ryan O'Neal as Tim Madden, a would-be writer who fears he may have committed murder during an alcoholic blackout. Crammed with ludicrous performances (Debra Stipe and John Bedford Lloyd are particularly awful), tone-deaf hard-boiled dialogue ("I just deep-sixed two heads"), and macho Mailer-esque posturing that tumbles over the edge of self-parody, *Tough Guys* is never boring, but there's not a moment of recognizable human behavior in the entire film.

Hellraiser (1987)—British writer Clive Barker came to prominence in the early eighties when paperback copies of his *Books of Blood* series published in America carried a blurb from Stephen King reading "I have seen the future of horror, his name is Clive Barker." In Barker's directorial debut, an enchanted Rubik's cube sends a hedonist into a realm of demons, from which he can escape only by feeding on human blood. Barker gives his fascination with bondage and S&M a workout and creates some memorable demons in the Cenobites, but coherent storytelling is at a premium here. Nevertheless, *Hellraiser* has spawned a direct-to-DVD franchise every bit as inexplicably unkillable as the *Children of the Corn* series.

Stephen King is not the only horror writer to take a crack at directing. Clive Barker stepped behind the camera for his feature debut *Hellraiser*.

Lulu on the Bridge (1998)—Best known for postmodern novels like his *New York Trilogy*, Paul Auster broke into filmmaking as the screenwriter of Wayne Wang's *Smoke* and Wang's codirector on the improvisatory follow-up, *Blue in the Face*. Auster's first solo directorial effort stars Harvey Keitel as a jazz musician who takes a stray bullet in the chest during a nightclub shooting spree. The film takes a magical realist turn when a recovering Keitel finds a stone with mystical properties and falls in love with an aspiring actress (Mira Sorvino). Self-consciously arty to a fault, Auster's film contains little in the way of compelling drama, but it does include one of the hoariest clichés in all of cinema: It was all just a dream.

Stand by Me: Rob Reiner Exhumes "The Body"

In 1982, King published *Different Seasons*, a collection of four novellas, three of which were distinctly nonhorror offerings. One of them, "The Body," was inspired by a story King's college roommate had told about his childhood journey with friends a long way down the railroad tracks to see a dead dog. King decided to raise the stakes a bit by turning the dog's corpse into a human body and used the story as a hook to explore his own past. "For a long time I thought I would love to be able to find a string to put on a lot of the childhood experiences I remembered," he recalls in the DVD documentary *Walking the Tracks*.

Raynold Gideon and Bruce Evans, who had written the John Carpenter film *Starman*, were in the market for properties to produce and adapt for the screen, and "The Body" was at the top of their wish list. The option price was out of their financial league, so they brought in Adrian Lyne, a British filmmaker who had most recently directed the hit *Flashdance*, in hopes of attracting a studio's interest. Norman Lear's Embassy Pictures took the bait and purchased the screen rights on behalf of Gideon and Evans.

Lyne was forced to drop out of the project due to production delays on his film *9½ Weeks*, and Gideon and Evans were suddenly in the market for another director. They found one well known to Embassy's chief: Rob Reiner, who had costarred in Lear's long-running sitcom *All in the Family*. The artist formerly known as Meathead had transitioned into directing with the hilarious and groundbreaking mockumentary *This Is Spinal Tap*, which he'd followed up with the well-received romantic comedy *The Sure Thing*, starring John Cusack. Reiner wasn't much of a horror fan, nor was he familiar with Stephen King's work, but the script for *The Body* struck a chord with him, reminding him of some of his own childhood experiences.

Once he'd signed on as director, Reiner worked with the writers to shape the script around the personal connection he felt with the material. Specifically, Reiner wanted to turn Gordie LaChance, one of the four boys at the center of the story, into the film's point-of-view character. Reiner identified more closely with Gordie than with his friend Chris Chambers, the kid from the wrong side of the tracks who was a more central figure of the novella. Still, even with these changes, the final shooting script stuck closely to King's plot, characters, and dialogue.

Reiner felt the casting of the four childhood friends was essential to the success of the film, and that it would only work if he found young actors that matched up well with the personalities of their characters. Thus, sensitive, doe-eyed Wil Wheaton was cast as the budding writer Gordie, brooding River Phoenix became the leader Chris, exuberant Jerry O'Connell won the role of goofy Vern Tessio, and troubled Corey Feldman rounded out the group as the loose cannon Teddy Duchamp. Reiner spent two weeks rehearsing with the boys before filming began, essentially running an acting camp to ensure his young stars would be able to handle the demands of the shoot.

Once again, Stephen King's small-town Maine milieu was transplanted to the West Coast: In this case, most of the film was shot in Oregon. Reiner did retain the name of the town, Castle Rock, the setting of many King stories. Later, when Reiner established his own production company, he would name it Castle Rock. Only two days before shooting was to begin, Embassy Pictures was sold off to the Coca-Cola company, potentially putting the project in limbo. Rather than leave his former star hanging, however, Norman Lear put up the money for the production himself. (Coca-Cola later sold Embassy to—of course—Dino De Laurentiis.)

The film was shot in the summer of 1985 on a budget of $8 million. Despite his young cast (which also included Kiefer Sutherland in one of his earliest roles, as town bully "Ace" Merrill), Reiner had few problems on the shoot, only losing his temper once when he felt the kids didn't appear frightened enough by an oncoming locomotive (and even that anger was at least a partially calculated display). The only real issue concerned the wraparound segments involving the adult Gordie Lachance. Originally, the role was played by David Dukes, but Reiner felt the actor didn't have the right voice for the narration. Several other actors tried it, including Reiner's *Spinal Tap* star Michael McKean, before the director decided on his own childhood friend Richard Dreyfuss.

Columbia Pictures picked up the distribution rights to the film, and scheduled it for an August 1986 release, only a few weeks after the debut of *Maximum Overdrive*. Far from trumpeting the Stephen King connection, Columbia and Reiner were determined to downplay it as much as possible. The market had been saturated with so many bad King adaptations in recent years, they wanted no part of the stigma associated with the King-movie-of the-month club. First there was the matter of the title: *The Body* sounded like just the sort of horror movie they were trying to distance themselves from. Many different titles were considered, but Reiner finally settled on *Stand by Me*, after the Ben E. King song that closes the film. The marketing campaign was designed to play up the young stars and the fifties nostalgia angle of the story. Although the author's name appeared in the credit box on the posters and at the end of the trailers, there was no attempt to sell the film as "Stephen King's *Stand by Me*."

River Phoenix and Kiefer Sutherland both had star-making roles in *Stand by Me.*

The strategy paid off. *Stand by Me* was the best-reviewed King adaptation to that point, and it became an unexpected sleeper hit. After opening in just sixteen theaters on August 8, 1986, it went into wide release two weeks later and jumped to the number two slot on the box office charts. It took over the top spot on Labor Day weekend and stayed there for three weeks, eventually grossing more than $50 million, by far the biggest return on any King movie up until then. If the author took the studio's attempts to downplay his involvement personally, it didn't show. He called *Stand by Me* the "first really, completely successful adaptation of my work" and predicted it would be nominated for Best Picture at the Academy Awards.

That didn't happen, although the movie was nominated for Best Adapted Screenplay, ultimately losing to *A Room with a View.* But *Stand by Me* did demonstrate that it was possible to adapt Stephen King's work for the screen in a way that honored the spirit and intentions of the original while bringing his recognizable characters, milieu, and voice alive in a cinematic context. Dino De Laurentiis thought he could accomplish that simply by hiring King himself to write and direct, but it's not as if there's a great body of evidence to indicate that a talent for one art form so easily translates to another. (Again, look to Prince's *Under the Cherry Moon* or, if you can endure it, Bob Dylan's 1978 film *Renaldo and Clara.*) There's a reason no one has ever asked King to choreograph a ballet based on *Pet Sematary* or compose a *Salem's Lot* rock opera.

Stand by Me suggests that a better path toward a successful adaptation is simply finding the right filmmaker for the job: someone who is able to forge a personal or artistic connection with the story, or sees something in the material that fires his imagination in a way that serves both the source and the cinematic medium. That doesn't mean Rob Reiner is some kind of visionary, or that *Stand by Me* is a perfect film. It just means he was the right guy at the right time. *The Shining* is a far more brilliant movie, but King isn't wrong when he says *Stand by Me* is a more successful adaptation of his work.

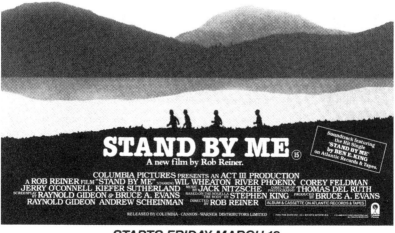

"A MAGICAL AND WHOLLY DELIGHTFUL SURPRISE."
DEREK MALCOLM (THE GUARDIAN)

"Brilliant recollection of a childhood journey…tough, realistic, painful and very funny…a superb film"
NEIL NORMAN (THE FACE)

"A magical and evocative recollection of childhood on the cusp of adolescence…"
GEORGE PERRY (SUNDAY TIMES)

"…Wonderful new movie…hot new young actor River Phoenix…"
BAZ BAMIGBOYE (DAILY MAIL)

"The brilliant performance of River Phoenix is mountain high…"
GARTH PEARCE (DAILY EXPRESS)

"A wonderful movie with remarkable performances."
JULIE SALOMON (WALL STREET JOURNAL)

"My favourite movie of the year."
JONATHAN KING (BBC TELEVISION)

STAND BY ME (15)
A new film by Rob Reiner.

Soundtrack featuring the Hit Single 'STAND BY ME' by BEN E. KING on Atlantic Records & Tapes

COLUMBIA PICTURES PRESENTS AN ACT III PRODUCTION
A ROB REINER FILM "STAND BY ME" STARRING WIL WHEATON RIVER PHOENIX COREY FELDMAN
JERRY O'CONNELL KIEFER SUTHERLAND MUSIC JACK NITZSCHE DIRECTOR OF PHOTOGRAPHY THOMAS DEL RUTH
SCREENPLAY BY RAYNOLD GIDEON & BRUCE A. EVANS BASED ON THE NOVELLA THE BODY BY STEPHEN KING PRODUCED BY BRUCE A. EVANS
RAYNOLD GIDEON ANDREW SCHEINMAN DIRECTED BY ROB REINER ALBUM & CASSETTE ON ATLANTIC RECORDS & TAPES

RELEASED BY COLUMBIA·CANNON·WARNER DISTRIBUTORS LIMITED

STARTS FRIDAY MARCH 13
CANNON HAYMARKET 839 1527 · **CANNON** TOTTENHAM CT. RD. 636 6148
CANNON CHELSEA 352 5096

The advertising campaign for *Stand by Me* played down its Stephen King connection and accentuated its critical acclaim.

In its weakest moments, *Stand by Me* exhibits the saccharine brand of senti-mentality that has plagued most of Reiner's work over the past two decades—such middle-of-the-road, feel-good dreck as *The Story of Us* and *The Bucket List*. The most egregious such instance is entirely Reiner's creation: Gordie's tearful speech about feeling misunderstood by his parents and Chris's encouraging words about his future. It's a moment that's too on-the-nose and touchy-feely, and it suffers in comparison to the scene in which Chris breaks down over his theft of the school's milk money and the bad-boy reputation he fears will dog him all his life. It doesn't help that Gordie's parents come off as caricatured pod people in our few glimpses of them. The film's passage-into-manhood moment, when Gordie holds a gun on Ace and calls him a "cheap, dime-store hood," is likewise less than convincing. (In the book, it is Chris who wields the weapon.)

Yet the movie as a whole works, partly because the portrait of boyhood friendship is grounded in the specificity of its time, as Reiner sprinkles the film with pop culture references to cherry Pez, the theme from *Have Gun, Will Travel*, and the eternal question of whether Mighty Mouse could beat up Superman. This sort of thing is done all the time now, often to excess (practically every comedy set in the seventies or eighties fetishizes the junk culture of the past), but here these touchstones represent the secret language of children. Even if we can't relate to the 1959-specific references, we can equate them to the toys and TV theme songs of our youth, and anyone can identify with the film's more general observations, like pinkie swears and secret treehouse knocks.

Without the framing story and the narration by Richard Dreyfuss, *Stand by Me* might have been overwhelmed by its tendency toward nostalgia and sentimental-ity. But Dreyfuss provides a certain wry, ironic distance to the proceedings, as well as a metatextual presence as the writer gazing back through the years, much as King did when he wrote the novella. There's a sense that he's collapsing all his most vivid childhood memories into one weekend suffused with the golden nostalgic glow that lights the summers of our youth in reflection. He may be embroidering some of the details—perhaps even putting that gun in his hands and that clunky one-liner in his mouth—in the same way King changed that dead dog into a human body. Think of it that way, and *Stand by Me* becomes a movie about a writer fictionalizing his own childhood that is itself adapted from a writer's fictionalization of his own childhood: an adaptation of an adaptation.

In the years since its release, *Stand by Me* has taken on an additional, unin-tended poignancy. Chris Chambers's final scene, in which he walks away from Gordie and disappears from view as Dreyfuss tells us of his untimely demise, can't help but resonate with the real-life tragedy of River Phoenix's drug overdose and death at the age of twenty-three. But the movie also represents the starting point of a new phase in the saga of Stephen King on the screen. Reiner would play a much larger role in that story than he could have imagined when he first read the screenplay based on "The Body," not only as a director, but as the cofounder of one of the most successful production companies of the nineties and beyond: Castle Rock.

Deep Cuts

- Dino De Laurentiis has taken a well-deserved beating in the last couple of chapters, but even a broken clock gets it right twice a day. At the same time Stephen King was filming *Maximum Overdrive*, David Lynch was also in Wilmington, North Carolina, making what many regard as his masterpiece: *Blue Velvet*. How did De Laurentiis come to produce such a moody, strange arthouse offering? He really had no choice, per the terms of the contract he signed with Lynch in order to secure his directing services for *Dune*. That movie was a notorious bomb, but it didn't matter: as long as Lynch delivered his next film on a specified budget (reportedly $6 million), he would get final cut and creative carte blanche. *Overdrive* and *Blue Velvet* shared some crew members, and King and Lynch did cross paths that summer: When King mentioned his problem with crossing the axis, Lynch cheerfully replied that he could do anything he wanted. "You're the director!"

- Those who have endured *Maximum Overdrive* may find it hard to believe that the film was meticulously planned, shot by shot, but the evidence exists in a thick folder within the Fogler Library's special collection of King's personal materials. King's shot cards—1,173 of them, to be exact—have been photocopied, three to a page. Each card is crossed out, with a handwritten date next to each, presumably indicating the day on which the shot was completed. (Some cards are marked "OMIT," while others indicate "Tom Cranum will draw this" in reference to the storyboard artist.) King may not have distinguished himself as a director, but no one can say he didn't take the task seriously.

  Sample card:

SHOT 5

1st BANK OF WILMINGTON, MEDIUM

People go in, people go out. In the front, a man is using the Automatic Bank Teller. CAMERA PANS UP to the digital time and temperature. From 9:48 A.M. and 79° it starts flashing FUCK YOU.

Bare Bones

Through the Lean Years with *The Running Man* and *Pet Sematary*

Being Bachman

T he late eighties saw a sharp decline in the number of Stephen King projects adapted for the big screen. It's safe to say that the glut of King movies in the earlier part of the decade, and the generally poor quality (and poor performance) of many of the adaptations that did make it to the screen, contributed to this fallow period. It certainly wasn't due to any lack of material: Not only was King more prolific than ever during this period, but it turned out that he had already published more material than his loyal readers could have guessed.

Actually, at least a few of those readers *did* guess that King had been even busier than his publishing schedule suggested. In 1984, a novel called *Thinner* by Richard Bachman was released, and it didn't take a Washington, D.C., bookstore employee named Steve Brown very long to deduce that Bachman had to be a pseudonym for Stephen King, even though the book's jacket included a photo of its supposed author. To that point, Bachman had published four other novels, all paperback originals that quickly went out of print: *Rage* (1977), *The Long Walk* (1979), *Roadwork* (1981), and *The Running Man* (1982). The suspicious Brown decided to check on the copyright documents for all of these books at the Library of Congress. Most of the copyright registrations included the name of Kirby McCauley, King's longtime literary agent. *Rage*, however, also included the name of one Stephen King of Bangor, Maine.

The jig was up, and King soon confessed that he was indeed the author of the Bachman books, the first four of which were reissued in a 1985 omnibus edition titled, appropriately enough, *The Bachman Books*. King explained his reasons for adopting the alter ego in an introduction to the collection, and in a second introduction included with a reissue of *The Bachman Books* (minus *Rage*, a school-shooting story King disavowed after several real-life instances that may have been influenced by it). One of his reasons was pragmatic: The publishing industry at that time had no interest in putting out more than one book a year by a given author, and King was already amassing a sizable back catalogue of work. (By the mid-eighties, of course, King could release as much product as he pleased.) Releasing additional material under a pseudonym seemed like an appropriate compromise.

In addition, King enjoyed the role-playing aspect of Bachman, including his invention of a backstory for the author, complete with a wife (Claudia Inez Bachman) and a phony photo (the man pictured on the *Thinner* jacket was actually Kirby McCauley's insurance agent, Richard Manuel). Bachman's work tended to be darker, more angry and cynical, than King's usual fare, and until *Thinner*, the supernatural played no role. "Bachman had become a kind of id for me," King wrote in his second *Bachman Books* introduction. "[H]e said the things I couldn't, and the thought of him out there on his New Hampshire dairy farm—not a best-selling writer who gets his name in some stupid *Forbes* list of entertainers too rich for their own good, or his face on the *Today* show or doing cameos in movies—quietly writing his books, gave him leave to think in ways I could not think and speak in ways I could not speak."

Even after Bachman's death by "cancer of the pseudonym," King did not completely abandon his alter ego. In 1996, the author published the novel *The Regulators* under his old pseudonym, and in 2007 he issued another early unpublished work, *Blaze*, as Bachman. And although Bachman never attracted much critical attention or sold many books before he was exposed, he did have one thing in common with Stephen King: When he wrote, Hollywood came calling.

Running with Arnold

George Linder was the CEO of a wheelchair company called Quadra Medical Corporation when he happened upon a copy of the original paperback edition of *The Running Man* in a bookstore. Linder was looking to break into the movie business, and he thought the story of a futuristic game show in which the contestants are pursued by deadly "Hunters" had the makings of a successful motion picture. Linder was somewhat taken aback when he contacted author Richard Bachman's agent, Kirby McCauley, and was told that the option on the novel would cost him $20,000. After all, Bachman was an unknown author, and the book had sold fewer than 100,000 copies. Still, Linder bit the bullet and paid up, only to be happily surprised when it was revealed that Bachman was in fact Stephen King. "I felt like I'd found a Rembrandt at K-Mart," Linder told *Inc.* magazine.

It didn't take long for Linder to sell the rights to what was now a far more bankable project to Taft/Barish Productions, attaching himself as a coproducer on the project. Steven E. de Souza, screenwriter of *48 Hrs.* and *Commando*, was hired to adapt the book, and George Pan Cosmatos, fresh off *Rambo: First Blood, Part II*, signed on to direct. Former Superman Christopher Reeve was cast as the everyman hero of *The Running Man*, Ben Richards.

Early in preproduction, it became clear to executive producer Rob Cohen that Cosmatos was not going to work out. The success of *Rambo* had gone to

Cosmatos's head, and when he insisted on budget-busting changes to the script, Cohen let him go and began the search for a new director. He hired Carl Schenkel (*The Mighty Quinn*), who lasted three weeks before deciding *The Running Man* wasn't his kind of film. Next came *Nate and Hayes* director Ferdinand Fairfax. "Fairfax wanted to redevelop the script to have the picture say that American culture, especially our TV, is a cancer on world society," Cohen told Vernon Scott of UPI. "After two months, I had to let him go." Even cult director Alex Cox (*Repo Man*), who now insists he's been blacklisted by Hollywood, says he was offered the picture. "The last movie I was asked to direct

King wrote *The Running Man* under the pseudonym Richard Bachman, but by any name the author couldn't have imagined Arnold Schwarzenegger in the lead role.

was *The Running Man* . . . which was actually quite a good film, I thought," Cox told Noel Murray of *The A.V. Club*. "I would have liked to have done *The Running Man*. It was just that *Walker* happened at the same time."

By now Christopher Reeve had departed the project, and de Souza had done several more drafts of the screenplay. When Arnold Schwarzenegger was brought aboard to take Reeve's place as Ben Richards, the script had to be rehauled again with the new star in mind. "When writing it for Reeve, the character could be much more talkative because he's a stage actor," de Souza told Edward Gross of *Starlog* magazine. "You want Arnold to be a man of action and not of words . . . Plus Arnold, as demonstrated in *Commando*, can be very funny. Christopher Reeve can't."

Next up on the directing carousel was Andrew Davis, now best known for *Under Siege* and *The Fugitive* but then coming off a low-budget Chuck Norris picture called *Code of Silence*. Shooting actually began with Davis behind the camera, but, according to Cohen, "after eight days of shooting we were four days behind schedule and $400,000 over budget. The scenes just couldn't be edited together." Davis was fired, and Cohen dug even deeper into his rolodex, emerging with the name Paul Michael Glaser.

Glaser became a television star in the seventies on the cop-buddy show *Starsky and Hutch*, for which he directed several episodes. He'd helmed a few *Miami Vice* episodes and the feature *Band of the Hand* by the time he got the call from Cohen to take over *The Running Man* on two days' notice. "When I first came on board and looked at what I had to work with, I thought to myself, this is bizarre," Glaser told interviewer Dan Scapperotti. "It's like doing a commercial version of *Brazil* attached to *Network*." Finally, however, Cohen had solved his director problem, as Glaser managed to stick to the sixty-one-day schedule even though the $18 million budget had by now ballooned to $28 million. But even when it was finally in the can, the movie's problems weren't over.

Cohen had departed Taft/Barish during production, and the picture was now set for release by Tri-Star. The studio hoped to have the movie in theaters for the summer of 1987, but their star blocked that plan, as he didn't want *The Running Man* to compete with his already scheduled summer release, *Predator*. The movie was bumped to November, and upon its release, became the second King adaptation in a row (following *Stand by Me*) to downplay its connection to its source material. This time, however, the producers didn't have much choice. They'd purchased the rights to a novel by Richard Bachman, after all, and they'd done so before the author's true identity had become public knowledge. If he'd felt like it, King surely could have given the production his blessing to use his real name in the publicity, but he wanted nothing to do with the film. As he said in 1990, "It doesn't have much in common with the novel at all, except the title."

That's absolutely true. If anything, *The Running Man* is an object lesson in the pitfalls of tailoring a project specifically for a star. Arnold Schwarzenegger was easily the most larger-than-life screen presence of the 1980s, and after starring in such huge hits as *The Terminator* and *Commando*, he had the clout to match.

Whatever else you might say about him, he could never be confused for an everyman, yet that's exactly what the novel (and the early drafts of de Souza's screenplay) called for. In the book, Ben Richards is an unemployed resident of the dystopian Co-Op City in the year 2025. Desperate to earn money to care for his sickly daughter, Richards volunteers to participate in *The Running Man*, the world's most dangerous game show. For thirty days, a contestant must evade Hunters who are dispatched to kill him, but no one has ever lasted longer than eight days. The book ends with one of King's darkest visions, particularly from a post-9/11 perspective, as Richards crashes a plane into the skyscraper housing the headquarters of the *Running Man*'s TV network.

This was nobody's idea of an Arnold Schwarzenegger character, and the film's Ben Richards bears little resemblance to his literary equivalent. In the movie, Richards is a helicopter pilot for the police state government of 2017 who refuses orders to fire on innocent civilians in a food riot. The footage is doctored to make it look like Richards instigated the attacks on the rioters, and he is captured and sentenced to a labor camp. Richards and several of his fellow inmates escape, and he returns to his brother's former apartment, now occupied by Amber Mendez (Maria Conchita Alonso). With Amber as his hostage, Richards attempts to flee the country, but he is captured again and forced to participate in the number one television game show, *The Running Man*, produced and hosted by Damon Killian (longtime *Family Feud* host Richard Dawson).

Released into a game zone covering forty city blocks, Richards and his cronies must evade the Stalkers—comic book executioners with names like Buzzsaw and SubZero—in order to escape with their freedom and fabulous prizes. This being a Schwarzenegger movie, the Stalkers are dispatched in increasingly violent manner, with each kill accompanied by a groan-inducing one-liner. "Give you a lift?" he asks a security guard before tossing him over a railing. "How about a light?" he queries of the Stalker called Fireball, tossing a flare at him. He even hauls his signature *Terminator* line, "I'll be back," out of cold storage.

The Running Man somehow manages to be both prescient and incredibly dated at the same time. The film anticipates the reality TV genre by more than a decade: Such series as *Survivor* and *The Amazing Race* may not be quite as dangerous as the fictional game show depicted here, but the spectacle of ordinary people competing in contests of elimination and having their every move recorded and transmitted into living rooms nationwide is commonplace today. De Souza's script displays flashes of wit, as in its references to court-appointed theatrical agents and the Justice Department's Entertainment Division. Dawson, for one, is on the right wavelength, goosing his buttery game-show host persona into a caricature of unctuous evil.

But director Glaser's *Miami Vice*-honed aesthetic results in a "futuristic" movie rooted in the MTV-saturated eighties. With its smoke machines, colored light gels, latex-and-big-hair fashion, and squawking synthesizer score, *The Running Man* might as well be a Duran Duran video. The supporting cast, including Yaphet Kotto, Jesse Ventura, Jim Brown, Mick Fleetwood, and Dweezil Zappa in addition to Alonso and Dawson, suggests an unmade *Cannonball Run* sequel. But really, the movie is all about Schwarzenegger, who isn't playing any character at all besides "Arnold Schwarzenegger, Action Superstar." He wears Gold's Gym t-shirts and puffs cigars and spits out corny one-liners in his inimitable Teutonic tones. He might as well be on an actual game show, and the extent to which *The Running Man* has been refitted into a vehicle for his persona renders the entire enterprise impossible to take seriously.

Certainly that's the way Stephen King saw it. In his second introduction to *The Bachman Books*, King noted that his "scrawny pre-tubercular protagonist" was "about as far from the Arnold Schwarzenegger character in the movie as you can get." King hadn't softened his stance as of December 2012: In an appearance at the University of Massachusetts in Lowell, he made offhand reference to *The Running Man* as "a really awful movie."

The Running Man was no box office disaster, but by Schwarzenegger standards, it was a bit of a disappointment. The film earned close to $40 million in American theaters, a dropoff from the $54 million *Predator* had brought in the previous summer, especially considering the movie's hefty price tag. For once, however, no one could blame Stephen King for the film's performance. But the next time one of his works was adapted for the big screen, the author was all in—and the results would come as a surprise to almost everyone.

Pet Sematary Unearthed

On Stephen King's personal list of frequently asked questions, "Have you ever written anything so scary that you scared yourself?" would certainly rank in the top ten. His answer is always the same: *Pet Sematary*. The story of a man who discovers an Indian burial ground that brings his cat—and eventually his toddler son—back to life, the novel was drawn from some of King's real-life experiences, and cut very close to the bone. After writing the book in the early eighties, King stuck it in a drawer, hinting in interviews that it was too frightening to publish. But when he departed his longtime publisher Doubleday in 1983, he agreed to give them *Pet Sematary* to fulfill his contractual obligation.

Even after the novel's publication, King resisted the temptation to sell the book to Hollywood. He told the *New York Times* in 1984 that he'd turned down offers from every major studio, as well as "a firm $1 million from a consortium." But King found he couldn't turn down his old friends Richard Rubinstein and George A. Romero. He agreed to sell the movie rights to the duo's Laurel Entertainment on a handshake deal for $10,000 and a share of the eventual profits. King had two conditions, however: He would write the screenplay, and, as Rubinstein put it, "as additional icing on the cake, we'll make the movie in Maine, because Steve is concerned about Maine's depressed economy."

King had long bristled at the fact that, although most of his works were set in Maine, none of the movies adapted from them had actually been shot there. This time he insisted upon it, hoping that a film crew spending several months

A veces, la muerte es lo mejor.

EL CEMENTERIO MALDITO

PARAMOUNT PICTURES PRESENTA UNA PRODUCCION DE RICHARD P. RUBINSTEIN UN FILM DE MARY LAMBERT "PET SEMATARY" ELLIOT GOLDENTHAL MICHAEL HILL y DANIEL HANLEY PETER STEIN MITCHELL GALIN TIM ZINNEMANN STEPHEN KING RICHARD P. RUBINSTEIN MARY LAMBERT   UNA PELICULA PARAMOUNT

Distribuida por: UNITED INTERNATIONAL PICTURES

This vintage international lobby card for *Pet Sematary* features a rather graphic spoiler.

in the Pine Tree State would provide a much-needed boost to local businesses. That would prove to be the case, but it would be four years before the cameras started to roll in Downeast Maine, and by then, George Romero would no longer be onboard.

Pet Sematary wasn't a priority because King and Romero were already wrestling with another adaptation: the mammoth prospect of bringing *The Stand* to the screen. That process will be detailed in a later chapter, but suffice it to say, by the mid-eighties they had still not gotten a handle on it. By then, the multiplexes had been flooded with inferior and underperforming King adaptations, and that, along with the author's insistence on script and location approval, kept *Pet Sematary* on the back burner.

By the time financing came together (courtesy of Paramount Pictures, which had already passed on the project twice) and shooting was scheduled for the summer of 1988, Romero had left Laurel Entertainment and was preoccupied with postproduction on his feature film *Monkey Shines*. Although he had spent more than a year preparing King's *Pet Sematary* script for shooting, he was forced to bow out—not for the first or last time on a King project. (In fact, some enterprising soul could schedule an entire film festival of King adaptations Romero had once been slated to direct.) The search for a new director was on.

Given King's conditions, a big-name filmmaker was probably out of the question, as few established auteurs would agree to shoot the author's script as-is. Still, the name that was eventually announced came as a surprise: Mary Lambert, director of several Madonna videos and the offbeat 1987 indie *Siesta*, starring Ellen Barkin. Lambert had no experience in the horror field (although her few weeks of shooting *Under the Cherry Moon* before being fired by Prince may have qualified as a horror show), but she and King hit it off, and he and Rubinstein felt confident about her vision for the film. "Stephen and I just really saw eye-to-eye on the material," Lambert recalls on her *Pet Sematary* DVD commentary. "And Stephen liked me. I think it was because I knew the Ramones quite well, partly because of my music video career and partly because they were in my circle of friends." (King had specifically written a Ramones song into one of the movie's key scenes.)

Per King's wishes, filming began in coastal Maine in the summer of 1988, on a budget of roughly $10 million. The cast and crew were based in Ellsworth, about thirty minutes from King's Bangor home, with much of the shoot taking place in nearby Hancock. (The Creed house from the film still stands on Hancock Point and is a popular Maine attraction for fans of the movie.) Dale Midkiff (*Elvis and Me*) and Denise Crosby (*Star Trek: The Next Generation*) were cast as Louis and Rachel Creed, with twins Blaze and Beau Berdahl as their daughter Ellie and twenty-seven-month-old Miko Hughes as infant Gage Creed. For the pivotal role of neighboring old salt Jud Crandall, Lambert had only one actor in mind and couldn't have been happier when former *Munsters* star Fred Gwynne agreed to take on the role.

Although the interiors of the Creed and Crandall houses were sets in a warehouse, everything else was shot on location. King was often on set, conferring with Lambert on any changes required due to time, budget, or logistics. As with *Cat's Eye*, a number of identical-looking felines were required to play Church, the cat who comes back after being buried in the ancient Micmac grounds. (Since cats can't really be trained, each was chosen for its ability to perform a certain task; hence, there was a scratching Church, a hissing Church, a jumping Church, and so on.) For the undead Gage Creed, who performs a number of deadly deeds upon his return from the grave, a fully articulated puppet double was built (although Lambert used shots of both the young actor, made up to look mildly cadaverous, and the puppet in the film's final minutes).

Pet Sematary was initially set for release in February 1989 but was delayed several months in order to allow additional postproduction time, and also because the film had run afoul of the MPAA ratings board. The censors demanded cuts before it would grant an R rating, a process that frustrated Lambert. "I think what the MPAA is reacting to is that the film works," she told interviewer Frederick C. Szebin. "The scenes when the child comes back are very chilling." When the movie was released on April 21, 1989, it soon became apparent that audiences agreed. *Pet Sematary* debuted in first place at the box office with a $12 million weekend en route to a $57 million total. It was King's biggest moneymaker to date, and nobody had seen it coming.

Although it was well received by many fans and has accrued a cult following over the years, today *Pet Sematary* looks more like a near-miss than a fully realized dramatization of one of King's darkest horrors. Dale Midkiff is almost surreally bland as Louis Creed; his screen presence is more like a screen absence, leaving a gaping hole in the heart of the movie. Denise Crosby has her moments, as when Rachel recounts her childhood horror of being left alone with her severely deformed sister, but together, she and Midkiff don't begin to generate the empathy required to make the story's terrors tangible. Only Fred Gwynne, boasting an impeccable Pepperidge Farm accent, delivers a fully human performance. He resists the temptation to portray Jud as the lovable codger next door; it is Jud's darker impulses that set the story in motion, and Gwynne doesn't shy away from that aspect of the character.

For all the fuss made over shooting in Maine, the picture makes surprisingly little use of its remote locations. A few sequences stand out, notably the initial trek to the Micmac burial ground and a flashback shot of a weatherbeaten house under low grey skies, but most of the action is confined to two farmhouses on a remote stretch of road. Aside from a few brief glimpses of picturesque Frenchman's Bay behind the Creed house, it could be rural Arkansas for all the downeast flavor Lambert wrings out of the location. The entire film feels oddly underpopulated, except for one jarring scene set at the college where Louis works, and much of the backstory involving the Creed marriage and Louis's poor relations with his in-laws is underdeveloped.

And yet the film retains enough of the primal power of King's story that it's a shame it's not just a little bit better. King admittedly drew on the classic tale "The Monkey's Paw" as much as his own experiences with his daughter's cat dying and his son nearly running into the path of an oncoming truck, and the "three wishes" structure lends *Pet Sematary* a grim inevitability. There's no real reason Jud Crandall should show Louis the Micmac burial ground, given his own dreadful experiences with bringing the dead back to life, but he does it anyway. The path to the burial ground makes no real geographic sense—it goes from deep woods to rocky coastal cliffs to the top of a mountain—but as a sort of regression to a primitive world of ancient spirits, it works. (Of course, the "old Indian burial ground" is one of the hoariest conceits in horror, but given *Pet Sematary*'s dark fairy-tale context, it's a serviceable archetype.)

As the movie goes along, death begins to seep into nearly every frame. Missie, the Creeds' housekeeper, hangs herself after receiving a terminal cancer diagnosis. An overheard TV newscast mentions dolphins beaching themselves on the Maine coast. Rachel recalls her sister choking to death. And eventually, of course, Gage is killed by a Ramones-loving truck driver, prompting Louis to tamper with forces beyond his reckoning. Lambert composes a few classic horror visuals: Jud, waiting for Louis across the road, his sunken eyes peering out from beneath a parka hood; an overhead shot of the Micmac grounds atop a mountain; a *Night of the Living Dead*–inspired flashback that acts as a nod to original director George Romero.

But the movie is ultimately undermined by its lead performances, a somewhat leaden pace, and a few unfortunate choices. The character of Pascow, the dead, decomposing student who haunts the Creeds, is too reminiscent of Griffin Dunne's similar turn in *American Werewolf of London*. (Recall that John Carpenter cut the character of Roland LeBay from *Christine* precisely to avoid such comparisons.) And while Miko Hughes is used to creepy effect in a few shots, his rampage as a pint-sized killing machine (with an improbably intact corpse) is too reminiscent of Chucky the *Child's Play* doll.

Despite its flaws, however, the movie's financial success and a handful of positive reviews helped put the dark days of the De Laurentiis era in the rearview mirror. Bad Stephen King movies would still be made, but *Pet Sematary*'s strong performance only served to increase the author's already estimable clout. More and more, the movies made from his work would be made on his terms.

Deep Cuts: Q&A with Filmmakers John Campopiano and Justin White

Pet Sematary's cult following has grown over the years, but few fans have taken their interest as far as John Campopiano and Justin White, a pair of New England filmmakers. Campopiano and White agreed to answer a few questions about their documentary *Unearthed & Untold: The Path to Pet Sematary*.

Q: *Have you always been Stephen King fans? Do you remember how you first got into his work?*

John Campopiano: I was six or seven years old and a childhood friend who lived across the street from me for many years invited me over to watch Stephen King's *It*, which he had just rented on VHS. This friend was a couple of years older than me, which, at that age, can make all the difference. We watched it and the only real vivid memories I have from that screening and the proceeding hours involve tears, a ripe-for-the-pickin' nightmare that night, and a groggy morning. A few years later when I was a bit older I realized that being scared like that was actually a lot of fun, and so I revisited not only *It* but also many other films. I was, and still am, hooked on Stephen King and the horror genre.

Justin White: *Pet Sematary* was one of the first examples of King's work that I ever experienced, the first I believe being *Stand by Me*. I actually haven't read that many of Stephen's books, maybe six at best, but I have always been a big fan of his film adaptations, favorites including *Carrie*, *Pet Sematary*, *Misery*, and of course *The Shining*. There was always an element to those films that separated them from the other horror films of the day, in that they didn't always rely on the gore and the blood to produce the fear. Instead the fear came from your association with the main characters of these tales, as many of these films revolve around their personal story that King had created for them. They are more psychological thrillers in my opinion and at least for me, were able to sustain the fear throughout the entire movie rather than films that would make you jump due to shock every couple of minutes.

Q: Do you remember the first time you saw Pet Sematary? What were your first impressions of the movie?

JC: I do remember the first time I saw *Pet Sematary*. I was at a friend's house and remember being scared senseless by Zelda—not only actually seeing Zelda on the screen but her voice. There's a great flashback scene of young Rachel standing on the stairway of her parents' Chicago home, listening to Zelda call her name and laugh demonically. As I recall I looked at my other pals in the room and laughed—suggesting that the terror on the screen was more comical to me than scary. Of course this was a complete façade, an attempt to seem tougher than I was, because inside I was trembling like a schoolgirl.

JW:The first time I saw *Pet Sematary* was during its initial run on HBO. I remember watching it by myself in the middle of the night, which looking back, was probably not the best idea for a thirteen-year-old to do, but once I got into it I just couldn't look away. The scene that really sent a wave of fear through me above all else in the film was when Spot, Jud's childhood dog returns. The sound of that dog growling and the look of fear in that boy's eyes were enough to make me cover my ears and close my eyes. I've been a fan of the film ever since, and now doing this documentary I've rediscovered it in so many ways and developed a much greater appreciation for this timeless story.

Q: What made you choose Pet Sematary as the subject of your documentary?

JC & JW: It started out as something fun to do for ourselves. As mutual fans of the horror genre as well as movie location junkies, we thought spending a day in Maine finding the *Pet Sematary* filming spots on a warm May Saturday was going to be time well spent. Well, on this trip we encountered locals who had a hand in the film and realized that many of the locations remained unchanged almost twenty-five years later. Similarly, the relatively low number of online references to *Pet Sematary* filming locations only punctuated the fact that a comprehensive look at where this movie was made, the impact it had, and the cult legacy it has acquired was very much needed. I think we pretty much decided on the drive home that day that we needed to go back and continue filming, talking to people, and digging up whatever stories we could. Since then the project has evolved, rather organically, and taken us to places we never imagined. It has been a great ride so far.

Another piece of the puzzle is the freshness of the stories. By and large *Pet Sematary* has been an overlooked eighties horror cult classic. With the exception of Paramount's 2006 special edition DVD, which featured a small segment on the making of the film, there exists no other extensive look at the film and the memories of the cast and crew that made it possible. The fact that Justin and I aren't just reinventing the wheel or retelling the same stories, showing the same photos, and featuring rehashed behind-the-scenes video footage is what partly drives our motivation. In the last decade the horror genre has seen some incredible making-of documentaries about other horror favorites such as *Return of the Living Dead*, *Friday the 13th*, and others. Even cooler is the fact that many of these documentaries are made by the fans themselves. We just want to add our names to this already impressive list.

Q: *What is the general impression you got from the locals who were involved with the making of the film? Were they happy with the finished movie and/or its effect on their community?*

JC & JW: Not surprisingly it's a mixed bag. You have folks who love King's work and so it was an exciting and anticipated event. Others who don't care for his work could have done without the rigmarole that is a Hollywood production. The economic impact was something that pretty much everyone appreciated, that's for sure. In terms of impressions of the film, that, too, is a mixed bag. As you can imagine, recreating intricate regionalisms such as style of speech is never an easy thing. We feel that the locals' impressions on these and other related topics are fairly well represented in the documentary.

Q: *Were there any particularly surprising untold nuggets you unearthed while making the documentary?*

JC & JW: Absolutely—and we think for the sake of trying to keep the film's content as fresh as possible, we'll hold off on revealing them!

The 1990s

The Castle Rock Era

Rage

The Violent Mood Swings of *Graveyard Shift* and *Misery*

Doing Time on *Graveyard Shift*

Following the success of *Pet Sematary*, the Stephen King movie industry cranked back into gear. And while it would never again reach the King-movie-of-the-week pace of the early eighties, late 1990 would see a concentrated burst of activity reminiscent of that prolific period. The ABC miniseries of *It* debuted on November 18, bookended by two theatrical releases: one big hit that would go on to win the first major Academy Award ever for a King movie, and one that went all but unnoticed by the moviegoing public—and rightfully so.

Graveyard Shift began with the best of intentions, as part of King's ongoing effort to support Maine filmmakers and boost the local economy. William Dunn was a former schoolteacher who had worked as location manager on *Pet Sematary*. He and King had both played a role in launching the Maine Film Office in 1987, and both were eager to see more of the author's works produced in his home state. King had earlier sold an option on his short story "Graveyard Shift" to George Demick, a friend of George Romero's he'd met while making *Maximum Overdrive*. Demick commissioned a script from first-time screenwriter John Esposito, but his option ran out before he could make the film.

When the rights to the story reverted to King, he turned around and sold them

SCREAMIN' TRADERS

Like *Pet Sematary* before it, *Graveyard Shift* was shot in Maine on a low budget. Unlike its predecessor, it did not connect with audiences or critics.

STEPHEN KING'S

GRAVEYARD SHIFT

PARAMOUNT PICTURES PRESENTS
A LARRY SUGAR PRODUCTION A RALPH S SINGLETON FILM
STEPHEN KING'S GRAVEYARD SHIFT
DAVID ANDREWS KELLY WOLF STEPHEN MACHT
AND BRAD DOURIF EXTERMINATOR MUSIC BY ANTHONY MARINELLI
AND BRIAN BANKS COSTUMES BY SARAH LEMIRE
EDITED BY PETER STEIN PRODUCTION DESIGNER GARY WISSNER
VISUAL CONSULTANTS HAROLD MICHELSON SPECIAL MAKEUP EFFECTS ALBERT J. WHITLOCK
FILM EDITORS JIM GROSS AND RANDY JON MORGAN
ASSOCIATE PRODUCERS JOAN V. SINGLETON AND ANTHONY LABONTE
EXECUTIVE PRODUCERS BONNIE AND LARRY SUGAR SCREENPLAY BY JOHN ESPOSITO
BASED ON THE SHORT STORY STEPHEN KING PRODUCED BY WILLIAM J. DUNN
AND RALPH S SINGLETON DIRECTED BY RALPH S SINGLETON
R RESTRICTED   A PARAMOUNT PICTURE
COMING OCTOBER 26
FROM PARAMOUNT PICTURES

The world premiere of *Graveyard Shift* was held at the Bangor Mall Cinema. Not exactly Grauman's Chinese Theatre in Hollywood.

to Dunn for $2,500. Again, it was understood that the movie would be shot on location in Maine, although King would not take as strong a creative hand as he did with *Pet Sematary*. Dunn retained the Esposito script and hired a novice director, Ralph Singleton, who had been an associate producer on *Pet Sematary*. The budget was roughly the same as that of its predecessor, $10.5 million, with financing supplied by Larry Sugar Entertainment, the company that had released the *Salem's Lot* miniseries theatrically in Europe. Shooting would take place in Bangor and surrounding areas in the summer of 1990.

Given that "Graveyard Shift" was a fifteen-page story, Esposito had his work cut out for him in expanding it to feature length. King's story, based on his own experiences working in a knitting mill during high school, concerned a "college boy" employed by just such a mill. When the operation shuts down for a week during the summer, a cleaning crew is assembled to go down to the basement with high-powered hoses and clear out the rats that have infested it. As the crew moves deeper and deeper into the basement, the rats grow larger and larger, until finally a gigantic bat is unleashed from the subcellar. Esposito added characters (such as a quirky exterminator), an unlikely romance, and an *Alien*-like "disappearing crew" structure to the piece to flesh it out to an acceptable length.

With Brad Dourif (*Deadwood*) as the lone name actor aboard, production got underway, much of it centered around the Bartlettyarns woollen mill in Harmony, Maine. (The mill, built in 1821 on the banks of Higgins Stream, is still standing, and although it was sold in 2007, is still operational.) The production utilized a combination of real, mechanical, and puppet rats as the film's villainous vermin, according to the American Humane Society's website. "When a rat runs from an exterminator's spray (actually plain water), it is responding to the sound of a clicker that signals where his rat chow is. When a soda can is thrown by sling-shot and hits a rat, the can actually hits an area in front of the rat and the rat is pulled out of sight by the trainer, who is unseen by the camera. The vacuum hose sucking up rats is sucking up fake rats."

Production wrapped in July after seven weeks of filming, leaving only three months to edit the movie and prepare it for its Halloween release. Paramount Pictures was onboard to distribute the film, clearly hoping the *Pet Sematary* lightning would strike twice. The red-carpet premiere was held at the Bangor Mall Cinema, surely a first and a last in the annals of cinema. King attended, along with Dunn and Esposito, and everyone was all smiles, even enjoying a cake in the shape of a giant rat. But that was the end of the good times as far as *Graveyard Shift* was concerned. The movie was savaged by critics, and although it opened in the top slot in a very soft weekend at the box office, it quickly disappeared from sight. It went on to earn only $11.5 million, barely enough to cover its production budget.

"I got spanked in *People* magazine for allowing *Graveyard Shift* to be made, which is ridiculous," King told Daniel Cerone of the *L.A. Times*. "Ralph Singleton had never directed a film. John Esposito had never written a film. Now they both have a movie credit. They'll do better next time. This is why you do it." That's a generous attitude, although King's generosity doesn't extend to saying anything good about the movie itself. He's trashed it at every opportunity since its release, which is really the only sensible reaction to such a dismal effort.

Graveyard Shift does a (very) few things right. The background is populated with authentically rough-and-ready rural Mainers; there are no Beverly Hills bodies on display here. The production design of the mill's interior is appropriately dank and cavernous: With its dark clutter of ancient machinery, half-flooded nooks and crannies, and walls seething with rats, it's a nightmarish setting . . . for some other movie. This one, however, is at least twice as long as it needs to be and leaves us rooting for the rodents.

Dourif delivers a typically wild-eyed, intense performance as the Exterminator, but once he's gone, he leaves us in poor company. David Andrews is so opaque in the lead role of John Hall, he makes Dale Midkiff in *Pet Sematary* look like the life of the party. Stephen Macht is a complete disaster as the gruff foreman Warwick; it's never clear whether he's trying to do a Maine accent or a German one. Singleton's inexperience shows: The camera rarely seems to be in the right place, and the action doesn't cut together well. The grand finale features a giant rubber bat that even Roger Corman would have found chintzy and unconvincing. But the movie's biggest problem is that it's a perfectly adequate *Creepshow* segment that's been allowed to mutate into a dreadful feature-length film. Fortunately, King fans wouldn't have to wait long before washing the bad taste of *Graveyard Shift* out of their mouths.

No rats were harmed in the making of this motion picture.

Reiner's Company Loves *Misery*

Rob Reiner was riding high in the years following *Stand by Me*. His next two directorial efforts, *The Princess Bride* and *When Harry Met Sally*, were both crowd-pleasing hits, and in 1987, he'd founded his own production company, named Castle Rock Entertainment after the town featured in *Stand by Me* and so many other Stephen King works. One of his first orders of business in this new capacity was to option the rights to King's 1987 novel *Misery*, but as with *Pet Sematary*, the author was reluctant to sign on the dotted line unless he received some assurances. In this case, because he'd been so pleased with *Stand by Me*, he wanted it in writing that Reiner would either produce or direct the film himself.

King was hoping for the latter, but Reiner wasn't so sure he was the man for the job. He was not a fan of the horror genre, and not interested in making a film loaded with graphic violence. Still, per the terms of the deal, he agreed to oversee the production and began developing a screenplay. Reiner reportedly went through eight other writers before sending King's novel to William Goldman, the well-regarded screenwriter of *Butch Cassidy and the Sundance Kid* and *All the President's Men*.

Goldman was intrigued by King's story of a writer's worst nightmare—being held captive by an obsessed fan—but it wasn't until he reached the "hobbling" scene that he knew he wanted to adapt the book for the screen. In King's novel, writer Paul Sheldon realizes just how psychotic his captor Annie Wilkes is when she uses a blowtorch and axe to remove his feet. Goldman went to work on the screenplay, and he and Reiner landed their dream director. "Our first choice is George Roy Hill and he says *yesss*," Goldman wrote in his memoir *Which Lie Did I Tell?* "Nirvana."

But after thinking about the hobbling scene a little more, Hill decided it wasn't nirvana for him. "Gentlemen, she lops his fucking feet off," he told Reiner and Goldman. "And I can't direct that." Reiner briefly considered sending the script to Barry Levinson, then decided he'd direct it himself after all. (In the end, Reiner ended up changing the hobbling scene anyway, to Goldman's initial dismay and eventual gratitude.)

Casting the two leads was a study in contrasts. Goldman knew immediately he wanted to tailor the part of Annie Wilkes for stage actress Kathy Bates, and Reiner agreed with no debate. The role of Paul Sheldon proved far more problematic. For much of *Misery*, Sheldon is immobilized in a bed, and of course, he gets his feet lopped off; this combination did not exactly prove irresistible for Hollywood's A-list talent. Among the actors Reiner approached were William Hurt, Kevin Kline, Michael Douglas, Harrison Ford, Dustin Hoffman, and Reiner's old school chum Richard Dreyfuss. All of them turned him down, but surprisingly, Warren Beatty was interested. Of course, Beatty has a long-standing reputation for getting involved in a project and then waffling for as long as possible, and *Misery* proved no exception. After many meetings and script consultations, he bowed out, leaving Reiner and Goldman in a bind.

One actor was still interested in the part, although he was no longer on the A-list, was rumored to have a substance-abuse problem, and didn't appear to be a good fit for the role: James Caan. Still, at this point the movie needed Caan as much as Caan needed the movie (he told Reiner he'd pee in a bottle every day, but that didn't prove to be necessary), and *Misery* finally had its Paul Sheldon.

King's novel was essentially a claustrophobic two-hander until the very end, but Goldman's screenplay opened up the story a bit by expanding the character of the sheriff, Buster, who only arrives in the last few pages of the book. Reiner cast Richard Farnsworth (*The Grey Fox*) as Buster and Frances Sternhagen as his wife and partner in law enforcement, Virginia. Lauren Bacall rounded out the cast as Paul's agent. Principal photography took place in Los Angeles and Reno, Nevada (subbing for Colorado, not Maine this time) in the summer of 1990 in anticipation of a late November release.

Christmas isn't traditionally the season for horror movies, but that's not how Reiner saw *Misery* anyway. He described it as a "suspense/thriller," telling interviewer Gary Wood, "What I hope is that we don't fall into the cracks between people who are going to be hardcore Stephen King fans—horror fans who are going to be disappointed that there aren't enough blood and guts—and people who are expecting me to give them another comedy." But while *Misery* may have spent less of its budget on gore than any King adaptation since *Stand by Me*, it did have a visceral shock in its hobbling scene.

Reiner felt King's version of the hobbling, with the blowtorch and axe, would overpower the film, leaving no room for the audience to empathize with Annie Wilkes. Instead, he and his effects crew devised an alternate scene in which Annie uses a sledgehammer to break Paul's ankles. Caan stuck his legs through holes drilled in the bed, and gelatin legs created by the effects team were used to create the horrific moment. For a later scene in which Paul beats Annie over the head with his typewriter, the crew built two prosthetic heads to substitute for Bates's real noggin.

Shooting wrapped in July, with postproduction completed in time to meet a November 30, 1990, release. Although Reiner had downplayed the Stephen King connection on *Stand by Me*, he and distribution partner Columbia Pictures had no intention of doing so this time around. Despite some doubts about releasing a horrific thriller into the Christmas marketplace, *Misery* opened to strong reviews and box office. Its $10 million opening weekend couldn't knock *Home Alone* out of its top perch, but the film remained in the top ten for six weeks, eventually garnering over $61 million—a new record for a King adaptation.

The critical praise tended to cluster around Kathy Bates's performance as Annie Wilkes, and true to King's prediction, Bates was nominated for a Best Actress Oscar. On March 25, 1991, Bates prevailed against a field that included Meryl Streep (*Postcards on the Edge*), Anjelica Huston (*The Grifters*), Joanne Woodward (*Mr. and Mrs. Bridge*), and Julia Roberts (*Pretty Woman*). In her acceptance speech, she thanked "William Goldman for bringing the wonderful, crazy Annie Wilkes to the screen, and Stephen King for thinking of her in the first place."

As embodied by Bates, Annie isn't a particularly fearsome presence; in fact, the actress invests a comic sensibility in the role, flirting with caricature at times. That suits the tone Reiner brings to the film perfectly. True to his word, the director has not made a pure horror movie but rather a suspense thriller with both comedic and horrific elements. There's a dusting of Hollywood glaze coating the whole enterprise, although it's nowhere near as gooey as such later Reiner works as *The Bucket List* and the diabetic shock that is *The Magic of Belle Isle*. The suspense sequences are a bit mechanical, like Hitchcock-by-numbers: Reiner has clearly studied the master, but the results come off as . . . well, *studied*. And the counterintuitive casting of James Caan, a physically expressive actor confined to a bed, is problematic. He never suggests the life of the mind in the way that William Hurt or Richard Dreyfuss might have, and it's tough to buy him as the author of a series of bodice-rippers.

And yet none of these flaws are fatal enough to keep *Misery* from being a perfectly enjoyable light entertainment. Bates's performance grows richer as it progresses, and it becomes clear that she's portraying Annie as an overgrown little girl: the tantrums, the romantic swooning, the fake swears like "dirty birdie" and "cockadoodie" all add up to an extreme state of arrested development. Hamstrung as he is, Caan makes an amusing foil for Bates, delivering Paul's sarcastic retorts just subtly enough to ensure they pass over Annie's head.

Goldman's method of opening up the story by including the sheriff's investigation into Paul's disappearance not only allows for some warm, comic banter between Farnsworth and Sternhagen, it adds another layer to the movie's symmetry with *The Shining*. Both films concern writers trapped in claustrophobic conditions in the snowy Rockies—one haunted by his own demons, one terrorized by his self-proclaimed "number one fan." Both movies explore fears specific to writers (or other creative types): In *The Shining*, it's writer's block, and in *Misery*, it's every successful artist's fear of becoming a prisoner or puppet of the audience. (*Misery* also addresses the common writer's nightmare of losing the only copy of a manuscript, although that one is almost obsolete in our electronic age.) And in both movies, the most sympathetic character is the aging would-be rescuer who spends the second half of the film closing in like the cavalry but is killed immediately upon arrival.

In addition to its critical and financial success, *Misery* was a hit with King himself, and also an important turning point in the author's filmography. As if

Although he had directed *Stand by Me*, Rob Reiner didn't initially see himself as a good fit for *Misery*. William Goldman's screenplay helped convince him otherwise.

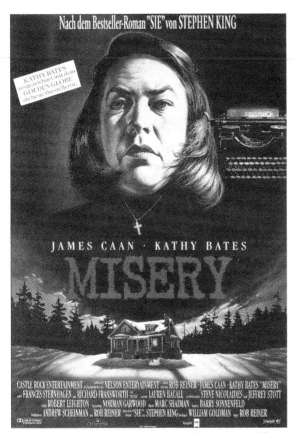

Nach dem Bestseller-Roman "SIE" von STEPHEN KING

KATHY BATES
ausgezeichnet mit dem
GOLDEN GLOBE
als beste Darstellerin

JAMES CAAN · KATHY BATES

MISERY

CASTLE ROCK ENTERTAINMENT In Zusammenarbeit mit NELSON ENTERTAINMENT ein Film von ROB REINER · JAMES CAAN · KATHY BATES "MISERY"
und FRANCES STERNHAGEN · RICHARD FRANSWORTH Musik von LAUREN BACALL Co-Produzenten STEVE NICOLAIDES und JEFFREY STOTT
Kamera ROBERT LEIGHTON Ausstattung NORMAN GARWOOD Musik MARC SHAIMAN Schnitt BARRY SONNENFELD
Produzenten ANDREW SCHEINMAN und ROB REINER Roman "SIE" von STEPHEN KING Drehbuch WILLIAM GOLDMAN Regie ROB REINER

Kathy Bates won an Oscar for her performance in *Misery*, the one and only time such an honor has been bestowed upon a King adaptation.

it was meant to be, Castle Rock Entertainment became the primary producer of theatrical features based on King's work, even as ABC was establishing itself as home base for King product on the small screen. The Castle Rock era would prove to be a substantial upgrade over the De Laurentiis days. Not all of the King films produced under Reiner's shingle would turn out to be classics, but several would rank among the best adaptations of the author's work, and at least one would go on to become an unlikely candidate for the most beloved movie of all time.

Bloodlines: Five Movies about Obsessed Fans

For Stephen King, Annie Wilkes was the embodiment of his worst fears about his fans (as well as, he would later admit, a metaphor for his addiction issues of the 1980s). But Annie is only one member of the cinematic rogues' gallery of obsessed fans that has made for a number of memorable movies over the years. Here are five more.

Play Misty for Me (1971)—Clint Eastwood's directorial debut introduced audiences to the threat of stalking long before the word "stalker" had become common currency. In a change of pace from his usual monosyllabic gunslingers, Eastwood plays a smooth jazz DJ with a whispery voice and an eye for the ladies. One of his conquests, Evelyn (Jessica Walter), doesn't see herself as a one-night stand, however: She insinuates herself into his life in ways both seemingly benign (showing up unexpectedly to cook dinner) and eventually horrifying (slashing his housekeeper with a butcher knife). Eastwood's languorous direction is an odd fit for the material; he lingers over the Monterey-Carmel scenery like he's making a travelogue and takes an extended break for a jazz festival late in the film. Still, Walter makes for a memorably unhinged cinematic ancestor of Annie Wilkes.

The King of Comedy (1983)—One unintended side effect of Martin Scorsese's *Taxi Driver* was its influence on John Hinckley, whose obsession with the film's Jodie Foster manifested in an assassination attempt on Ronald Reagan. Scorsese and *Taxi Driver* star Robert De Niro explored the dark side of celebrity worship in this pitch-black comedy about failed comedian Rupert Pupkin and his worship of late-night talk show host Jerry Langford (Jerry Lewis). Frustrated by his inability to get on Langford's show, Pupkin and fellow obsessive Masha (Sandra Bernhard) kidnap the host and ransom him in exchange for the coveted guest appearance. Pupkin and Masha are both indelible creeps thanks to disturbing turns by De Niro and Bernhard, but Lewis is the real surprise here, stripped of his usual goofy screen persona to reveal the showbiz monster we always suspected was lurking inside.

Tony Manero (2008)—Against the backdrop of Augusto Pinochet's brutal dictatorship in 1978 Chile, fiftysomething Raul Peralta (Alfredo Castro) develops an unhealthy fascination with *Saturday Night Fever*. The glamorous world on the screen bears no relationship to his life of poverty and petty crime, but Peralta tries to will that world into being by joylessly mimicking John Travolta's dance moves in a replica of his famous white disco suit. His efforts to build a glass disco floor on which to strut his stuff lead him to ever more shocking and violent extremes in director Pablo Larrain's fascinating but often difficult to watch film.

Chapter 27 (2007)—*Misery* was partially inspired by a story King often told about signing an autograph for his "number one fan," a young man named Mark Chapman, who would go on to assassinate John Lennon. (In the years since, King has realized it couldn't have been the same Chapman, as the dates don't match up. Weirdly enough, another obsessive fan named Steven Lightfoot has insisted for more than two decades that it is King, not Chapman, who shot Lennon.) J. P. Schaefer's repellent indie film imagines Chapman's life in the days leading up to the assassination, but never develops a compelling reason we should care. Jared Leto packed on the pounds to play the unbalanced killer, but his strained performance adds nothing to our understanding of a man who probably isn't worth understanding in the first place.

The Assassination of Jesse James by the Coward Robert Ford (2007)—Nearly a hundred years before Chapman gunned down Lennon, another "number one fan" ended the life of his one-time hero in what could be called America's first celebrity assassination. Andrew Dominik's adaptation of the historical novel of the same name stars Brad Pitt as Jesse James at the end of his outlaw days and Casey Affleck as Robert Ford, the man who first worships him, then turns against him. Dominik is only partially successful at creating a mood piece from this scenario, and his film is too languid at times, but the cinematography by Roger Deakins is often breathtaking, and Affleck is mesmerizingly twitchy as the admirer turned murderer.

Big Fan (2009)—Former editor in chief of *The Onion* Robert D. Siegel wrote and directed this downbeat indie starring Patton Oswalt as a New York Giants fan with more than a little Rupert Pupkin in him. As "Paul from Staten Island," Oswalt's character is a regular caller to sports talk radio who delivers epic rants he's scripted in longhand, but after an encounter with his favorite player goes awry, Paul finds himself in danger of becoming a pariah among his fellow Big Blue rooters. Oswalt gives a surprisingly poignant yet unsentimental performance as an underachiever who has invested his entire sense of self-worth in a team that wants nothing to do with him.

Danse Macabre

Sleepwalkers, The Dark Half, and Needful Things

Sleepwalking With Mick Garris

By 1992, Stephen King had scripted two anthology films (*Creepshow* and *Cat's Eye*) and adapted several of his own published works for the screen (*Silver Bullet, Maximum Overdrive*, and *Pet Sematary*). As King writes in the introduction to *A Life in the Cinema*, a short story collection by Mick Garris, "I decided to take what I'd learned and write an original screenplay, and I had a bloody good time doing it. Adapting a novel like *Pet Sematary* for the screen is tough—like swiping all the hotel towels out of your room and trying to cram them in a medium-sized attaché case. Compared to that, writing an original screenplay—something meant from the first to fit the movies' two-hour time frame—was a piece of cake."

This particular piece of cake turned out to be *Sleepwalkers*, the story of an unusually close mother and son who aren't quite human. Columbia Pictures optioned the screenplay, which King had written on spec, and offered a choice of two directors: one who had directed, in King's words, "an arty-farty gangster film," and one who would go on to become one of the author's key collaborators in future film and television projects.

Mick Garris had worked in a variety of capacities in and around the film industry since the 1970s: a freelance writer for genre magazines like *Starlog* and *Cinefantastique*; a receptionist for George Lucas; a publicist for the PMK agency; and even host of a public-access talk show called Fantasy Film Festival, through which he met and interviewed some of the biggest names in the business, including Steven Spielberg. Years later, when Spielberg was ramping up production on his anthology series *Amazing Stories*, he remembered Garris and hired him as a writer and story editor. Garris directed one episode of the series, "Life on Death Row," and had two horror sequels under his belt when the opportunity to direct *Sleepwalkers* arose. Garris believes it was his direction of *Psycho IV: The Beginning*, with its focus on the relationship between the young Norman Bates and his mother, that brought him to Columbia's attention.

Madchen Amick followed her run on *Twin Peaks* with a scream-queen role in *Sleepwalkers*.

The studio was still leaning toward the other director, but King was so dismayed by the unnamed auteur's ideas for the film, which entailed some kind of "Planet of the Sleepwalkers" prequel, that he insisted on Garris. The newly hired director, who had worked as a publicist on the 1981 adaptation of Peter Straub's *Ghost Story*, pursued that film's star, Alice Krige, for the role of the mother, Mary Brady. Brian Krause, a teen idol type who had starred in *Return to the Blue Lagoon*, was cast as her son Charles, and *Twin Peaks* star Madchen Amick as his love interest/intended victim Tanya. Budgeted at roughly $15 million, the fifty-day shoot took place in Los Angeles, primarily on Columbia's Culver City lot. Alterian Studios handled the practical makeup effects, with Apogee Effects providing the then-cutting-edge digital morphing.

Garris had few problems on the shoot, but many more when it came time to screen *Sleepwalkers* for the MPAA ratings board. Four separate times the movie was awarded an NC-17 rating for its graphic violence, forcing Garris and his editors to go back and trim a little more. One of the main points of contention was a scene in which Krige's shape-shifting Mary bites the fingers off a policeman played by Ron Perlman. In the original cut, Krige spits out the fingers, which then hit the ground; the final R-rated version offers an abbreviated, less gory version of the scene.

Despite largely negative reviews, *Sleepwalkers* enjoyed a strong opening weekend when it was released in April 1992. The film debuted at the top spot, taking in over $10 million en route to a $30.5 million total. That's a surprisingly strong performance for what is, in retrospect, one of the very worst entries in the King filmography. The story is so simplistic and unambitious, it's hard to see what excited the author enough to pursue it as his first original screenplay. An opening title card lays out the basic premise: "sleepwalkers" are nomadic, shape-shifting creatures with human and feline origins. They feed on the life force of virginal human females, and mother and son Mary and Charles Brady may be the last of their kind. Shortly after arriving in their new home in small-town Indiana, Charles sets out to find a victim to keep himself and his mother/lover alive.

King's script appears to make up the rules about sleepwalkers as it goes along. We learn that their one weakness is cats (which seems odd, since they're supposedly part feline themselves) and that Charles can not only turn invisible but turn his car invisible and transform it from a blue Trans-Am into a red Mustang. He can also absorb his victim's life essence by stealing her breath—a trope King already used in two earlier screenplays: *Cat's Eye* and his *Tales from the Darkside* segment. Although King initially sketches Mary and Charles in somewhat sympathetic terms, they quickly devolve into cartoon villains; about the time Charles jams a pencil in a police officer's ear and pronounces him "cop-kebab," any hint of subtlety is out the window.

Garris compounds the problem with his casting choices. Krige is icy and remote, and Krause gives a lightweight performance suitable for a toothpaste commercial. Amick briefly provides the movie a jolt of life as she is introduced swaying and bopping to the Contours' "Do You Love Me?," but she is soon reduced to scream-queen status. Although there's no shortage of gore, Garris and his effects team aren't able to make the sleepwalkers into genuinely frightening antagonists: Once Mary and Charles have morphed into their true forms, they look like rubbery chew toys. It doesn't help that the climactic cat attack looks like an outtake from a Monty Python episode. (Really, though, how scary can a monster be if it can be defeated by Fluffy and friends?)

King's first original screenplay was also the occasion for his first collaboration with Mick Garris, who would go on to direct a number of King projects.

The movie may be short on scares, but Garris packs in plenty of in-jokes. In addition to casting King in his usual cameo, Garris finds room for John Landis and Joe Dante as lab technicians, Clive Barker and Tobe Hooper as forensic workers, and even Mark Hamill in a droopy mustache, for some reason. Garris only met King in person once during the shoot, for a few hours on the day the author flew in to do his cameo, but he must have made quite an impression. It was the beginning of a friendship and working relationship that would continue for more than two decades.

Romero Goes Dark

Stephen King fans could be forgiven for greeting the news that George Romero was set to write and direct an adaptation of King's 1989 novel *The Dark Half* with a healthy dose of skepticism. After all, Romero had been slated to direct both *It* and *Pet Sematary*, both of which made it to the screen without him, and he was still attached to *The Stand*, which was lingering in Development Hell. With the backing of Orion Pictures (to the tune of a $15 million budget), however, Romero began principal photography in his home stomping grounds of Pittsburgh on October 15, 1990. He had escaped Development Hell, but rocky days were still ahead for *The Dark Half*.

King's novel was a riff on *Dr. Jekyll and Mr. Hyde* filtered through the author's own experiences with his pseudonym, Richard Bachman. Like King, *Dark Half* protagonist Thad Beaumont is a writer who has published several books under a pen name, in this case George Stark. Unlike King, Beaumont has had little success with the novels published under his own name, but has achieved best-seller status with the darker, grittier Stark novels. When a blackmailer threatens to expose his secret, Beaumont goes public, giving Stark a burial in the pages of *People* magazine. But Stark refuses to stay dead: He somehow manifests in the real world as Beaumont's shadow-self, taking his revenge on those who conspired to bury him.

King was happy to sell the rights to Orion for a hefty fee, and even happier that his old friend would be directing the project, but otherwise the author had nothing to do with the production. Romero adapted the novel himself, sticking close to King's story line, and began his search for an actor who could play both Beaumont and his alter ego Stark. With Orion's backing, Romero discussed the project with a number of actors who would ordinarily be out of his price range, such as Gary Oldman and Willem Dafoe. In the end, Timothy Hutton (*Ordinary People*) was cast rather late in preproduction, with Amy Madigan taking on the role of Elizabeth Beaumont and Michael Rooker cast as Castle Rock sheriff Alan Pangborn.

Despite the novel's Maine setting, Orion agreed on the Pittsburgh-area locations Romero had preferred since kicking off his career with *Night of the Living Dead*. Romero felt comfortable working with old friends in familiar environs, but less so with the more established actors, particularly Hutton. As part of

Timothy Hutton proved to be a handful on the set of *The Dark Half*, employing a second, garbage-strewn trailer for his scenes as Thad Beaumont's evil twin George Stark.

his preparation, Hutton required two trailers: a normal one for his Beaumont days, and one trashed with pizza boxes and empty beer cans, where he blasted heavy metal music to pump himself up to play Stark. Romero and Hutton butted heads, with the actor reportedly even quitting the production briefly. In interviews at the time of the film's release, Romero praised the give-and-take he had with Hutton, but he later told Rick Curnette of *The Film Journal* that "the experience was hell." Part of that had to do with working for a studio for the first time; even though Orion was a "mini-major," Romero missed his independence. "It takes longer to tell 100 people something than 20," he told interviewer Charles Leayman during a break in shooting.

Although it begins as a sort of psychological thriller, *The Dark Half* becomes an effects-heavy picture by the end. Stark begins deteriorating, both mentally and physically, requiring Hutton to wear extensive prosthetics. An animatronic puppet was substituted for the actor for shots in which Stark is attacked by birds that rip the flesh from his body (a change from the original ending, mandated by Orion). And then there were the birds themselves: 4,500 live cut-throat finches cast as the sparrows that tear Stark apart. Bird wrangler Mark Harden trained the birds to attack, while special makeup effects artist Larry Odien designed and built mechanical birds for close-up shots. More birds were added digitally in postproduction.

Romero's troubles weren't over when the grueling shoot wrapped in March 1991. "Orion was sorta running out of money, and they didn't really let us finish the film the way we wanted to," the director told Alex Sorondo of *The Examiner* in 2010. "I really like *The Dark Half* up until the last reel. And then, you know, the truth is: we never had enough money to score the last reel. . . . So it's really that final sequence that bugs me the most." Worse yet, Romero would have to wait nearly two years to see his film reach theaters. By 1991, Orion was in financial trouble: Deep in debt and facing lawsuits from its shareholders, the studio filed for bankruptcy in December of that year. All of its releases were put on hold while Orion went through Chapter 11 proceedings. *The Dark Half* finally reached theaters on April 23, 1993, but it didn't stay in them long. A sixth-place opening weekend brought in only $3.2 million; by its third weekend, it had dropped out of the top ten. Its final total of just over $10 million didn't even recoup its production costs.

It deserved a better fate, although it would be a stretch to call it a complete creative success. Romero's fidelity to the source material pays off in *The Dark Half*'s first hour but becomes a liability as the story approaches its climax. Like a number of mid-period King works, *The Dark Half* doesn't so much come to a satisfactory conclusion as dissolve into arbitrary hocus-pocus. The implications of George Stark's existence, and Thad Beaumont's culpability in unleashing his dark side, aren't really dealt with. What begins as a metaphor for the creative process ends with a grislier variation on Alfred Hitchcock's *The Birds*.

Romero excels at the buildup but can't find a way to make the climax work (not that the studio interference helped any). The best moments come early on: the operation on young Thad's brain that reveals the blinking eyeball of the twin he absorbed in the womb; an artificial leg getting hung up on the car window through which Stark has just pulled his first victim; a dream sequence in which Madigan's jigsaw-puzzle face shatters to reveal a skull beneath. Romero lets the story unfold at a deliberate pace, and his film is intriguing as long as its mysteries are allowed to simmer. But he tips his hand too early: Instead of playing with the idea that Thad may be committing the murders himself, he makes it all too clear that Stark is a separate (albeit psychically connected) entity. Thad never seems to be in too much danger; the fact that he isn't arrested immediately after his fingerprints are discovered all over the first crime scene is hard to swallow. Rooker's Sheriff Pangborn is almost completely ineffectual, to the point that his extensive screen time feels gratuitous.

Orion went through bankruptcy proceedings. The film was never completed to director George Romero's satisfaction.

The bubble completely bursts in the last twenty minutes or so, but King is more to blame for that than Romero. This is one case where the filmmaker would have been better off deviating from the source material to find a more satisfying conclusion. The sparrow attack is visually arresting, but it's a narrative botch and ends the film so abruptly that it almost feels unfinished. *The Dark Half* has its moments, but in the end it might as well be called *Half-Baked*.

This Spanish postcard promotes *Needful Things*, a plodding adaptation of one of King's least inspired efforts.

The Long and Short of *Needful Things*

When *Needful Things* was published in 1991, it was billed as "the last Castle Rock story," so who better than Castle Rock Entertainment to bring it to the screen? That doesn't mean King gave it away to his old friend Rob Reiner; in fact, Castle Rock paid a reported $1.75 million to acquire the film rights to the novel before it was even published. Lawrence D. Cohen, by now a veteran at adapting King for the screen, was hired to write the screenplay. This time, Reiner would not be directing or even overseeing the production. That task fell to production chief Martin Shafer, who hired Hollywood veteran Peter Yates (*Bullitt, The Friends of Eddie Coyle*) to direct.

When Yates backed out of the project, Shafer brought in first-time filmmaker Fraser Heston, son of Moses himself, Charlton Heston. (In fact, Fraser Heston had played Moses as a baby in the 1956 version of *The Ten Commandments* that starred his father.) Feeling that Cohen's draft was a bit *too* faithful to King's sprawling novel, Heston and Castle Rock brought in W. D. Richter (*Big Trouble in Little China*) for a fresh take on the adaptation. "The book is a complicated spider web of interwoven hot wires, and it needed to be simplified," Heston told John Stanley of the *San Francisco Chronicle*. "Rick focused on the most important characters and the exciting parts and we then had a realistic shooting script."

On paper, at least, the cast was perhaps the most impressive yet assembled for a King production. Former son of God and demon exorcist Max Von Sydow agreed to play against type as Needful Things proprietor Leland Gaunt, demonic purveyor of antiques and curios. Ed Harris signed on as Castle Rock sheriff Alan Pangborn (a familiar name to *Dark Half* viewers) and Bonnie Bedelia as his fiancée Polly Chalmers. Amanda Plummer, J. T. Walsh, Ray McKinnon and Don S. Davis filled out the supporting cast. Gibson's Landing, British Columbia, was cast in the crucial role of small-town Maine.

Richter's script may have streamlined King's novel, but the version of *Needful Things* that was shot in the fall of 1992 was still too unwieldy for Castle Rock's liking. In the editing room, subplots were reduced or excised entirely, scenes were shifted around, and an extensive (and presumably expensive) action sequence meant to open the film was deleted entirely. The theatrical version of *Needful Things* clocked in at exactly two hours when it was released on August 27, 1993, but the extra showtimes gained by the tight running time didn't prevent it from becoming another King-related box office disappointment. With an opening weekend of just over $5 million, it finished a distant second behind *The Fugitive* and ended its run with a domestic gross of $15 million.

At any length, *Needful Things* was probably doomed from the start, if only because its source material was one of King's weakest efforts—a bloated *Twilight Zone* riff fueled by cheap cynicism and easy moralizing. The story concerns devilish shopkeeper Leland Gaunt, who will be happy to sell you that rare baseball card or magical arthritis-curing necklace, if only you will agree to do a deed in return. Such deeds include but are not limited to: throwing rocks at a neighbor's windows; skinning a neighbor's dog; and pasting citations for "embezzlement," "fraud," and "cornholing your mother" all over a neighbor's house. In each case, a long-standing grudge or unresolved dispute will result in the offended party blaming the wrong neighbor for the deed, such misunderstandings inevitably escalating into violence. Before long, the entire town is in chaos, and it's up to Sheriff Pangborn to save Castle Rock from destroying itself.

Since this is, after all, the last Castle Rock story, you can't like his chances. Especially since Gaunt can't resist dropping coy hints that he just might be Ol' Scratch in the flesh. (At least, subtle quips like "You've been having a devil of a time" or "I have a tendency to turn up the heat" tend to support this reading, although with all of Hell at his disposal, you'd think Satan could enlist a better gag writer.) Much of the town goes up in flames, but while Castle Rock may have a long, rich history on the page, Heston's filmed version exists in a vacuum. Readers of the book could at least amuse themselves by charting the connections to other King works—"Hey! It's Ace Merrill from 'The Body'! And isn't that the bandstand from *The Dead Zone*?"—and perhaps the accumulation of these references supplied some weight to the apocalyptic events that transpire, but little or none of this makes its way into the movie.

Instead, this Castle Rock is a town that could only have been imagined by someone who once glanced through a glossy Maine wall calendar. It's all colorful autumn leaves drifting past white-columned porches and swooping helicopter shots of waves crashing upon rocky shores illuminated by lighthouse beacons. There's nothing about the place that feels lived-in, which is a problem since the story springs from long-simmering resentments boiling over in a tight-knit community. Few of the characters seem to be occupying the same planet, let alone the same small town. (As usual, Amanda Plummer makes her contributions from somewhere in the vicinity of Pluto.) Other actors, including Harris and Bedelia, are victimized by the two-hour edit, which also makes for a choppy, disjointed narrative.

When *Needful Things* aired on the TBS network in May 1996, more than an hour of footage cut from the theatrical release had been restored. Among the additions were the deleted opening sequence, including Pangborn's pursuit of Gaunt's car and the car's subsequent explosion; a number of additional scenes between Harris and Bedelia; an entire subplot concerning Cora Rusk (Lisa Blount) and her obsession with Elvis; and more details concerning other subplots, such as "Buster" Keeton's embezzlement from the town funds. This extended version (which has never been released on DVD, although bootleg copies can easily be tracked down) is certainly a fuller, more complete adaptation of King's novel, with somewhat deeper characterizations of Pangborn and Polly in particular. But it's so repetitive and poorly paced, it's hard to call it an improvement on the theatrical cut. At any length, it's a needless thing.

Deep Cuts

- If the house Charles and Mary Brady share in *Sleepwalkers* looks familiar, you're probably old enough to remember *The Waltons*. The same house, located on the Warner Bros. lot in Burbank, was used for both productions.
- *The Dark Half*'s George Stark was mostly inspired by King's own experiences with his pseudonym, Richard Bachman, but Stark is also a homage to the great mystery writer Donald Westlake. Westlake wrote a series of darker, grittier novels about a ruthless criminal named Parker—novels he published under the pseudonym Richard Stark.
- Although *The Dark Half* and *Needful Things* share a character in Alan Pangborn, there's no continuity to speak of between the two movies. But there is one amusing casting connection: Amy Madigan stars in *The Dark Half*, in which Pangborn is played by Michael Rooker, while Madigan's real-life husband, Ed Harris, plays Pangborn in *Needful Things*.

"Get Busy Living or Get Busy Dying"

Human-Scaled Horror in *The Shawshank Redemption* and *Dolores Claiborne*

Home Video Redeems *Shawshank*

When speaking at colleges or libraries, Stephen King has a handful of go-to anecdotes that have gotten a lot of use over the years. In one of them, King is picking up a few items at the grocery stores when an elderly woman recognizes him.

> "I know who you are," she says. "You're the one who writes those scary stories." King acknowledges that she's got the right man, to which the woman replies, "I don't like that stuff. I like uplifting things, like that *Shawshank Redemption*."
> "Well, ma'am, I wrote that."
> "No, you didn't!"

By 1994, King's constant readers knew he wasn't just the guy who wrote the scary stories, but to the moviegoing public, he was still America's number one horror-meister. Only one of the films adapted from his writing had been a non-horror movie, and that one, *Stand by Me*, had downplayed the author's connection in all its publicity. In the mid-1990s, however, the company owned by the director of *Stand by Me* would release two back-to-back King adaptations in which nary a hint of the supernatural could be found. The horrors in *The Shawshank Redemption* and *Dolores Claiborne* were rooted in reality, and while neither of them would set box office records, both would bring a new respectability to the tarnished reputation of the King filmography. One, in fact, would blossom from a theatrical flop into one of the most beloved movies of all time. As King himself put it in the introduction to the published version of the *Shawshank Redemption* screenplay, "Castle Rock Pictures has more or less rescued my film-associated reputation from the scrap heap."

Stephen King first heard the name Frank Darabont when the latter was a film student who approached the author about adapting one of his short stories, "The Woman in the Room." (That story is told in chapter 22.) King had been so impressed with the resulting short film that when Darabont inquired in 1987 about the rights to one of the novellas from the *Different Seasons* collection, King gave him the option for a song. For four years, Darabont did nothing with the story, "Rita Hayworth and Shawshank Redemption." As he told Robin Rauzi of the *Los Angeles Times*, this was "a massive case of work avoidance . . . It's like solitary confinement: You know you're going to be there a while."

In this case, "a while" turned out to be roughly eight weeks. Darabont sent his completed script to King, who was both delighted and skeptical. "It was great—too great, I thought, to be produced by any company in California. I did not feel there was a place for *Rita Hayworth and the Shawshank Redemption* in an industry consumed with Predators and Terminators." Nevertheless, King renewed Darabont's option on the story, and the screenwriter began shopping the script around Hollywood. It turned out to be one-stop shopping, as Castle Rock, the production company Darabont had in mind from the beginning, jumped at the chance to make the movie. This time, Rob Reiner was very interested in directing what was now known as *The Shawshank Redemption* himself, but Darabont resisted a strong financial incentive to give up the director's chair. According to an October 5, 1994, *L.A. Times* story, Castle Rock offered Darabont $2.4 million for the script if he would agree to let Reiner direct. "Ultimately, what kind of price tag do you put on your passion?" Darabont told interviewer Irene Lacher. "What's it worth to you to sell your dream away to somebody else, even if it's somebody as great as Rob Reiner?"

Instead, Castle Rock paid $750,000 plus a percentage of future profits for *Shawshank* with Darabont attached as director. While Reiner had eyed Tom Cruise and Harrison Ford for the central roles of Shawshank inmates Andy Dufresne and "Red" Redding, Darabont would go a different direction. Based largely on the enigmatic quality he'd displayed in movies like *Jacob's Ladder*, Tim Robbins was cast as Andy, while the part of Red, conceived by King as a white Irishman, went to an unlikely candidate: Morgan Freeman. The all-male supporting cast was filled out with character actors Bob Gunton, Clancy Brown, William Sadler, James Whitmore, and Gil Bellows.

Another important casting decision involved the prison itself. With nearly every scene set inside the walls of Shawshank, Darabont knew he couldn't use a working prison. "I know people who have shot in a real prison, and for the first two hours it was security checks going in and for the last two hours security checks going out," Darabont told Rauzi. Producer Niki Marvin spent five months scouting correctional facilities before selecting the ideal spot: the Ohio State Reformatory in Mansfield, Ohio. The prison had been closed since 1990, when the new Mansfield Correctional Institute opened, and its imposing stone facade was the perfect setting for the film's exteriors. "It's big, it's Gothic, it's old, it's bleak and it's not something that had a town around it," Darabont told the

Despite its initial failure at the box office, *The Shawshank Redemption* went on to become one of the most beloved movies of all time.

Columbus Dispatch. "I feel so lucky that this place was here and hadn't been torn down. The prison, if not a character in the movie, is at least a constant, embracing presence."

Interior sets were built in a nearby warehouse, and shooting began in the summer of 1993. Filming lasted for three months under sometimes grueling conditions. The simulated prison life felt a little too real at times for the actors: Actual guards from the nearby correctional facility worked as extras on the film, and a scene in which the men swab tar onto the roof was shot in sweltering heat. The movie's final scene, set in Mexico, was shot in St. Croix in the Virgin Islands. This reunion scene between Andy and Red was filmed under protest by Darabont, but Castle Rock insisted; later, when audiences responded well to the scene, he relented and left it in the picture.

Shawshank's future looked promising when it opened in limited release on September 23, 1994. The opening-day reviews were among the best ever for a King adaptation, and the weekend box office was strong for a film showing in only thirty-three theaters: $750,000, for a per-screen average of over $22,000. But as the film expanded into wide release, the hoped-for mass audience never arrived. The movie peaked at the number nine spot on the charts on the weekend of October 14–16, bringing in a very disappointing $16 million in its initial run. *Shawshank* got another chance at connecting with the moviegoing public when it was nominated for seven Academy Awards in February 1995—an unprecedented total for a King film. Castle Rock rereleased the film in theaters in hopes of capitalizing on the award buzz, but it was shut out at the Oscars and added only another $9 million to its coffers.

Despite its initial failures, however, *The Shawshank Redemption* went on to have an afterlife as impressive as those of *Citizen Kane* and *It's a Wonderful Life* (both box office flops upon release). To the surprise of everyone, including Warner Bros., which released the movie on VHS, *Shawshank* went on to become the top-rented home video of 1995. For whatever reason, the home audience proved more willing to accept both a two-and-a-half hour prison film and one of the clunkiest titles of all time. (On one of the DVD extras, Clancy Brown chuckles about people approaching him on the street to praise his performance in "The Scrimshaw Rejection.") And many of those home viewers didn't just *like* the film—they became evangelists for it, watching it over and over and pushing it on their friends.

Shawshank's home video afterlife also coincided with the rise of the Internet. When the Internet Movie Database began tracking user ratings in order to determine the top 250 movies of all time, some of the titles at the top were obvious choices: acclaimed popular favorites like *The Godfather, Star Wars*, and *Schindler's List*. But more often than not, the movie in the number one spot on the list was *The Shawshank Redemption*; in fact, it's still there as of this writing. It's clear that the film has struck a chord with an entire generation of movie fans, but why?

In part, it's because Darabont's direction is a throwback to a classical Hollywood style. *Shawshank* doesn't sugarcoat the prison experience: Andy is raped by the Sisters, there are a number of violent assaults and several murders, and a general coarseness of language and interaction (at least early on). Yet the director aestheticizes the more brutal moments, artfully hiding them in shadow or pulling the camera away, folding them into the overall elegant presentation. No one is ever going to confuse *Shawshank* with gritty portrayals of prison life like *Hunger* or *A Prophet*, or even the HBO series *Oz*. Even the "Dracula's Castle" look of the prison itself adds to the film's elevation of reality to a more mythical realm. On the *Shawshank* DVD, Darabont describes the movie as "a tall tale," which sounds about right.

It's telling that he doesn't describe it as a prison movie, because that's not really what *Shawshank* is about. If it were made today, it would be called a "bromance," because it's essentially a study of male friendship using the tropes of the prison movie as a framework. Certainly Darabont isn't trying to score any points for originality with his portrayals of the corrupt warden, the sadistic guard, thirty days in the hole, and so on. And he's definitely not crafting a prison escape procedural for the ages; Andy's plot is only revealed in retrospect and relies heavily on the dumb luck of being assigned a cell at the end of the block. (A more procedural version of *Shawshank* might have revealed the answer to one of the film's great unanswered questions: How the hell did Andy hang his Raquel Welch poster back up after climbing into the tunnel?)

What really drives the movie (in addition to its overall excellent craftsman-ship, including the typically outstanding cinematography of Roger Deakins) are the central performances by Tim Robbins and Morgan Freeman. Robbins's introverted, low-key turn clarifies why casting Cruise in the role would have been a fatal mistake: The *Top Gun* star's cocky energy would have left no doubt that Andy would get the best of his prison tormentors and escape Shawshank in the end. Freeman proves to be a surprisingly natural match for King's distinctive voice, making wry, hard-won wisdom from turns of phrase that might otherwise fall flat. Together, the two actors lend Red and Andy an ease and comfort level with each other than never feels forced.

Every critical impulse suggests that Darabont's (and King's) original ending, with Red heading south on the bus, hoping that he'll see Andy again and that the Pacific is as blue as it is in his dreams, is the right one. And if *Shawshank* were a different kind of movie; it *would* be the right one. But a throwback "male weepie" like this needs the cathartic reunion on the beach, and it would be a hard-hearted viewer indeed who didn't get a little choked up at the end.

The Shawshank Redemption doesn't belong at the top of any list of the best movies ever made, but that's not really what the IMDb Top 250 is. It's a crowd-sourced list, so by definition it's a list of the most crowd-pleasing movies ever made, and it's hard to argue that *Shawshank* doesn't belong near the top of *that*. Its message of hope is easily digested, but it comes from a place of sincer-ity. There's always been a populist, sentimental streak in King's writing; it's something he proudly admits, and it's something Darabont honors here. In that sense, *Shawshank* is among the truest of King adaptations: It gets straight to the heart of the matter.

Bloodlines: Five Great Prison Escape Movies

As discussed above, there's more to *The Shawshank Redemption* than its prison escape sequence. Still, Darabont's film is the heir to a long-standing Hollywood tradition, as exemplified by the following five films.

I Am a Fugitive from a Chain Gang (1932)—This pre-Code drama directed by Mervyn LeRoy is surprisingly tough-minded and positively thrilling at times. Paul Muni (*Scarface*) stars as a World War I veteran who is inadvertently involved in robbery and sentenced to ten years on a chain gang. His escape makes for a breathless, nail-biting sequence, but it's the aftermath that sets *Chain Gang* apart, as Muni's character becomes a productive, thriving member of society only to find himself back in chains through the machinations of an unforgiving state. The social commentary is powerful enough to change minds about the prison system, but never gets in the way of a taut, propulsive narrative.

***Brute Force* (1947)**—Burt Lancaster stars in Jules Dassin's prison noir as a convict determined to escape the clutches of a sadistic warden (Hume Cronyn). Through its flashback structure, *Brute Force* is one of the few prison films to include the stories of the women Lancaster and his friends have left behind. (A bit too conveniently, all of these men committed their crimes for love.) Dassin stages several set pieces that are shocking in their violence considering when the film was made, with the climactic escape sequence truly living up to the movie's title.

***A Man Escaped* (1956)**—Robert Bresson was known for his minimalist approach and attention to the smallest details, and this based-in-fact story of a French Resistance officer's efforts to escape his Nazi captors encapsulates his style perfectly. François Leterrier is Fontaine, whose methodical approach to escaping Fort Montluc prison unfolds with such bare-bones precision and clarity as to exert a hypnotic fascination. By the final half-hour, we are so attuned to Fontaine's meticulous planning and patient execution, the tension becomes nearly unbearable.

***Cool Hand Luke* (1967)**—At first blush, the prison road crew in director Stuart Rosenberg's film would appear to have a better time of it than the one Paul Muni escaped thirty-five years earlier. There are no leg irons, unless you've tried to escape, and the minimum-security facility housing Dragline (Oscar winner George Kennedy) and company allows for plenty of raucous good times in the off-hours. Enter Luke (Paul Newman), the original rebel without a clue and one of the first antiheroes to signal the rise of the New Hollywood. Luke's stubborn brand of contrarianism is almost completely pointless: He's arrested for cutting the heads off parking meters, and he agrees to eat fifty eggs on a bet with no idea whether he can do it or not. He is good at escaping, however, pulling it off three times with increasingly dire consequences. Best known for the line "What we've got here is failure to communicate," *Cool Hand Luke* boasts a distinctly sixties brand of antiauthoritarianism and a magnetic lead performance from Newman, not to mention a peerless supporting cast of character actors, including Harry Dean Stanton, Strother Martin, Dennis Hopper, Clifton James and Joe Don Baker.

***Escape from Alcatraz* (1979)**—No one who has seen Don Siegel's fact-based thriller about what may or may not have been a successful escape from America's most notorious island penitentiary will be inclined to give the prison-break scenes in *The Shawshank Redemption* any points for originality. Many of the elements of Andy Dufresne's escape are lifted straight out of this picture starring Clint Eastwood as one of his signature men of few words and bold action. Siegel combines Bresson's attention to detail with Hollywood-honed suspense and a more colorful cast of characters, notably Patrick McGoohan, who delivers a twisted turn as the by-now-stock sadistic warden.

Dolores Claiborne's Maine Character

Stephen King's 1992 novel *Dolores Claiborne* was one of his more unlikely candidates for big-screen adaptation. The entire book took the form of a monologue by its title character, a Maine cleaning woman defending herself against charges of murdering her employer and, years earlier, her husband. It had no supernatural elements to speak of, aside from a brief telepathic interlude during an eclipse, which was essentially a device designed to tie the novel, however tenuously, to the even more unfilmable *Gerald's Game*. Still, that didn't stop Castle Rock from snapping up the movie rights for $1.5 million not long after the book's publication.

Once again, Rob Reiner would abstain from directing, although it was clear that his *Misery* star, Kathy Bates, was the only real choice to play the title role. *Misery* screenwriter William Goldman was brought aboard as a consultant, and it was Goldman who recommended Tony Gilroy for the tricky task of adapting King's book for the screen. According to a 2009 *New Yorker* profile of Gilroy, the screenwriter

> liked the character of Claiborne, a woman suspected of murdering her husband on a small island off Maine. She had an unusual voice and a toughness that appealed to him. The problem with the story, he realized, was that "she confesses to the crime at the outset. The mystery was: Is this a reliable narrator? And that doesn't seem intrinsically very dramatic to me onscreen." Gilroy made *Claiborne* a movie by foregrounding Dolores's daughter, Selena, who was sexually abused as a child. She is a secondary figure in King's book; Gilroy made her an equal protagonist . . . This trick even impressed King, who wrote to Castle Rock to say that he wished he'd thought of it.

Gilroy's script also impressed director Taylor Hackford (*An Officer and a Gentleman*), who agreed to take on the project. Bates was already aboard, but Hackford had no problem with that. His choice for the role of Selena, based on her work in Robert Altman's *Short Cuts*, was Jennifer Jason Leigh. David Strathairn (*Matewan*) would play Claiborne's late husband in flashbacks, with Christopher Plummer, John C. Reilly, Judy Parfitt, and Eric Bogosian filling out the supporting cast. Hackford shot the film in Nova Scotia, just across the Bay of Fundy from Downeast Maine. (Some of the same locations, notably Lunenburg, were later used for the King-based SyFy series *Haven*.)

Hackford's biggest technical challenge during the shoot was recreating the eclipse that figures into the movie's big set piece: Claiborne's final showdown with her drunken, abusive husband. For this scene, Hackford optically combined shots of the actors on a green-screen set with location footage and a

Director Taylor Hackford evoked a convincing Maine landscape, both geographical and psychological, in *Dolores Claiborne*.

computer-generated eclipse to create an eerie effect. Hackford also alternated film stocks to differentiate between flashbacks (shot in warm Fuji color) and the present-day scenes (for which he used cold, desaturated Kodak stocks).

Released on March 24, 1995, *Dolores Claiborne* met with much the same fate as *The Shawshank Redemption*: generally warm notices from critics but a chilly reception at the box office. After debuting in third place with a $5.7 million opening weekend, the film finished its run with a little over $24 million total. Unlike its predecessor, *Claiborne* wasn't remembered at Oscar time, nor did it develop a rabid following on home video, although it's generally well regarded among King fans.

Like *Shawshank*, *Dolores Claiborne* is a throwback to an earlier Hollywood style—in this case, the "women's pictures" made popular by directors like George Cukor and Vincente Minnelli and stars like Bette Davis and Barbara Stanwyck. Hackford leans too heavily on the melodrama at times, and like many King adaptations, the film is overlong, but it's among the most successful realizations of the Maine landscape—both physical and mental—to reach the screen. When Dolores is accused of murdering mean old Vera Donovan, her estranged daughter Selena, now a New York journalist, returns to the island to aid her mother's defense against detective John Mackey (Plummer). Selena is reluctant to do so, as she and Mackey are both convinced Dolores murdered her husband (and Selena's father) Joe some twenty years earlier.

As we learn through flashbacks, Joe (Strathairn) was an abusive drunk with an unseemly interest in his daughter. Dolores arranged for him to fall down a well during a solar eclipse because, as Vera Donovan insists, "Sometimes being a bitch is all a woman has to hold onto." A crude brand of feminism to be sure, but in this case, a highly effective one. The bulk of the movie is a two-woman show about the reunion of mother and daughter, which is not what King had in mind when he wrote the book. In his interview with Tony Magistrale for the book *Hollywood's Stephen King*, the author notes, "If there's anything wrong with *Dolores Claiborne*, it was the decision on the part of the filmmakers to try to tack on this artificial reconciliation between Dolores and her daughter. It's a very human desire, and it's understandable that producers would want to cater to it."

Leigh is the movie's weak link, although the fault lies less with her than with Gilroy and Hackford's conception of the character. The pale, fast-talking chain-smoker dressed all in black is more a caricature of how someone from insular Maine community would picture a New Yorker than a three-dimensional human being. Bates, on the other hand, delivers a much richer, more believable flesh-and-blood portrayal than in her (admittedly entertaining) Oscar-winning *Misery* turn. (The fact that she wasn't even nominated for *Claiborne* surely owes more to the film's box office failure than the relative quality of her work.) And Strathairn totally nails a particular Maine type, possessed of a stony meanness brought on by hard work, little money, boredom, and drink; his resentful sneer of an accent is pitch-perfect.

In its detailing of the housekeeper's relationship with her boss "from away," *Dolores Claiborne* hints at the thorny relationship between Maine natives and the summer people—the rich folks who invade for a few months, clog up the roads, dump some cash into the local coffers, and vanish with the fall foliage. *Claiborne* shows us the world they leave behind: a frigid gray landscape of isolation, all barren trees and boarded-up houses. It's the flip side of Vacationland, and it has a lot to do with the taciturn demeanor and dry, bleak humor (often directed at those summer people) so often associated with the Maine character. In the dead of winter, when the sun goes down in mid-afternoon and the harbor fog creeps in, it's easy to think that Stephen King could have come from nowhere else.

15

Full Dark, No Stars

The Mangler, Thinner, and The Night Flier

Mangled

Horror movies are often described as "roller coaster rides," but that comparison works especially well with the Stephen King filmography as a whole. It seems as though every time King movies reach a new height of popularity, artistic accomplishment, or critical respect, there is an immediate plunge back into the depths of cheap exploitation, gratuitous gore, and a haphazard approach to adaptation. Not that those are *necessarily* bad qualities in a horror movie, but more often than not, they result in the kind of completely forgettable films discussed in this chapter.

First up is *The Mangler*, based on another one of the *Night Shift* short stories optioned by Milton Subotsky in the late 1970s. As mentioned earlier, Subotsky had planned an anthology film called *The Machines*, which would have been adapted from three of the stories he owned: "Trucks," "The Lawnmower Man," and "The Mangler." King had based the latter story on his experiences working in an industrial laundry during his summer hiatus from his pre-*Carrie* teaching job. The laundry's speed-ironing machine was known as "the mangler," with good reason, as King explains in his introduction to the story in the *Stephen King Goes to the Movies* collection: "One of the floor foremen, Harry Cross, had hooks instead of hands . . . One Saturday during World War II, he fell into it while it was running."

At twenty pages, the story was just about the right length for one segment of an anthology film. As the basis of a full-length feature, it was a little thin. That proved no obstacle to Allied Vision, which purchased the rights to several of the Subotsky-owned properties after the producer's death in 1991. Allied had already run into trouble with their first attempt at a King adaptation, "The Lawnmower Man" (a case that will be discussed in chapter 34), which deviated too greatly from the original story for the author's liking. In this case, Allied (along with coproducer Distant Horizon and distributor New Line Cinema) brought aboard a ringer of sorts in director Tobe Hooper.

Hooper had already directed one Stephen King adaptation, the CBS-TV version of *Salem's Lot*, of which the author generally approved. As Hooper worked on the screenplay with his visual effects supervisor Stephen Brooks and

A familiar makeup-encased face, *Nightmare on Elm Street* star Robert Englund, couldn't save *The Mangler* from box-office disaster.

executive producer Harry Alan Towers (writing under the name Peter Welbeck), he stayed in touch with King to ensure that the script would be faithful enough to satisfy him, and that he would approve the changes necessary to expand the story to feature length. Those changes included the radical expansion of the character of Bill Gartley, who is referenced in passing in the short story but becomes the chief villain of the movie, as embodied by former Freddy Krueger Robert Englund.

Originally set to shoot in Toronto, *The Mangler* instead turned into "a grueling shoot in South Africa," as Tobe Hooper described it in his introduction to Englund's memoir, *Hollywood Monster*. It would be another makeup-intensive role for Englund, who was relieved to have his *Nightmare on Elm Street* makeup man, David Miller, aboard. The other name of note in the cast was Ted Levine (best known for his unsettling performances as Jame Gumb in *Silence of the Lambs*) as the ostensible hero, Officer John Hunton. The director's son William Hooper designed the title character, the demon-possessed speed-ironing machine that develops a taste for blood.

New Line may have believed that the combination of Hooper, King, and their own *Elm Street* star Englund added up to a horror movie trifecta that would prove irresistible to audiences, but if so, they badly miscalculated. Released on March 3, 1995, in 800 theaters, *The Mangler* barely cracked the million-dollar mark in its opening weekend. By the following weekend, it had virtually disappeared from theaters. With a total gross of $1.7 million, it's arguably the biggest flop in the entire King catalog.

It's not hard to see why. Like *Graveyard Shift*, another low-budget *Night Shift* adaptation, *The Mangler* can't sustain its thin conceit for nearly two hours. Hooper and his production design team give us an impressively Dickensian setting, all clanking pipes and blasts of steam and nearly medieval-looking chains and gears grinding away. And even the R-rated theatrical version provides ample fodder for gorehounds as the demonic laundry machine folds, spindles, and mutilates its victims. (The unrated DVD version is even more graphic.) Levine is entertainingly unhinged as the cop investigating the laundry, while England, encased in layers of old-age makeup and clunky mechanical hands and legs, delivers a performance sponsored by Honey Baked Ham. But the story makes less sense as it goes along, and it's padded with pointless, endless scenes in which Hunton confers with his New Age buddy and an ailing old crime-scene photographer about how to defeat the evil. (Here's an idea: Why not just stay out of the laundry?) This time, the audience was right to stay home: *The Mangler* easily ranks among the least essential Stephen King movies.

It's a verdict the author himself agrees with. In *Stephen King Goes to the Movies*, he writes, "Tobe Hooper, who directed it, is something of a genius . . . *The Texas Chain Saw Massacre* proves that beyond doubt. But when genius goes wrong, brother, watch out . . . The movie's visuals are surreal and the sets are eye-popping, but somewhere along the way (maybe in the copious amounts of steam generated by the film's mechanical star), the story got lost."

Thin Gruel

Thinner was the Richard Bachman book that blew Stephen King's cover. Published in 1984, the story of an obese lawyer whose pounds start melting away after he's cursed by an ancient Gypsy sold only twenty-eight thousand copies until a story in the *Bangor Daily News* revealed that Bachman was actually King's pseudonym. In the late eighties, King's longtime collaborator Richard Rubinstein of Laurel Entertainment optioned the rights to the novel and hired Michael McDowell (*Beetlejuice*) to adapt it for the big screen.

The project was set up at Warner Bros. with *Child's Play* helmer Tom Holland attached to direct, but it never got past the development stage. A number of studios showed interest over the years as the script went through several rewrites, but all eventually passed, either because they felt the ending was too dark or because the extreme weight-loss effects proved too daunting. After the ratings success of ABC's *The Langoliers* (produced by Rubinstein, written and directed by Holland, based on King's novel), Paramount Pictures finally agreed to take on *Thinner* at a budget of $17 million.

For years, Stephen King movies set in Maine had been shot in disparate locations, but now, for once, the author's home state would fill in for another setting. *Thinner* mostly takes place in Connecticut, but Holland and Rubinstein settled on Camden, Maine, as the shooting locale. Although King had once speculated that John Candy would be the ideal choice for the lead character of Billy Halleck ("He'd have to lose some weight, and maybe it'd save his life"), the role went to Robert John Burke, who had taken over for Peter Weller in *Robocop 3*. Burke lost twenty pounds for the role, but since Halleck is only skinny for part of the film, he also had to endure a number of long days in the makeup chair.

The weight-loss effects were a crucial component of the shoot, which began in August 1995. Makeup effects artist Greg Cannom, an Oscar winner for *Mrs. Doubtfire* and Francis Coppola's *Dracula*, had the task of slimming Halleck from around 300 pounds to a low of 120. Cannom created a variety of fat suits and latex pieces for Burke's face for the eight stages of Halleck's deterioration. For one shower scene, Cannom designed a full flesh suit for Burke, complete with silicone breast implants. The Halleck character was not the only makeup challenge on the shoot: Cannom and his team were also responsible for turning Michael Constantine into a 106-year-old Gypsy and Howard Erskine into the lizard-faced Judge Phillips for a dream sequence.

Shooting wrapped in November, and it appeared *Thinner* was set for a May 1996 theatrical release. After preview audiences at test screenings overwhelmingly rejected the movie's ending, however, Holland and his cast and crew returned to Camden to shoot a new one, delaying the film's release. The novel had ended with a dark but mordantly humorous twist: Halleck, with the help of a mobster client, convinces the old Gypsy to remove the curse. But first Halleck must pass the curse to someone else via a special pie. Believing that his wife is having an affair, Halleck seeks revenge by leaving the pie out for her to eat. But after his beloved daughter, who he'd believed to be staying with a friend, also eats a piece of the pie, a despondent Halleck cuts a slice for himself.

In some interviews, Holland has described his original ending as being faithful to the book, although in his DVD commentary, he states that the first version had shown Halleck eating the pie himself, thus sparing his wife and daughter. Either way, the studio felt the audience wanted to see more gore in the finale. Holland reshot the ending to include the grisly corpses of both the wife and daughter. In the final version, however, only the wife's corpse is seen; the daughter is still alive, although the implication is that she'll soon be dead. Halleck is also given a last moment of triumph, as he invites the man he believes to be his wife's lover inside for a slice of pie. As late as 2012, while in preproduction on another King adaptation, *The Ten O' Clock People*, Holland was still fuming about the postproduction meddling on *Thinner*.

When it was finally released on October 25, 1996, it quickly became apparent that no amount of tinkering was going to turn *Thinner* into a hit. Opening in third place with a $5.6 million opening weekend, the movie dropped out of the top ten after only two weeks; in the end, it barely recouped its production budget with a $15 million domestic gross. Critical reception was mixed, although few reviewers passed up the opportunity to spin the title into wordplay: Positive

King chats with director Tom Holland on the set of *Thinner*, in which the author played the small role of pharmacist Dr. Bangor.

reviews tended to call it "lean and mean," while negative ones preferred variations on "weightless."

Holland's film has two major flaws it can't quite overcome. First, no matter how well designed and expertly constructed it may be, even by Oscar winners, a fat suit is still a fat suit. The obese version of Billy Halleck is never convincing: Burke's face is restricted by the latex applications, and his shape simply doesn't conform to the contours of an actual human being. The skinny version of Halleck is, if anything, even worse. Burke may have lost a few pounds for the role, but it's not as if he's as skeletal as, say, Christian Bale in *The Machinist*; his end-stage makeup makes him look more old and wrinkly than emaciated. This is one instance where CGI might have been a better option than traditional methods, if *Thinner* had been made only a few years later.

The second major problem is that Holland and screenwriter McDowell are unable to duplicate King's feat of building a gripping story around some very nasty, unlikable characters. King's tale is a morality play in which the gluttonous and greedy get their comeuppance; its "hero" is, after all, an obese mob lawyer who gets off without even a slap on the wrist after running over an old lady while receiving oral favors from his wife. It's a rare actor who can turn an essentially despicable character into a magnetic protagonist, and Burke is not that actor. Joe Mantegna has some fun as Halleck's mobster pal, the sort of role he's played a dozen times in his career, but he's the only one who seems to be on the story's darkly comic wavelength. We're left watching a handful of very unpleasant characters (including the Gypsies, who were hoary stereotypes even in the novel) come to a very unpleasant end, which hardly seems worth the seven years it took to bring *Thinner* to the screen.

Fly-by-Night

The Langoliers was the last production from Laurel Entertainment, but the company's cofounder Richard Rubinstein had no plans to get out of the movie business—or the Stephen King business, for that matter. Rubinstein formed a new production company, New Amsterdam Entertainment, with partner Mitchell Galin. The company's first feature production would be *The Night Flier*, based on a short story from King's *Nightmares and Dreamscapes* collection.

"The way we've worked with Steve is that we informally identify projects we'd like to do and then wait," Rubinstein told *Variety* in May 1996. In the case of *The Night Flier*, the impetus for proceeding with the project arrived in the mail at both Rubinstein's office and the Bangor home of Stephen King. A recent film school graduate named Mark Pavia had decided to make a calling card film and send it around Hollywood in hopes of landing a job. "I knew nothing about the inner workings of the industry at that time being from the midwest and all," Pavia told Jason Bene of the website Killer Film, "but I *was* aware that several directors that I admired had gotten their break in this manner, including Steven Spielberg with his short *Amblin.*"

Pavia made a short zombie film called *Drag* with the help of some friends from film school and sent copies of it to the Hollywood studios, as well as some individuals in the industry he admired. As Rubinstein recalled, "Steve calls me and said he'd gotten a 40-minute short film, an homage to George Romero's zombies, and it turned out we'd gotten the same film by Mark Pavia. He and his partner pitched us. They had every scene on index cards and brought music, and we waited a day, called them, and I'm sure it was the second time in a week they thought they'd died and gone to heaven."

It's rare that a plan like Pavia's pays off in the movie business, yet by July 1, 1996, he was behind the camera directing the adaptation of *The Night Flier* he'd scripted with partner Jack O'Donnell. Miguel Ferrer, who King and Rubinstein had worked with on *The Stand*, signed on to play the lead, a cynical tabloid reporter named Richard Dees. Pavia had heavily storyboarded the film, which reassured Ferrer that the first-time director knew what he was doing, and ensured that the tightly budgeted, thirty-day shoot would go smoothly. Like a number of King adaptations from the Dino De Laurentiis days (including King's own directorial effort *Maximum Overdrive*), the film was shot in Wilmington, North Carolina. Despite nearly collapsing from heat exhaustion, Pavia brought the film in a day early and under budget.

The movie may have been finished, but it still didn't have a distribution deal. Rubinstein screened it for the Hollywood studios, but found the offers wanting.

According to Pavia, "Paramount bit. They wanted it. But the catch was, the film would have to wait until the following year to be released because the studio had no available slots in their schedule." Rubinstein felt his investors couldn't wait that long, so he struck a deal with HBO instead. After the pay-cable network aired *The Night Flier* in November 1997, New Line Cinema picked up the film for theatrical release the following year. Opening on only ninety-five screens on February 6, 1998, the movie took in less than $100,000 in its opening weekend.

It would be a stretch to call *The Night Flier* a great overlooked King film, but it deserved a little better than that. Miguel Ferrer is his usual enjoyably acerbic self as the sarcastic, ill-tempered Dees, a reporter for the *Weekly World News*-esque *Inside View*. Dees and a rival cub reporter (Julie Entwisle) are investigating a series of murders at small airports, all committed by "the Night Flier," a vampire who swoops down in his black Cessna, emerges in a black-and-red Dracula cloak, and eviscerates the unlucky inhabitants. Once again, the strain of expanding a short story to feature length is palpable; the movie's first hour is not particularly eventful, although Pavia demonstrates a gift for establishing a sinister mood.

Pavia ratchets up the creepiness—and the gore—in the last half-hour, as Dees finally catches up to the Night Flier in an airport full of slaughtered victims. A scene in which Dees stares into a bathroom mirror, afraid to turn around, while his unseen vampire quarry enters the room and unleashes a stream of blood into a urinal is particularly unsettling. A nightmare sequence in which the dead bodies in the airport rise to stalk Dees is shot as a black-and-white homage to *Night of the Living Dead*. The spell is broken, however, when the Night Flier's face is finally revealed as just another latex fright-mask. Pavia's film is at its best when it sticks to the shadows.

Deep Cuts

- *The Night Flier* features a clever inside joke for King fans: a gallery of *Inside View* covers with tabloid headlines ripped straight from the author's works. For instance, the headline "Springheel Jack Strikes Again!" refers to the *Night Shift* short story "Strawberry Spring." Other covers include "Ultimate Killer Diet" (referencing *Thinner*) and "Satanic Shopkeeper Sells Gory Goodies" (*Needful Things*).

- Mark Pavia hasn't had much luck getting another project off the ground since *The Night Flier*. One potential follow-up, a homage to '70s slasher films called *Slice*, had its financing fall through on the eve of production. In 2005, Pavia penned a sequel called *Night Flier 2: Fear of Flying* and sent it to Stephen King, hoping for his approval. He got more than he bargained for when King responding by asking if Pavia would mind if he took a crack at rewriting it. Of course, Pavia was thrilled, and he and King ended up sending the script back and forth, doing several drafts together. They are now cocredited with the script, which has been in development at New Amsterdam for years. While it seems unlikely that a sequel to a movie few people saw will ever get off the ground, *Night Flier 2* does not mark the end of the King/Pavia collaboration. Pavia is writing the script for a new anthology film called *The Reaper's Image*, which will adapt four existing King stories—two chosen by Pavia and two by the author himself. In addition to the title story, the segments will include "Mile 81," "The Monkey," and "N."

16

Faithful

Apt Pupil and *The Green Mile* Stick to the Story

Apt Pupil Tested

S tephen King's novella collection *Different Seasons* seemed to have a charmed existence as far as film adaptations were concerned. *Stand by Me* and *The Shawshank Redemption* were both drawn from its pages, and both rank among the most acclaimed and beloved of all the King movies. But whatever magic pixie dust had enchanted those two films was in short supply when it came to bringing a third novella from the collection, "Apt Pupil," to the screen. King's story of a boy who befriends a Nazi war criminal in exile went before the cameras in 1987 but didn't reach movie screens until more than a decade later.

The saga began when Richard Kobritz, who had produced *Christine* and the CBS miniseries version of *Salem's Lot*, purchased the screen rights to *Apt Pupil* from King in the mid-1980s. Kobritz had his *Salem's Lot* star James Mason in mind for the role of Dussander, the former Nazi now living under an assumed name in a Southern California suburb. Mason died before Kobritz had even finalized his deal with King, so the search for a new Dussander began. "Alec Guinness and Paul Scofield were both talked to," Kobritz told interviewer Gary Wood. "Both had no desire to portray realistic villains this late in their careers."

After John Gielgud also passed, the role went to Nicol Williamson, who played Merlin in John Boorman's 1981 *Excalibur*. Seventeen-year-old Ricky Schroder, then best known for the sitcom *Silver Spoons*, was the producer's only choice for the part of Dussander's young protégé, Todd Bowden. After rejecting a draft by B. J. Nelson, Kobritz hired brothers Ken and Jim Wheat (*A Nightmare on Elm Street 4*) to write the screenplay and British filmmaker Alan Bridges (*The Shooting Party*) to direct. Shooting got underway in Los Angeles in July 1987 and continued for ten weeks before suddenly shutting down with the film still incomplete.

Granat Releasing, the production company financing the film, had run out of money. Cast and crew paychecks were bouncing, and Bridges was preparing to shoot the film's climax, in which Todd goes on a shooting spree before being killed himself, when the production shut down. Reports vary on how much of the 1987 version of *Apt Pupil* was actually filmed. Stephen King describes seeing "a rough assemblage of about three-quarters of the film," while other accounts indicate anywhere from forty minutes to two-thirds of the movie had been completed.

Regardless of how much had been shot, it clearly wasn't enough. Bridges claims the production nearly started up again in early 1988 and again a year later. But this version of the movie hit a dead-end when Schroder aged past the point where new footage could have matched what had already been shot. If the footage still exists, it has never surfaced; it's not among the stacks of videotaped dailies housed in the Fogler Library collection of King materials. Of his viewing of the rough assembly, King has said, "That sucker was *real* good!" The rest of us will probably never know.

In 1995, the screen rights reverted back to King. Bryan Singer, a longtime fan of the novella, had been waiting for this opportunity. He'd already asked his friend Brandon Boyce to write a screenplay adaptation of "Apt Pupil," which he sent to King along with a copy of his then-unreleased film *The Usual Suspects* in hopes of convincing the author to give him a chance to make the movie. It worked: King optioned the story to Singer for a dollar against a share of future profits, but *Apt Pupil* wasn't out of the woods yet.

Brad Renfro plays Todd Bowden, a suburban American boy who falls under the sway of a former Nazi in Bryan Singer's *Apt Pupil*. Ricky Schroeder had played the role in a never-completed adaptation of King's novella.

Singer made a deal with Scott Rudin and Spelling Films, and cameras were set to roll in June 1996, with Ian McKellen and Brad Renfro as Dussander and Todd. Once again, however, it was not to be: Rudin and Singer clashed, and the start date was pushed back. Eventually, the production was canceled completely. Rudin described the problem to *Entertainment Weekly* as "somewhat financial, somewhat creative, somewhat chemical. To force everybody to do it together seemed pointless."

Just when it seemed the project might be cursed, Mike Medavoy, the former head of TriStar who had just formed his own production company, approached Singer about working together. *Apt Pupil* was resuscitated again, with McKellen and Renfro still aboard, and shooting got underway in February 1997 in Altadena, California. This time, filming was actually completed on the project, although the production was not entirely without incident. On April 2, a locker room shower scene was filmed in which Todd Bowden imagines his fellow gym students as concentration camp inmates. Two weeks later, fourteen-year-old extra Devin St. Albin filed a lawsuit claiming he and other minors had been ordered to strip for the camera. Two other extras joined the lawsuit, but after an eight-month investigation, the Los Angeles District Attorney's office determined there was no cause to file charges. Although the lawsuit was dismissed, Singer reshot the scene with adult extras.

Originally scheduled for release in February 1998, *Apt Pupil* was pushed back to the fall in hopes that it would compete for awards consideration with the year's prestige projects. On October 23, the hex was finally lifted as the completed film debuted on nearly 1,500 screens. But the curse returned when the weekend box office was reported the following Monday morning: *Apt Pupil* debuted in ninth place, with a total of $3.6 million. It finished with less than $9 million in its domestic run. There would be no boost from the Academy Awards (the film received no nominations), nor would the film get a second lease on life from its home video release.

It's not surprising that Singer's film wasn't embraced by the public in the same way its *Different Seasons* predecessors were. In the end, *Stand by Me* and *Shawshank* were essentially sentimental, feel-good fables, whereas *Apt Pupil* is never heartwarming and never tries to be. Its message is not one of uplift; it's that evil is evil wherever you find it, whether in the concentration camps of Nazi Germany or in the suburbs of 1980s Southern California. But what ultimately makes *Apt Pupil* fall short of the best Stephen King movies is that Singer pulls his punches in the end: He goes for downbeat but doesn't go for the jugular.

For most of its running time, the film is as faithful to its source material as any King adaptation. The time frame has been shifted from the mid-1970s to 1984, but young Todd Bowman's discovery that his neighbor Arthur Denker is actually a Nazi war criminal in hiding named Kurt Dussander plays out much as it does in the novella. Bowman plies Dussander for stories about his days in the SS, threatening to expose the old man if he doesn't play along. He even finds a Nazi officer's uniform, which he forces Dussander to wear as he goosesteps around for Todd's amusement. A twisted friendship of sorts is formed, and Dussander helps Todd out of some trouble at school by posing as his grandfather. Through his actions, Todd has reawakened the murderous impulse within the old man, while at the same time, an evil seed within the boy appears to have taken root.

Todd's obsession with the Holocaust leads the film into some dicey territory. On one level, the above-mentioned shower scene is almost an in-joke for Stephen King fans in the way it inverts the locker room sequence from *Carrie*. Contrary to the implication of the filed lawsuit, the scene here isn't played for eroticism but for horror, as Todd's classmates fade into emaciated, elderly concentration camp inmates. (As with Carrie, it's an "innocence lost" moment, but unlike the tormented Spacek character, the popular Todd is the author of his own descent.) But the use of Holocaust imagery for horror-movie effect (here and in a separate dream sequence) is an exploitation movie technique that cheapens its subject: It's real-life tragedy as window dressing. (Singer would encounter similar criticism with *The X-Men*, in which McKellen's Magneto character is given the backstory of an Auschwitz survivor.)

Apt Pupil doesn't delve deeply into Dussander's own feelings about the Holocaust, Jews, and his Nazi past; it's more concerned with how his relationship with Todd reveals the monster that may have been inside the boy all along. Renfro is well cast, not because he's a particularly expressive actor but because his limitations play to the character's favor. His dead-eyed, affectless presence suggest the sort of soulless suburban boy who would have found some way to go bad even if he'd never met the neighborhood Nazi. For his part, McKellen is at his best when playing Dussander-as-Denker, as when he's charming Todd's parents at a dinner party or posing as the kindly grandpa for guidance counselor Edward French (a miscast David Schwimmer). At other times, a campy strain of mustache-twirling villainy creeps into his performance.

Boyce's screenplay hews closely to King's story until its climax, at which point *Apt Pupil* suffers from a loss of nerve. As in the novella, Todd is called to Dussander's house late one night after the old man suffers a heart attack while killing a homeless man he's invited into his home. Todd comes over and finishes the job, and Dussander is taken to the hospital, where he's spotted by a witness who finally exposes him as a Nazi in hiding. But the film omits Todd's own murderous tendencies (he begins killing cats and then later, homeless people), as well as the finale in which he kills Mr. French, who now knows Todd's "grandpa" is a Nazi, and goes on a shooting spree before being gunned down himself. In the movie, when French comes to Todd's door, the boy threatens to ruin him by going to the authorities with false accusations of sexual advances. Despicable, yes, but far too commonplace to serve as an effective shocker in this context; plenty of people who never hung out with Nazis have come up with that move. It's a flat ending for a film that's well crafted but oddly remote—a study of evil that never gets a grip on its subject.

Doing Time on *the Green Mile*

The Green Mile grew out of a conversation between King's literary agent Ralph Vincinanza and his friend Malcolm Edwards, a British editor. After Vincinanza showed him the first few installments of *The Plant*, a limited-edition serialized story King had started writing (but abandoned) as a Christmas card for friends and family, Edwards suggested the idea of a published serialized novel. King was intrigued by the notion as a throwback to the Dickens era and had a story he thought might work for the project: a Depression-era death row tale of a convicted murderer awaiting his date with the electric chair. It was a publishing experiment that might have backfired, but it succeeded spectacularly: When the final volume of *The Green Mile* was published in September 1996, all six installments shared space on the *New York Times* best-seller list.

Even before he'd finished writing the story, King had a director in mind for the eventual film version. Really, there was only one obvious choice. "Frank Darabont jokes and says that he has the world's smallest specialty, and that he only makes Stephen King prison movies that are set in the past," the author explained while celebrating his birthday on the set of *The Green Mile*. Darabont received the novel in installments, just like everybody else, but only needed to read the first before agreeing to make the film. Once King had finished the final chapter, Darabont sat down to write the script, a process that took eight weeks. Given how well Castle Rock had treated him on *The Shawshank Redemption*, Rob Reiner's company was again his first shopping stop. "I love Castle Rock," Darabont told interviewer Audrey Kelly for *Fade In*. "There is no tier of executives—baby executives, mini-executives and people whose job it is to make sure that nothing ever actually happens."

Darabont also had his star in mind from the jump: Tom Hanks. Hanks had heard the buzz over the *Green Mile* script and was not disappointed when he read it. "I can honestly say that reading the better screenplays is not like looking at the blueprints for a house," Hanks told interviewer Frederick C. Szebin. "It was very much like reading an all-encompassing story unto itself that was an extraordinary surprise and a brand new thing." For his services, Hanks would be paid a cool $20 million, only $5 million short of the entire budget of *The Shawshank Redemption*.

The key role of John Coffey, the enormous black man convicted of murdering two little girls, proved a more difficult casting decision. The answer came from an unlikely source: Bruce Willis, who had recently worked with Michael Clarke Duncan on *Armageddon*. Having read the books, Willis encouraged Duncan to audition for the role. Although Duncan was clearly physically right for the part, Darabont was concerned about his relative lack of acting experience and considered several other actors. In the end, however, Duncan won the director over. David Morse, Barry Pepper, and Doug Hutchison were cast as the other guards on the mile, along with James Cromwell as the warden and Sam Rockwell, Michael Jeter, and Harry Dean Stanton as the other death row inmates.

As with *Shawshank*, the prison itself had to be cast. In this case, the shuttered Tennessee State Prison, with its castle-like facade, was used for exterior shots. But most of the film takes place on "the mile" itself, Cell Block E, which was built on a soundstage at Warner Hollywood Studios. The final member of the cast, the mouse known as Mr. Jingles, was actually played by twenty-four different real mice, as well as radio-controlled and cable-operated puppets and a CGI version. Shooting began in July 1998 and wrapped in December, although additional "wraparound" scenes featuring Dabbs Greer as the elderly version of Hanks' character, Paul Edgecomb, were shot the following summer. (The original plan had been for Hanks to play the character in old age makeup, but it was determined that audiences would be too distracted by his appearance. His screen test can be found on the special edition DVD.)

Although his screenplay had been 126 pages, a length that normally translates to a two-hour movie, the version of *The Green Mile* that emerged from the editing room ran three hours and eight minutes. Darabont dismissed the criticism that such a running time was self-indulgent. "The truth is, I don't know where the length of a movie is determined to be two hours or less," Darabont told *Fade In*. "If you want to qualify *Schindler's List* as indulgent. If you want to qualify *Lawrence of Arabia* as indulgent, or *Bridge on the River Kwai* as indulgent. I mean, the list goes on. *Godfather, Godfather II*—these are all great, great movies." Exhibitors are generally wary of three-hour movies, as they lose one showtime per day in comparison to two-hour films, but when *The Green Mile* debuted in theaters on December 10, 1999, its length didn't appear to be an issue with audiences. An opening weekend tally of $18 million placed it a hair behind *Toy Story 2* for first place, and *The Green Mile* went on to gross over $136 million, by far the most money any King-related film had earned. When the Academy Award nominations were announced in February 1999, *The Green Mile* earned nods for Best Picture, Supporting Actor (for Duncan), Adapted Screenplay, and Sound; however, it won none of those Oscars.

Darabont's film makes a great case for being the most faithful Stephen King adaptation ever: Given its gargantuan running time, it's hard to believe Darabont left anything out at all. Its opening hour is particularly deliberate in the way it unspools the various plot threads: E Block supervisor Paul Edgecomb's struggle with a bladder infection; death row inmate Eduard Delacroix's adoption of a talented mouse; a rehearsal for the execution of another inmate, followed by his date with "Ol' Sparky," the electric chair; the warden's despair over his wife's losing battle with cancer; and the arrival of the dangerous-looking John Coffey. It's the sort of novelistic sprawl that terrifies studio executives who believe the "inciting incident" should arrive no later than page 12 of the screenplay, lest viewer attention start to wander. Gradually the threads come together, as it is revealed that Coffey has a supernatural healing ability he applies first to Edgecomb, then to Mr. Jingles, and finally to the warden's wife.

As John Coffey's initials suggest, this is a Christ allegory of sorts; the demonized black man is in fact a gentle giant innocent of the crimes for which he is condemned to die. Edgecomb comes to believe Coffey is not guilty and has his belief confirmed by a psychic flash he shares with the condemned man during a handshake. Coffey is resigned to his fate, however, and Edgecomb is powerless to prevent his execution.

Inevitably, perhaps, *The Green Mile*'s most powerful moments revolve around Ol' Sparky. For most of the film, stark realism is the furthest thing from Darabont's mind, and he's certainly not crafting any sort of coherent anti–death penalty polemic, but the execution scenes build intensity through a methodical, procedural accumulation of horrific details. What King termed "the bad death of Eduard Delacroix" in the title of *The Green Mile*'s fourth volume transports the electric chair into the

Frank Darabont followed up *The Shawshank Redemption* with another Stephen King period piece set in prison, *The Green Mile*.

realm of Gothic horror—it's like *Frankenstein* in reverse as smoke and sparks pour from Delacroix's flailing body until he finally bursts into flames.

But after a while it starts to feel like Darabont has designed every scene within an inch of its life in an attempt at piling one tour-de-force set piece on top of another: the botched execution; the smuggling of John Coffey out of the prison; the healing of the warden's wife; the killing of Sam Rockwell's "Wild Bill" Wharton; the flashback revealing that Wharton is actually responsible for the murders pinned on Coffey; and on and on. The three-hour running time alone may not be confirmation of the director's self-indulgence, but when nearly every scene is straining for significance and crying out for attention, it's a clear indication that we're dealing with what critic Manny Farber termed "white elephant art."

Some of *The Green Mile*'s biggest problems, however, are inherent in King's original text. Director Spike Lee, never one to shy away from controversy, called out the movie for its use of the "Magical Negro" trope. As Lee described it in an interview for *Cineaste*, *The Green Mile* and other films like *The Legend of Bagger Vance* and *What Dreams May Come* "all have these magical, mystical Negroes who show up as some sort of spirit or angel but only to benefit the white characters . . . this character has such magical powers that he can touch Tom Hanks and cure him of his urinary tract infection, why can't he use those gifts to walk out of prison? . . . He'd rather die with Tom Hanks looking on. Get the fuck outta here! That's that old grateful slave shit."

King himself vehemently disputed this charge in his 2002 interview with Tony Magistrale. "It's complete bullshit," said King. "Coffey was black for one reason only: It was the one sure thing about his character that was going to make certain that he was going to burn . . . I am not surprised that this is Spike's reaction. It's a knee-jerk reaction of a man who sees everything in terms of his race. And for an artist of his stature, it's a hobbling factor in his creative life."

Yet it's undeniable that the Magical Negro turns up time and time again in King's works: Dick Hallorann in *The Shining*, Mother Abigail in *The Stand*, and even a real-life Red Sox pitcher in his short novel *The Girl Who Loved Tom Gordon*. It's hard to imagine there's any racist intent behind all this—it's more likely an overreliance on a narrative device that may be expedient but is also, intentionally or not, patronizing. (It doesn't help King's case that his vast cast of characters is overwhelmingly white, but that can at least be chalked up to the fact that most of his works take place in Maine . . . which is overwhelmingly white.)

What ultimately sinks *The Green Mile* (as a work of art, if not as a popular success) is Darabont's egregious sanitization of the Depression-era death row setting. Aside from Rockwell's over-the-top Wild Bill, E Block is home to the nicest, most likeable bunch of death row inmates ever assembled. Eduard Delacroix, Mr. Jingles's best friend, is particularly lovable, and at no point during the film are we told of what crime he's been convicted (in the book, he's an arsonist, rapist, and murderer). Likewise, with the notable exception of the sadistic Percy Wetmore, the prison guards (as well as the warden) are a sweet, friendly group of guys, and Edgecomb is downright saintly. This Disneyfied death row stacks the deck in a way that ultimately cheapens the film's brutal depiction of its executions: It's as if *The Green Mile*'s message is that capital punishment is bad only when its victims are pure at heart. This is manipulative filmmaking at its most cloying, and it's particularly unnecessary because Duncan's performance is heartbreaking enough to deliver all the emotion the story needs without Darabont's excessive string-pulling. *The Green Mile* is undoubtedly one of the most well made of all Stephen King adaptations, but that's not to say it's one of the best.

2000 to Present

The Golden Years

Just After Sunset

Hearts in Atlantis, Dreamcatcher, and *Secret Window*

Dealing Hearts

In his 2002 interview with Tony Magistrale, Stephen King explained his longtime working relationship with Castle Rock Entertainment. "I have told them that you can have my work for a buck. What I want from you is script approval, director approval, cast approval, and I want to have the authority to push the stop button at any point . . . What I get on the back end, if things work out, is 5 percent from dollar one."

By the early twenty-first century, it seemed King was working almost exclusively with Castle Rock. In November 2000, the company purchased the movie rights to *Hearts in Atlantis*, which had been published only two months earlier. Comprised of two long novellas and three shorter stories, all of which were loosely linked, the book was King's ambitious attempt at reckoning with the decade of the 1960s. Its structure posed some challenges in adapting it for the screen, so Castle Rock put its top screenwriter, William Goldman, on the case.

After reading *Hearts in Atlantis*, Goldman determined that trying to adapt the book as a whole wasn't going to work. He decided to focus on the first story in the collection, "Low Men in Yellow Coats," and use the final story, "Heavenly Shades of Night Are Falling," as a framing device. "[T]he thing that appealed to me was the story of Bobby and Carol. It was that relationship and the father-son thing with Ted," Goldman told Daniel Argent for *Creative Screenwriting*. "The other three stories [in the anthology] are marvelous but they didn't fit. I'm convinced, as I get older, that movies are only about story. And that sometimes when you get fucked up is when you try to include too much."

Even "Low Men" presented certain obstacles to adaptation, in the way it ties in with King's larger *Dark Tower* mythology. In the original story, the title characters are supernatural agents of the Crimson King, the main villain of the *Dark Tower* series. Goldman removed all of those references, leaving the low men in the script as a much less defined force of evil. Australian-born director Scott Hicks (*Shine, Snow Falling on Cedars*) signed on to direct the film on the strength of Goldman's script. The screenplay also convinced Anthony Hopkins to take on the role of Ted Brautigan, although the supernatural may have also played a role: While on the set of *Hannibal*, Hopkins had been reading about *Misery* in Goldman's book *Which Lie Did I Tell?* and thought to himself, "I'd like to do a Stephen King novel, and I'd like to work with William Goldman again." A few days later, the *Hearts in Atlantis* script arrived, and Hopkins immediately signed on.

With eleven-year-old Anton Yelchin (who would later play Ensign Chekov in J. J. Abrams's *Star Trek* movies) aboard to play young Bobby Garfield, King movie veteran David Morse as Bobby's older self, and Hope Davis as Bobby's mother Liz, filming got underway in October 2000 in Richmond, Virginia. Castle Rock set the film's release for September 28, 2001, in hopes that it would compete with other fall prestige releases for awards consideration. *Hearts in Atlantis* opened to respectable reviews and box office, earning $9 million in its opening weekend, but could not sustain its strong start. Even after adding more than 250 screens in its second weekend, the film's grosses plummeted by 44 percent en route to a final domestic total of $24 million, well short of its reported $31 million budget.

Although visually rich and featuring several strong performances, *Hearts in Atlantis* struggles on a narrative level and suffers by comparison to several other King adaptations it resembles. Its flashback structure, with Morse appearing at the beginning and end to reminisce about his youth in the sixties and mourn the death of a childhood friend, immediately recalls the way Rob Reiner used Richard Dreyfuss in *Stand by Me*. But the visual choices—a chilly gray palette for the present-day scenes and warm, rich tones for the flashbacks—echo the pattern used by Taylor Hackford in *Dolores Claiborne*.

The *Stand by Me* parallels become impossible to ignore once we're transported back to the early 1960s to the tune of golden oldies like "Ain't That a Shame" and "Sleepwalk." The nostalgic glow of a childhood spent riding bikes, playing catch, and evading the neighborhood bullies is familiar enough, but even the young actor cast as Bobby's friend Sully bears a striking resemblance to River Phoenix's Chris Chambers. The problem is that the *Hearts in Atlantis* kids aren't nearly as sharply drawn or memorably acted as the ones in *Stand by Me*.

The movie gets a lift from Hopkins's arrival as Brautigan. The actor is incapable of delivering the sort of sentimental "grampa" performance that would have made *Hearts* unbearably cloying; he's too cagey for that, as if tuned into another frequency nobody else can hear. His interactions with young Yelchin are refreshingly free of condescension, neither warm and fuzzy in the Jack Lemmon mode nor creepy in a way that would suggest unwholesome interest on Brautigan's part.

The story, however, remains frustratingly elusive. Hope Davis is fine as Bobby's oft-absentee mother, but her arc is too vaguely sketched: For much of the movie, it's unclear whether she's actually working hard to better her life and Bobby's, or if she's just a flake who's carrying on with her boss. (A jarring rape scene late in the film clarifies the situation.) The threat to Brautigan is just as fuzzy; the supernatural element has been removed (although Brautigan still possesses psychic abilities), but it hasn't been replaced with anything. The low men are simply phantom figures in fedoras, stripped of any context, so it's hard to feel particularly invested in Brautigan's fate.

Goldman's original ending followed King's lead from "Heavenly Shades of Night Are Falling" by reuniting Bobby with his first love, Carol, whom he'd believed to be dead. Halfway through production, Hicks decided to change the ending; Carol actually *is* dead, and Bobby instead meets her daughter (played by the same actress who portrayed young Carol). In his *Creative Screenwriting* interview, Goldman laments the loss of the original ending, while conceding that it might not have worked on the screen. Interviewer Daniel Argent notes, "For me, that was the most powerful scene in the script." But

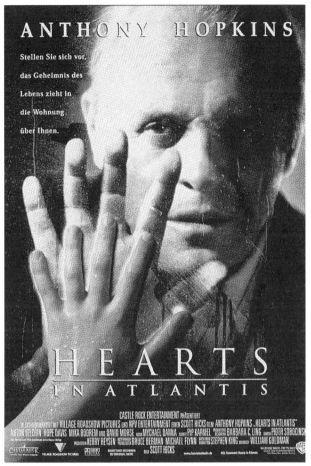

With Anthony Hopkins and *Snow Falling on Cedars* director Scott Hicks aboard, *Hearts in Atlantis* suggested a prestige production. Instead it played like Stephen King leftovers.

the problem with *Hearts in Atlantis* isn't that it leaves out so much of King's book. It's that it never finds its own identity as a movie.

Catching Kasdan

Another year, another Castle Rock production scripted by William Goldman. King wrote the novel *Dreamcatcher* in longhand while recovering from his 1999 accident, and Castle Rock optioned it (not for a dollar this time, but a cool million) before its publication. Once again they put Goldman to work on the adaptation. "What they didn't have was a director," Lawrence Kasdan told *Screenwriting* magazine. Kasdan had heard that the novel involved a group of

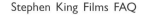

Lawrence Kasdan was an odd fit for *Dreamcatcher*, which earned terrible reviews upon its release. There are certainly worse King adaptations.

childhood friends reuniting later in life to battle an alien invasion. To the director of *The Big Chill*, it sounded like one of his movies combined with a big-budget special effects extravaganza, and he wanted in.

The powers-that-be at Castle Rock were happy to have Kasdan aboard, with the understanding that he and Goldman would write a second draft together and Kasdan would pen the final shooting script alone. As he had done with *Hearts in Atlantis*, Goldman had streamlined King's sprawling, digressive novel considerably. When Kasdan took over, he reintroduced a few things Goldman had left out. "A lot of it takes place in the head of the characters, and Bill was reluctant to show that in the movie," Kasdan told interviewer Todd Longwell. "I kept all the elements that I liked, that I thought were fun."

As the central foursome of friends, Kasdan cast Jason Lee (with whom he'd worked on *Mumford*), Timothy Olyphant (*Justified*), Damian Lewis (*Homeland*), and Thomas Jane (*Hung*). He had a Stephen King veteran in mind for the part of the crazed Col. Curtis (changed from the novel's Kurtz, a none-too-subtle nod to *Heart of Darkness* and *Apocalypse Now*): Morgan Freeman. With Donnie Wahlberg aboard as the adult version of the foursome's mentally challenged childhood friend Duddits, shooting got underway in British Columbia, five hundred miles north of Vancouver. After six weeks of location shooting in frigid subzero temperatures in early 2002, the production relocated to Vancouver for soundstage work.

While some special effects were done practically on the set, notably the puppet "shit weasels" used in the film's grotesque bathroom centerpiece, most of them, including the two incarnations of the alien "Mr. Gray," were created digitally in postproduction. *Dreamcatcher* was originally scheduled for a January 2003 release but was bumped to March 21 when Kasdan decided to reshoot the ending. Encouraged by early test screenings, distributor Warner Bros. sprang for additional digital effects in hopes of a big box office opening.

That never materialized. *Dreamcatcher* debuted to a $15 million weekend, which would have been a solid figure for a lower-budgeted film but spelled doom for a would-be blockbuster's long-term prospects. Most reviews were terrible, with critics calling it "a bloated mess," "a head-scratchingly silly B-movie," and in one of its kinder notices, "a likable disaster." It was no surprise when the second weekend grosses plummeted more than 55 percent. The movie's final domestic haul of $33.8 million amounted to less than half of its reported budget. Years later, Kasdan would tell the *L.A. Weekly* that the movie's failure left him "wounded careerwise . . . I was planning to do *The Risk Pool* with Tom Hanks. I had written the script from a great book by Richard Russo (*Nobody's Fool*). And it didn't happen. Then another one didn't happen. Meanwhile, two years have passed here, two have passed there. That's how you're wounded."

Although most of his fans would dismiss *Dreamcatcher* as one of the worst King adaptations, the author himself disagreed, telling interviewer Thomas Quinn about Kasdan, "what he did I thought was really wonderful." While "wonderful" may be an overstatement, *Dreamcatcher* is actually far more entertaining than its reputation suggests. The critics quoted above are all correct—the movie *is* a bloated mess, and head-scratchingly silly, and a likable disaster. It's less a coherent horror/science fiction tale than it is a monster mash-up that tosses a dozen familiar Stephen King tropes into a blender along with elements of classic films like *Alien*, *The Thing*, and *Invasion of the Body Snatchers*. The fact that the movie reinvents itself every fifteen minutes or so makes for a bumpy ride, but a fun one nevertheless.

In its opening scenes, *Dreamcatcher* deliberately echoes *Stand by Me* and *It*, even as it draws on King's real-life brush with death (for the first time in his work but not for the last). Four adult friends convene for a weekend at a remote cabin in Maine six months after one of them was run down by a car on a Boston street. Their manly camaraderie, and the flashbacks to their childhood bonding with the disabled Duddits, suggests a movie in King's sentimental, nostalgic mode, a notion that is rudely dispelled with the introduction of the shit weasel—a variation on the *Alien* chest-burster that emerges instead from its host's rear exit. What follows is one of the most overtly gross sequences in the entire King oeuvre, one the author predicted would "do for the toilet what *Psycho* did for the shower." (Then again, King predicted Dee Wallace would be nominated for an Oscar for *Cujo*; no one ever confused him for a showbiz pundit.)

From this point, the craziness quotient of *Dreamcatcher* increases exponentially. Morgan Freeman, sporting a high brush cut and eyebrows like tufts of steel wool, seems to relish the opportunity to play the bad guy. His General Curtis leads a helicopter assault on a crash-landed UFO and its occupants that intentionally evokes the Normandy Beach invasion from *Saving Private Ryan*.

Damian Lewis, as the alien-possessed Jonesy, carries on numerous conversations with himself using his (real) British accent as the voice of Mr. Gray. Bodies, both human and alien, explode into churning geysers of blood and viscera on a regular basis. Donnie Wahlberg's magical mentally challenged man turns out to be (in Kasdan's revised ending) an alien himself.

Kasdan clearly bit off more than he could chew and in hindsight might wish he'd stuck to William Goldman's more streamlined vision of *Dreamcatcher* instead of trying to stuff every element of King's overextended novel into a two-hour feature. But the movie he ended up making is flat-out *nuts* in a way that none of Kasdan's other films ever attempts to be. It doesn't end up making much sense, but it works as a goofy, pumped-up, digitally enhanced version of a fifties creature feature. No wonder Stephen King enjoyed it.

Depp Opens *Secret Window*

Columbia Pictures acquired King's novella "Secret Window, Secret Garden" (from the *Four Past Midnight* collection) through somewhat unconventional means. King had seen Lars von Trier's miniseries *The Kingdom*, made for Danish television, while on location in Colorado during production of the *Shining* remake. He hoped to adapt it for American television, but the rights were held by Columbia, which was trying to put together a big-screen version of the series. After a number of false starts, Columbia agreed to a "barter" deal with King: The studio would grant him the rights to *The Kingdom* in exchange for one of the author's properties that had not yet made it to the screen.

That turned out to be "Secret Window, Secret Garden," the story of a writer accused of plagiarism by a mysterious stranger. As of 2002, King was under the impression that Anthony Minghella (*The Talented Mr. Ripley*) would be helming the film, but if that was the case, Minghella's attachment didn't last long. *Jurassic Park* screenwriter David Koepp, who had been working on several projects at Columbia, got a call from an executive asking if he'd like to write and direct what came to be known as *Secret Window*. Koepp read the novella and immediately agreed.

Although King retained all his usual rights in terms of script, director, and cast approval, he never used them. As Koepp explains on the *Secret Window* DVD's supplemental materials, the author reserves those rights for nightmare scenarios only. "He wants you to go make your movie." In any case, as Koepp tells it, King was enthusiastic about his screenplay. "I like your script, man! Everyone in it is a rat bastard!"

Koepp's first choice for the leading role of Mort Rainey was Johnny Depp, who was then filming what would become his biggest hit to date, *Pirates of the Caribbean: Curse of the Black Pearl*. "So much of this movie is a guy in a cabin alone," Koepp told Glenn Whipp of the *L.A. Daily News*. "So I needed a really charismatic actor who could make taking a nap look entertaining. And that's Johnny. He's never boring." It took some time to land the star, but Koepp was finally able to cut through the Hollywood red tape and lure Depp aboard. Depp, who had famously modeled his *Pirates* performance after Keith Richards, had another musician in mind for the role of Rainey. "Brian Wilson," Depp told Whipp. "I remember hearing those famous stories or maybe myths about him in this very reclusive period where he didn't leave his house and had sand brought in to cover his living-room floor."

As Depp's nemesis, Mississippi farmer John Shooter, Koepp cast John Turturro, whose son had encouraged him to take a role in a Stephen King film. The supporting cast included Maria Bello as Rainey's ex-wife Amy, Timothy Hutton as her lover Ted, and Charles S. Dutton as Rainey's ex-cop friend Ken Karsch. Filming got underway in the summer of 2003 in and around Montreal, with the lake house exteriors being shot at Lake Sacacomie in Quebec. Koepp worked from detailed "animatics," or animated storyboards, in carefully con-

structing the film's suspense sequences. After a few days of shooting in New York, production wrapped in October.

Columbia opened *Secret Window* on March 12, 2004, hoping to capitalize on Depp's *Pirates* popularity. The film opened in second place for the weekend with $18.2 million, not a bad start for a movie budgeted at around $40 million. Reviews were mixed (although generally better than those that greeted *Dreamcatcher*), and *Secret Window* experienced the same sophomore slump as its predecessor, falling nearly 50 percent in its second weekend. Its final domestic gross of $47 million wasn't disastrous, but it certainly wasn't the hit Columbia and Koepp had been hoping for.

Although much more compact and coherent than Kasdan's film, *Secret Window* is another bowl of Stephen King leftovers spiced with ingredients from other familiar genre pictures. The story of a writer

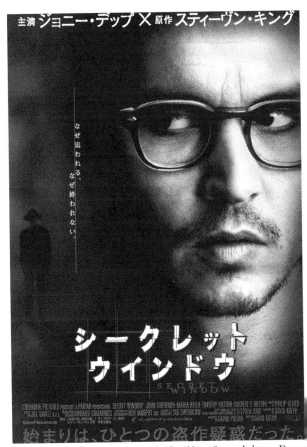

At the height of his *Pirates of the Caribbean* fame, Johnny Depp starred in *Secret Window*, a mind-bending thriller with a too-familiar twist.

who may or may not have a murderous alter ego inevitably recalls *The Dark Half*, a resemblance Koepp perversely plays up through his casting of Hutton in a supporting role. (The fact that said alter ego is played by Turturro, who famously played a psychologically unsound writer in *Barton Fink*, is the icing on the gravy.) But *The Shining* is also evoked in the "Redrum"-like revelation wherein Rainey's ex-wife realizes that "Shooter" (the name of Rainey's tormenter) actually means "shoot her," and that her husband intends to kill her. (Writing has been very good for Stephen King, but it rarely turns out well for his protagonists.)

In his director's commentary, Koepp cites Roman Polanski, and *The Tenant* and *Rosemary's Baby* in particular, as influences on *Secret Window*. But *Psycho* also looms large over the picture, with its motel room violence, disposal of a car and its evidence of murder, and climactic split-personality revelation. (There's even a shot of a cop in sunglasses peering through Rainey's car window that's lifted straight out of Hitchcock's film.)

That third-act reveal is problematic for several reasons. By 2004, after *Fight Club*, *Memento*, *Identity*, and a number of other "mind-bending" thrillers, it no longer came as a surprise to learn that the protagonist has actually been the killer all along; in fact, it had become a rather groan-worthy cliché. It still might have worked had Depp given a halfway relatable performance for the movie's first hour, but his Mort Rainey features just as many personality quirks and oddball mannerisms as Jack Sparrow, Willy Wonka, or Ichabod Crane. Right from the beginning, he seems perfectly capable of burning down his ex-wife's house or carrying on extended conversations with himself. It doesn't help that Turturro delivers such a broad take on his imaginary nemesis Shooter: This *O Brother, Where Art Thou?* character in a *Children of the Corn* hat never seems real to begin with. Koepp's film is stylish and watchable enough, but it's as insubstantial as the Muzak version of a favorite tune.

Four Past Midnight

Riding the Bullet, 1408, The Mist, and Dolan's Cadillac

Bullet Misses the Target

It may be hard to believe in this age of Kindles, Nooks, and other e-readers, but it wasn't long ago that conventional wisdom suggested reading books on computers wouldn't catch on. Although the music business was already in the process of migrating to the web, the publishing industry was much slower to react to changes in technology. Stephen King was in an experimental mood in 2000, not long after his life-threatening accident. Having published the serialized *Green Mile* a few years earlier, he now released an audio-only short story collection (*Blood and Smoke*), and on March 14, an electronic-only novella called *Riding the Bullet*.

King optimistically hoped for sixteen thousand downloads; instead, over four hundred thousand downloads were recorded in the first twenty-four hours, crashing the servers of Simon and Schuster's technology partner SoftLock. Within a few days, it would pass the half-million mark. One of its first readers was one of King's most trusted collaborators, Mick Garris. Although their first pairing, *Sleepwalkers*, had been a theatrical release, their subsequent efforts (including *The Stand* and the remake of *The Shining*) had all been for the small screen. Garris immediately optioned the rights to the story from King and got to work on the screenplay, finishing the first draft in two weeks.

Garris had the big screen in mind for the project, but his agent was unable to interest any of the studios. Finally, after three years of trying to get the movie off the ground, Garris struck a deal with independent production company Motion Picture Corporation of America, which had had its biggest success with *Dumb and Dumber*. Jonathan Jackson, then best known for a long run as Lucky Spencer on *General Hospital*, was cast in the lead role of Alan Parker. Despite the low budget, Garris was able to corral a number of name actors for small roles, including Barbara Hershey, Cliff Robertson, David Arquette, and Nicky Katt.

Riding the Bullet was shot on a tight schedule in Vancouver in November and December 2003. A new independent distributor, Freestyle Releasing, picked up the American theatrical rights and scheduled a limited release for October 15,

This Mick Garris adaptation of the experimental electronic-only novella "Riding the Bullet" remains one of the least-seen King movies.

2004. Opening on one hundred screens, the movie had the softest debut of any King film to date, finishing in thirty-third place with just over $100,000 total. The initial plan had been to platform the release, increasing the number of screens over the next several weekends. That never happened; instead, by the following weekend, the movie had completely vanished from theaters. It remains one of the least-seen King movies ever made.

Rest assured, however, that *Riding the Bullet* is no undiscovered gem. Set in 1969, with a K-Tel style soundtrack of all the most obvious groovy sixties tunes, Garris's film stretches a thin premise past the breaking point, becoming a barely coherent fever dream of automotive anxiety in the process. Alan Parker (Jackson, a third-string Johnny Depp) is a student at the University of Maine, dating cute free-spirit Jessica (Erika Christensen). Fearing he's losing her, Alan makes a half-hearted suicide attempt. Shortly afterward, he learns that his mother (Hershey) has had a stroke and is recovering in the hospital.

Alan decides to hitchhike home, a course of action that puts him in close contact with every creep, pervert, and weirdo on the road. A "weekend hippie" (Katt), a batty old farmer (Robertson), and a literal speed demon (Arquette) all stop to give him a lift. Will Alan make it home, or will he be killed in a car wreck like his father before him? That's the extent of the story, so Garris throws everything but the kitchen sink at the screen. The movie is so crowded with flashbacks, flash-forwards, dreams, hallucinations, and apparitions, it quickly becomes a chore to sit through. It's hard to tell what's really happening, and even harder to care.

Cusack Checks into *1408*

In November 2003, Dimension Films optioned the rights to "1408," a haunted hotel-room story that had first appeared on the audio anthology *Blood and Smoke* and was later collected in *Everything's Eventual*. Matt Greenberg, who had scripted *Halloween H20* for Dimension, was hired to write the screenplay. The *Ed Wood* team of Scott Alexander and Larry Karaszewski were later brought in to rewrite Greenberg's draft. In October 2005, Swedish filmmaker Mikael Hafstrom (*Derailed*) won the directing job. The following March, John Cusack signed on to play the lead role of paranormal investigator Mike Enslin. "This film is so much a one-man show," Hafstrom told *Variety*. "It's quite a contained drama. It is a horror film if you want to put a label on it, but the way I see it, it's much more an inner-journey of this character."

The second major piece of casting came courtesy of an unlikely source: Quentin Tarantino. The *Pulp Fiction* director and frequent collaborator with Dimension's Harvey and Bob Weinstein had read the *1408* script and loved it. He suggested to the Weinsteins that Samuel L. Jackson would be perfect for the role of Olin, the hotel manager. Olin had been conceived by King (and subsequently by the screenwriters) as a very proper British sort: a Michael Caine or Ian Holm. But as Alexander and Karaszewski noted, Jackson brought a different energy to the role: If Samuel Jackson tells you to stay out of a room, there must be something very wrong with it.

In July 2006, the third major role, that of Enslin's ex-wife Lily, went to *Grey's Anatomy* star Kate Walsh. Scheduling conflicts with the series forced her to bow out, however, and in August she was replaced by Mary McCormack. The bulk of the film was shot in and around London, primarily at Elstree and Pinewood studios. On his director's commentary, Hafstrom notes that "11 or 12" different versions of the titular hotel room had to be built: a frozen version, a burnt-out version, one on gimbel that would allow the room to rotate, and so on. A sequence in which room 1408 is flooded was shot on the underwater stage at Pinewood. A few exteriors were shot in New York (with the Roosevelt Hotel substituting for the film's fictional Dolphin) and in Hermosa Beach, California.

After test screenings of *1408* revealed that audiences felt the ending was too downbeat, the cast and crew reassembled to shoot a new finale. Dimension and releasing partner MGM set a June 22, 2007, release date—a show of confidence for a relatively low-budget film ($25 million) in a crowded summer marketplace. They were rewarded with a $20.6 million opening weekend, good for second place behind the far more expensive *Evan Almighty*. Although that figure dropped by nearly 50 percent in the film's second weekend, *1408* was able to hang around the top ten long enough to accrue a total of nearly $72 million, making it one of the biggest hits in the King filmography. The movie drew generally positive reviews, as well as the praise of the author himself: In his introduction to the story in the collection *Stephen King Goes to the Movies*, King calls *1408* "a horror movie that actually horrifies . . . Like one of the great old Val Lewton films, this baby works on your nerves, not your gag reflex."

Hafstrom's film (and the story on which it's based) inevitably recalls *The Shining*, as *1408* finds another troubled writer checking into another spooky hotel. Perhaps under the same management as the Overlook, the luxurious Dolphin Hotel on the East Side of Manhattan has a long, tragic history. In this case, the dark deeds are confined to room 1408, which has seen more than its share of suicides, mutilations, and unexplained deaths. Hotel manager Olin never rents the room anymore, but that changes when Mike Enslin, a once-promising novelist turned cynical hack responsible for a series of supernatural guidebooks, checks in.

Despite his profession Enslin is no believer, but that starts to change when mints mysteriously appear on the pillows, paintings on the wall shift in place, and most unnervingly of all, the clock radio keeps switching itself on and playing the Carpenters' "We've Only Just Begun." Mild unease turns to mounting dread when Enslin finds himself unable to leave the room. Malevolent ghosts appear and vanish, and the room transforms itself into a chamber of horrors from which there appears to be no escape.

For the first hour or so, Hafstrom keeps finding inventive ways to make *1408* a creepy and entertaining funhouse, balancing brain-teasing visuals with jump-out-of-your-seat scares. (There's even a suspenseful callback to "The Ledge" segment from *Cat's Eye* as Enslin tries to make an escape through the window.) It's virtually a one-man show by Cusack for

Samuel L. Jackson warns John Cusack to stay out of another creepy Stephen King hotel room in Mikael Hafstrom's *1408*.

long stretches, and he's up to the task, sketching Enslin's transformation from skeptic to basket case with sly humor. Unfortunately, *1408* simply doesn't know when to quit. A backstory involving Enslin's estranged wife Lily and their late daughter Katie is shoehorned into the proceedings, and a series of false endings ensues, each more unsatisfying than the last.

The original ending, which is included as part of the "director's cut" on the DVD release, has Enslin dying in a fire he sets in the room, sacrificing himself to destroy room 1408. This is followed by a "Boo!" moment after Olin tries and fails to return Enslin's charred belongings to Lily: When Olin gets back into his car, a crispy Enslin appears in his rearview mirror. In the theatrical version, Enslin survives the fire and is reunited with Lily; the film ends as he plays back his tape recording from the Dolphin, revealing that the ghost of Katie really had been in the room with him. The original is preferable, but neither entirely works. Ideally, *1408* would have made a fine one-hour episode of a horror anthology series like *Nightmares and Dreamscapes*. As the protracted finale goes on and on, the old line about another haunted hotel comes to mind: You can check out anytime you like, but you can never leave.

The Mist Gets Darker

The novella "The Mist" was first published in a horror anthology called *Dark Forces* in 1980, but King had the movie in mind even before that. In a *Fangoria* interview with Michael Rowe, the author called his story "my homage to the B-pictures of my childhood . . . I always saw it as a film that would be black-and-white, widescreen." In the early eighties, King worked with writer Dennis Etchison, with whom he shared an agent, on an adaptation of the novella. Although it was never produced as a movie, this version of *The Mist* later became an audio drama released on cassette tape (discussed further in chapter 35.)

Frank Darabont had read "The Mist" in the *Dark Forces* collection and had considered approaching King about making it his directorial debut before deciding on *The Shawshank Redemption* instead. After completing that film, Darabont optioned the rights to "The Mist," hoping to make it his next movie. But script problems, particularly with the ending, forced the director to postpone the project in favor of *The Green Mile* and the non-King film *The Majestic*. King's novella had ended on an ambiguous note, with the survivors of an attack on a supermarket by extradimensional creatures driving away into an uncertain future. Darabont and King agreed the movie needed a punchier wrap-up, as the author explained to Joe Mauceri of *Shivers*. "We need to find an ending that works in terms of the story and that will please people in Hollywood . . . No one is looking for a sugary ending, but they need a sense of closure."

Darabont eventually solved the problem with an ending that was anything but sugary; in fact, it caused a potential roadblock to *The Mist*'s production. "One big producer offered me a great deal and a $30 million budget—on condition that I change the ending," Darabont told John Patterson of *The*

Guardian. Darabont refused but later found a kindred spirit in Bob Weinstein of Dimension Films. Oddly enough, after changing the ending of *1408* because audiences found it too downbeat, Weinstein embraced Darabont's dark denouement, agreeing to finance *The Mist* for $17 million and guaranteeing that the ending would not be changed.

Although a lot of money by indie film standards, $17 million was a drop in the bucket compared to most big-budget effects movies. It was clear that Darabont would have to alter his usual deliberate working methods to adapt to a thirty-seven-day schedule, so he took a job directing an episode of the FX series *The Shield*, known for its run-and-gun handheld visual style. The gig gave Darabont confidence that he could pull off *The Mist* using similar techniques, and it didn't hurt that he poached *The Shield*'s cinematographer and camera operator for his own shoot.

In December 2006, Thomas Jane, who had starred in *Dreamcatcher*, agreed to headline his second Stephen King adaptation as illustrator David Drayton. The following month, Andre Braugher and Laurie Holden joined the cast, followed in February by Marcia Gay Harden and Toby Jones. Darabont filled out the cast with some of his regulars, including William Sadler and Jeffrey DeMunn, as well as Frances Sternhagen, making her third appearance in a King-related work following *Misery* and *Golden Years*. Filming got underway in February in Shreveport, Louisiana, and surrounding areas, substituting for Maine (convincingly enough for King, who asked Darabont if he'd shot some of the film in his home state).

For the primary supermarket setting, Darabont used an actual supermarket in Vivian, Louisiana, which he and his crew matched exactly for the interiors shot on a Shreveport soundstage. The creatures were a collaborative effort between illustrator Bernie Wrightson, creature designer Greg Nicotero, and the digital effects studio CafeFX. While most of the creatures seen in the film are CGI creations, animatronic puppets were used in certain shots and digitally enhanced in others. Although Darabont had always hoped to shoot *The Mist* in black and white, just as King initially imagined it, Dimension wouldn't go that far. Instead it was shot on Fuji 400ASA, a film stock that gave the movie a grainy, retro look in places.

Dimension set *The Mist* for a Thanksgiving 2007 release on over twenty-four hundred screens. The film opened to generally strong reviews but a somewhat disappointing $12.8 million over the five-day weekend. It finished with a $25.5 million domestic total, a lukewarm performance for a relatively low-budget production. The following March, a two-disc special edition DVD was released, featuring a black-and-white version of the movie on the second disc. Inspired by the Coen Brothers' *The Man Who Wasn't There*, which was shot on color film but released in black and white, Darabont and his color timer Keith Shaw used digital postproduction techniques to transform *The Mist* into what the director called his "preferred version."

In either version, but especially in black and white, *The Mist* ranks as one of the best King adaptations. It's not without its flaws, as Darabont can't seem to resist

This promotional snow globe for *The Mist* is a rare collector's item.
Courtesy of Shasta Blaustein

underlining his themes rather than letting them play out through the movie's action. The supermarket under siege becomes a microcosm for the breakdown of society, with the patrons splitting into different factions: the rationalists, the religious, the militant, and so on. But it's clear enough that this is happening without all of the overt speechifying Darabont stuffs into his character's mouths. Marcia Gay Harden's religious fanatic Mrs. Carmody is the most egregious offender: On the DVD's deleted scenes commentary, Darabont explains that several of Carmody's appearances were trimmed because "a little of her goes a long way." Even less of her in the finished film would have been preferable.

But *The Mist* does a lot of things right, too. Darabont effectively builds tension by withholding the revelation of the creatures (apparently released from a nearby military installation during the testing of an interdimensional gateway), allowing the encroaching mist itself to act as a free-floating signifier of dread. Even once the creepy-crawlies are unleashed, they're often shrouded in fog or revealed only in part, as in the intense loading-dock scene in which the tentacles of an otherwise unseen creature cause havoc. The movie finds an ideal balance between suspense and splatter; as a monster-movie throwback enhanced with up-to-the-minute visual effects, it's everything a horror fan could hope for.

That's especially true of the beautifully textured black-and-white version. The combination of retro visuals and modern digital technique works wonders: In the color version, the creatures are sometimes too cartoonish or videogame-like, but CGI really does look better in black and white. Scenes in which characters are swallowed up by the mist or make their way through dark aisles with only flashlights to guide them deliver a thrilling, old-school creature-feature charge.

The controversial ending is what truly elevates *The Mist* to the first rank of King adaptations, although that's certainly not a universally held opinion. (Readers who, for whatever reason, haven't seen the movie yet should probably skip to the next section.) The scene is a gut-punch that some see as nothing more than a sick joke, but as Darabont explains in his commentary, it's actually the logical extension of King's story. The author himself had forgotten his narrator noting that, if all was lost, he had a gun and enough bullets to mercy-kill the other survivors before the creatures could get them, and "I'd find some other way out for myself." In the movie, this worst-case scenario actually plays out . . . just before the cavalry arrives with flamethrowers and the mist begins to clear. It's a feel-bad ending that channels that old EC Comics spirit by way of *The Twilight Zone*, and a deliciously dark, ironic capper that makes *The Mist* unforgettable.

Burying *Dolan's Cadillac*

The story "Dolan's Cadillac" was first published in serialized installments in the now-defunct Stephen King newsletter *Castle Rock* and later collected in *Nightmares & Dreamscapes*. In 2001, per the *Hollywood Reporter*, Sylvester Stallone and Kevin Bacon were set to star in an adaptation from Franchise Films, to be directed by Stacey Title (*The Last Supper*) from a script by Title and her husband, three-time *Survivor* competitor Jonathan Penner. Stallone dropped out of the project in November, and *Dolan's Cadillac* disappeared from the radar until 2004, when Freddie Prinze Jr. told reporters he would be starring in the film with Gabriel Byrne.

With the movie still unmade as of 2005, the rights reverted back to King. "He was incredible and very generous about the whole thing," Title told *Fangoria*. "He loved the script when he first read it and then, all of a sudden, he changed his mind. I did a lot of drafts for free, so it was disappointing . . . He waited a long time for this to happen. It wasn't his fault. I thanked him for the rights when I had them. All I can say is that I tried."

Two years later, *Dolan's Cadillac* was back in the news when *Production Weekly* reported Dennis Hopper would star as villainous mobster Jimmy Dolan. Once again, the casting report proved unfounded, and when production on the film finally got underway in May 2008, it was with Christian Slater in the role of Dolan and Wes Bentley (*American Beauty*) as Robinson, the schoolteacher seeking vengeance on Dolan for the murder of his wife. Richard Dooling, King's collaborator on the ABC limited series *Kingdom Hospital*, wrote the screenplay. Erik Canuel was initially announced as the director, but it was Canadian filmmaker Jeff Beesley behind the camera when filming began in Regina, Saskatchewan. The shoot continued in Moose Jaw and wrapped up in Las Vegas in mid-July.

The movie's production company, Film Bridge International, peddled *Dolan's Cadillac* at the American Film Market in November 2008, hoping to reel in a theatrical distributor. Although Film Bridge was able to sell the movie in some foreign territories, no U.S. distributors bit. Instead, with little or no fanfare, *Dolan's Cadillac* was released directly to DVD on April 6, 2010. As it turns out, that was an appropriate fate.

King's story is a simple revenge tale: After Las Vegas mobster Dolan has Robinson's wife killed to prevent her from testifying against him, the grieving widower puts an elaborate, Poe-inspired scheme into play. He gets a job doing road construction in the Nevada desert, then uses the tools of his trade to dig and conceal a pit that becomes a tomb for Dolan when his Cadillac falls into it. Dooling's screenplay adds a human trafficking element not present in King's story: Instead of simply being a crime and casino boss, Dolan is now a virulent racist dealing in sex slaves smuggled over the Mexican border. Dennis Hopper might have made something memorable of this character, but even Sylvester Stallone would have been more convincing than Slater, who is no more an imposing presence now than he was in the brat-pack flop *Mobsters* nearly two decades earlier.

As the vengeful Robinson, Wes Bentley seems to be under heavy sedation for the first half of the movie, before flipping the switch and going into all-yelling, all-the-time mode. What should have been the centerpiece of any *Dolan's Cadillac* adaptation, Robinson's methodical construction of Dolan's death-trap, is here reduced to a brief, semicoherent montage of random images. At least the Cadillac company has to be pleased with their product's placement in the film: Dolan's SUV comes equipped with all the modern conveniences and survives a barrage of bullets with nary a scratch. Sure, the Caddy becomes Dolan's coffin, but as we've seen in many of the films discussed in these pages, there are worse places to spend your final moments.

Bloodlines: Five Great 21st-Century Horror Movies

For the past decade-plus, horror cinema has been dominated by endless sequels (notably the *Saw* and *Final Destination* franchises) and so-called torture porn, a blanket term for a wave of films taking a graphic approach to human suffering. But for hardcore genre buffs, the second century of horror has produced its share of unforgettable additions to the pantheon of classics. Here are five that will stand the test of time.

***Audition* (2001)**—Although released in his home country of Japan in 1999, Takashi Miike's supremely unnerving bait-and-switch qualifies for this list by virtue of its U.S. release date. Ryo Ishibashi stars as Aoyama, a middle-aged widower whose friend sets up a phony casting call in hopes of helping Aoyama find a new love. It seems to work, as Aoyama hits it off with a younger woman, Asami (Eihi Shiina). But what appeared to be a poignant romance is turned inside-out in *Audition*'s second half, as Miike reveals Asami to be severely damaged and disturbed, and more than willing to turn the tables on someone she perceives to have slighted her. The last half hour is so bizarre and horrific, it has sent many a moviegoer fleeing for the exits, but those who can take it will find Miike's audacity awe-inspiring to behold.

***Wolf Creek* (2005)**—This Australian thriller opens with a title card informing us that it is "inspired by actual events." A more truthful statement might be "inspired by actual movies," as *Wolf Creek* often plays like *Deliverance* in the Outback or a Down Under version of *Texas Chain Saw Massacre*. What it lacks in originality, however, it makes up for in execution. When their car breaks down in remote Wolf Creek National Park, three young adventure-seekers are rescued by Mick (John Jarrett), a larger-than-life bushman who makes Crocodile Dundee look like a shrimp on the barbie. Unable to fix their ride, Mick tows it to his remote, ramshackle base camp, where he treats the threesome to the kind of backwoods hospitality popularized by Leatherface and his family. Writer/director Greg McLean ratchets up the intensity—not to mention the gore—to stomach-churning levels in the film's third act. It may be too gruesome for the faint of heart, but *Wolf Creek* is a creepy nail-biter that should satisfy any horror fan.

***The Devil's Rejects* (2005)**—One of the decade's more unlikely horror auteurs, Rob Zombie made the transition from razor-throated White Zombie vocalist to genre filmmaker with the barely coherent *House of 1000 Corpses*. But Zombie made a huge leap forward with this second effort, a relentless riff on seventies horror tropes set to a good-time classic-rock soundtrack. Bill Moseley, Sid Haig, and Sheri Moon Zombie are the depraved members of the Firefly family, responsible for the greatest mass slaughter in American history. William Forsythe is the sheriff trying to bring them down. Ultraviolent and gleefully amoral, *The Devil's Rejects* doesn't lack for gut-churning gore, but there's beauty here too, as Zombie coaxes trippy visuals from his sun-bleached desert settings. Quentin Tarantino and Robert Rodriguez tried to make the ultimate seventies sleazoid mash-up with *Grindhouse*, but this is the real deal.

***The Strangers* (2008)**—Not much happens for the first thirty minutes of Bryan Bertino's directorial debut, as unhappy couple James (Scott Speedman) and Kristen (Liv Tyler) mope around their vacation retreat. At four in the morning there's a knock at the door, and Bertino has you right where he wants you. The deliberately paced quietude of the movie up until this point serves to make what follows so effective; our senses are sharpened, every nerve raised. Bertino is a minimalist who creates unbearable suspense and genuine dread from a few raw materials: sudden loud noises, lingering tracking shots, a hulking, shadowy figure in a burlap mask. *The Strangers* eventually becomes repetitive, and the plot, such as it is, doesn't hold up to much scrutiny, but for a long stretch it's as unnerving as any horror movie of this century.

The House of the Devil (2009)—Like Bertino, Ti West favors slow-burn horror over graphic violence . . . although he's not above the occasional exploding head. Every now and then a movie comes along that seems explicitly designed to make you yearn for a drive-in theater revival, and *House of the Devil* is one of them; it wouldn't look out of place on a double bill with the likes of *The Omen* or *Burnt Offerings*, and that's entirely intentional. Not so much a homage to the horror flicks of the seventies and eighties (with all the wink-wink kitschiness that implies) as a meticulous re-creation of same, *House* stretches nail-biting suspense to the breaking point. West uses deliberately grainy stock and an ominous synth-rock score to evoke the early 1980s in this tale of a down-on-her-luck college student (Jocelin Donahue) who unwisely accepts a babysitting job from a creepy couple (Tom Noonan and Mary Woronov). The ending offers more of a hasty bloodbath than the truly mind-roasting finale the movie deserves, but for the most part, West displays uncommon skill at milking maximum dread from seemingly innocuous events.

Skeleton Crew

Short Subjects

The Vault of Horror

The Anthology Films *Creepshow* and *Cat's Eye*

The Legacy of EC Comics

George A. Romero grew up in the Bronx and Stephen King (mostly) in rural Maine. But although their childhoods may have been very different, they did share certain cultural touchstones: black-and-white creature features, early rock 'n' roll, and the horror comics published by William M. Gaines in the early fifties.

Max Gaines, William's father, founded Educational Comics, which published such pulse-pounding fare as *Picture Stories from the Bible*. Eventually the "Educational" in EC was changed to "Entertaining," but it was not until William Gaines took over the company following his father's death that EC Comics began publishing its signature titles: *The Vault of Horror*, *The Haunt of Fear*, and *Tales from the Crypt*.

These horror comics pushed the boundaries of good taste far beyond anything that was being shown in cinemas or on television at the time. Gory imagery, grisly turns of fate, and pitch-black humor fueled the stories, which often borrowed liberally from the work of popular genre writers like Ray Bradbury. Gaines and writers Al Feldstein and Harvey Kurtzman scripted most of the stories, handing the illustrating chores over to an impressive roster of artists, including Jack Davis, Will Elder, Wally Wood, and Graham Ingels. Each issue featured several stories, with corny, pun-packed introductions provided by the host associated with the particular title: the Crypt Keeper, the Vault-Keeper, or the Old Witch.

Kids ate them up, but parents hated them, and the EC line soon drew the ire of Dr. Frederic Wertham, the anti-comic book crusader who penned *Seduction of the Innocent*. (Wertham was perhaps best known for perceiving an inappropriate sexual relationship between Batman and Robin.) Congress held hearings to determine whether the EC Comics (and the many imitators they'd spawned throughout the early fifties) contributed to juvenile delinquency. Gaines made himself a target by testifying at the hearings, and soon the other comics publishers capitulated to the political pressure by forming a self-censorship board, the Comics Code Authority.

Gaines resisted joining the CCA but found he could no longer get his comics on newsstands. He put an end to the horror titles in 1954 and eventually abandoned comics entirely to focus on *Mad*, which had begun as a comic before becoming a black-and-white magazine. *Tales from the Crypt* and *The Vault of Horror* resurfaced in the early seventies in the form of horror anthology films produced by Amicus Productions, the main rival to Hammer Films for the British horror market. It was these omnibus horror films, as well as the comics that inspired them, that sparked a budding collaboration between George Romero and Stephen King.

Romero and King Team Up for a Creepshow

Romero and King were introduced when the director was being considered for the theatrical version of *Salem's Lot* that never materialized. When that opportunity fell through and the project headed to television, Romero and his producer Richard Rubinstein visited King at his home in Maine to discuss other collaborative possibilities. King offered the pair their choice of his available properties, and they seized on *The Stand*.

The long, tortuous development saga surrounding that project will be detailed in a later chapter. Suffice it to say that Romero, Rubinstein, and King soon came to the conclusion that producing a smaller-scale picture as a test run for *The Stand* might be the way to go. In theory, this low-budget film would reap big box office, convincing potential investors that *The Stand* was a viable proposition.

In brainstorming this canary in a coal mine, Romero hit on the idea of an anthology film akin to the Amicus efforts of the sixties and seventies. Given the poor track record for such omnibus pictures, both creatively and commercially, the author was wary. "In the past, the trouble with this type of film has often been that one of the segments will be good, but the other two or three will be sort of lukewarm and not very interesting," King told Paul Gagne. "So we're trying to make each one of these strong and punchy."

To that end, King suggested going all the way back to the source that had influenced them in the first place and making a homage to the EC horror comics. He even had a title for the anthology: *Creepshow*.

Romero agreed, and only two months later, King presented him with a completed screenplay, consisting of five horror tales in the EC vein, surrounded by a wraparound story. Romero took the script to United Film Development, which had already agreed to finance his 1981 film *Knightriders*. He walked away with an $8 million budget, modest by most standards but gargantuan by Romero's. *Creepshow* was a go, and after several misfires, Stephen King would finally see a screenplay of his own go before the cameras.

But King's participation in the project didn't stop there. Romero cast him as the lead in the second segment, "The Lonesome Death of Jordy Verrill." King had played a small role in *Knightriders*, and the director was confident that the part of a luckless Maine farmer was well within the author's limited acting wheelhouse. The rest of the cast included Leslie Nielsen, Hal Holbrook, Ed Harris, Adrienne Barbeau, Ted Danson, and E. G. Marshall, who shared his scenes with thousands of live cockroaches.

Principal photography began in July 1981 in and around Romero's home base of Pittsburgh. Most interiors were shot at Penn Hall Academy in Monroeville, not far from the shopping mall made famous in *Dawn of the Dead*. Tom Savini, who had created the zombie makeup effects for that picture, turned down the opportunity to direct his own feature in order to rejoin Romero for *Creepshow*. His work included a number of reanimated corpses, a furry creature discovered inside a mysterious crate, and The Creep, the skeletal "host" of the movie à la EC's Crypt Keeper. Shooting lasted for seventeen weeks, wrapping in November 1981. Romero employed a different editor for each segment (with the exception of "Father's Day" and "They're Creeping Up on You," which were both edited by Michael Spolan), handling the chores himself on "Something to Tide You Over." The director commissioned an animation company in the same building as his production offices to create interstitial segments tying the film together.

Released on November 12, 1982, by Warner Bros., which had purchased the domestic rights after a screening at the Cannes Film Festival, *Creepshow* debuted at the top of the box office charts with a $5.8 million opening weekend. Why it wasn't released a month earlier in order to capitalize on Halloween is anybody's guess, but the film went on to have a moderately successful run, finishing with a $21 million total. It wasn't quite the game-changer King and Romero had been hoping for, in terms of attracting financial backing for *The Stand*, but it was profitable enough (particularly in its home video release) to inspire a sequel a few years later.

As King himself noted, horror anthologies tend to be mixed bags, and *Creepshow* proved no exception. King called the first segment, "Father's Day," a "deliberate EC pastiche," and this tale of a murdered patriarch returning from the grave to exact vengeance on his ungrateful kin is easily the slightest of his contributions. "The Crate," based on the author's short story of the same title, offers an amusing turn by Barbeau as a drunken harridan, but it's by far the longest of the five stories, and ends up being too slack and predictable.

For the most part, however, *Creepshow* achieves what it set out to do, which was to recreate the disreputable fun of the EC comics. Romero gives each of the segments a slightly different tone, just as each story within an issue of *Tales from the Crypt* was illustrated by a different artist yet still hewed to the house style. "The Lonesome Death of Jordy Verrill" is the broadest of the bunch, taking its cue from Stephen King's absurdly cartoonish performance as the hapless rube who becomes infected with "meteor-shit" and soon finds his body covered with green moss. "Something to Tide You Over" is the most reality-based story (at least until the reanimated corpses show up at the end), playing on the primal terror of being buried alive as vengeful Leslie Nielsen entombs his wife (Gaylen Ross) and her lover (Ted Danson) up to their necks on a deserted beach as the tide rolls in.

The final segment, and the most memorable, takes a minimalist, antiseptic setting straight out of a Kubrick movie and marries it to one of the signature gross-out sequences of the eighties. Even a gorehound like Savini found it hard to stomach "They're Creeping Up on You," in which E. G. Marshall's Howard Hughes–like germophobe finds his penthouse apartment infested with cockroaches. Romero hired entomologists to travel to Trinidad and dig around in a cave full of bat guano for six thousand giant roaches and ordered another sixteen thousand standard-issue American roaches from a catalogue. (You never know what you're going to find when you peruse the Skymall listings.) The *Creepshow* crew had to build their own roach motel of sorts to keep the

This original British newspaper ad for *Creepshow* promises "the most fun you'll ever have being scared."

insects from escaping the set, but even styrofoam walls smeared with Vaseline could not contain them. The money shot, in which hundreds of roaches burst out of Marshall's mouth and neck, required Savini to build a life-size dummy of the actor equipped with air bladders (to suggest the roaches massing under his skin) and flesh-colored toilet paper (through which the roaches could escape). Savini watched the filming of the sequence from behind a Plexiglass partition, refusing to step on the set while the tiny stars were at work.

Romero has a lot of fun with the comic-book conceit. He uses optical effects to put the scenes within panels and to pan between them; animation to create page-turning effects and yellow-boxed captions; gels to saturate certain shots with bold primary colors, mostly vivid shades of blue and red; and background scrims painted with zigzag patterns to enhance crucial close-ups. It's a somewhat more sophisticated variation on a technique that's been around at least since the sixties *Batman* TV show ("Bam! Pow!"), and although it's not quite on par with the remarkably fluid comic-book editing style Ang Lee would bring to his 2003 *Hulk*, it's a big part of what makes *Creepshow* an enjoyably nostalgic exercise.

Reflections in a Cat's Eye

Dino De Laurentiis was convinced Drew Barrymore was going to be a star. (He was right about that, although his timing was a little off: Dino's powers of prognostication apparently didn't extend to anticipating Barrymore's wild-child years of alcoholism and drug addiction.) Even before *Firestarter* was released in theaters, De Laurentiis was looking for another project for his young prodigy to headline. At the same time, the minimogul was continuing his Stephen King feeding frenzy, buying up every available property as well as a few that had already been sold. De Laurentiis acquired the rights to several stories from King's *Night Shift* collection from a production company in California that had purchased them in hopes of producing an NBC TV-movie that never made it past the scripting stage, as well as stories that had been sold to Milton Subotsky of Amicus Productions. (Subotsky had produced a number of horror anthology films, including the 1972 adaptation of *Tales from the Crypt*.)

De Laurentiis decided to combine his two mid-eighties obsessions by asking King to script a film with Barrymore in mind. King had been toying with a short story idea about a cat that protects a little boy from the monster that invades his bedroom at night, and it was easy enough to swap the child's gender in order to accommodate the young star. De Laurentiis was intrigued and asked the author if he could use the cat as a linking device between Barrymore's story and a couple of tales from *Night Shift*. King figured out a way to weave the cat in and out of "Quitters, Inc." and "The Ledge," and gave him the starring role in "The General," the screenplay's final segment.

Cat's Eye went into production in the summer of 1984, with *Cujo* director Lewis Teague at the helm. Teague was eager to work with King in a more direct fashion (the two had never met during the production of *Cujo*), and saw in the

Cat's Eye screenplay an opportunity to bring a more lighthearted tone to the proceedings than the grueling killer-dog movie had allowed. (Indeed, *Cat's Eye* would become the first Stephen King film to earn a PG-13 rating.) The entire film was shot in Wilmington, North Carolina, primarily on the soundstages De Laurentiis had built during the production of *Firestarter.*

The movie originally began with a prologue called "A Death in the Family" that set up the cat's motivation before setting him loose to wander through the three stories. In this opening sequence, a Wilmington couple finds their daughter (Barrymore) in bed, not breathing. Suspecting the family cat has stolen her breath, per the old wives' tale, the mother (Patti Lupone) fetches an automatic weapon from the basement and opens fire, destroying the house as the cat escapes to pursue the real culprit, a tiny troll. According to Teague's DVD commentary, executives at MGM/UA (which acquired the U.S. distribution rights from De Laurentiis) felt this prologue was too over-the-top and ordered it excised.

Cat's Eye now opens with a bit of self-referential humor as the cat, already on the loose, evades both Cujo and Christine before escaping on a truck bound for New York City. Unfortunately, Teague hangs a lantern on the gag by cutting to the bumper of the 1958 Plymouth Fury, where a sticker reading "I am Christine!" is plastered. It's a small matter, perhaps, but an early indication of the movie's uncertain tone. *Cat's Eye* isn't really trying to scare us, and it's not going for a *Creepshow*-style blend of gory effects and cartoonish humor. Most of the time, its goal seems to be mild amusement. You could dub in a laugh track without substantially altering the viewing experience. Its rhythms, and its visuals, are strictly from sitcom-ville.

The first segment, "Quitters, Inc.," is the most successful, largely thanks to a wry, wired performance by James Woods as a man trying to quit smoking through extreme measures. "The Ledge," in which an Atlantic City wiseguy forces the tennis bum who's been sleeping with his wife to circumnavigate a hotel on a tiny ledge thirty stories above street level, is more interesting for its low-budget special effects than its lukewarm execution. Shot entirely on a soundstage, "The Ledge" appears to take place high above Atlantic City despite the fact that star Robert Hays was never more than seven feet above the ground. The skyline was recreated using giant photographic transparencies lit from behind, while the closer buildings were actually hanging miniatures designed and built by Emilio Ruiz and shot in forced perspective. Fog and wind machines helped complete the illusion, which today would likely be rendered entirely in digital pixels.

The third segment, "The General," uses the same sort of pre-CGI trickery to the opposite effect. Instead of miniatures, giant props were used to make the troll who terrorizes Drew Barrymore appear to be only a few inches tall. In fact, the creature was portrayed by a four-foot-tall actor, who wore an animatronic headpiece designed by Carlo Rambaldi, the man who built E.T. for Steven Spielberg. A handful of puppeteers hidden out of frame manipulated the troll's facial expressions with a series of levers and pulleys. Again, had *Cat's Eye* been made even a decade later, the creature would likely have been composed entirely of ones and zeroes. This is why DVD commentary tracks and "making of" features are almost always more interesting if the movie in question is more than a couple of decades old. Learning about this sort of Hollywood magic is inherently more fascinating than watching a row of geeks enter code on their iMacs.

Unfortunately, the result of these efforts is not particularly satisfying in the case of "The General," which is neither scary enough to work as horror nor funny enough to work as comedy. The segment is also a poor fit with the two *Night Shift* stories, both of which are reality-based tales with mobster antagonists and no supernatural elements. The film as a whole suffers from De Laurentiis's legendary cheapness: While Teague and his team did an admirable job with the special effects, the budget deficiencies show up in other areas. The score by Alan Silvestri is a painfully dated collection of Casio bleats and tinny drum machines, and on those occasions Teague opts to use a pop song, as in a fantasy sequence scored to the Police's "Every Breath You Take," cheesy soundalike remakes are substituted for the originals Dino refused to shell out for.

The connecting material involving the cat feels a little strained, perhaps because the prologue setting it all up was excised before the movie's release. In any event, *Cat's Eye* failed to buck the conventional wisdom that audiences stay away from horror anthologies in droves. The movie opened in third place on the box office charts in April 1985, well behind the immortal *Police Academy 2: Their*

James Woods goes to extreme measures to shake his smoking habit in "Quitters Inc.," one segment of the anthology film *Cat's Eye.*

First Assignment. It dropped out of the top ten after only two weeks, finishing its run with a little over $13 million total. The next attempt at anthologizing the works of Stephen King would happen not at the movies but on the small screen.

Five Hair-Raising Horror Anthologies

Dead of Night (1945)—Martin Scorsese named this granddaddy of horror anthology films one of his five scariest movies of all time in 2009. That may be a bit of an overstatement, but this Ealing Studios production boasts its share of eerie moments, even as it demonstrates the inconsistency that would come to characterize such efforts. In the wraparound story, an architect arrives for a scheduled appointment at a house he's never visited before and soon realizes he remembers the place and everyone gathered in it from a dream. Each guest relates a personal experience with the uncanny, ranging from the mildly amusing ("Golfing Story," adapted from an H. G. Wells story) to the downright spooky ("The Haunted Mirror"), but *Dead of Night* is best remembered for "The Ventriloquist's Dummy," starring Michael Redgrave as a performer haunted by his wooden partner.

Black Sabbath (1963)—Mario Bava is best known as the godfather of "giallo" cinema, the Italian suspense-horror subgenre that spawned the modern slasher film, but this early work is closer in spirit to Roger Corman's Poe series. Boris Karloff introduces this anthology's three stories and also stars as a Russian patriarch-turned-vampire in "The Wurdalak," based on a novella by A. K. Tolstoy (not to be confused with his cousin Leo). The English-language version of the film varies greatly from the Italian original (particularly in the case of "The Telephone," which is transformed from a tale of spurned lesbian love into a barely coherent ghost story), but both "The Wurdalak" and "The Drop of Water" are effectively atmospheric chillers in the Gothic mode.

Trilogy of Terror (1975)—Dan Curtis, producer of *Dark Shadows* and *The Night Stalker*, directed this trio of tales based on short stories by Richard Matheson. (William F. Nolan scripted the first two segments, with Matheson himself taking on the third.) This TV-movie served as a showcase for Karen Black, who starred in all three parts. In the first installment, "Julie," Black is a college teacher in the "sexy librarian" mode who draws seemingly unwanted attention from one of her students. The segment's ironic comeuppance would have fit right in to an old *Tales from the Crypt* issue had it been a bit grislier. But the evil twin story "Millicent and Therese" features a hoary twist any viewer should have seen coming from the top of Mt. Everest, even in 1975. It's the third segment, "Amelia," that haunted the nightmares of every child of the seventies who saw it. Curtis and Matheson expertly blend horror and hilarity as Black is terrorized by a Zuni fetish doll come to life. "Amelia" no doubt influenced the similar third act of *Cat's Eye*, "The General."

Trick 'r Treat (2007)—Although its opening credits borrow the fake-comic-book gimmick from *Creepshow*, Michael Dougherty's interlocking omnibus of Halloween horror recalls *Pulp Fiction* in the way its stories dovetail in nonchronological fashion. Fans of Anna Paquin on *True Blood* will get a kick out of her turn as a virginal Red Riding Hood-turned-supernatural being, but the creepiest segments involve a busload of severely disturbed children and Dylan Baker as a school principal with a dark side. Buried by Warner Bros., which had originally planned to release it in theaters for Halloween 2007, Dougherty's clever film went direct-to-DVD in 2009 and has since amassed a deserved cult following.

V/H/S (2012)—In the years since *The Blair Witch Project* became an unexpected sensation, the "found footage" technique has become the genre's most overused gimmick. This collaboration from five young horror filmmakers (and the collective known as "Radio Silence") proves there are still a few scares to be found in grainy, shaky camcorder images. In the wraparound story, a criminal gang breaks into a house in search of a VHS tape that will fetch big bucks. They find a dead body in a chair and a cache of tapes, each of which contains a short found-footage film. While all of them have their creepy moments, the most effective are Radio Silence's "10/31/98," which follows a group of costumed revelers to an ill-fated Halloween party, and David Bruckner's truly unnerving "Amateur Night," about a one-night stand gone very awry. On the whole, *V/H/S* is very successful at exploiting a fear for our times: the way

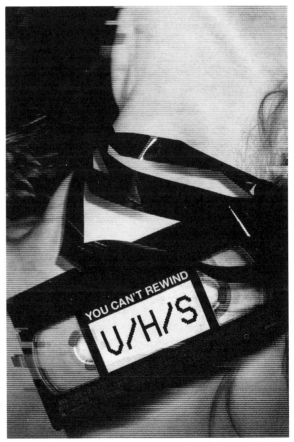

Despite its overused "found footage" technique, *V/H/S* is one of the scariest anthology films in recent memory.

our precious electronic gadgets have eradicated any expectation of privacy in our lives.

Deep Cuts

- The little boy in *Creepshow*'s wraparound story is played by Stephen King's son, Joe, who was nine years old at the time. Romero had seen Joe while visiting the Kings in Maine and felt he looked like the kid on the preliminary poster for the film. Joe read for the part and won it. Joe King is now known as Joe Hill, a horror novelist in his own right. The first film adaptation of his work, *Horns*, directed by Alexander Aja and starring Daniel Radcliffe and Juno Temple, premiered at the Toronto International Film Festival in 2013.
- Although *Creepshow* was based on a fictional comic book, it became a real one when Stephen King declined to write a novelization of the film. Instead, a trade paperback comic adaptation, featuring artwork by illustrator Bernie Wrightson (best known for his work on *Swamp Thing* and the horror-comic magazines of the sixties *Creepy* and *Eerie*), was commissioned. This should not be confused with the prop comic book used in the interstitial segments of the movie, which was illustrated by original EC artist Jack Kamen and animated by Rick Catizone.
- In addition to the cameos by Cujo and Christine, *Cat's Eye* contains several other in-jokes referencing other Stephen King works. During "Quitters, Inc.," James Woods watches a scene from *The Dead Zone* on television before snapping it off and muttering, "I dunno who writes this crap!" Later, during "The General," Candy Clark is seen reading a copy of *Pet Sematary* in bed.
- Just as Lewis Teague had needed a dozen or more St. Bernards to bring Cujo to life, he and his animal wranglers required sixteen cats to portray the feline star of *Cat's Eye*. The difference, according to Karl Miller, the animal trainer who worked on both films, is that "you train a dog, but you con a cat." While dogs are eager to please their human companions, cats can't be bothered—but they *can* be bribed with food. Lest anyone worry that any kitties were harmed in the making of this motion picture, Teague explains on his DVD commentary that the scene in which the cat is jolted with an electrified floor was achieved using only gentle blasts of compressed air.

Nightmares and Dreamscapes

Short Stories on the Small Screen

As far back as the late seventies, network executives and television producers have been trying to involve Stephen King in a horror anthology series for the small screen. When NBC aborted a proposed TV-movie based on stories from King's *Night Shift* collection due to Standards and Practices concerns, the producers behind the project tried to resurrect it as a weekly series, to no avail. And when television powerhouse Aaron Spelling (*Charlie's Angels, Beverly Hills 90210*) approached the author with a similar offer, King made his position clear. "I've always remembered an episode of Boris Karloff's *Thriller* where the hero's murdered brother came walking downstairs with an ax sticking out of his head," King told Bill Kelley of the *Ft. Lauderdale News & Sun-Sentinel*. "I told Spelling, 'Boy if we could get away with anything like that on network TV, you've got yourself a deal.'" Needless to say, there was no deal.

The idea certainly had merit, given the plethora of available King stories, and it's easy to picture the author strolling onto a haunted house set and introducing the evening's tale of terror, in the tradition of *Alfred Hitchcock Presents* and *The Twilight Zone*. But the weekly grind held little appeal for King. "My own feeling is that television ate up Rod Serling and spit him out," he told Paul R. Gagne in 1980, "and I don't want to get into something like that."

Following *Creepshow*'s theatrical run in 1982, a weekly small-screen version of the horror anthology seemed like a natural. The problem for George Romero and partner Richard Rubinstein was that Warner Bros., the studio that released the film, had a claim on some of the rights, including the title. Instead, Romero and Rubinstein's Laurel Entertainment launched *Tales from the Darkside* with a 1983 Halloween special, "Trick or Treat," scripted by Romero and directed by Bob Balaban. A weekly syndicated series, adapting stories by famous horror and sci-fi writers including Harlan Ellison, Clive Barker, and Stephen King (as we'll soon see) followed a year later and lasted four seasons.

Darkside sparked something of a horror anthology revival in the eighties and nineties. Steven Spielberg created *Amazing Stories*, which aired from 1985 to 1987 on NBC (and helped launch the career of frequent King collaborator Mick Garris). After *Darkside* ended its run, Richard Rubinstein produced the very similar *Monsters* from 1988 to 1991. Revivals of *The Twilight Zone* and *The Outer*

Limits may not have made anyone forget the originals, but they did have lengthy runs (the former for three seasons, the latter for seven). And in 1989, HBO launched its very successful *Tales from the Crypt*, based on one of the EC comics that had inspired *Creepshow* in the first place.

In 2005, Garris conceived a new horror anthology series for Showtime called *Masters of Horror*. For years, Garris had been hosting gatherings of the genre's leading lights, including John Carpenter, Wes Craven, Tobe Hooper, and Dario Argento. Garris took this impressive rolodex to the pay-cable network, and a deal was struck for a series of one-hour films, each directed by an

Television networks spent decades trying to launch a Stephen King anthology series before *Nightmares & Dreamscapes* finally premiered on TNT in 2006. Unfortunately, it lasted only one season.

established horror filmmaker. The series (and in particular, the Iraq-themed satire "Homecoming," directed by Joe Dante) was a critical success and ran for two seasons on Showtime. Also in 2005, TNT made its initial foray into the world of Stephen King–based entertainment with its remake of *Salem's Lot*, which proved to be a ratings success. When TNT decided to pursue further projects involving the author's work, the stars were finally aligned for a Stephen King anthology series.

The network commissioned Bill Haber's Ostar Enterprises to develop eight scripts based on King's short stories. "We picked eight that we thought we could adapt most successfully." Haber said in a TNT press release. "We had to pick the ones that were available because some had already been adapted into motion pictures." The series would take its name from King's 1993 collection *Nightmares & Dreamscapes*, even though only five of the eight scripts that eventually went into production were based on stories from that book. Although Mick Garris penned a script based on "Home Delivery" from the collection, and was set to direct it for the series, he had to drop out due to scheduling conflicts with the second season of *Masters of Horror*. "Home Delivery" was replaced with "Autopsy Room Four," based on a story from the *Everything's Eventual* anthology.

The final roster of behind-the-camera talent assembled for the project didn't quite match up with the *Masters of Horror* lineup, but the cast boasted some impressive names, including William Hurt, William H. Macy, Claire Forlani, Tom Berenger, and Kim Delaney. The entire series was shot in Melbourne, Australia, which doubled for Boston, Maine, San Francisco, and London, among other locations, with the help of extensive green-screen. TNT decided to air the eight episodes in two-hour blocks over the course of four weeks in the summer of 2006.

The series opened on the night of July 12th, with "Battleground," airing entirely without commercial interruption, followed by "Crouch End." Ratings for this premiere outing were quite good by basic cable standards, averaging five million viewers over the course of two hours. But the July 19th airing of "Umney's Last Case" and "The End of the Whole Mess" failed to hold the audience, losing two million viewers from the previous week. After two more weeks, the series wrapped, and although a second season was discussed in some quarters, it never materialized. The eight existing episodes are collected on a three-DVD set, and they are:

"Battleground"—The earliest story adapted for the series, "Battleground" was first published in *Cavalier* magazine in 1972 and later collected in *Night Shift*. This adaptation was scripted by Richard Christian Matheson, son of one of King's writing heroes, Richard Matheson. It's an appropriate connection, as this story of a hit man pursued around his apartment by living toy soldiers is reminiscent of the senior Matheson's "Amelia" segment from *Trilogy of Terror*, in which Karen Black is terrorized by a Zuni fetish doll. (In fact, that doll makes a cameo appearance in this episode.) Directed by Muppet heir Brian Henson, "Battleground" sets a high bar for the rest of the series in several ways: It stars William Hurt, an

Oscar-caliber actor coming off a Best Supporting Actor nomination for David Cronenberg's *A History of Violence*, and it tells its story without a single line of dialogue. This is a stunt of sorts, but an unobtrusive one: There is sound, but it's all ambient noise, music, and the occasional grunt or scream. Those come courtesy of Hurt, who plays Renshaw, a hit man who whacks a toy company executive, then comes home to his San Francisco apartment to find a package containing living (and heavily armed) toy soldiers. The CGI and green-screen work is effective, and Hurt gives a witty performance as a cold-blooded killing machine who unravels under attack from tiny plastic figures. Fans of *Cat's Eye* may also detect a homage to "The Ledge" segment when Hurt takes cover outside his skyscraper apartment.

"Crouch End"—King's H. P. Lovecraft homage was originally published in the Arkham House anthology *New Tales of the Cthulhu Mythos* before being collected in *Nightmares & Dreamscapes*. The story's Lovecraft references may have been a bit too esoteric for a television audience, and the resulting episode suffers from the same sort of vague hocus-pocus that has characterized some of the author's later works. Claire Forlani and Eion Bailey star as Doris and Lonnie, a couple honeymooning in London and looking for a neighborhood called Crouch End, where a client of Lonnie's has invited them to dinner. None of the Londoners they meet wants anything to do with Crouch End, which is described by one cabbie as a "thin spot" between our world and another. Director Mark Haber conjures a mounting sense of anxiety with the help of cinematographer Ben Nott's bleached, cloudy imagery; Jeff Beal's hypnotic, Indian-flavored score; some creepy kids (always a reliable King device); and a swirling vortex of doom. But the spell is broken by the appearance of an incredibly cheesy CGI creature at the episode's climax, and "Crouch End" ultimately amounts to little more than pastiche.

"Umney's Last Case"—Pastiche again—but this time, pastiche with a purpose. William H. Macy is Umney, a private eye in a 1938 Los Angeles straight out of a classic film noir. Actually, it's more like a highly stylized Coen Brothers-esque Raymond Chandler parody, lit through the slats of Venetian blinds and populated by chatty elevator operators, wisecracking newsboys, and shadowy femmes fatale. It doesn't feel quite real because it's *not* real, as Umney learns when he meets Sam Landry (also played by Macy), a novelist who claims Umney is the lead character of his private eye series. The writer who meets his own creation is a device King has used several times, notably in *The Dark Half* and *The Dark Tower* series (in which the writer in question is King himself), but this is a particularly fun example, especially once Umney escapes his fictional world for the real one. Macy was born to deliver Umney's rat-tat-tat dialogue, and of all the episodes, "Umney's" is the one that might benefit most from expansion to feature length, as the possibilities of Umney as fish out of water in our modern age are barely tapped.

"The End of the Whole Mess"—It took *The Stand* eight hours to end the world, but "The End of the Whole Mess" pulls it off in only one. Ron Livingston (*Office Space*) stars as a documentary filmmaker recalling the life of his genius brother (Henry Thomas), whose plan to save humanity has actually brought about its doom. Thomas manages to isolate a chemical found in the water source of an unusually peaceful small town and spread it globally, bringing years of peace to the world. This being a Stephen King story, however, the peace is only temporary, as a latent side effect of the chemical brings dementia and eventually death to everyone who has been exposed to it. Screenwriter Lawrence D. Cohen (*It*, *The Tommyknockers*) updates King's story in order to make the events of 9/11 the impetus for Thomas's quest for peace, and director Mikael Salomon (the *Salem's Lot* remake) does a creditable job of rendering a worldwide apocalypse on a TNT budget.

"The Road Virus Heads North"—Tom Berenger stars as a famous horror novelist from Maine who bears absolutely no resemblance to any actual persons, living or dead. Or maybe it's plausible to assume that this character pestered by questions like "Where do you get your ideas?" or "Have you ever scared yourself?" from his adoring fans is vaguely autobiographical. But if "The Road Virus Heads North" is King's *Stardust Memories*, at least he's diabolical enough to cook up a comeuppance for his doppelganger. After getting some potentially bad news from his doctor in Boston, Berenger stops at a yard sale on his way home to Maine and purchases a morbid painting of a devilish character driving across the Zakim Bridge. As Berenger heads north, so does the character in the painting, leaving a trail of dead bodies in his wake. The most overtly King-like episode of the series, "Road Virus" is all creepy buildup and no real payoff.

"The Fifth Quarter"—Perhaps the *least* King-like episode of the bunch, this tale of small-time criminals trying to make a big score plays more like an Elmore Leonard adaptation in the hands of director Rob Bowman (who also helmed "Umney's Last Case"). Jeremy Sisto plays an ex-con who gets his hands on one scrap of a treasure map that's been ripped into four pieces. Samantha Mathis is his wife, who becomes the unexpected beneficiary of the map after the previous holders of its four quadrants all end up dead or in jail. "The Fifth Quarter" could use a little Leonard-style ironic humor, but Bowman keeps it dark and gritty, resulting in a somewhat plodding installment.

"Autopsy Room Four"—Although it was a last-minute substitution ordered up when Mick Garris had to back out of adapting "Home Delivery," this adaptation of a story from the *Everything Eventual* collection is one of the strongest entries in the series. A clever variation on the "buried alive" chestnut, the story concerns a man bitten by a poisonous snake while golfing and subsequently paralyzed to such an extent, he is believed to be dead. After awakening in a hospital's autopsy room, he is unable to alert the attending medical staff of his condition and forced to watch helplessly as they prepare to cut him open. Richard "John-Boy" Thomas, who had previously starred in the *It* miniseries, may not have been the most inspired casting choice (a more overtly comedic actor might have mined more black humor from the character's increasingly frantic voice-over monologue), but director Mikael Salomon (who also helmed "The End of the Whole Mess") hits on just the right tone of giddy suspense.

"You Know They Got a Hell of a Band"—The series' last episode is also its weakest. Like several other King stories, this one finds a squabbling couple getting lost on a road trip and ending up in very bad place. (*Children of the Corn* is the best-known example, but Steven Weber, who stars in this segment with Kim Delaney, had played a nearly identical role a few months earlier in the ABC TV-movie of *Desperation.*) Here, the bad place is a fifties-style small town that turns out to be Rock 'n' Roll Heaven, populated by the pantheon of rock gods taken before their time, including Buddy Holly, Janis Joplin, Jimi Hendrix, and the mayor himself, Elvis Presley. It's a one-joke premise, and most of the impersonators gathered here are second-rate at best. Since TNT only shelled out for one real rock classic—Roy Orbison's "Oh Pretty Woman"—an already thin premise becomes translucent.

It's a shame the series ended on a low note, and that it never continued beyond the initial eight episodes. But as we'll see in the next chapter, the stories anthologized in *Nightmares and Dreamscapes* are not the only Stephen King short subjects to reach the small screen.

One for the Road

The X-Files, Tales from the Darkside, and Other One-Shots

The Twilight Zone: "Gramma"

Stephen King has always expressed a certain ambivalence about the original version of *The Twilight Zone*, which ran from 1959 to 1964 on CBS. In his survey of the horror genre, *Danse Macabre*, King compares the series unfavorably to *The Outer Limits*, noting that *Twilight Zone* episodes tended to be "moral tales, many of them smarmy" or "well meant but simplistic and almost painfully corny." But he also acknowledges that some episodes "generated a kind of existential weirdness that no other series has been able to match." The series did lead King to discover some of his favorite authors, most notably Richard Matheson, after seeing their names in the credits. Regarding creator and host Rod Serling's work, King noted in an interview with Ben Herndon that "a third of what he wrote for the series was crap. I also think a third of what he wrote was inspired, and the rest was pretty good." What is undeniable is that *The Twilight Zone* refused to die. Long after its cancellation, it lived on in the twilight zone known as perpetual syndication.

After Serling sold his share of the *Twilight Zone* rights to the network, CBS began to explore the notion of reviving the series. Several attempts fell through, but a new *Twilight Zone* finally got the green light in 1984, a year after a theatrical film based on the series (with segments directed by Steven Spielberg and John Landis, among others) exposed a new generation to the brand name. Overseen by producer Philip DeGuere, the new version of the series would feature hour-long episodes consisting of two or three different segments each week. DeGuere wanted to launch the revival with an adaptation of Harlan Ellison's short story "Shatterday," but the author was reluctant to get involved with television again following a number of bad experiences. After several meetings, however, Ellison not only gave his blessing, but came aboard the project as a creative consultant.

Ellison scripted several segments during the first season, including an adaptation of Stephen King's short story "Gramma" from his *Skeleton Crew* collection. In a sense, Ellison was putting his money where his (considerable) mouth was. In October 1984, he'd written an installment of his "Harlan Ellison's Watching" column called "In Which We Scuffle Through the Embers," praising King's writing but noting that the films made from his work "turn out, for the most part, to be movies that look as if they'd been chiseled out of Silly Putty by escapees from the Home for the Terminally Inept."

The "Gramma" episode isn't terminally inept, nor does it particularly distinguish itself from the pack. The story upon which it's based is semiautobiographical, but like "Crouch End," it also draws on H. P. Lovecraft's Cthulhu Mythos. When King was a child, his family took in his ailing grandmother, who proceeded to make life hell for his mother. King was home alone with the old woman when she passed away. The same thing happens to Georgie, the young hero of "Gramma," except that his grandmother turns out to be a soul-sucking witch in league with Lovecraftian demons.

The segment is a virtual one-boy show for twelve-year-old Barret Oliver, as his mother (Darlanne Fluegel) only appears briefly at the beginning and end. Ellison's script renders Georgie's interior monologue from the story as a voice-over conversation with himself, interspersed with remembered arguments between his mother and her brother regarding which of them will get stuck taking care of their remaining parent. Director Bradford May visualizes Georgie's fear of approaching his grandmother's bedroom by playing perspective tricks with the hallway, making it appear to elongate before him. When Gramma finally appears, however, she does look a bit like she's been chiseled out of Silly Putty. The final twist, in which Gramma's demons appear to have infected Georgie, is mildly subversive by eighties network television standards. But as it turned out, "mildly" was about as far as the new *Twilight Zone* was prepared to go.

After the network rejected Ellison's adaptation of Donald Westlake's dark Christmas fable "Nackles," the author did what he'd done every other time he'd tried to work in television: He quit. "I didn't come back to TV after 10 years to maintain the status quo," Ellison said at the time. "I came back to give Jerry Falwell nightmares." The *Twilight Zone* revival lasted two seasons on CBS and one more in syndication. In 2002, the series was resuscitated yet again, this time for the short-lived UPN network, for a single season of forty-four episodes.

Tales from the Darkside: "Word Processor of the Gods," "Sorry, Right Number," and "Cat from Hell"

As mentioned earlier, *Tales from the Darkside* was basically *Creepshow: The Television Series* in all but name (and, of course, with far less gore). Stephen King was not involved with the development or production of the series, but once it was up and running, he did make several contributions. The eighth episode of the first season, "Word Processor of the Gods," was based on a short story first published in *Playboy* in 1983 and later collected in *Skeleton Crew*. Adapted by Michael McDowell (who would later pen the screenplay for *Thinner*) and directed by Michael Gornick (an associate producer of *The Stand* miniseries), the episode stars Bruce Davison as a writer who receives a word processor built by his beloved nephew shortly before his death in a car accident. (Yes, kids, back in the Reagan era you could buy a computer the size of a grand piano, solely dedicated to word processing. It was truly an age of wonders.)

Until the arrival of this machine, Davison lives a life of quiet desperation with his nagging shrew of a wife and brain-dead, guitar-mangling teenage son. But once he fires up the word processor, he finds it possesses special powers: The "execute" key can make his fondest wishes come true, while the "delete" key can wipe any object—or person—from existence. It's a shrewd update of the classic "Monkey's Paw" tale, but the biggest surprise is the twist ending that never comes. Davison receives no comeuppance for tampering with the forces of fate; instead, the horrible family he hates is replaced by the woman he always pined for and the nephew he adored. Yet to say "Word Processor" has a happy ending wouldn't quite be accurate either. Because Davison gives such a warm, likable performance, it's easy to gloss over the fact that his character has just erased the lives of two annoying but basically innocent human beings. The episode is a cookie full of arsenic, to quote *Sweet Smell of Success*, and its use of what is now dinosaur tech adds an extra (albeit unintended) level of amusement to the proceedings. When Davison unboxes his new toy, with its monitor as big as a dorm fridge and its pizza-sized diskettes, anyone who remembers the early days of home computing will be unable to suppress a smile.

In his endnotes to *Nightmares & Dreamscapes*, King recalls the process that led to his second *Darkside* contribution, "Sorry, Right Number." The story came to him in strongly visual terms, so he decided to write it up as a "teleplaylet," without any particular outlet in mind. His agent sent it to Steven Spielberg for consideration for his anthology series *Amazing Stories*, which was just gearing

Tom Savini called *Tales from the Dark Side: The Movie* "the real Creepshow 3." King wrote the middle segment, "The Cat from Hell."

up at the time. Spielberg thought the script wasn't upbeat enough for his show, so King sent it to his old friend Richard Rubinstein, producer of *Tales from the Darkside*. Rubinstein "bought it the day he read it and had it in production a week or two later. A month after that it was telecast . . . as a season premiere, if my recollection serves. It is still one of the fastest turns from in-the-head to on-the-screen that I've ever heard of."

King's recollection doesn't exactly serve, as "Sorry, Right Number" actually aired as the ninth episode of the fourth season; moreover, his account doesn't quite jibe with the timeline. He says *Amazing Stories* was in production but had not yet begun to air when he sent his script to Spielberg, but that series debuted in the fall of 1985 and lasted two seasons. Its final episode aired in April 1987, seven months before "Sorry Right Number" premiered on *Tales from the Darkside*. In any case, Rubinstein bought the script and handed it off to director John Harrison, who had composed the music for *Creepshow* and would later direct *Tales from the Darkside: The Movie*.

Like "Word Processor of the Gods," "Sorry, Right Number" concerns a writer and a haunted (and dated) piece of home technology, in this case a two-line telephone with light-up buttons. Unlike "Word Processor," it also features a twist so obvious, it's probably visible from the moon. While on the phone with her sister, Katie (Deborah Harmon) gets a call on the other line—a very familiar voice, apparently in great distress. Her husband, horror novelist Bill (Arthur Taxier),dismisses it as a prank call, but Katie is convinced that the voice she heard is someone very close to her. After checking with her daughter and sister, however, it seems everything is all right. But Bill dies in his sleep that night, at which point savvy viewers anticipating a twist will deduce that, somehow or another, Katie has called herself from the future in an attempt to save his life.

It's the mechanics of this twist that fail the episode, at least in its aired version. In the future-set scene that ends the story, Katie is overcome by emotion after inadvertently viewing a videotape of a movie adapted from one of her late husband's novels. In King's first-draft teleplay, which he published in *Nightmares & Dreamscapes*, it is explained that "the depth of her grief has allowed a kind of telephonic time travel." That's admittedly a little thin, but even that much doesn't come across in the televised version, in which Katie's dialing of her old phone number is completely unmotivated. In this case, the twist ending feels like the tail wagging the dog.

Tales from the Darkside concluded its four-season run in July 1988, but producer Richard Rubinstein wasn't quite finished with it yet. A big-screen version of the show had been in development for years, but it wasn't until the success of *Pet Sematary* in 1989 that Paramount gave the project a green light, albeit at a bargain-basement budget of $3 million. Longtime Rubinstein associate John Harrison got the directing job, and two of the three segments of the anthology film, along with the wraparound story, were scripted by Michael McDowell. The middle segment, "Cat from Hell," based on a Stephen King story written in 1977, was adapted by George Romero, who originally intended it for *Creepshow 2*. It was dropped for budgetary reasons, but Rubinstein held onto it, and included it in *Darkside* without Romero's knowledge. Still, when he eventually learned about it, Romero gave his blessing. "I like John [Harrison] a lot," he told interviewer Alan Jones, "and I wish him all the luck in the world with it."

Given the involvement, however tangential, of Romero and King, many fans (including Tom Savini) consider *Tales from the Darkside: The Movie* to be "the real *Creepshow 3*." (If only a magical word processor could delete the actual *Creepshow 3* from existence . . . but that's a story for later.) Indeed, the big-screen version of *Darkside* is much more in line with the gory, EC comics–derived tales of comeuppance from the first two *Creepshow* films than the much tamer version of same from the TV series. There is no comic-book style connective tissue in *Darkside*, however; instead, the wraparound story is a modern riff on "Hansel and Gretel," in which Debbie Harry plays a witch planning to cook and serve a little boy for her dinner guests. The boy stalls for time by reading selections from a *Tales from the Darkside* anthology, and it is those three stories that play out in the film.

The first segment, "Lot 249," based on a story by Sherlock Holmes creator Arthur Conan Doyle, concerns a collegiate nebbish who uses a resurrected mummy to enact revenge on his classmates, and is mostly notable now for its before-they-were-stars performances by Steve Buscemi and Julianne Moore. The final story, "Lover's Vow," is the movie's standout: a dark-hearted romance with an effectively vicious twist. But oddly, the King-Romero collaboration "Cat from Hell" is the weakest link in the chain.

William Hickey, a gravelly-voiced character actor who always appeared to be at least three hundred years old, stars as a wealthy man plagued by a cat he feels is responsible for the deaths of the three other people who lived with him (one of whom died when the cat stole her breath, in a callback to "The General" segment from *Cat's Eye*). He hires a hit man (David Johansen) to whack the cat, a task that proves more difficult than the professional killer could have dreamed. Like "Battleground" and "They're Creeping Up on You," it's another story of a man fighting a tiny enemy in a confined space, and easily the least compelling of the three. Even the gross-out ending is lifted whole-cloth from the E. G. Marshall segment from the original *Creepshow*, as the cat defeats Johansen by crawling down his throat and later bursting out of his body. It's a nasty little gag (no pun intended), but we've seen it all before.

Monsters: "The Moving Finger"

The last episode of *Tales from the Darkside* aired in July 1988, but by October of that year, Rubinstein was back on the air with a very similar anthology series called *Monsters*. There were only two real differences between *Monsters* and its predecessor: Per its title, every episode had to contain some sort of monster, and per its budget, it was even cheaper looking than the already low-rent *Darkside*. You may have noticed that the King stories adapted for these anthology series tend to revolve around domestic situations, all the better to confine the action to one or two sets. The *Monsters* episode based on King's 1990 short story "The Moving Finger" takes that cheapo aesthetic to an extreme.

Airing as the series finale (*Monsters* lasted three seasons and seventy-two episodes, wrapping in April 1991), "Finger" concerns an ordinary guy whose only real passion in life is his favorite game show. (In the short story, it's *Jeopardy*, but for reasons you can probably guess, it remains nameless in the episode.) That this everyman is played by Tom Noonan, an actor who has never had a "regular guy" setting in his arsenal, is our first clue that the character will be a raving loon by episode's end.

His troubles begin when he spies what appears to be a human finger emerging from the drain in his bathroom sink. As the title foretold, the finger is moving in a way that suggests it's still attached to a human being, which is impossible given the configuration of pipes under the sink. The man attempts to rid himself of this infestation by pouring drain cleaner on the finger, but the appendage only grows more elongated and vicious. His next step is to attack the finger with an electric saw, with surprisingly bloody (for television at the time) results. By the time a police officer shows up at his apartment in response to noise complaint, he is a gibbering wreck cowering in the corner and advising her not to lift the toilet seat.

"The Moving Finger" is yet another variation on the "Battleground" formula of a man facing off with an unexpected threat in his own home, and not an especially inspired one. The self-consciously wacky "sad trombone" music that accompanies the action doesn't help matters much, nor do the bargain-basement special effects. The scene in which Noonan is reduced to urinating in the kitchen sink may have pushed the boundaries of acceptable television behavior, but it's a minor victory at best.

The Outer Limits: "The Revelations of 'Becka Paulson"

"Nominally science fiction, more actually a horror program, *The Outer Limits* was, perhaps, after *Thriller*, the best program of its type ever to run on network TV," writes King in *Danse Macabre*. Of course, he's referring to the original version of the show, which ran from September 1963 to January 1965, but like its contemporary *The Twilight Zone*, *Outer Limits* would be revived decades later for a new generation of fans. Rights-holder MGM produced the new series in conjunction with Trilogy Productions, with Showtime signing on to carry the new *Outer Limits* in America. (The show moved to the Sci-Fi Channel for its final season.) A total of 154 episodes were produced, more than three times as many as made up the original series.

The fifteenth episode of the third season, first airing in June 1997, was "The Revelations of 'Becka Paulson," based on King's 1984 short story. (First published in *Rolling Stone*, the story was later reworked into a subplot in the novel *The Tommyknockers*.) Like the King stories adapted for *Twilight Zone*, *Monsters*, and *Tales from the Darkside*, "Revelations" is a domestic drama with few characters, largely confined to one location. Catherine O'Hara stars as Becka, a trailer-park housewife who lives a life of quiet desperation with her unfaithful, abusive husband Joe (John Diehl). While searching the top closet shelf for Christmas ornaments, Becka happens upon a gun Joe has stashed there and manages to shoot herself in the head with it. The bullet doesn't kill her, however; instead, it imbues her with what are either psychic visions or powerful hallucinations.

Specifically, the photograph of a smiling, tuxedoed man that comes with the purchase of an 8×10 frame begins speaking to Becka, spilling the beans about her husband's transgressions with his coworker at the post office. (Most people, upon purchasing such a frame, replace this picture with one of their own photographs, but Becka is not particularly bright.) Mr. 8×10 is played by Steven Weber, who also directed this episode, mere months after playing Jack Torrance in the miniseries of *The Shining*. "Revelations" is not only Weber's directorial debut, but his only turn behind the camera to date.

As she has done so often in Christopher Guest's mockumentaries (such as *A Mighty Wind* and *Waiting for Guffman*), O'Hara finds the balance between humor and pathos in her characterization. Weber's direction tends to emphasize the comic aspects of the story over the horrific ones, but although the supporting players tend toward caricature, O'Hara's performance ensures we never lose our empathy for Becka. "Revelations" is a decidedly minor work in the King canon, but it's worth seeking out.

The X-Files: "Chinga"

In 1995, Stephen King appeared on a special celebrity edition of *Jeopardy* with actor David Duchovny. (King eked out a win for his charity, the Bangor Public Library, over Duchovny and the third contestant, Lynn Redgrave.) As they chatted backstage, Duchovny suggested that King write an episode of the series he was then starring in, *The X-Files*. King hadn't seen the show at that point, but after catching up with it, found himself hooked.

Created by Chris Carter and airing on the Fox network, *The X-Files* concerned two FBI agents assigned to investigate cases involving paranormal activity. Duchovny played Fox Mulder, the true believer, and Gillian Anderson was his partner Dana Scully, the skeptic. Fusing the supernatural investigations of *Kolchak: The Night Stalker* with the quirky FBI agents of *Twin Peaks*, *The X-Files* helped pioneer the concept of an overarching "mythology" for later sci-fi/horror-themed shows such as *Lost* and *Buffy the Vampire Slayer*. If Stephen King was going to write an episode of any continuing series, this one seemed like a natural fit.

It took a while, though. In 1996, an *X-Files* spin-off of sorts, *Millennium*, debuted. When King made his first call to Carter, it was the somewhat darker, more overtly horrific *Millennium* that the author expressed interest in writing. He later changed his mind, however, reasoning that it would be easier to jump into the world of *The X-Files*. King set to work on a script that could serve as a stand-alone episode, unconnected to the show's larger mythology.

His screenplay, "Chinga," didn't exactly blow Carter's mind. "Chris is a real gentleman," King told *TV Guide*, "but basically he came back to me and said, 'This isn't what we wanted.'" King took another whack at it, and he and Carter exchanged several phone calls in an effort to iron out what Carter felt were some inconsistencies in the characterizations of Mulder and Scully. Finally, Carter ended up rewriting the episode himself, and the credits for "Chinga" list him and King as coauthors of the script.

The truth is, there's nothing very unusual about this in the world of auteur-driven television. Shows such as *Buffy*, *The Sopranos*, and *Deadwood* may have their scripts credited to a variety of writers, but the creator/showrunner almost always does the final draft, which can range from a mere polish to a total overhaul of the original. An outsider like King can't be expected to know the characters as well as their creator, so it's not really such a slap in the face that Carter rewrote his work.

In some ways, the finished version of "Chinga" plays like a Stephen King tribute episode. The very first shot is a close-up of a Maine license plate, and the reveal of Scully in a "The Way Life Should Be" t-shirt confirms that one of our heroes is on vacation in a very King-esque small Maine town. (Mulder is back at the office, making only occasional appearances via phone calls to Scully; a comment on the King/Carter working relationship perhaps?) Sure enough, this town has a supernatural secret, in this case a young autistic girl with a creepy doll. Either the girl or the doll has the power to cause people to do harm to themselves, and it's up to Scully and her temporary partner, a laconic Maine cop straight out of a Stephen King story, to solve the case.

It's a lightweight episode of the show that might have benefited from more humor. Mulder supplies some comic relief in his brief appearances, but Carter ends up taking the hoary "killer doll" scenario more seriously than is warranted. In the end, neither King fans nor X-Philes were very satisfied with "Chinga" when it aired as the tenth episode of the fifth season. Even the title proved controversial when it became clear that, unbeknownst to King, "Chinga" was a vulgar Mexican slang term. For overseas broadcast, the episode was retitled "Bunghoney," a nonsense word Fox executives apparently found completely innocuous.

Michael Jackson's *Ghosts*

After Michael Jackson's death in 2009, Stephen King recounted the events that led to his collaboration with the *Thriller* performer in his *Entertainment Weekly* column, "The Pop of King" (itself a play on Jackson's self-appointed moniker, the King of Pop). He'd been on the set of *The Stand* in 1993 when he received a phone call from a breathless fan who turned out to be Jackson. "What he wants, it develops, is for me to write the *scariest*, the absolute SCARIEST, music video ever, called *Ghosts*," King writes. "It will be like the old Frankenstein movies, he explains, only scarier! TERRIFYING!"

King had no illusions that he and Jackson were going to create the scariest thing ever, but he took the pop star up on his offer anyway, just to try something new. He and Jackson hashed out a story over the phone, and King wrote it up in screenplay form, but it's hard to say how much of his draft actually made it into the final version of *Ghosts*. The film credits the story to King, Jackson, Mick Garris (the video's original director), and Stan Winston (the video's credited director), with the screenplay attributed to Winston and Garris. "The story had wandered a far distance from my original script," writes King in his column, "but that hardly matters."

Garris, by an odd coincidence, had played a zombie in Jackson's *Thriller* video, thanks to an invitation from his friend (and the video's director) John Landis. "Later on, when I was shooting *The Stand*, Stephen King and Michael put together a script for another scary music video—one with huge scale, even compared to *Thriller*," Garris told *Movieline* in 2009, following Jackson's death. "King recommended me for it, and that's where I really met Michael on a one-to-one basis."

Garris hired Winston to handle the makeup and special effects, and production on the video began in 1993. The first of the child sex-abuse scandals involving Jackson hit during the filming, and production shut down after two weeks. It remained dormant for three years, and when it resumed in 1996, Garris was no longer at the helm. In the midst of directing *The Shining* miniseries, Garris had no time to return to the *Ghosts* project, and instead recommended that Stan Winston take over as director. He did so, and this time, the video was completed. Running over thirty-eight minutes (and winning a spot in the *Guinness Book of World Records* as the longest music video ever), *Ghosts* was released as a preshow attraction with prints of *Thinner* playing in Sony Theaters.

As a music video, *Ghosts* is basically *Thriller* all over again, but with far less memorable music. (The three songs used in the video, "2 Bad," "Is It Scary?," and "Ghosts," aren't exactly Greatest Hits material.) But as an accidental exploration of a very strange celebrity's psyche, it's both fascinating and disturbing. *Ghosts* begins as a pastiche of an old, black-and-white Universal monster movie, with an angry, torch-wielding mob of citizens from Normal Valley charging the gates of "Someplace Else." This scary mansion is home to a "weirdo," and according to the portly, middle-aged, white mayor leading the mob, "there's no place in this town for weirdos."

The children in the group wonder why they can't leave the poor weirdo alone. Once the mob enters the haunted mansion, the film turns to full color, *Wizard of Oz* style. Michael Jackson, his physical appearance about halfway between Original MJ and the final version of Horrifying Waxen MJ, greets his visitors. This exchange of dialogue actually occurs:

Kid 1 (to Jackson): "Show him the neat stuff you did for us."

Kid 2 (to Kid 1): "Shut up! That's supposed to be a secret!"

Bear in mind that *Ghosts* was made after the initial allegations of Jackson's sexual misconduct with young boys had been made public. In that context, it's hard to know quite what to make of the video. Is it a self-satire? A secret confession? Or was Jackson completely oblivious to the video's parallels with his real life? This seems unlikely, especially since his character goes on to peel his face off and reveal the skeleton beneath, and later pounds his face into the floor until it completely disintegrates into dust. It's as if he was aware of the public's perception, and clearly saw the fate that awaited him, but was powerless to do anything about it except use it as raw material for his art.

Adding to the psychodrama is the fact that Jackson also portrays his own persecutor in the video. The end credits reveal (if you hadn't already pieced it together) that the mayor was played by Jackson, under layers of latex. Again, Freudians could have a field day with the spectacle of the increasingly pale pop star playing a white man in the video, particularly one who could be taken as a stand-in for his real-life prosecutor, Thomas Sneddon. But as fascinating as all this subtext may be, it doesn't turn *Ghosts* into a video anyone but a Jackson fanatic would want to watch more than once or twice. It's bloated, incredibly repetitive (there's no clearer sign of Jackson's rampant narcissism than the endless reaction shots of the mob to his performance), and far too derivative of the superior *Thriller*. And yet this version of Jackson, caught in limbo between his heyday as a music superstar and his sordid end as a freak show in disgrace, holds a unique fascination. He would have made for a great Stephen King character.

"Dollar Babies"

Short Stories on a Shoestring

The Boogeyman and the Woman in the Room

In his introduction to the published edition of Frank Darabont's screenplay for *The Shawshank Redemption*, Stephen King recalls 1977 as the year that student filmmakers began writing him letters about his short stories, "wanting to make short films out of them. Over the objections of my accountant, who saw all sorts of possible legal problems, I established a policy which still holds today." For the price of a dollar, a student filmmaker could secure permission to make a film based on one of King's short stories. However, the author insisted on certain stipulations. He would retain all future rights to the stories, including the ability to reassign them to future student or commercial filmmakers. In addition, the filmmaker had to agree not to commercially exhibit the resulting film without King's authorization. Finally, the filmmaker would have to supply the author with a videotape (or later, a DVD) of the finished work for his collection.

At the time King wrote that introduction, 1996, he estimated that he'd made this deal "sixteen or seventeen times," and he has made it at least fifty times since then. Some stories, notably "The Boogeyman," "Mute," and "Popsy," have been adapted multiple times over the years. These short student films have come to be known as "Dollar Babies," and collectively they represent a virtually unprecedented display of generosity by a popular artist.

The first known Dollar Baby is 1982's "The Boogeyman," directed by Jeffrey Schiro. A Bangor, Maine, native, Schiro had been making home movies since he was thirteen years old. In 1977, he won a prize at the first annual Maine Student Film Festival for his claymation short "Evolution II." After graduating from Bangor High School, Schiro studied film at New York University, choosing King's story from the *Night Shift* collection as his final project. "[H]aving always been obsessed with psychological drama," Schiro told his hometown *Bangor Daily News*, he "thought it would make an interesting and intense film." After obtaining permission from King and a student waiver from the Screen Actors Guild, Schiro produced, wrote, directed, and edited a $20,000, twenty-eight-minute adaptation of "The Boogeyman."

Long before he made *The Shawshank Redemption*, Frank Darabont bought the rights to Stephen King's short story "The Woman in the Room" for a dollar. It proved to be a sound investment.

Michael Read stars as Lester Billings, a man whose three young children have all died, supposedly of crib death. While the police suspect Billings of murdering the children, he tells his psychiatrist Dr. Harper (Bert Linder) that the Boogeyman killed them. Although Read's performance suggests that Billings has suffered a break with reality, the twist ending reveals that he was right, and that Dr. Harper is actually the Boogeyman in disguise. Although all of this is clear enough to anyone who has read King's story, Schiro's interpretation is rather muddled, and his otherwise low-key film is overpowered by John Cote's electronic score. Schiro went on to direct an episode of *Tales from the Darkside*, and has spent the past decade or so editing TV-movies for Morningstar Entertainment.

In 1980, King received a letter from twenty-year-old Frank Darabont, asking for permission to adapt the short story "The Woman in the Room," also from the *Night Shift* collection. Knowing nothing about the author's Dollar Baby policy at the time, Darabont was surprised when King said yes. It took Darabont three years to raise the money to make his short film, during which time he worked as a production assistant on the low-budget slasher movie *Hell Night* and a prop assistant on television commercials. Darabont financed the postproduction himself, telling the fan site Lilja's Library, "I spent that entire year with a borrowed Moviola in my bedroom, editing the film. I had heaps of 16mm film piled all over the place. At night, I had to move all the piles of film off my bed onto the floor so I could go to sleep. In the morning, I'd have to move the piles of film from the floor back onto my bed so I could walk to the bathroom. Very glamorous!"

King's story contains no supernatural elements, but it's no less horrifying for that. It concerns a man whose mother is in the hospital wasting away from cancer, and his torment as he comes to the decision to end her suffering with an overdose of pills. Darabont's film is a stark, matter-of-fact re-creation of the story but for a couple of additions: a new scene in which the main character is revealed as a lawyer consulting with a death row inmate and a dream sequence incorporating a corpse borrowed from the set of *Hell Night*. The prison scene almost plays as an inside joke now, knowing what we know about the later Darabont/King collaborations, but the nightmare is an effectively staged "Boo!" moment breaking up what is otherwise a rather static adaptation.

Darabont submitted the film for Oscar consideration in the live-action short category, but although it made the Academy's short list of contenders, it was not among the four films nominated. "The Boogeyman" and "The Woman in the Room" were released together on home video in 1985 as *Stephen King's Nightshift Collection*, an experience Darabont does not remember fondly. "Unfortunately, the video distributor we originally got into business with totally fucked us . . . this bottom-feeder with no integrity who made a shitload of money on the video but never paid us a dime of it, even though we had signed contracts."

Still, the short film paid off for Darabont in other ways. King was very impressed with it, writing in his *Shawshank* introduction that he "watched it in slack-jawed amazement . . . 'The Woman in the Room' remains, twelve years later, on my short list of favorite film adaptations." Several years later, when Darabont wrote to inquire about the rights to King's novella "Rita Hayworth and Shawshank Redemption," the author was happy to oblige, in the process launching one of the most fruitful ongoing collaborations of his career. For Frank Darabont, it was a dollar well spent.

Disciples of the King

A second volume of *Stephen King's Nightshift Collection* was issued on VHS in 1987. In addition to a short called "The Night Waiter," which has nothing to do with Stephen King at all, the videotape included the first-ever adaptation of "Children of the Corn." Retitled "Disciples of the Crow," this nineteen-minute version of the story was adapted, directed, and edited by John Woodward. While the later *Children of the Corn* movies (including the endless parade of sequels) suffered from padding the story to feature length, "Disciples" has the opposite problem. Woodward adds a prologue set in 1971, with the children of Jonah, Oklahoma, plotting the murders of their parents. The action then cuts to 1983 and the familiar sight of squabbling couple Burt and Vicky driving through corn country. From here the film plays out as an extremely truncated version of King's story, as Burt and Vicky make their escape from the corn children without much trouble at all. There's a hint of further menace at the end via a shot of a corncob weapon protruding from their car's hood, but King's downbeat ending is abandoned.

More intriguing is a 1986 adaptation of "Battleground," an animated short from the Soviet Union called "Srazhenie" (sometimes spelled "Srajenie"). Directed by Mikhail Titov, assisted by a team of four animators, the ten-minute film employs a hand-drawn rotoscope style that works extremely well for the story of a hit man menaced by toy soldiers. Titov lends the story a future-noir quality not present in King's original, and although briskly paced, his rendition doesn't feel rushed or incomplete.

Darabont isn't the only Dollar Baby filmmaker who has gone on to enjoy a successful career in Hollywood. Michael De Luca, producer of over sixty movies including *The Social Network* and *Moneyball*, earned his first screen credit by adapting "The Lawnmower Man" for a twelve-minute short film. Directed by then-NYU student James Gonis, who now makes a living booking Playboy Playmates for promotional appearances, the short is crudely made but far more faithful to King's story than the later feature film of the same name. (Oddly, De Luca spent several years as the president of production for New Line Cinema, the company that released the feature version of *The Lawnmower Man*, although that movie preceded his tenure.)

Compiling a comprehensive list of the Dollar Babies is a nearly impossible task. Only King and his accountant know for sure how many times they have granted the dollar license, and it's entirely possible (indeed, probable) that some of the short films made from his work are completely unauthorized. Aside from the early works found on the *Nightshift Collection* tapes, none of the Dollar Babies are officially available on home video. Although a number of the films have turned up on YouTube, the only authorized public exhibitions of most of these works are at film festivals.

In 2004, James Renner, who directed a short based on "All That You Love Will Be Carried Away," organized the first Dollar Baby Film Festival at King's alma mater, the University of Maine at Orono. The charity event included screenings of eight Dollar Baby films and a Q&A with the filmmakers. The festival returned in 2005 with an expanded lineup, this time featuring more than twenty shorts, including *Gotham Cafe*, to which King himself had contributed a voice-over. Since then, Dollar Baby Festivals have been held all over the world. In May 2013, Houston's Comicpalooza hosted a Dollar Baby Festival organized by Shawn Lealos.

Deep Cuts: Q&A with Dollar Baby Filmmaker/Historian Shawn S. Lealos

Shawn Lealos is an Oklahoma-based freelance writer and filmmaker who directed the 2005 Dollar Baby "I Know What You Need." Lealos, who is also working on a book called *Dollar Deal: The Stories of the Dollar Baby Filmmakers*, agreed to share some insight on the Dollar Baby phenomenon.

Q: *Have you always been a Stephen King fan? Do you remember how you first got into his work?*

A: I started reading Stephen King when I was starting college (1988). Before that, I really was shut off from a lot of entertainment due to growing up in a pretty strict religious household, but once I was out on my own I decided to give him a try. The first book I read was the unabridged version of *The

Stand, and I was hooked. That remains my favorite King story of all time, and I ended up joining a Stephen King book club where I got a new book each month and just absorbed them all.

Q: *How did you first hear about King's Dollar Baby program?*

A: In 1999, I was in my senior year at college at the University of Oklahoma (this was my second go-around and was ten years after I started reading King) and was studying journalism with an emphasis on professional writing. I was just reading everything that I could about writing itself and grabbed the screenplay book for Frank Darabont's *The Green Mile.* In the introduction, King talked about how he gave Darabont the rights to make a short film based on one of his short stories for only $1. That was the dollar baby deal. Of course, I knew about Darabont's movie, "The Woman in the Room," because I had watched it on a VCR tape years before, but I had no idea it was a Dollar Baby. Darabont is not the oldest Dollar Baby (Jeff Schiro's "Boogeyman" was actually made before the Darabont film, and there were ones before that which only King knows about), but Darabont has done more than anyone to get the word out that this opportunity exists.

Q: *Can you describe the process of securing permission to make your film?*

A: When I learned about the Dollar Baby program, the first thing I did was e-mail a woman who put out a Stephen King online e-mail newsletter called SKemers. This was before the Internet exploded, and it was really just message boards, chat rooms, and stuff like that. She got me the address of King's office, and I sat down to write a letter requesting permission. I read in *The Green Mile* that most request letters were barely readable, so my first thought was to make mine as professional as possible. I sent it off and waited. About nine months later, the permission came in the form of contracts. Now, people can just go to his website, click a button, and choose one, getting their acceptance or denial in less than a week. Things were different for me.

Q: *How did you decide on "I Know What You Need" as the story you wanted to adapt?*

A: While I was in college, I was working as a sports journalist for the school's yearbook. I chose the yearbook over the paper because I was more interested in feature stories and not news articles. Well, I was covering the Big 12 football championship and had to drive to Kansas City from Norman, Oklahoma, by myself. I knew I needed to decide which King story I wanted to make, so I bought *Night Shift* as a book on tape to listen to on my drive. When I got home I had two that I wanted to choose from. My stipulations were a small cast, limited locations, and no special effects. It was either "Last Rung on the Ladder" or "I Know What You Need." I chose "I Know What You Need" because I didn't want to have to find kids to work with. After seeing James Cole and Daniel Thron's "Last Rung," I am glad I didn't choose it because their version is great.

Q: *Tell us a little about the making of the film. Did you have to submit your script to King for approval?*

A: No. King really doesn't care about anything other than giving us permission to make the short film, making sure we don't make any money off it (because that hurts his ability to option it to actual studios), and watching it when it is completed. He just lets us make the movie our way, for better or worse. We got the contracts in 2000 and started to make the movie immediately. After we shot some scenes, we realized that we were in way over our heads. We stopped production and made a couple of other short films to cut our teeth and then in 2003, started up again. This time we were ready and shot it over three weeks with a cast of local drama students and student actors. It was an interesting experience, that is for sure. If I could do it all over again, there are a lot of things I would change, but it is what it is, and it helped me network with some great filmmakers when all was said and done. Despite problems (sound problems and difficulties with one specific person involved), I thought we did a decent job with it.

Q: *You're involved with a festival of Dollar Babies at Comicpalooza in Houston. About how many of the other Dollar Babies have you seen? What are your favorites (aside from your own, of course)?*

A: The Dollar Baby filmmakers are almost a fraternity. The first person to contact me after I began promoting my movie online was James Cole ("Last Rung on the Ladder"), and then Jay Holben ("Paranoid") quickly followed. We have all kept in contact, even if many of us have never met face-to-face. Thanks to the festivals previously held in Bangor, Maine, and Los Angeles, many of the filmmakers have connected, although this will be my first screening to attend with them. There will be nineteen Dollar Baby movies screening at the festival, and I saw over twenty-five that were submitted to me for possible inclusion.

I'd say the best one I have seen hands down is "Umney's Last Case" by Rodney Altman. It is funny because that was also made for the TV miniseries *Nightmares and Dreamscapes* and starred William Macy, and I think Altman's version is better. I also really liked "Paranoid" by Jay Holben, which is the only Dollar Baby to screen online with King's permission (any other is illegally uploaded). That one was just fantastic. I also have a soft spot for James Cole's "Last Rung."

Q: *Tell us about your book* Dollar Deal.

A: It started about five years ago when I thought it would be nice to tell the story of the Dollar Baby filmmakers and reached out to find out who was interested. I got a few interested responses, but it didn't go very far at that time. Well, last year I decided to try again and reached out to all the Dollar Baby filmmakers I knew, plus a man named Bernd Lautenslager, who runs the website *stephenkingshortmovies.com*. He sent the word out as well, and I received over twenty-five responses from people wanting to tell their stories.

Some were not ready and others did not follow up, but I interviewed seventeen Dollar Baby filmmakers and they told me their stories, both of making their movies and what that led to in their lives. This book is not so much about Stephen King's work but about how Mr. King helped all these people realize their dreams.

One filmmaker is now making those fun monster movies you see on the SyFy Channel, another created a TV show that aired on NBC a couple of years ago, another is now writing true-crime novels, and two of these filmmakers actually teamed up to make another movie together. When I set out to write this book, I had no idea these directors' stories would be so amazing. There have been a lot of books dealing with King's works, but most only touch on the Dollar Babies. I am proud to be the first person to actually tell the story of these Dollar Baby filmmakers, with the first interviewee making his film in 1979 and the newest making theirs in 2012. We'll also be taking cameras to the festival and will work on a complementary documentary telling these amazing filmmakers' stories. It is all very exciting. The book will come out later this summer [2013], altho ugh the date is still up in the air.

Creepshows

Miniseries, TV Series, and TV-Movies

"They All Float"

It and *The Tommyknockers* Go Long

It: Prime-Time Coulrophobia

W hen Stephen King's massive novel *It* was published in the fall of 1986, it was immediately clear that adapting it for the screen would pose a challenge. At 1,138 pages, the hardcover edition could double as a deadly weapon, and with its story revolving around an ensemble of characters and unfolding in two distinct timelines, it was hard to envision *It* squeezing into a two-hour running time. A television miniseries seemed a more viable option, but King remained extremely skeptical about the prospect of horror in prime-time.

The only one of his books to be adapted for the small screen at that point was *'Salem's Lot*, and that had started as a theatrical project which fell to the television department by default after several failed attempts at a feature version. A proposed *Night Shift* miniseries was canceled before production began due to irreconcilable differences with the Standards and Practices department. Even after selling the *It* rights to ABC, King remained pessimistic about its prospects. "Don't hold your breath," he told Gary L. Wood in 1989. "ABC is one of the networks that still has a fairly strong censorship code . . . I thought when they offered to buy it, 'This will probably never get made.'" Spoken like a man who had no idea *It* was only the beginning of a partnership with the network that would last nearly two decades.

For a while, however, it looked like King was going to be proven right. Lawrence D. Cohen, who had written the screenplay for Brian De Palma's *Carrie*, was hired to pen the script for what was at first envisioned as a seven-hour miniseries. George Romero, whose relationship to Stephen King adaptations was beginning to resemble Charlie Brown's relationship with Lucy's football, was the first director attached to the project. And to hear Romero tell it, it was more than just a token attachment. "I was involved," he said in 1990. "I put in a hell of a lot of time. It's like *Pet Sematary* revisited." Romero worked with Cohen in cutting the miniseries down to six hours and finally down to four, but as preproduction stretched on, the director was forced to leave the project due to other commitments. Tommy Lee Wallace, who had directed the horror sequels

Fright Night, Part 2 and *Halloween III: Season of the Witch*, took Romero's place behind the camera.

Wallace thought Cohen's script for the first night of the miniseries was masterful in the way it devoted each of the seven acts of a two-hour TV time-slot to one of the seven main characters. He was less enamored of the second part, which he felt took too many liberties with King's text. With Cohen unavailable, Wallace rewrote the second half himself, keeping the focus on the adult characters with only a few flashbacks to childhood.

The cast could have been confused with that of a 1990 *Hollywood Squares* episode. Richard Thomas, John Ritter, Tim Reid, and Harry Anderson, all staples of long-running TV series in the seventies and eighties, were joined by Annette O'Toole, Dennis Christopher, and Richard Masur to form the adult version of the Losers Club. The real casting coup, however, proved to be Tim Curry, whose Pennywise the Clown is easily the miniseries' most memorable element. Once again, the West Coast would have to stand in for Stephen King's Maine—in this case, the west coast of Canada, as shooting took place in and around Vancouver in the summer of 1990.

ABC had already taken a deep dive into a pool of weirdness with *Twin Peaks*, which became a sensation in the spring of that year. That series had pushed the envelope in a number of ways, notably in its portrayal of graphic violence on network television, and *It* was one of the first beneficiaries of these relaxed standards. ABC scheduled the miniseries for its November sweeps period and allowed Wallace a bit more leeway in terms of blood, terror, and children in peril than would have been possible even a year or two earlier. But only a *bit* more: Inevitably, the finished product was a homogenized horror show, with fleeting moments of genuine terror and suspense.

The ABC miniseries *It* featured a number of familiar television faces, including John Ritter.

Airing on November 18 and 20, 1990, the two-night event drew inspiration from both *Stand by Me* and *The Big Chill*, two movies we can all agree could only be improved with the addition of a malevolent supernatural clown. The story centers on the same group of characters in two different time periods:

schoolmates in 1960, adults reuniting in 1990. As youngsters, the self-proclaimed Losers are outcasts who band together for survival against not only the town bullies but Pennywise the Dancing Clown. Only the kiddies can see this terrifying balloon-wielding harlequin, who drags his victims into the sewers beneath Derry and devours them. He's sort of a magical, shape-shifting John Wayne Gacy, with better dance moves.

When Pennywise kills his younger brother George, Bill Denbrough leads the rest of the Losers down into the sewers to do battle with the evil clown. They emerge victorious, but their triumph is a temporary one. Thirty years later, the Losers have all grown up to become successful and famous, not to mention instantly recognizable to regular TV viewers. In fact, our acquaintance with the actors as longtime television regulars is both an asset and a hindrance to the production. On the one hand, their familiarity enhances the reunion scenes, as it's easy to believe this was once a tight-knit group (indeed, on the commentary track, the actors indicate that they'd all worked together in various combinations over the years, and were no more than "one-and-a-half degrees of separation" apart, to quote Thomas); on the other hand, their presence makes it easier to dismiss *It* as mere television product. How seriously can we take an ensemble comprised of Jack Tripper, Venus Flytrap, the wacky judge from *Night Court*, and John-Boy Walton in a dorky ponytail?

The kids' scenes work best, although again, it's hard to shake the *Stand by Me* similarities, particularly when the Losers are menaced by greaser Henry Bowers. But the first half of the miniseries does resonate with the hysteria surrounding recovered memory of child abuse in the late eighties and early nineties. In *It*, the adults have lost all recollection of their childhood trauma, only regaining it when they are reunited upon returning to Derry. From 1987 to 1990, the McMartin preschool trial dominated headlines; it was a case in which the "recovered" memory of many now-adults who had attended the preschool eventually proved to be false memories. Some of these "memories" were as bizarre as anything in *It*: teachers flying like witches, molestation in a hot-air balloon over the desert, identifying actor Chuck Norris as one of the abusers. Intentionally or not, *It* mirrored this real-life social phenomenon, although of course, in the reality of the story, the recovered memories are all too real.

It also played a huge role in making the fear of clowns a legitimate pop culture phenomenon. Clowns have been around for thousands of years, and it's likely they've always scared at least as many children as they've delighted, but Pennywise represented some sort of tipping point in the representation of clowns in popular media. Bart Simpson's declaration "Can't sleep—clowns will eat me" became one of *The Simpsons*' many oft-quoted catchphrases (and eventually, a song title for Alice Cooper). A string of evil clown movies, including *Killjoy*, *Clownhouse*, *Dead Clowns*, and *Fear of Clowns*, have cluttered DVD shelves in recent years. The rap group Insane Clown Posse has spawned an entire subculture, Juggalos, modeled after evil clowns. In 2000, the fear of clowns even got its own psychiatric designation in the revised fourth edition of the Diagnostic and

STEPHEN KINGS

ES

HARRY ANDERSON · DENNIS CHRISTOPHER · TIM CURRY · OLIVIA HUSSEY · RICHARD MASUR · ANNETTE O'TOOLE · TIM REID · JOHN RITTER
RICHARD THOMAS · "IT" · Ausführende Produzenten: JIM GREEN, ALLEN EPSTEIN · Produktionsleitung: MATTHEW O'CONNOR · Fernsehdrehbuch von LAWRENCE D. COHEN
The Konigsberg/Sanitsky Company · Regie: TOMMY LEE WALLACE

Evil clowns have become a staple of the horror genre, but Pennywise (Tim Curry) is still the most memorable.

Statistical Manual of Mental Disorders: coulrophobia.

Indeed, Curry's performance as Pennywise is probably the single reason *It* is remembered as a scary picture, especially among those who saw the miniseries as children. With his shock of Bozo hair, cartoon-Brooklyn accent, and sharpened teeth, he's certainly a vivid presence, yet Pennywise, like the real-life Gacy, operates on the premise that children not only *aren't* afraid of clowns but are delighted by them. Pennywise, after all, is only a manifestation of a greater evil—one chosen specifically because of its appeal to youngsters. There's no overt suggestion of child sexual abuse in the miniseries, but the specter of a clown dragging a small boy into a sewer to devour him speaks for itself. (Wallace wanted no part of the most controversial scene from King's book, in which the six pubescent boys in the Losers Club take turns having sex with the one girl in the sewer as some sort of team-building exercise. "It just didn't ring true to me," Wallace says on the DVD commentary. "It felt like a major fantasy, that the writer for a moment let himself get carried away." It's hard to believe the network would have gone along with such a scene, even if Wallace had wanted to include it.)

The clown doesn't resonate so well with the adult characters, which is one reason the second half falters. Part two has a few effective moments, as when the reunited Losers open their fortune cookies to find a variety of nasty surprises, including a roach, an eyeball, and a chicken fetus. But it builds to a climax that satisfies absolutely no one, including the director and the cast. When the adults convene in the sewer for their final confrontation with the fearsome "It," they find themselves face-to-face with . . . a giant spider. In the book, Stephen King could make the case that this creature is the earthly manifestation of a much greater force of evil (and honestly, it still wasn't a very satisfying finale), but none of that came across on the TV screen. Instead, we see our heroes going to battle against a rickety special effect (stop-motion animated in some shots, a man in a costume in others) and defeating it far too easily.

But by the time that spider appeared at the end of the miniseries' second night, ABC already had a hit on its hands. The first part of *It*, airing on a Sunday night, drew over seventeen million viewers and finished as the fifth highest rated program of the week. Part two, airing the following Tuesday, did even better: nineteen million viewers and a second-place finish for the week. It didn't take a high-powered network executive to see that staying in the Stephen King business could be very good business indeed for ABC.

Knocking on *The Tommyknockers*

ABC originally planned to follow-up *It* with a multipart adaptation of *The Stand*. As development on that massive project dragged on (a process detailed in the next chapter), it became clear that the miniseries was not going to be close to production in time to air during the crucial May sweeps period in 1993. Instead, the network decided to go with an adaptation of a decidedly less iconic King work: his 1987 novel *The Tommyknockers*. Several members of the *It* team, including executive producers Frank Konigsberg and Larry Sanitsky and screenwriter Lawrence D. Cohen, reunited to produce a four-hour version for television.

As with *It*, TV-friendly faces were cast in the leading roles: Jimmy Smits (*L.A. Law*) would play the typically King-esque hero, alcoholic poet Jim "Gard" Gardner, while Marg Helgenberger (*China Beach*) won the role of his girlfriend Bobbi Anderson, who discovers the secret of the Tommyknockers. The eclectic supporting cast included Robert Carradine, Joanna Cassidy, Allyce Beasley, John Ashton, and, in what was surely their only screen appearance together, E. G. Marshall and former porn star Traci Lords. Lewis Teague, who had helmed *Cujo* and *Cat's Eye*, was hired to direct. Although *The Tommyknockers* was yet another King work set in small-town Maine (this time in one of his recurring fictional hamlets, Haven), the production found another most unlikely substitute filming location: Auckland, New Zealand.

According to Helgenberger in a 1993 interview with the *Toronto Star*, it was a difficult shoot. Teague was fired after one week and replaced by TV-movie veteran John Power. "We had to shut down production for a week to regroup, then pressed on with a whole lot of script changes." New Zealand's rainy season played havoc with the production, causing further delays. "The weather was always uncertain, meaning rain anytime, so we learned to change the shooting schedule on a moment's notice."

The Tommyknockers was described as a change of pace for King, in that it is primarily science fiction rather than horror, but it's really just one of his periodic reworkings of *'Salem's Lot*: a Peyton Place taken over by unspeakable evil, and the one good man who tries to stop it. In this case, the evil is not vampires but aliens—specifically, a spacecraft discovered buried in the cursed Indian woods.

While walking her dog, Bobbi literally stumbles upon this UFO and begins to unearth it; the more of it is exposed, the stranger the town's residents become. The only one unaffected by the weird, green energy emanating from the spaceship is Gard, who has a metal plate in his head as the result of a skiing accident. While the other Havenites are reading each other's thoughts and building strange new devices powered by alien technology, Gard finds himself in an *Invasion of the Body Snatchers* scenario wherein all his friends and neighbors are becoming . . . something else.

The novel was one of King's lesser efforts, and in his nonfiction book *On Writing*, the author sheds some light on why that might have been. "In the spring and summer of 1986 I wrote *The Tommyknockers*, often working until midnight with my heart running at a hundred and thirty beats a minute and cotton swabs stuck up my nose to stem the coke-induced bleeding." The story became a metaphor for King's drug abuse: The author assigned his nosebleeds to his alcoholic hero, and his addiction became the Haven townspeople's unhealthy obsession with the alien artifact.

The miniseries makes wholesale changes to King's story, almost all of them in service of making *The Tommyknockers* less dark, depressing, and violent. In the book, the Havenites are irredeemably transformed into psychotic, murderous creatures. Gard is forced to kill Bobbi, and his escape in the alien spacecraft ignites a blaze that kills nearly every character in the novel. In an epilogue, government agents arrive on the scene to kill or capture the few remaining survivors. It's not King's most charitable view of humanity, and it's certainly not the brand of horror-lite ABC would have been comfortable with.

In the miniseries, only a few of the characters become as craven and evil as they are in the book, and generally speaking, they're the ones that get killed off. Bobbi snaps out of her spell after she and Gard access the spaceship, and they reaffirm their love for each other. Most of the Havenites survive and are little the worse for wear after the ordeal, give or take a few teeth. Gard sacrifices himself for the greater good by psychically flying the ship into space and blowing it up, and life goes on in Haven.

Viewed today, *The Tommyknockers* could be interpreted as an allegory for the growing methamphetamine problem in some rural parts of Maine, right down to the rampant tooth loss among the Haven residents, but that couldn't have been the intent at the time. (By most accounts, meth manufacture and use was a rarity in New England until the early twenty-first century.) In any case, it seems absurd to ascribe any sort of serious purpose, metaphorical or otherwise, to such a silly, shoddy production. Smits is a reliable presence, and surprisingly, Traci Lords makes for an amusing cartoon femme fatale, but for the most part, the actors struggle to make the best of underdeveloped roles. To the extent that it makes sense at all, the plot seems to have been cobbled together from bits and pieces of the King filmography. As in *Maximum Overdrive*, man's technology falls under an alien influence and turns against him; there's even a virtual replay of

Overdrive's soda machine attack. The haunted Indian ground is straight out of *Pet Sematary*. There's even a joking reference to Cujo that lands with a thud.

If the giant spider was a letdown at the end of *It*, the rubber aliens that figure into the anticlimax of *The Tommyknockers* are a bad joke. Smits knocks the head off one of them with a shovel, using no more effort than would be required to step on a cockroach, and his sudden ability to telepathically pilot the spaceship out of Haven is an all too convenient head-scratcher. (What happened to the metal plate in his head?) But if audiences minded this overdose of nonsense, it wasn't reflected in the ratings when the miniseries aired on May 9 and 10, 1993. Both installments finished in the top ten for their respective weeks, each pulling in an audience share of over 25 percent. The Stephen King miniseries

This Australian poster for *The Tommyknockers* suggests something far more interesting than the actual miniseries turned out to be.

was poised to become a staple of ABC's May sweeps programming, and the network was finally ready to go ahead with the most ambitious adaptation of them all: *The Stand.*

Deep Cuts

- Pennywise the Clown not only inspired a string of terrible evil clown movies, he also served as the muse for a punk band formed in Hermosa Beach, California in 1988. The band called Pennywise released its first (self-titled) album in 1991 on Epitaph Records and is still active to this day. Although none of Pennywise's ten albums has sold in huge numbers, several (including *Straight Ahead* and *From the Ashes*) have cracked *Billboard's* Top 100 chart. The song "Pennywise" from the first album pays explicit tribute to the band's inspiration, with lyrics about "the clown they call Pennywise" with evil in his eyes.
- *Tommyknockers* viewers who followed the nineties revival of *The Outer Limits* may have experienced a strong feeling of déjà vu when an episode titled "The Revelations of Becka Paulson" aired in 1997. Based on a short story that became, with a few changes, a subplot in *The Tommyknockers,* the episode starred Catherine O'Hara in the title role, played by Allyce Beasley in the miniseries. The major differences between the two: In the *Outer Limits* episode, Becka develops telepathic powers after accidentally shooting herself in the head, rather than from exposure to the Tommyknockers. And while it's a game show host who begins speaking directly to Becka and instructing her to kill in the miniseries, it's an 8×10 photo sitting on top of the television in the O'Hara version (as discussed at greater length in chapter 21).

The Long Walk

The Stand Escapes Development Hell

Soon to Be a Major Motion Picture

he Stand is Stephen King's longest novel (at least in its expanded edition, released in 1990), so it's perhaps appropriate that its journey to the screen became a drawn-out, epic quest in itself. First published in 1978, King's take on the end of the world soon became his most popular work, and over the years, as its millions of fans watched his other books get the Hollywood treatment, they could only wonder: When would *The Stand* become a movie?

On May 7, 1980, an ad published in the industry bible *Variety* proclaimed, "The Laurel Group, Inc. is pleased to announce the acquisition of the motion picture rights to Stephen King's best-selling novel of ultimate horror *The Stand*." The ad went on to announce the screenwriter (King himself), the producer (Richard P. Rubinstein), and the director (George A. Romero). When the paperback edition of *The Stand* was released later in 1980, the back cover blurbed, "Soon to be a major motion picture directed by George Romero." Needless to say, "soon" never arrived. So what happened?

The saga began in the late seventies, when *Salem's Lot* was still in development as a theatrical feature at Warner Bros. Romero, best known for his *Living Dead* movies, was under consideration to direct the potential film, so he traveled to Maine to meet King and kick around some ideas. Of course, the Warners theatrical department eventually passed the *Salem's Lot* project down to the TV division, but Romero and King had hit it off in the meantime. King offered Romero and his partner in Laurel Entertainment, Richard Rubinstein, the chance to purchase the screen rights to any of his novels that had not yet sold to Hollywood. Romero jumped at *The Stand*.

Two major obstacles stood in the project's way: time and money. King had conceived *The Stand* as a sort of American *Lord of the Rings*, and the end of the world was only the beginning. The first part of the book traces the spread of the lethal "Captain Trips" virus from a top-secret government facility in California to a gas station in East Texas and then throughout the continental United States. After 99.44 percent of the population is wiped out by the plague, the survivors begin to split into two camps: the good guys, who congregate around 108-year-old Mother Abigail in Nebraska, and the bad guys, who convene in Las Vegas at the behest of "the Walkin' Dude," Randall Flagg. The novel builds to a climactic confrontation between good and evil.

Distilling this sweeping tale into a feature film's two-hour (or even three-hour) running time would be a challenge for any screenwriter, and this time King was determined to take it on himself. "I wouldn't trust it to anyone else," he told interviewer Paul Gagne in 1980. "In fact, I've been offered option deals on *The Stand* before and I've turned them down. Some of them have been for pretty good money. But this is maybe the one thing I've done where I want as much creative control over the movie as I can get. If it's gonna get bitched up, I want to do the bitching up."

Bitched up or not, *The Stand* was going to be an expensive proposition. Romero had ended the world on the cheap before in *Dawn of the Dead*, but he'd done it in microcosm, with a small handful of survivors making their stand in a shopping mall. *The Stand* would require a large cast and numerous shooting locations, as well as big action set pieces and special effects. Sensing it might be a hard sell, Romero and King decided to do a "tune-up" project first to entice potential investors. That became *Creepshow*, discussed in chapter 19.

Turning his own epic novel into a workable screenplay proved a more arduous task than King had bargained for. By 1983, he'd completed two drafts but still hadn't managed to boil the story down to a manageable length. His second draft would have translated into a four-hour running time—"40 minutes longer than *Godfather II*," as he put it—and he and Romero were mulling the idea of splitting *The Stand* into two films. They still hadn't approached any studio with the project or even worked out a budget (although they'd

Stephen King's most mammoth novel, *The Stand* defied many attempts to bring it to the big screen.

contemplated trying to rent Francis Ford Coppola's Las Vegas set from his flop *One from the Heart* as a cost-cutting measure), and their reluctance to cede any creative control over the movie seemed to have a paralyzing effect on *The Stand*'s progress to the screen.

One possible solution to the length problem, turning the proposed feature into a TV miniseries, struck King as unrealistic. "The networks don't want to see the end of the world, particularly in prime time," he told Charles L. Grant in 1985. "Advertisers don't want to sponsor the end of the world." (Two years earlier, ABC had broadcast the end of the world, in the form of the TV-movie *The Day After*, in prime time. True to King's words, however, advertisers didn't want to sponsor it, and no commercials were shown after the bombs dropped on-screen.) King knew he had to cut his three-hundred-page script in half in order to get the film made, but that was easier said than done. Finally, five drafts and several years after announcing he'd trust the task to no one else, the author decided *The Stand* needed fresh blood.

The Pallenberg Script

In 1985, George Romero left the Laurel Group to pursue his own projects, but the rights to *The Stand* remained with Laurel and Richard Rubinstein. By the late 1980s, Warner Bros. had taken an interest in the project. The studio put up the money to develop the screenplay with another writer, and Rubinstein's search began. He interviewed a number of screenwriters, finally settling on Rospo Pallenberg, who had written *Excalibur* and *The Emerald Forest* for director John Boorman. Rubinstein was impressed that Pallenberg was such a fan of the book, he'd brought the first paperback edition to their meeting. (Memo to struggling screenwriters: If you're ever up for an adaptation gig, stop by the used bookstore on your way to the interview and pick up the oldest, most battered copy of the novel you can find.)

Pallenberg's task was to ignore King's attempts at adapting his own work and go back to the source, somehow finding a way to squeeze the story into a running time of three hours or less. To his credit, he managed to do this. But although Pallenberg's second draft (which is just a Google search away, if you're curious) met with the approval of all parties, it hardly reads like the basis for a successful adaptation. In trimming the story down to a manageable size, Pallenberg stripped away the backstories for many of the major characters, reducing them to little more than bit players. Frannie Goldsmith, Harold Lauder, Nick Andros, and Tom Cullen are the important figures who lose the most in translation (poor mentally challenged Tom is even deprived of his signature claim that M-O-O-N spells everything), but even Stu Redman, whose arc is more or less intact, is barely developed as a character.

The dialogue is another victim of the compression process, as the characters are reduced to explaining their motivations and expressing their interior mono-logue with little regard for subtlety or realistic speech rhythms. Much of it reads like placeholder dialogue, as though the actual lines had yet to be filled in. The biggest problem with Pallenberg's script may well have been inevitable with any adaptation of the novel running under 150 pages: It reads more like a collection of sketches from *The Stand* than an epic, sweeping narrative.

At the very least, Rubinstein and King felt Pallenberg's draft could serve as a workable blueprint. "We've gotten ourselves at least within shouting distance," Rubinstein told Gary Wood in 1991. "The point is, I think Rospo was successful where Steve wasn't in terms of being able to get some distance on the material and make those decisions that needed to be made, in terms of what stays in the movie and what gets left out." But although Rubinstein insisted Warner Bros. was happy with the work as well, the bean counters had the final say. The studio backed out of the project, leaving Rubinstein and the Laurel Group once again without financing and distribution for their crown jewel.

ABC Takes the Stand

Stephen King's dim view of network television's handling of the horror genre softened somewhat in the early nineties, after *It* and *The Tommyknockers* both enjoyed ratings success on ABC. "I liked *It* very much," King told the *Hartford Courant*. "The way that *It* was adapted was largely instrumental in my decision to go ahead and run with *The Stand* on ABC. I liked *Tommyknockers* a little bit less. . . . But I thought they did a pretty decent job with a book that wasn't top drawer to begin with." The network clearly wanted to stay in the Stephen King business, and since *The Stand* had still not been produced as a feature, it inevitably rose to the top of ABC's wish list. Although King and Rubinstein had turned down television offers before, they finally relented when the network offered six hours (eight with commercials) to tell the complete story.

The Pallenberg script was tossed, and Stephen King went back to work on the adaptation freed of the time constraints that had bedeviled him for years. His final draft totaled more than four hundred pages and restored many of the subplots he'd had to excise from the proposed feature version. He and Rubinstein became co-executive producers of the miniseries, ensuring their creative control . . . up to a point. ABC's Standards and Practices division would still have the final say over exactly what kind of apocalypse could be presented on prime-time network television.

Fans who had been waiting more than a decade for the film were less than thrilled when King and Rubinstein chose their director for the project. Gone was George Romero, who had been associated with the film for so many years; instead, Mick Garris, who had directed King's script for *Sleepwalkers*, got the nod. Every fan of *The Stand*, including King himself, had mentally assembled a casting wish-list over the years (King had envisioned Robert Duvall as his demonic villain, Randall Flagg), but the final roster was a mix-and-match selection of familiar faces from film and television. Gary Sinise won the pivotal role of Stu Redman on the strength of his performance as George in an adaptation of

Steinbeck's *Of Mice and Men* that he directed. Former teen star Molly Ringwald was cast as Frannie Goldsmith, while her fellow brat-packer Rob Lowe was the somewhat unlikely choice for deaf-mute Nick Andros. Supporting roles were filled by Miguel Ferrer, Matt Frewer, Laura San Giacomo, Corin Nemec, and Ruby Dee (the only logical choice for Mother Abigail).

The five-month shoot began in Utah in February 1993, and the production would ultimately travel to six states and ninety-five locations, including Las Vegas, New York, and Ogunquit, Maine. While a shoot of that length would be considered luxurious for most feature-length films, it was a breakneck schedule for a six-hour epic. The $28 million budget was huge for a television production of the time (although ABC didn't cover all of it; Laurel made up the balance with international

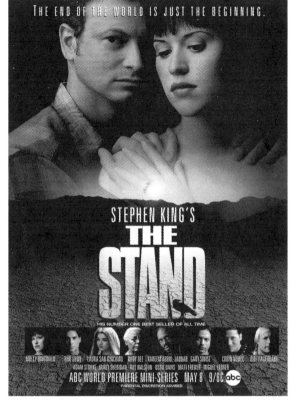

The end of the world in prime time? It happened in 1994, when the miniseries version of *The Stand* aired over four nights on ABC.

sales), but given the hectic pace of shooting, Garris still felt he was engaged in "guerrilla filmmaking" much of the time.

Expectations were high when ABC scheduled *The Stand* to air during the May sweeps period in 1994. The ratings did not disappoint: Each two-hour episode drew around nineteen million viewers, with the final three installments ranking as the top three shows of week, according to A. C. Nielsen. That made it the highest-rated ABC miniseries in eight years (since *North and South, Book II*) and ensured that Stephen King would remain a staple of the network for some time to come. Although reviews were mixed, many fans pronounced themselves satisfied that so much of the story had made it to the screen intact.

Nearly two decades on, it's hard to see *The Stand* as a success on any level besides its relative completeness. The opening sequence is promising enough, as Garris efficiently traces the release of the superflu bug from the government facility via security guard Charlie Campion (Ray McKinnon). When Blue Oyster Cult's creepy "Don't Fear the Reaper" (quoted at length in King's novel) strikes up on the soundtrack as Garris's camera tracks through offices and laboratories full of dead bodies, there's momentary reason to hope that King's apocalyptic vision has arrived on the small screen more or less intact. It's a high point the miniseries never reaches again.

The show's problems begin with the very aspect of the production that was so hard-won in the first place: its length. There's a big difference between sweep and sprawl, and *The Stand* comes down on the wrong side of it. So many characters are introduced, and so many different acting styles are in play, that it rarely seems they are all occupying the same movie. Gary Sinise delivers exactly the sort of taciturn Gary Cooper/Henry Fonda performance King envisioned, but it's hard to reconcile his American-made stoicism with Matt Frewer's Trashcan Man, who's pitched somewhere between a *Road Warrior* villain and a *Roadrunner* cartoon. Minor characters come and go before we really get a sense of how they fit into the big picture, whereas a somewhat trimmer *Stand* might have eliminated them entirely.

It's not easy to take the end of the world seriously when Garris has populated it with so many pointless celebrity cameos. A few of them work, such as an uncredited Ed Harris, who brings a cold-blooded steeliness to the role of a general overseeing the Project Blue cover-up. At the other end of the spectrum, casting Kareem Abdul-Jabbar as New York's nutty Monster Shouter does nothing but jar the viewer out of the show's already threadbare reality. But the most crucial casting error—even more so than Molly Ringwald's googly-eyed, tremblylipped turn as Frannie—concerned *The Stand*'s embodiment of evil.

The role of Randall Flagg was offered to a number of high-profile actors, including Jeff Goldblum, Willem Dafoe, and Christopher Walken. Any one of them could have made Flagg into an idiosyncratic, memorable villain, but none accepted the role. Instead, clean-cut, granite-jawed Jamey Sheridan was fitted for a denim jacket and a mullet wig, and turned in an entirely fright-free performance. On his DVD commentary track, Stephen King notes with amusement Sheridan's resemblance to a romance novel cover-boy with demonic eyes, but it's unlikely any reader of *The Stand* had pictured the Walkin' Dude as a Satanic Fabio.

The miniseries' biggest flaw, however, is the one King and his fans had feared from the beginning: It looks like television. ABC's *The Stand* offered a compromised, sanitized apocalypse over four nights in May 1994. Had the miniseries been made even a decade later, around the time the *Lost* pilot premiered on ABC, it could have benefited from better production values, a higher grade of digital effects, more cinematic (and high-definition) visuals, and somewhat looser content restrictions. Instead, the production looks slapdash and rushed (which it was), flat and visually uninspired, and utterly incapable of depicting King's more horrific visions from the novel.

Take the Lincoln Tunnel sequence, which nearly every reader remembers as a white-knuckle highlight of the book. Garris was faced with certain logistical problems (a location that looked exactly nothing like the Lincoln Tunnel, a scene that unfolded in total darkness in the novel), but even those challenges could have been overcome in a feature film or pay-cable production. But hamstrung by the network's stringent Standards and Practices guidelines, the director struggled in vain to convey the mounting terror of Larry Underwood's journey through a passage choked with rotting corpses. Although *The Stand* won an Emmy for its makeup work, the special effects in general are cheesy and unconvincing, particularly the then-cutting edge CGI and "morphing" visuals. Nothing looks quite so dated now as the earliest digital effects—and even Garris concedes, on his DVD commentary, that the grand finale's "hand of God" image is "chintzy."

The Stand was always going to be compromised in one way or another. Ultimately, King and company made the decision to prioritize sheer length and comprehensiveness over a format that might have proved more artistically rewarding. Thus, "George Romero's *The Stand*" becomes one of those mythical lost films that may actually be more fun to ruminate about than it would have been in reality. We all have our own idea of what that movie might have looked like, but of course, our imaginations have unlimited budgets and no time constraints. Maybe Romero should consider himself lucky. An unmade movie can never disappoint.

Bloodlines: Five Apocalyptic Plagues

The Stand was hardly the first time the world ended (or narrowly escaped its doom) by deadly disease in pop culture, and it wouldn't be the last. Here are five other notable explorations of this theme, including one that helped inspire *The Stand* in the first place.

The Earth Abides (1949)—This novel by George R. Stewart served as one of King's initial inspirations for *The Stand* and is likewise divided into three sections. In the first, "World Without End," lead character Isherwood "Ish" Williams returns from his remote mountain cabin to find that he is apparently the last man on earth. Gradually he learns that, while most of civilization has been wiped out by a virulent disease, a few survivors remain. They form a new society, and the second section, "The Year 22," catches up with them twenty-two years later. In Part III, "The Last American," an eldery Ish witnesses civilization's return to a primal state. Interesting but not especially gripping, Stewart's novel suffers from an often unlikable lead character. As King noted, the book is weighed down by its focus on ecological issues rather than the human element.

The Andromeda Strain (1971)—Based on a novel by Michael Crichton, and directed by Robert Wise (*The Day the Earth Stood Still*), this low-key sci-fi film takes a methodical, scientific approach to the deadly plague problem. A satellite bearing an alien virus crashes to earth in a small New Mexico town, killing all but two of its inhabitants. A team of scientists is assembled in a high-tech facility

9:00 PM COLOR NBC

The Stand was not the first work of popular fiction to warn against the dangers of a global pandemic. Author/director Michael Crichton explored a similar scenario in 1971's *The Andromeda Strain*.

to study the Andromeda strain and find a way to eradicate it before it can spread worldwide. Wise hasn't exactly made a nail-biter here—the suspense doesn't really kick in until the end, when a team member must race against the clock to disable a self-destruct sequence—but the seventies futurism of the Wildfire complex is appealing, and the casting of lumpy, middle-aged actors as the scientific team is a concession to reality that would never be made today. (In fact, the film was remade as a TV miniseries with a far more photogenic cast in 2008.)

Survivors (1975–1977, 2008–2010)—*Doctor Who* writer Terry Nation created this postapocalyptic BBC series, which springs from a similar premise as *The Earth Abides*. After a Chinese scientist releases a deadly virus that nearly wipes out the world's population, scattered British survivors gather to try to rebuild civilization. Nation left the show after the first series and wrote a 1976 novel based on the same premise, also called *Survivors*. (King saw Nation's novel in a bookstore while he was still writing *The Stand* and thought, "Great, this guy has just written my book," but decided his story was different enough to continue.) In 2008, the BBC began airing a new series of *Survivors*, based on the book rather than the original show. By then, in the wake of *The Stand* miniseries and other postapocalyptic series like *Jeremiah* and *Jericho*, the material simply felt too familiar.

12 Monkeys (1995)—Chris Marker's 1962 short film *La Jetée* is a miraculous, one-of-a-kind piece of cinema that cannot be improved upon, but Terry Gilliam's loose adaptation (written by David and Janet Peoples) stands on its own as an idiosyncratic piece of big-budget science fiction. Bruce Willis stars as James Cole, a prisoner in a future civilization that has been driven underground by a deadly plague. Cole is sent back in time in hopes of developing a cure for the virus, but ends up in mental institution in 1990 America, throwing into doubt everything we have seen. His psychiatrist (Madeleine Stowe) must determine if he is truly from the future or delusional and dangerous. Brad Pitt was nominated for a

Supporting Actor Oscar for his twitchy performance as Cole's fellow patient, who may be responsible for unleashing the virus. Gilliam's film is as visually baroque as the rest of his work, but has a core of melancholy lacking in most time-travel brain-teasers.

Contagion (2011)—Steven Soderbergh put his own spin on the old Irwin Allen all-star disaster movies with this cool, clinical examination of a deadly pandemic. Soderbergh tracks the progress of the outbreak from its first known carrier (Gwyneth Paltrow) through the search for a cure and the deaths of millions worldwide. The cast includes Matt Damon as Paltrow's devastated husband, Kate Winslet and Lawrence Fishburne as scientists working on the antidote, and Jude Law as a blogger questioning the official story and spreading potentially danger- ous misinformation. *Contagion* is methodical, almost Kubrickian as it unfolds in cool blue and golden hues, and Soderbergh wrings surprising levels of dread from the quotidian gestures of everyday life—a glass passed from a waiter, a woman blowing on dice for luck—that could easily carry the seeds of our doom.

Deep Cuts

- Pennywise is not the only band to pay tribute to the works of Stephen King. In 2009, prog-rock outfit Shadow Circus released the album *Whispers and Screams*, featuring a thirty-three-minute opening suite called "Project Blue." Divided into sections with titles like "Captain Trips," "The Seduction of Harold Lauder," and "The Hand of God," the track is an overt homage to *The Stand*. Guitarist John Fontana told the website Sea of Tranquility, "the idea of basing an epic on *The Stand* was settled during the writing of 'Project Blue,' so I had the opportunity to compose as if writing a score for an imaginary film, which I found a very inspirational way to write. The characters, emo- tion, and story provided a much more determined purpose for the mood and action of the music."
- It's hard to imagine stranger bedfellows than Stephen King and the Osmonds, yet *The Stand* represents a (very tenuous) intersection of these two very different worlds of entertainment. In the 1970s, the Osmonds built soundstages in Orem, Utah, where *The Donny & Marie Show* as well as various Osmond-related TV specials were taped. In 1989, the Osmonds sold the soundstages to Ventura Entertainment Group. A few years later, much of *The Stand* miniseres was shot on those stages.

Fair Extension

The Langoliers, Storm of the Century, Rose Red, and Bag of Bones

The Langoliers Invade Bangor

Following the ratings success of *The Stand*, there was no question that the relationship between ABC and Stephen King would continue to flourish. King enjoyed the creative freedom he'd been given to tell his tale at epic length (even if he bristled a bit at the restrictions imposed by Standards and Practices), and the network loved the numbers his work pulled in. The only real question concerned how to follow up an adaptation of one of the author's most beloved books.

Richard Rubinstein, King's longtime collaborator who had produced *The Stand*, purchased the rights to "The Langoliers," a novella from the *Four Past Midnight* collection, in 1992. King's inevitable take on the fear of flying, the story concerned a passenger jet slipping through a time-rift that causes all but ten passengers to disappear from the plane. It fitted ABC's need for a May 1995 King miniseries nicely, and Rubinstein had a director in mind for the project: Tom Holland. Rubinstein had been working with the *Child's Play* director on a proposed feature based on King's *Thinner*, but with that project on the back burner, Holland turned his attention to *The Langoliers*.

The two-part miniseries would become the first King production to shoot entirely in the author's hometown, at the actual location where most of the story takes place: the Bangor International Airport. Unable to find a set suitable for the airplane scenes, the production purchased an actual L1011 aircraft, parked it in a hangar at BIA, and cut it into sections to allow the crew to shoot the interior from multiple vantage points. Another (functional) L1011 was used for shots of the plane taking off and landing; other shots of the plane in midair were computer generated.

Holland adapted King's story for the small screen himself, and he and Rubinstein assembled another cast composed primarily of familiar television faces; among them, David Morse (*St. Elsewhere*) as pilot Brian Engle, Patricia Wettig (*thirtysomething*) as passenger Laurel Stevenson, and Bronson Pinchot (*Perfect Strangers*) as the insane Craig Toomey. For the miniseries' title "characters," Holland and Rubinstein turned to Image Design, the same effects house that had contributed the morphing and "hand of God" effects to *The Stand*. King had described the Langoliers, extradimensional entities that eat reality as it fades into the past, as "sort of like beachballs, but balls which rippled and contracted and expanded again" and had "high-speed teeth, whirring and crunching." On-screen, they would be entirely CGI creations.

King wasn't nearly as involved with the production as he had been with *The Stand*, but given that the shoot was practically happening in his backyard, he did visit the set occasionally and played one of his usual cameo roles. Filming generally went smoothly, aside from the usual headaches associated with shooting at an airport—mainly, waiting for planes to take off and land. (Bangor doesn't have the busiest airport in the world, but traffic does pick up quite a bit in the summer, which is when *The Langoliers* was shot.) The miniseries premiered in 1995, in the May sweeps slot now reserved for King, and attracted the usual strong ratings: 17.5 million for the first episode, placing it fourth for the week, and 19.5 million for the conclusion.

Part one of *The Langoliers* is relatively successful at conveying the tone Holland was going for, which he described as "a four-hour *Twilight Zone*." The mystery of the disappearing passengers is a strong hook, and Holland doles out the suspense and the backstories of the characters (although not all of them) skillfully enough to hold our interest. The plot mechanics become strained, however, once the writer character played by Dean Stockwell starts explaining what's happening for the benefit of his fellow passengers and the viewing audience. This is a built-in flaw of King's novella, but still, it's almost impossible to believe Stockwell's character could unravel all the science-fictional happenings (and yet no other way for us to get the information necessary to understand the story). *The Langoliers* does offer a unique spin on the time-travel narrative, with its conceit that the past is an empty shell that's left behind and eventually eaten by weird blobs with teeth to make way for the future, but this isn't explained very well in the miniseries and doesn't hold up to much scrutiny anyway.

What really sinks *The Langoliers*, even more than the absurdly over-the-top performance by Bronson Pinchot (who consumes more of the scenery than all of the Langoliers put together), are its digital villains. Even making allowances for technology that was in its infancy at the time, the time-eating entities are laughable creations. With their round, blobby contours and gaping maws full of tinsel-teeth, they appear to have escaped from some hyperviolent mid-nineties Pac-Man knockoff. By the time order is restored and our heroes are skipping happily into a freeze-frame, the spell cast by the first installment has long since worn off.

"A Real Novel for Television": *Storm of the Century*

ABC followed *The Langoliers* with a three-night remake of *The Shining* (discussed in chapter 30) in 1997. The next Stephen King miniseries for the network would not be an adaptation of an existing work but an original called *Storm of the Century*, scripted specifically for the network by King. In his introduction to the published version of the teleplay, King described it as "a *real* novel for television" and explained how it came to be. He'd begun work on a new project he'd assumed would become his next novel. But the story kept coming to him in visuals, notably the central image of a man "sitting on the bunk of his cell, heels drawn up, arms resting on knees, eyes *unblinking*." King envisioned the cell in the back of a general store on the fictitious Little Tall Island, the setting for *Dolores Claiborne*, and imagined the island buffeted by a massive winter storm.

It felt more like a movie than a novel to King but too lengthy for a theatrical release. He asked Mark Carliner, his producer on *The Shining*, and Maura Dunbar, his contact at ABC, if they'd be interested in an original miniseries. To no one's great surprise, they were, and King went to work on the teleplay in December 1996. He wrote *Storm of the Century* in three "acts," to unfold over three nights in six hours of TV time (or about four and a half hours sans commercials). ABC committed $35 million to the project, and the search for a director began. King didn't think they'd have to look far: He'd been perfectly happy working with Mick Garris on *The Stand* and *The Shining*, and hoped to have him helm the new project as well. Garris, however, was busy with the TV-movie *Host* and would be unavailable.

After watching and enjoying the direct-to-video movie *Twilight Man*, King suggested its director, Craig R. Baxley, for the job. Baxley read the script and impressed King over a dinner meeting with his ideas and enthusiasm for the project. The job was his and the casting process began. Tim Daly, who had met with King about the *Shining* role that eventually went to his *Wings* cast-mate Steven Weber, won the Gary Cooper-esque lead role of Constable Mike Anderson. Debrah Farentino would play his wife Molly and Casey Siemaszko his right-hand man Hatch. For the part of the antagonist, Andre Linoge, ABC execs tossed around a lot of big names King knew were pie-in-the-sky suggestions, like Anthony Hopkins. He preferred a relative unknown in the role, and he got his wish when Colm Feore, an actor Carliner had liked in the movie *Thirty Two Short Films About Glenn Gould*, signed on to play Linoge.

Shooting began in February 1998 in Southwest Harbor, Maine. Although the real town stood in for Little Tall Island in some exteriors, a replica of Southwest Harbor was built on a stage in a former sugar-beet storage facility outside of Toronto, in order to allow the production greater control over the snowstorm. The snow itself was a mixture of the real stuff, the man-made variety, shredded polyethylene, some digital work, and "a food compound similar to Cheez-Its," according to Baxley's DVD commentary. Some shots of the storm, notably those involving a lighthouse and a boat crashing against the docks, were created in miniature. After eighty days of shooting, the production wrapped in San Francisco, where the miniseries' final scenes take place.

ABC pulled out all the stops to publicize *Storm of the Century* when it premiered during February sweeps in 1999, even weaving the blizzard through its daytime soap operas and some prime-time shows. The promotion didn't quite translate into the ratings bonanza the network had been hoping for, however. Although the first two episodes won their time slots and the third drew the network's biggest Thursday night audience in five years, the miniseries overall drew a smaller audience than any of ABC's prior King adaptations.

An original novel for television not based on an existing King work, *Storm of the Century* proved to be the most enjoyable of the ABC miniseries.

From a creative standpoint, however, *Storm of the Century* is easily the strongest of the ABC miniseries efforts. True to the author's intentions, it plays like a Stephen King novel in visual form, with both the strengths and weaknesses that implies. To the latter point, it offers the full array of familiar King tics: the folksy, cornball humor; the repetition of sing-song catchphrases ("born in sin, come on in"); and characters with the irritating habit of calling each other by their full names ("That's about enough out of you, Robbie Beals!," "Don't you be sassing me, Ursula Godsoe!"). It also shares the author's tendency toward bloat: No one who skipped the middle segment of this three-night affair would find it terribly difficult to fill in the gaps.

But the fact that *Storm* isn't based on an existing King work pays off in the ways the author hoped it would. It couldn't disappoint in comparison to the book because there *was* no book (although obsessives could buy the published version of the screenplay and search for deleted and altered scenes), and more importantly, no one watching it would know how it ended, allowing *Storm* to "authentically shock" King fans in a way previous films and TV productions hadn't. Visually, the miniseries is a big step up from the likes of *The Stand* and *The Langoliers*: Baxley works in icy blues and steely grays, more or less seamlessly blends the Southwest Harbor exteriors with the Toronto stagework, and integrates the weather as a major character of the piece. (The Maine accents are again problematic, however, with only Jeffrey DeMunn doing a creditable job as town manager Robbie Beals.)

The plot is basically one long delaying tactic, as Linoge, a Randall Flagg–like demon in human form, allows himself to be captured by the Little Tall residents just as the titular storm hits. Linoge knows all the dark secrets of the townspeople and shares with Leland Gaunt of *Needful Things* the ability to turn them against one another. "Give me what I want and I'll go away," he vows, over and over again. If not, he will bring down a cataclysm that will wipe out every resident of Little Tall Island. The miniseries sags a bit in the middle, as the question of what Linoge wants continues to linger (what if he simply wants some waffles?), and it is not until the third night that we learn his demands. It's a credit to King's storytelling abilities that the answer is just about worth the wait.

The final hour is riveting, as Linoge demands a child to carry on his legacy, and a twist on Shirley Jackson's lottery is held to determine which one will be sacrificed to save the rest. Only the square-jawed constable protests, and ends up paying the biggest price. The diabolical final act of *Storm* finds King doing what he does best, using the supernatural to amplify domestic and community dramas. Here he flips over the stoic New England platitude ("We've always stood together on the island") to reveal the bitter reality hidden beneath ("Better you than me, buddy").

It's one of King's darker visions of humanity, and not every viewer appreciated it. But on his DVD commentary, the author is not exactly sympathetic to that point of view. "If you don't like it, put it on your Tough Shit List and send it to your chaplain."

Rose Red Reunion

In 1996, Steven Spielberg told Stephen King he'd like to make the scariest haunted house movie ever, and he'd like King to write it. "I said yeah, I'll take a shot at it," King says on the making-of documentary included on the *Rose Red* DVD. Spielberg, as is his habit, moved on to other things, but King remained intrigued by the idea of making "the *Moby Dick* of haunted house stories . . . big and scary, that sticks in people's minds as *the* haunted house movie."

Spielberg and King didn't see eye-to-eye on what *the* haunted house movie would look like, however, and after the director passed on the project, King had the idea of getting the *Storm of the Century* band back together. In June 1999, he sent his script for a three-night version of *Rose Red* to producer Mark Carliner, with a note that he should pass it on to Craig Baxley. Only a few days later, however, King was hit by a minivan and nearly lost his life, putting the project on indefinite hold. After about six months of recovery, the author was ready to make it a priority again. "I was using the work as dope," he told Kim Murphy of the *L.A. Times*, "because it worked better than anything they were giving me to kill the pain."

With Baxley onboard, the search began for a house that could double as the Rimbauer mansion, known as Rose Red. Just as Shirley Jackson's "The Lottery" had served as one inspiration for *Storm of the Century*, *Rose Red* was loosely based on Jackson's *Haunting of Hill House*. But King was also inspired by stories of the Winchester Mystery House, a supposedly haunted mansion in San Jose, California. According to legend, a psychic told the owner, Sarah Winchester, that she would live as long as she continued building the house but would die if she stopped. The mansion was under construction for thirty-eight continuous years, and King lifted the details for the ever-expanding Rose Red.

Baxley and his crew scouted the actual Winchester Mystery House but found it was too close to the freeway and that the rooms inside were too small and cramped. After an extensive search, they settled on Thornewood Castle in Tacoma, Washington, for the exterior shots. Since the castle wasn't nearly as sprawling as Rose Red was supposed to be, production designer Craig Stearns and his team built intricate miniatures, which were digitally composited with background plates of downtown Seattle, the setting for the miniseries. Stearns and his crew also built massive sets in a hangar at Sand Point Naval Air Station, replicating King's descriptions of the "freaky" interior of Rose Red.

Having spent so much of the $35 million budget on the look of the film, Baxley and the producers had to assemble a cast of familiar but not budget-busting faces. Nancy Travis, then best known for the TV series *Almost Perfect*, agreed to play Joyce Reardon, a psychology professor specializing in the paranormal who leads a team of ghostbusters into Rose Red. Julian Sands, Judith Ivey, Kevin Tighe, Melanie Lynskey, and Emily Deschanel signed on as members of her team, with David Dukes as Reardon's antagonist, department chair Carl Miller. Filming began in August 2000 and went relatively smoothly until

October 9, when Dukes suddenly died on location, having only completed about two-thirds of his performance.

Rather than let this tragic turn completely derail the production, Baxley and King huddled to rework the script, rewriting some of Dukes' scenes for another character. Baxley also used stuntmen, body doubles, a face double wearing a mask, and unused footage of Dukes for scenes in which his character's presence

Originally intended as a big-screen collaboration with Steven Spielberg on "the ultimate haunted house movie," *Rose Red* ended up as just another ABC miniseries.

was still required. Principal photography wrapped in December 2000, and six months of postproduction, including extensive digital effects work, began.

Again ABC planned an elaborate promotional campaign for the miniseries, this time featuring a tie-novel called *The Diary of Ellen Rimbauer: My Life at Rose Red*. (Despite speculation that King himself has penned the book, it was actually written by best-selling author Ridley Pearson.) Taking a page from the success of *The Blair Witch Project*, ABC marketed *Rose Red* as if it had been based on actual events, even airing a half-hour faux-documentary special called *Unlocking Rose Red: The Diary of Ellen Rimbauer* to build the hype. It paid off initially, as *Rose Red* got off to a better start in the ratings than the previous two King miniseries, reeling in twenty million viewers for its Sunday night premiere. But the two subsequent installments each saw a substantial drop-off, with the concluding segment finishing third in its Thursday night time slot.

It's not hard to figure out why viewers abandoned *Rose Red* as it went along. The production design is undeniably impressive; as he did with *Storm of the Century*, Baxley seamlessly integrates real locations with sets and miniatures. The Rose Red interiors, including false-perspective hallway, trick mirrors, upside-down room, and staircase to nowhere, are a lot of fun. But there are no worthwhile characters to populate them, nor a story compelling enough to hold our attention for more than four hours. In a way, *Rose Red* is exactly what Stephen King always accused Kubrick's *The Shining* of being: a good-looking Cadillac with no engine.

King expanded the feature-length screenplay he worked on with Spielberg to miniseries proportions, with predictable results: *Rose Red* feels at least twice as long as it really needs to be. The first installment is overloaded with backstory, not only of the mansion but of the various characters, who don't even arrive at the house until the end of the episode. Once they've entered Rose Red and things start to go bump in the night, the miniseries settles into a predictable pattern of "Boo!" moments, few of which are genuinely frightening. Part of the problem is that we've seen variations on this story done so many times before, from Robert Wise's *The Haunting* to the 1999 remake (another offshoot of the aborted Spielberg/King collaboration) to *The Legend of Hell House*, based on a Richard Matheson novel with a number of similarities to Shirley Jackson's original.

Another major problem is that it's hard to muster much sympathy for the characters, because unlike the residents of *Storm of the Century*'s Little Tall Island, who were put in an impossible situation quite against their will, these people have put themselves in potential danger on purpose. It doesn't help that most of the characters are at best mildly irritating and at worst thoroughly unlikable. The miniseries is rendered almost completely unwatchable by the intolerable performance of Matt Ross (in makeup and a fat suit, because apparently it's impossible to find an actual overweight actor) as Emery Waterman, the eternally whining, condescending, mama's-boy knockoff of *The Stand*'s Harold Lauder. By the end, the biggest disappointment is seeing how many of the characters have actually survived the ordeal.

To date, *Rose Red* is the last Stephen King miniseries to air on ABC, and the last overall for nearly a decade. The network wasn't quite out of the King business yet: By the time *Rose Red* aired, plans were already in the works for a limited series based on Lars von Trier's *The Kingdom* (to be discussed in chapter 27). But in 2011, when the opportunity arose for ABC to get back in the game, the network couldn't quite pull the trigger.

A Creaky *Bag of Bones*

King's 1998 novel *Bag of Bones* represented a turning point of sorts: It was his first book published by Scribner following a parting of the ways with his longtime home Viking, and it was a major part of a rebranding effort designed to get King taken more seriously. The novel was marketed as a more literary, mature effort than the author's earlier works, even though it was not much of a departure content-wise: A novelist in a small Maine town deals with supernatural forces.

Bruce Willis and his producing partner Arnold Rifkin purchased the movie rights to the novel in 2001, with an eye toward Willis starring as the writer Mike Noonan in a big-budget feature. Willis and Rifkin got at least as far as selecting a director, Peter Care (*The Dangerous Lives of Altar Boys*), but the project failed to gain any traction, and after a few years, the rights reverted to King. That was good news for Mick Garris, who had long wanted to direct a feature version of *Bag of Bones*. Garris and partner Mark Sennet optioned the rights and hired Matt Venne, who had written an episode of Garris's *Masters of Horror* series, to adapt the novel for the screen.

Like Willis and Rifkin before them, Garris and Sennet spent several years trying to set *Bag of Bones* up as a feature film and finding no takers. In 2010, they decided to try television instead. Venne expanded the screenplay into a two-nighter, and Garris took it to the longtime home of the Stephen King miniseries, ABC. The project remained in limbo at the network for about six months before the *Bones* team moved on, this time finding a taker at A&E. Once the basic cable network gave the green light in July 2011, the miniseries went into production almost immediately in order to meet a scheduled December airdate.

Pierce Brosnan, whose work in the film *The Matador* Garris had particularly admired, was cast as Noonan, and Annabeth Gish, who the director had worked with on the TV-movie *Desperation*, as his wife Jo. Melissa George, Matt Frewer (*The Stand*'s Trashcan Man), and Tony Award–winner Anika Noni Rose rounded out the cast. The thirty-nine-day shoot in Nova Scotia was immediately followed by a six-week crash postproduction schedule, for which Garris employed two editors for the first time. They finished in time for the miniseries' scheduled premiere on December 11, 2011. It's a measure of how much the television landscape had changed in the decade since *Rose Red* that the ratings were considered a success for A&E. The first installment drew 3.4 million viewers, a drop in the bucket compared to the ABC heyday but enough to make *Bag of Bones* the top-rated cable program of the night.

Garris had long spoken of his desire to make *Bag of Bones* as "a ghost story for grownups . . . something much more adult and passionate than studios are making now." The story opens with successful author Noonan finishing his latest best seller with the help of his wife Jo (who, as Noonan's lucky charm, always types the last sentence). A few months later, while Noonan is signing books for fans, Jo is struck by a car and killed. A despondent Noonan retreats to their summer cottage on Maine's Dark Score Lake, where he begins to experience strange visions and supernatural visitations. During his stay, he is inadvertently drawn into a custody battle between town bigwig Max Devore (William Schallert) and his daughter-in-law Mattie (George), and begins to unravel a decades-old mystery surrounding the disappearance of torch singer Sara Tidwell (Rose).

Early on, Garris establishes an effective mood of melancholy as Brosnan broods about the lake house, trapped in his memories of Jo. But the story's spooky elements aren't introduced in a way that gels with that atmosphere; they're too frantic, so that *Bag of Bones* is constantly ping-ponging between slow, quiet contemplation and fast, furious mayhem. The visions and dream sequences pile up like cordwood: One dream-within-a-dream turns out to be another dream-within-a-dream, to the point where Brosnan is constantly popping awake in a cold sweat.

By its final hour, *Bag of Bones* has become an exercise in unintentional camp. At one point, Brosnan is knocked into the lake by an elderly woman who then pelts him with stones; later, he battles a possessed tree with a shovel. It's to the actor's credit that the he's able to keep a straight face through all of this, although it would have been nice if, at some point amid the mayhem, we'd gotten an explanation for his British accent. (How he and Matt Frewer could be brothers may be *Bag of Bones*' greatest mystery.) All of which is to say it doesn't play much like a "ghost story for grownups," which is a shame. Cable television would seem to be an ideal landing place for Stephen King's brand of expansive storytelling with graphic elements, but so far that potential hasn't been tapped.

Night Shift

Sometimes They Come Back and Other TV-Movies

De Laurentiis Makes a *Comeback*

After the disappointment of *Maximum Overdrive* in 1986, Stephen King was through with Dino De Laurentiis . . . but De Laurentiis wasn't quite finished with King. The Italian minimogul still held the rights to several stories from the *Night Shift* collection, including "Sometimes They Come Back." By the late 1980s, however, his DEG production company had gone bankrupt, and the producer's clout was greatly diminished. After spending more than two years trying to set up *Sometimes They Come Back* as a theatrical release, De Laurentiis struck a deal with CBS president Jeff Sagansky. He would produce the King adaptation as a TV-movie for the network and sell it theatrically overseas.

Screenwriters Lawrence Konner and Mark Rosenthal were tasked with expanding the short story to feature length. Although "Sometimes They Come Back" was one of the longer stories in *Night Shift* (running forty-five pages in the paperback edition), it still needed to be fleshed out—and, because network television was now involved, toned down a bit. King's story concerns Jim Norman, a high-school teacher who returns to his hometown sixteen years after his brother was stabbed to death by juvenile delinquents who were themselves killed in a car accident shortly after the murder. As students in Norman's class disappear, the greasers begin to return from the grave. After they kill his wife, Sally, Norman studies a book on the occult and summons a demon to get rid of his tormentors once and for all. The screenplay gives Norman a son he didn't have in the story, does away with the demon, and allows Sally to live.

Tom McLoughlin (*Friday the 13th, Part IV: Jason Lives*) signed on to direct the film, which would be shot over five weeks at the end of 1990 in Kansas City and surrounding areas. Tim Matheson (*Animal House*) was cast as Jim Norman, and King veteran Brooke Adams (*The Dead Zone*) agreed to play Sally Norman after the script was tweaked by McLoughlin and Tim Kring. Encouraged by the high ratings of ABC's *It* miniseries, CBS hoped to have *Sometimes They Come Back* ready for February sweeps, but that proved too ambitious a schedule. Instead, the telefilm debuted on May 7, 1991, and fell well short of the network's expectations. It tied for thirty-fifth place in the weekly Nielsen ratings with the first part of *An Inconvenient Woman*, an ABC miniseries based on a novel by Dominick Dunne.

It was a forgettable performance for a forgettable production. As with *Children of the Corn* before it, the contortions necessary to stretch a short story to feature length are all too apparent. McLoughlin's film is padded with flashbacks, dreams, and visions, and its action is so repetitive, it feels much longer than its ninety-eight minutes. The greaser hoodlums from beyond the grave are about as menacing as *Happy Days* villains, and the network's Standards and Practices department ensures that their reign of terror is a bloodless one. The short story's downbeat ending has been replaced with an unambiguously happy finale: Norman even gets a tearful moment of goodbye with the ghost of his

Even after King stopped actively collaborating with him, Dino de Laurentiis retained the rights to several properties, including *Sometimes They Come Back*.

dead brother. Given its lackluster ratings performance and overall mediocrity, it's hard to imagine how *Sometimes They Come Back* could spawn two sequels . . . but as we'll see soon enough, that's exactly what happened.

Quick Turnaround on *Quicksilver Highway*

This one qualifies as half a Stephen King TV-movie. New World Television had asked Mick Garris to write the pilot episode of a potential horror anthology series the company was pitching to ABC. The rough idea behind the project was an ensemble show that would use the same actors in different roles every week. Garris wrote the pilot teleplay, adapting the King story "Chattery Teeth" (published in the *Nightmares & Dreamscapes* collection), as well as a second episode

Mick Garris directed *Quicksilver Highway*, a horror anthology that included an adaptation of King's "The Chattery Teeth."

based on a Clive Barker story called "The Body Politic" (from the fourth volume of the *Books of Blood* series).

When ABC passed on the series, Garris took the project to Fox, which commissioned a two-hour TV-movie (and potential backdoor pilot) based on the two existing scripts. Garris came up with a linking device to tie the scripts together, and production got underway shortly after work on *The Shining* miniseries wrapped, using much of the same crew. Christopher Lloyd signed on to play Aaron Quicksilver, "a collector of rare objects and dark tales, riding the back roads in search of the black heart of America." Raphael Sbarge, Missy Crider, and Garris favorite Matt Frewer all did double-duty in what was originally titled *Route 666* but came to be called *Quicksilver Highway*.

The telefilm aired on Fox on May 13, 1997, only a couple of weeks after *The Shining* miniseries had been broadcast on ABC. It finished a distant fourth in its time slot, scuttling any potential for an ongoing series. "Nobody saw it," Garris later told website IGN. "They had a small videotape release—I think they made like 10,000 copies. The good thing about the video version is that they let me recut it. When we aired it, they forced me to change the order of the two stories. I was able to put in a couple of things—and put the order right—that had not been in the broadcast. It is as intended on the video."

The video version of *Quicksilver* is one of Garris's more enjoyable outings, largely because it's more compact and takes itself much less seriously than his more elephantine King adaptations. "Chattery Teeth" is a goofy story to begin with: At a roadside gas station, a salesman buys an oversized set of wind-up metal teeth, which end up saving his life when he is attacked by a hitchhiker. The shot of the teeth hopping and dragging the body of the hitchhiker into the desert wouldn't have been out of place in an old issue of *Tales from the Crypt*.

The Clive Barker segment, in which Frewer plays a plastic surgeon whose hands literally rebel against him, is even more outlandish, and the wraparound story, with Christopher Lloyd hamming it up in a crazy wig and leather-bar outfit, is suitably bizarre. *Quicksilver Highway* is a minor entry in the catalogue to be sure, but not without its charms.

Hard Times in Desperation

On the set of *The Shining* miniseries, Stephen King and Mick Garris began discussing their next project together: *Desperation*. Based on King's 1996 novel about a psychotic sheriff in a Nevada mining town, the project would be mounted for the big screen—or so they thought. King adapted the novel himself in his usual fashion: by ripping the pages out of the book, a process that enabled him to break the story down into its component scenes and rebuild it as a screenplay. It worked well enough for New Line Cinema to option the script and green-light the project in 1998.

As the budget crept up over $30 million, New Line got cold feet and put the project in turnaround. King and Garris spent the next few years trying to set the film up with another studio, but when Garris started to worry about being pigeonholed as the guy who directs Stephen King movies, the author added a stipulation to any potential deal. As King explained to *Fangoria*'s Bill Warren, "what I'm saying is that if you want to make a deal on *Desperation*, first you have to do a *Mick Garris* picture. That's the deal—take both, or take neither." It was another generous display of loyalty by the author, but in the end, everyone decided to take neither. Everyone except King's old friends at ABC, that is.

Initially, the network hoped to do *Desperation* as another miniseries, four hours over two nights, but Garris resisted. He wanted to do the script King had written for the big screen, with only the most minimal changes for broadcast. It was another take-it-or-leave-it deal, and ABC took it. The director knew right away who he wanted to play the sheriff: Ron Perlman, who had already played a sheriff for Garris in another King adaptation, *Sleepwalkers*. Garris also picked a few other actors he'd worked with before: Steven Weber (*The Shining*), Charles Durning (*The Judge*), Matt Frewer (*The Stand*), and Henry Thomas (*Psycho IV*), as well as one he would work with on a future King adaptation, Annabeth Gish (*Bag of Bones*).

The mining town of Bisbee, Arizona, would fill in for the fictional Desperation, Nevada, while the interior sets were built in the nearby Tucson Convention Center. Filming began, appropriately enough, on Halloween night in 2004. It proved to be the most trying shoot Garris had ever experienced. The locations, weather, special effects, and stuntwork all presented the usual difficulties, but a couple of incidents pushed *Desperation* over the top. A scene in which a trained cougar leaps through a (candy) glass window took eight hours to complete when the animal basically went on strike. More seriously, a fire broke out on the mining set when a light shattered during a cave-in, igniting the dust and causing a giant fireball. The stunt performers and camera crew members were able to get everyone off the set safely, averting what could have been a tragedy.

Filming wrapped in January 2005, but it would be some time before *Desperation* reached the airwaves. Postproduction work wasn't completed in time for the telefilm to air during the May 2005 sweeps period, so an entire year passed before ABC finally scheduled it for a May 23, 2006, premiere. King, for one, was not happy with this decision and took to his website to issue a plea to his fans. "Those of you who are familiar with the wonderful world of television may have noticed that *Desperation*—probably the best TV movie to be made from my work—has been scheduled by ABC to run, not just against *American Idol*, but against the *American Idol* finals! When I see this kind of scheduling, my heart is warmed by how well I have been treated by all my friends at ABC. One can truly say that with friends like this, one doesn't need enemas. Little joke there. But am I bitter? HELL, YES, I AM BITTER!"

King's fears were well founded. While the *American Idol* finale drew over 30 million viewers, *Desperation* could only muster an audience of 7.5 million. (Coincidentally or not, King has not worked with ABC since.) Still, it's probably not fair to blame Simon Cowell and company entirely for the TV-movie's failures. *Desperation* wasn't one of King's better novels to begin with, and while the Garris adaptation has its moments of inspiration, for the most part it lives down to its title.

Desperation's best stretch comes at the very beginning, when Nevada sheriff Collie Entragian (Perlman) pulls over Peter and Mary Jackson (Thomas and Gish). Entragian is actually possessed by a demon called Tak, a scenario anyone who has ever been pulled over by a redneck cop on a deserted stretch of road can believe. Perlman, who describes his role as "15 years of MGM musicals wrapped in a Hitchcock character" on a DVD commentary, is equal parts menacing and amusing as he toys with the couple, and the "desert noir" visuals are effectively desolate. The biggest surprise comes about fifteen minutes into the picture, when Entragian pulls a gun on Peter, who has been set up as the hero of the piece, and shoots him in the gut, killing him. Garris cast his *Psycho IV* star Thomas specifically to play this "Janet Leigh moment," designed to upset audience expectations and create a mood where anything can happen.

Unfortunately, nothing much happens for quite a while. Entragian locks Mary up in the town jail with other unfortunates who have crossed his path: local Tom Billingsley (Durning) and the Carver family. Young David Carver (Shane Haboucha), who recently witnessed the accidental death of his best friend, has become very religious in the wake of the tragedy. Once the prisoners are joined by a few stragglers, including writer John Marinville (Skerrit) and his roadie Steve Ames (Weber), the stage is set for a confrontation between good and evil. How exactly that confrontation plays out is a little sketchy; Perlman disappears from the movie about halfway through, and his absence is keenly felt. Instead, our heroes take on a much more abstracted villain in Tak with the aid of an explicitly Christian God, an overwrought concept that isn't done any favors by the cheesy execution of its explosive finale.

Garris adds a few clever touches along the way, most notably in the way Tak's backstory plays out. Rather than rendering this as a traditional flashback, the director has David view the story of Chinese workers inadvertently releasing Tak from the mine on an old-fashioned nickelodeon viewer. The mine footage is digitally treated to resemble scratchy, sepia-toned film from a long-ago era. But in an effort to keep *Desperation* visually interesting, Garris gets carried away with wide-angle lenses and cartoonish close-ups. The showiness just draws more attention to the fact that there's not much of interest going on here. *Desperation* is too long, of course, but at least it's over with in one night. That would not be the case with a pair of limited-run series King created for network television, both of which would outstay their welcomes.

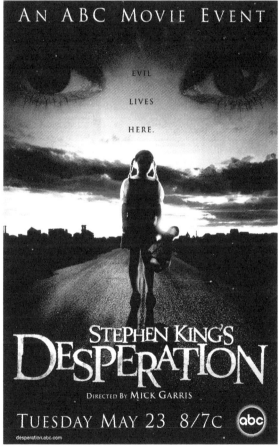

Stephen King's working relationship with ABC ended following *Desperation*, which sat on the shelf for a year before finally airing opposite the *American Idol* finale, much to King's dismay.

Something to Tide You Over

The Short Seasons of *Golden Years* and *Kingdom Hospital*

Running for the Shadows in *Golden Years*

nlike their British counterparts, the American television networks have generally shied away from the limited series. As Stephen King has noted on several occasions, the executives always have the same question: "What if it's a hit?" Of course, a hit TV show is a *good* thing, but in the minds of the suits, it's best if it can run forever, season after season, until every drop of creativity has been drained and every ratings point has been exploited. The vast majority of network shows exist in a state known as "the endless middle," where nothing ever really changes. (Even an acclaimed series like *M*A*S*H* kept the Korean War going for eleven years.)

Once in a blue moon, however, these executives can be persuaded to try something a little different, especially if an entertainment power player like Stephen King is involved. The networks were briefly receptive to new ideas after *Twin Peaks* premiered in the spring of 1990 to blockbuster ratings. Created by David Lynch and Mark Frost, the one-of-a-kind series exploded the traditional prime-time soap opera format, infusing it with Lynch's trademark surrealism, powerful emotional mood swings, and far darker sexual and violent content than network television generally allowed. The show burned brightly but briefly, as ABC buried the second season on Saturday nights and saw its audience dwindle by the week.

Stephen King was a fan, explaining to Peter Applebome of the *New York Times* that the show "turned the whole idea of that continuing soap opera inside out like a sock. If you think of *Twin Peaks* as a man, it's a man in delirium, a man spouting stream-of-consciousness stuff." Moreover, King felt the series might have opened the door for his own stab at weekly television. Over the years, he'd been approached many times about hosting a horror anthology show in the vein of *Alfred Hitchcock Presents*, but had always resisted the idea. When CBS

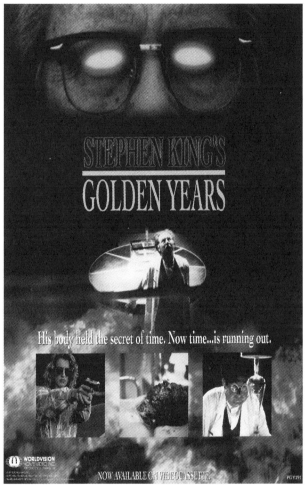

Stephen King envisioned *Golden Years* as a limited series with a beginning, middle, and end. The network saw it differently, until sagging ratings forced the show's premature cancellation.

came calling with such an offer in 1990, King and longtime associate Richard Rubinstein had a counterproposal.

"They wanted me to play America's best-loved bogeyman, to come out each week and say, 'I'm Stephen King. Come with me while I scare the hell out of you,'" King told Greg Baxton of the *Los Angeles Times*. Instead, he offered the network "a novel for television" that wasn't based on any existing work. *Golden Years* was an idea the author had toyed with for years but never committed to writing as a novel. He pitched it to CBS, and the network was willing to take a chance on it as a summer replacement series. The big question remained: How long would it run?

King would have preferred to lock down a limited number of episodes with which to tell the entire story. "A network definition of a TV series is a dramatic show with a beginning, a middle, a middle and a middle," he told Applebome. "I hate that. That's not storytelling as I understand it." But the network executives preferred to hedge their bet in case *Golden Years* turned out the be a golden goose: They approved an eight-hour summer run (a two-hour premiere followed by six weekly one-hour episodes), leaving the door open for the series to continue should the ratings prove irresistible.

King's story concerned a secret government facility where an experiment gone awry douses an elderly janitor with Marvel comics-esque green radiation that causes him to age in reverse. When The Shop (King's spy agency from *Firestarter*) is called in to clean up the mess, the old (but getting younger) man and his wife are forced to go on the run. King wrote the two-hour premiere as well as the next four episodes, then outlined the final two and turned them over to Josef Anderson (*China Beach*) for scripting. Keith Szarabajka of the long-running series *The Equalizer* was cast as the janitor, Harlan Williams. Szarabajka would have to endure up to six hours of makeup a day, depending on his character's age in a given scene. Frances Sternhagen (*Misery*) signed on to play Harlan's wife, Gina, and then-unknown Felicity Huffman won the role of Terry Spann, the facility's head of security. Ed Lauter, R. D. Call, and Bill Raymond filled out the supporting cast.

The series was shot in North Carolina, with Kenneth Fink directing the premiere episode and Allen Coulter and Michael Gornick directing subsequent installments. The network scheduled the premiere for July 16, 1991, with the next six episodes following on subsequent Thursdays. The two-hour opener scored big ratings, tying *Roseanne* for sixth place with a 22 share in the Nielsens. By the time the fifth episode aired, however, the show had dropped into third place in its time slot, and its fate was uncertain. In the August 8 issue of *USA Today*, CBS vice president of special projects Steve Warner was quoted as saying, "We're definitely thinking about bringing it back in the spring . . . What got on the air is what [King] wanted, and he acknowledged that if we brought it back, he could make some style changes."

He wouldn't get the chance. The seventh aired episode ended with a cliff-hanger that went unresolved, as King had envisioned the full story playing out over fourteen or fifteen hours. (If CBS had wanted to continue it beyond that point, King had a contingency plan. As the author explained in an *Entertainment Weekly* article, "We resolved it by creating a character, Terrilyn Spann, who if necessary could carry the series on when Harlan's tale was told. And although I wish Terry nothing but the best, I have to confess that it's still Harlan I care about. And because even his story can't be completely told in the eight-hour summer run of the series, I'm hoping people will like *Golden Years* well enough to bring it back for a full run."

Not enough people liked it well enough to satisfy CBS, which did not pick up an additional order of episodes. King and Rubinstein tried to negotiate a four-hour wrap-up for the series, but as King explained to *Fangoria*, the network was only willing to go as far as a two-hour finale. In the end, there would be no continuation of *Golden Years*, aside from an alternate ending appended to the video release of a heavily condensed four-hour version of the series. As of this writing, all seven episodes of the series are available for viewing on Netflix Instant, with the alternate ending in place of the original broadcast one.

Neither ending is particularly satisfying, but *Golden Years'* problems begin long before its concluding episode. The two-hour premiere establishes the pacing and plotting problems that dog the entire run of the series. After cartoonish mad scientist Dr. Toddhunter (Raymond) ignores the red-light warning on his control board and proceeds with his experiment in regeneration, janitor Harlan is caught in a blast of green light that gradually turns back the clock for him. This revelation doesn't come until the end of the two hours, however; instead, we are treated to an endless series of static interrogation scenes, as General Crewes (Lauter) and security chief Spann (Huffman) attempt to determine exactly what went wrong. The military facility in which most of the episode takes place is given an appealing stylized look in bold shades of red and blue, but the sameness of the scenes becomes numbing, and it's no wonder that audiences initially intrigued by the premise (and King's name) soon grew impatient.

It's not until the third episode that the structure of *The Fugitive* King hoped to emulate kicks in, as Harlan and his wife Gina go on the run with Spann and are pursued by Shop agent Jude Andrews (Call). But pacing remains an issue throughout the series. Initially, the relationship between Harlan and Gina has some emotional heft: She's an old woman watching her husband grow younger and more vital, and is understandably upset and worried that he'll fall out of love with her. Our empathy for her fades, however, as variations on the same scene play out over and over. It's to Sternhagen's credit that Gina doesn't become completely unlikable as she continually frets and nags at the eternally patient Harlan.

The emotional core of the series is also undercut by its cartoonish sci-fi trappings: With his Einsteinian frizz of hair and obsessive mien, Toddhunter is straight out of a 1940s serial. Science is never King's strong suit, but it's especially nonsensical here. At one point, a napping Harlan begins glowing with green light and causes an earthquake and a sunrise in the middle of the night; this happens at the end of an episode and is never referenced again. Later, Toddhunter bathes a clock with the green light, which causes it to run backward and then disappear. Is he experimenting with rejuvenation or with time travel—or is *Golden Years* saying they're the same thing?

We'll never really know, thanks to those two equally unsatisfying endings. In the broadcast version, Andrews and his Shop agents catch up to the fugitives at a hippie commune. Gina apparently dies, Harlan is taken into custody, and Crewes and Spann remain on the run. At episode's end, Andrews says, "There's more. Maybe a little and maybe a lot." That may have been King's little hint to the network, but of course, there was no more . . . at least on television. The video release offers a different outcome: Harlan and Gina escape the commune with Spann. As Andrews catches up to them, Harlan begins to glow green again, and he and Gina disappear. Spann shoots Andrews dead, and she and Crewes ride off into the sunset.

It's a resolution, if an abrupt, silly, and ultimately head-scratching one. Have Harlan and Gina traveled back through time? Teleported to another location? Slipped into an alternate reality? It's anybody's guess, but at least it's clear that *Golden Years* had been a learning experience for King. His next foray into weekly television would be made on his own terms, with no cliff-hanger ending. Ironically enough, it would be based on another television series that never completed its story.

Bloodlines: Lars Von Trier's *The Kingdom*

King was not alone in being inspired by David Lynch's short-lived experiment with *Twin Peaks*. Half a world away, Danish filmmaker Lars von Trier drew inspiration from Lynch when his country's national broadcast network DR approached him about doing a television series in the early 1990s. "I watched *Twin Peaks* on TV and I was thrilled, I must say," von Trier said in a short behind-the-scenes documentary. "It struck me that [Lynch] had very much used his left hand. You can write your name with your right hand, as most people do. Or you can try using your left hand, instead . . . That is the principle by which this series was made."

The series in question was called *Riget* in its home country and *The Kingdom* when released in the United States. Von Trier had been wanting to do a ghost story, and the network's offer put him in mind not only of *Twin Peaks* but of a French series he'd seen as a child called *Bellegegour, the Phantom of the Louvre*. "The advantage of setting a story like that in the Louvre was that the museum was so labyrinthine and difficult to get a grip on," he told interviewer Stig Bjorkman. "So I started wondering if I could think of a similar setting. And I ended up with a hospital, with all its wards and corridors and underground passageways."

Von Trier thought of a real hospital in Copenhagen called Rigshospitalet (Kingdom Hospital), or just Riget (The Kingdom) for short. A haunted hospital would allow Von Trier to employ the usual soap opera and medical drama story lines while kicking up the weirdness factor considerably. He enlisted a cowriter, Niels Vorsel, in the cause, and together they wrote the scripts for the first series of four episodes. Vorsel handled the heavy medical research, which took him into hospitals brimming with narrative possibilities. "When we wrote the series, we based it on true stories. Practically everything is based on events that we just rewrote a bit."

The cast included Ernst-Hugo Jaregard as dyspeptic Swedish consultant Stig Helmer, Kirsten Rolffes as spirit-world believer Mrs. Drusse, Holger Juul Hansen as the clueless hospital administrator Moesgaard, and Udo Kier in a dual role as a demon and an oversized baby. Von Trier shot the series on location in the actual Rigshospitalet, using 16mm film, available light, and a new handheld technique he'd picked up from another TV show. "[W]hat really opened things up for me was an American television series called *Homicide: Life on the Street* by Barry Levinson," von Trier told Lars K. Andersen in 1994. "Levinson started to cross-cut without any concern for which side of the axis the actors were standing on." The resulting visuals have been charitably called sepia-toned, but the show's sickly yellow pallor does suit its setting.

The series premiered on the DR network in 1994, with critics and audiences agreeing it was like nothing they'd ever seen before. The first season's story lines included Mrs. Drusse's attempts at contacting a little girl's ghost; a pathologist's insistence on having a tumor-ridden liver implanted in his own body to further his research; an intern cutting the head off a corpse in hopes of impressing a doctor with whom he's infatuated; and a pair of dishwashers with Down syndrome who act as a gnomic Greek chorus throughout the series. The insanity peaks with the birth of Dr. Judith Peterson's son, a deformed demon-spawn with the head of Udo Kier, whose head pokes out of the womb just in time to bring down the curtain on the first series.

It would take three years before the second of what von Trier envisioned as three series appeared on DR. The network was reluctant to bring *The Kingdom* back until von Trier began negotiating with other potential outlets, at which point the suits relented and backed another four episodes. The weirdness escalated into the realm of the truly bizarre in this second series, which took a more overtly comedic approach than its predecessor. Helger, who had previously taken to the roof of the hospital to issue profane rants against "Danish scum" now addressed his tirades to his own feces. Another doctor is presumed dead after drinking a voodoo potion, only to rise from his coffin days later as an evil version of himself. "Little Brother," as Kier's baby character is called, grows to grotesque proportions even as the relationship between him and his mother becomes oddly touching. Absurd cliff-hangers pile up toward the end, but alas, they would never be resolved.

Von Trier's third and concluding series never came to fruition, partially because DR was still reluctant to finance more of *The Kingdom*, but mostly because several important cast members, including Jaregard and Rolffes, died before the director could get around to it. Judging from his commentary track on the second series, however, it's possible that von Trier would never have followed up on it anyway: He seems genuinely dismayed by the direction of the later episodes. Still, the eight existing episodes, as funny, odd, and absorbing in their way as the best of *Twin Peaks*, are well worth a look . . . as Stephen King learned one night in 1996.

ABC Checks into *Kingdom Hospital*

King was in Colorado during the production of ABC's miniseries version of *The Shining* when he spotted the first series of *The Kingdom* on a video store shelf. It sounded interesting, so he took it back to his hotel room. He ended up watching all four and a half hours in one night, and enjoyed it so much, he approached his producer Mark Carliner the next day with the idea of remaking it for American television. "He said it was the most terrifying thing he'd ever seen, and it was also hysterically funny—an odd combination," Carliner told the *St. Louis Post-Dispatch.*

Carliner flew to Copenhagen to meet with von Trier about the idea. Although von Trier professed himself a fan of King's, he was more interested in seeing a big-screen version of the series, rather than an American television

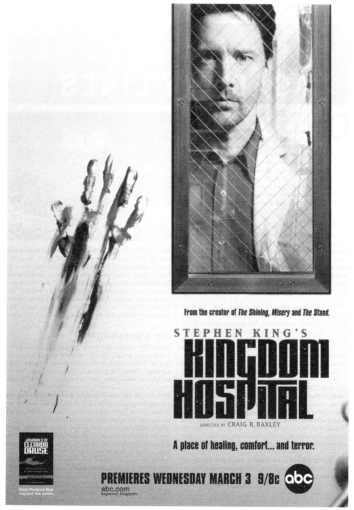

King's second shot at a limited series was based on Lars von Trier's wild and wacky Danish miniseries *The Kingdom*, but something was lost in translation.

adaptation. When Columbia Pictures bought the rights with an eye toward producing a feature film, it looked like the project was over before it got started. After spending a lot of time in the hospital following his 1999 accident, however, King was dead-set on making his own version of *The Kingdom* and incorporating his own experiences.

After Columbia failed several times at launching the project as a feature film, King was able to secure the rights in a swap: He granted the studio the rights to his novella "Secret Window, Secret Garden," which became a movie starring Johnny Depp, and in return he received the keys to *The Kingdom*. King envisioned a fifteen-week limited series that would work as a true novel for television. He approached Richard Dooling, a novelist with a background in medicine, to help him write the show's "bible" and serve as the show's medical consultant. As the writing progressed, Dooling ended up writing four of the episodes, with King himself tackling the other eleven hours.

With all fifteen hours scripted, King and Carliner brought the project to ABC, which agreed to finance and air the series to be called *Kingdom Hospital*. As with *Golden Years*, however, the network wasn't completely sold on the idea of a limited series. Despite King's wishes to tell a complete story with a beginning, middle, and end, ABC wanted to leave the door open a crack for a continuation of *Kingdom Hospital* should it prove to be a ratings success. Carliner agreed. "This should live as a weekly one-hour series," he told the *Post-Dispatch*. "If we're successful, then next season—and hopefully for the next seven seasons—you will see *Kingdom Hospital* on a weekly basis."

Although sticking to his plan to complete his story, King agreed to plant a seed in the final episode that could grow into a second season, with the idea that Dooling would take over as head writer. ABC originally scheduled *Kingdom Hospital* to debut in the fall of 2002. In a highly unusual move, all fifteen hours would be shot in one block, by a single director, as if the series were one long feature film. Craig Baxley, who had directed *Storm of the Century* and *Rose Red*, was brought aboard to take the reins of this ambitious effort.

Carliner noted that having the entire season scripted in advance made casting easier, as actors tend to respond well to seeing their characters' entire arcs play out. The ostensible lead of the ensemble piece went to Andrew McCarthy, the former Brat-Packer best known for *Pretty in Pink* and *Weekend at Bernie's*. "Stephen writes such wonderful, character-driven things that it gives us actors a lot of meat and potatoes to throw at one another," McCarthy told John Crook of the *L.A. Times*. Bruce Davison, a King veteran of *Apt Pupil* and the *Tales from the Darkside* episode "Word Processor of the Gods," also signed on, as did Diane Ladd, Jack Coleman, and Ed Begley Jr. Shooting took place in British Columbia, on stages in Vancouver and exteriors in Richmond. (Unlike *The Kingdom*, the U.S. version didn't shoot in an actual hospital; the Workers Compensation Board building was used for the exteriors.) The shooting schedule ran 150 days, with Baxter directing every scene using the same crew throughout.

Postproduction work on the series involved a great deal of computer-generated imagery, most notably in the creation of Antubis, an oversized supernatural anteater designed by Mark "Crash" McCreery. Artist Jamie Wyeth, King's fellow Mainer, was enlisted to provide the artwork that would be attributed to the character of Peter Rickman, a painter. After several delays, the two-hour premiere episode, "Thy Kingdom Come," was scheduled to air on March 3, 2004. ABC was feeling good enough about the series to commission a second season bible from King and Dooling, which they happily provided.

At first, it appeared the network had a hit on its hands. The two-hour premiere attracted fourteen million viewers, making it the second-highest-rated series debut of the season behind *Cold Case*. But viewership dropped drastically the following week, with only 8.5 million tuning in for the second episode, "Death's Kingdom." By episode five, that number had dwindled to just over five million, and ABC reacted quickly, shifting the series from Wednesday night to an 8:00 p.m. Thursday time slot widely viewed as a death sentence. As Bill Goodykoontz of the *Arizona Republic* put it, "scheduling a show on Thursday nights at 8 is TV's equivalent of pushing a baby carriage into the path of an oncoming train."

Sure enough, the series shed even more viewers over the next four weeks, dropping to a low of 2.6 million for the April 29 episode, "Butterfingers." ABC pulled the series from the schedule altogether, and heads at the fourth-place network began to roll. The final four episodes, including the two-hour finale (titled, appropriately enough, "Finale"), were burned off in June and July, by which time it was clear to everyone that *Kingdom Hospital* would remain the limited series it was originally intended to be.

King used his *Entertainment Weekly* column to sift through the ashes and figure out what went wrong. "So who's to blame for this el floppo? The network? That would be an easy answer—ABC has fallen on hard times—but it won't wash . . . Was it the story? Man, we all thought the idea of ghosts in a modern hospital was a groove, and European audiences flipped for the Lars von Trier version." King came to the conclusion that the series' slow, novelistic build turned off the potential audience. "I realize now, we were asking viewers to give us a week or two, maybe three, and that was more time than most were willing to give."

That may have been part of the problem, but the series' biggest flaw was its scattershot nature: It's never entirely clear what *Kingdom Hospital* is trying to be. For once, the shoe is on the other foot, and it is King adapting someone else's work rather than the other way around. In many ways, the ABC version is faithful to Lars von Trier's *The Kingdom* (first series only; it's not clear whether King ever saw the second series, but even if he did, nothing from the second series makes its way into King's version). The hospital has, of course, been transplanted from Denmark to Lewiston, Maine, but many of the characters and story lines are lifted directly from von Trier. Davison's Dr. Stegman is the arrogant outsider (from Boston rather than Sweden) appalled by the backward ways of Kingdom Hospital, particularly its cheerful dope of an administrator, Dr. Jesse James

(Begley). Diane Ladd is Sally Druse, the perpetual patient who communicates with the spirits trapped in "Swedenborgian space" between our world and the next. McCarthy is Hook, our roguish hero and foil for Stegman.

King also added new characters and story lines to the mix, in particular Peter Rickman, the successful artist and transparent King stand-in. While jogging along the side of the road one morning, Rickman is flattened by a van driven by a stoner distracted by two dogs in the back seat. This plays out almost identically to King's own 1999 accident, leading his wife Tabitha to ask," How many times are you going to relive that accident in your work?" (King's answer: Until I get it behind me.) After being struck by the vehicle, Rickman is visited by the bizarre supernatural entity Antubis, a talking anteater who acts as guardian between life and death. Von Trier's *Kingdom* had plenty of strange stuff in it, but no talking anteater.

The various story lines stagnate for too long while *Kingdom Hospital* gets distracted by tangential characters, such as a neighborhood priest who becomes a Christ figure or a disgraced ballplayer inspired by Bill Buckner's 1986 World Series gaffe. Too often, the series goes for the sort of gratuitous weirdness that characterized much of the second season of *Twin Peaks*. When the medical staff breaks into a song-and-dance routine based on "Na Na Hey Hey Kiss Him Goodbye," it feels completely unmotivated and falls flat. But the show's biggest problem are its characters, as King's gift for creating believable, relatable people largely deserts him here. The cast isn't much help; Davison is amusing enough, but McCarthy brings a smarmy, unlikable quality to Hook, and Ladd's dotty Mrs. Druse quickly grows tiresome.

King does deliver an ending, unlike von Trier, as the core characters venture into the "Old Kingdom," a spirit realm trapping the ghosts of Kingdom Hospital, and find a way to set them free. The final episode is padded with clips from earlier in the series, and it's a chore to get to the end for the "hint" of things to come in a potential second season: Stegman, who has been driven mad, in the company of a surviving evil spirit. The scene lands with a thud, but it doesn't really matter: There would be no second life for *Kingdom Hospital*.

Home Delivery

Week-to-Week with *The Dead Zone, Haven,* and *Under the Dome*

Recharting the Dead Zone

I n 2001, the now-defunct UPN network commissioned a pilot based on *The Dead Zone* (to which UPN's parent company, Paramount, owned the rights). Producer Lloyd Segan had pitched the network on an ongoing series about the book's main character, psychic Johnny Smith. Once UPN executives gave him the go-ahead, Segan brought longtime *Star Trek* writer Michael Piller aboard. "My agent called me to ask me if I would be interested," Piller told Ken P. of fan site IGN. "I had not read the book, and I don't recall seeing the movie—I might have seen it a long time ago—but I did go back and read the book and see the movie, and I was very intrigued."

To Piller, the most exciting aspect of *The Dead Zone* concept was its elasticity. A hero with psychic powers could find himself at the center of any number of stories. "The powers can take us anywhere we want to go—we can do medical mysteries, we can do legal mysteries, we can do police drama . . . We can do anything with this guy . . . Why limit him to one thing?" The network suits didn't see it that way. UPN president Dean Valentine wanted a defined franchise that would fit neatly under a particular genre umbrella. In addition, serialized dramas were on the outs at the time. Pulling extended arcs from King's novel (such as the search for the Castle Rock Killer) and playing them out over the course of a season or more wasn't going to fly.

Still, UPN agreed to finance the pilot. The first indication that the series was going to be a very different animal than either the book or the Cronenberg film came when Anthony Michael Hall won the leading role of Johnny Smith. According to Piller, Hall was his first choice for the part, based on his performance as Bill Gates in the TV-movie *Pirates of Silicon Valley*. Nicole de Boer, who Piller had worked with on *Star Trek: Deep Space Nine*, was cast as Johnny's fiancée Sarah, who marries another man while Johnny is in a coma. Sarah's husband Walt Bannerman (Chris Bruno) is a combination of two characters from the book: Walt Hazlett and Sheriff George Bannerman. Two new characters were created for the pilot. The part of Reverend Gene Purdy, both a father figure and a nemesis for Johnny, was played by Michael Moriarty in the (unaired) UPN pilot but taken over by David Ogden Stiers for the series. Relative unknown John Adams won the role of Johnny's physical therapist and eventual sidekick Bruce Lewis.

The pilot was shot in 2001, but when UPN's fall schedule appeared in May of that year, *The Dead Zone* wasn't on it. In July, the network announced tentative plans to premiere the series as a midseason replacement, but Valentine was already hedging, telling *USA Today*, "we're happy to have other networks pick up some of our development costs." That is, in fact, what happened. The Sci-Fi and USA networks both expressed interest in the project,

The weekly version of *The Dead Zone* was a decidedly lighter take on the material than David Cronenberg's film. Anthony Michael Hall starred as psychic Johnny Smith.

but it was ultimately the latter that took over *The Dead Zone* as a weekly series.

The show premiered on June 16, 2002, with the revised pilot "Wheel of Fortune." Cowritten by Piller and his son Shawn and directed by Robert Lieberman, the episode scored big numbers for the network, setting a record for the highest-rated basic cable drama series of all time with 6.4 million viewers. Ratings held strong as the first thirteen episodes played out over the summer, and in July, USA renewed the series for a second season.

If nothing else, the first season of *The Dead Zone* is a fascinating object lesson in the craft of translating a novel or film to the weekly television format. The plot that unfolds in "Wheel of Fortune" is familiar to any fan of King's book or Cronenberg's movie: After taking his fiancée Sarah to the carnival and proposing marriage to her, high school science teacher Johnny Smith has a near-fatal car accident that plunges him into a coma for six years. When he awakes, he finds that, as he explains in the teaser that opens each episode, "Everything has changed, including me." Sarah is married to the sheriff and they have a son, although Johnny is the biological father. And Johnny has been imbued with a gift (or curse): "With one touch, I can see things. Things that happened. Things that will happen."

By the end of the second episode, it's clear that UPN's dictate against heavy serialization has carried over to USA as well. The mystery of the Castle Rock Killer is wrapped up, leaving the rest of the season to play out as a series of stand-alone procedurals. All of the darker elements from the novel and film have been softened. Anthony Michael Hall may be a little quirkier than the traditional leading man for such a show, but he's certainly a warmer presence than Christopher Walken—all the better to invite him into your home week after week. And the character of Johnny Smith has had most of his rough edges sanded down: He may not be thrilled with what's happened to him, but he's far from the tortured soul King created.

To that end, Segan and the Pillers have supplied Johnny with a surrogate family of sorts to ensure he'll never become the embittered loner of the novel and film. In addition to his buddy Bruce, Johnny is also able to maintain a friendship with Sarah, and eventually Walt. Even his son J. J. eventually learns the truth about his parentage, and in later seasons, seems to spend as much time with his biological father as he does with his parents. Love interests are fleeting; the first two seasons feature an appealing flirtation with *Bangor Daily News* reporter Dana Bright (Kristen Dalton), but once their relationship is consummated, Bright soon fades from the scene.

The first season finale, "Destiny," introduces an ongoing antagonist for Johnny familiar to fans of *The Dead Zone*'s earlier incarnations: Congressional candidate Greg Stillson, played by Sean Patrick Flanery. As in King's book and the movie, Johnny shakes Stillson's hand and is overpowered by an apocalyptic vision. Unlike its predecessors, however, *The Dead Zone* television series exhibits no particular urgency about this turn of events. Stillson turns up several times each season for another close encounter with Johnny, but our psychic hero is never able to make anything stick, and the bleak future continues to lurk. In the second season episode, "Zion," we are treated to an alternate reality depicting what Johnny's life would have been like had he never met Bruce. Here and only here we see the darker, more desperate Johnny Smith who would resort to assassinating Stillson to prevent a future disaster. The implication is clear: This isn't the same Johnny, so don't expect the same outcome.

Despite the compromises made by the creative team, the weekly version of *The Dead Zone* is not without its pleasures. The flexible format Piller touted in his preair interviews may have been a bit overstated—most episodes settle into a familiar "psychic detective" mode—but Johnny's powers provide some visual variety to the series. (As in the movie, Johnny appears within his visions, sometimes as an observer and sometimes in place of one of the participants, a trick that allows Hall to play a variety of characters.) Episodes like "Precipitate," in which Johnny experiences visions from six different points of view, and "Shaman," in which he and a long-dead Indian seer are able to communicate across time, shake up the formula in fun ways. The cast is appealing and the actors have good chemistry, although none of them come close to suggesting actual Mainers. (The series is set in the fictional Cleaves Mills, Maine, and the first five seasons were shot in the Vancouver area, which doesn't do a particularly good job of simulating Maine either.)

Perhaps inevitably, the series grew stale over time. The fourth- and fifth-season episodes are particularly repetitive, and the overarching Armageddon

The supporting cast of *The Dead Zone* TV series included Nicole de Boer, Chris Bruno, and David Ogden Stiers.

plot only becomes more absurd as time goes on and the show keeps spinning its wheels. Michael Piller died in November 2005, while the fourth season was still airing, and by the time the fifth season ended its run in August 2006, the future of the series was in serious doubt. The fourth and fifth seasons had been shot together, as USA had originally ordered a twenty-two-episode season four before deciding to split those episodes between two seasons. By the time the network agreed to a sixth season, so much time had passed since the show had been in production that many members of the cast and crew, including the entire writing staff, had taken other jobs.

The search for fresh blood brought Lloyd Segan and Shawn Piller to the doorstep of Scott Shepherd, producer of shows like *Tru Calling* and *Reunion*. Shepherd agreed to join *The Dead Zone* as executive producer and showrunner, the first of many wholesale changes for the sixth season. The production relocated to Montreal, which made a much better match for the Maine setting, and as viewers learned in the sixth-season premiere "Heritage," the cast was trimmed. That episode saw the death of Walt Bannerman as well as the unceremonious departure of Bruce Lewis. It also brought the beginning of a change in Johnny's relationship to now-Vice President Greg Stillson: After the death of one of Stillson's shady advisors, Johnny has a new, Armageddon-free vision of the future.

As the season progresses, a love triangle develops among Johnny, Sarah, and Stillson, who has his eye on the presidency and could use a ready-made family like Sarah and J. J. In the final episode, "Denouement," Johnny learns that his father, long presumed dead, is still alive and being manipulated by Stillson. (Tom Skerritt, who played Sheriff Bannerman in the *Dead Zone* movie, guest stars as Herb Smith.) Stillson's "good guy" facade slips during a fight with Sarah, and he knocks J. J. to the floor, resulting in a "like father, like son" moment in which both Johnny and J. J. have visions revealing that Armageddon is back on track. The episode ends with Johnny, Sarah, and J. J. together but the potential apocalypse still unresolved.

No resolution was forthcoming. *The Dead Zone*, which had seen its viewing audience decline to little over two million viewers, was officially canceled in December 2007. Although there was some talk of a TV-movie that would tie up all the loose ends, that never materialized. But the creative team behind the series would soon find another Stephen King property to bring to the small screen on a weekly basis.

The Colorado Kid Finds a Haven

In 2005, a paperback-only novel by Stephen King was published by Hard Case Crime, a new imprint dedicated to the sort of hard-boiled crime novels with lurid covers King had grown up reading. *The Colorado Kid* was a short book by King's standards (184 pages), and it proved somewhat controversial when readers discovered that the author hadn't supplied a resolution to the story's murder mystery. That didn't stop ABC from exploring the possibility of turning the novel into a TV series, however. As King told *Entertainment Weekly* in November 2007, the pilot script by Jim Dunn and Sam Ernst for a show then titled *Sanctuary* was "closer to *The X-Files* than *Supernatural*." King further shared that he had a small stake in the potential series, "but it's not something that keeps me up nights, the way *Kingdom Hospital* did."

That's a good thing, because otherwise King wouldn't have slept for a while. Nearly two years would pass before E1 Entertainment announced plans for thirteen episodes of the show now titled *Haven*. Dunn and Ernst were signed as executive producers, along with the *Dead Zone* team of Lloyd Segan, Shawn Piller, and showrunner Scott Shepherd. *Variety*'s description of the show didn't sound much like *The Colorado Kid*, however. The trade paper reported that the series "centers on a spooky town in Maine where cursed folk live normal lives in exile. When those curses start returning, FBI agent Audrey Parker is brought in to keep those supernatural forces at bay—while trying to unravel the mysteries of Haven."

The deal with E1 meant that the series no longer had a home at ABC; rather, it would be shopped around to the highest bidder. In December 2009, SyFy (formerly the Sci-Fi Channel) announced that it had acquired *Haven* for broadcast in 2010. Emily Rose (*John from Cincinnati*) was cast in the lead role of FBI agent Audrey Parker, whose investigation of a murder in the small town of Haven, Maine, leads her to discover her own surprising personal connection to the town. Supporting roles were filled by Lucas Bryant (Haven police officer Nathan Wuornos), Nicholas Campbell (Nathan's father and boss, Police Chief Garland Wuornos), and Eric Balfour (smuggler Duke Crocker). The thirteen-episode season was shot in Nova Scotia, with the South Shore town of Lunenburg serving as the primary stand-in for Haven, Maine.

Haven premiered on July 9, 2010, with the appropriately titled "Welcome to Haven." In the episode, Audrey Parker's routine trip to a coastal Maine town takes a turn for the bizarre when she learns of "The Troubles," the residents' term for the supernatural powers afflicting many of the townspeople. (In this case, it's guest star Nicole de Boer's ability to control the weather.) When the editors of the *Haven Herald* show Audrey a photo from an old issue of the newspaper of a woman bearing a striking resemblance to the FBI agent, she decides to stick around town for a while.

In practice, this means *Haven*

The SyFy original series *Haven* is ostensibly based on King's short novel *The Colorado Kid*, but has little in common with its source.

essentially turns into a monster-of-the-week show. True to King's word, the series has much more in common with *The X-Files* than anything in his novel *The Colorado Kid*. As is typical for SyFy shows, the special effects tend toward the cheesier end of CGI. Rose is an appealing lead, and Bryant brings an almost subliminally dry humor to the proceedings, but there's not much chemistry between them. Balfour is the rogue with a heart of gold we've seen a million times before, and like *The Dead Zone* before it, *Haven* is short on authentic Maine characters. (As it did in *Dolores Claiborne*, however, Lunenburg makes an effective stand-in for coastal Maine.)

Still, *Haven* performed well enough to warrant a second season from SyFy. (Well enough by SyFy standards, that is: The audience declined from a high of 2.3 million for the premiere to 1.7 million for the season finale, "Spiral.") The first season ended with a cliff-hanger, as Audrey was confronted by a woman claiming to be FBI agent Audrey Parker. The second season placed a larger emphasis on the big-picture mythology, with Audrey coming to realize she is not who she thought she was all along. And while the series continued to have little to do with King's novel besides the similar newspapermen characters and the long-ago murder of the Colorado Kid, it did incorporate a growing number of references to King's other works. The second-season premiere, "A Tale of Two Audreys," featured a boy sailing a paper boat down the street and into the sewer (as in *It*), "Love Machine" revolved around machines coming to life (as in *Maximum Overdrive*), and so on.

Although ratings continued to dwindle, SyFy renewed *Haven* for a third season, which saw a slight boost in viewership. The series continued to improve creatively as well, with new revelations about Audrey's past and the history of the Troubles. On December 14, 2012, the penultimate season-three episode, "Reunion," was pulled from the schedule due to its echoes of the Sandy Hook shootings earlier that day. That episode, along with the season finale, "Thanks for the Memories," instead aired together a month later. By then, SyFy had renewed *Haven* for a fourth season, which began production in May 2013.

A Peek under the Dome

DreamWorks TV optioned the rights to Stephen King's 2009 novel *Under the Dome* within days of its publication, with an eye toward King and Steven Spielberg executive producing a cable miniseries based on the book. Two years later, Showtime announced that it would carry the series, to be written by Brian K. Vaughan, who created the long-running comic book *Y: The Last Man* and wrote for *Lost* in its third through fifth seasons. In 2012, Showtime put the series in turnaround when the cable outlet's entertainment president, David Nevins, decided it wasn't a good fit for the network. He recommended the project to Nina Tassler at CBS, and in November 2012, the Tiffany Network ordered thirteen episodes of *Under the Dome*, to air in summer 2013.

A familiar question arose: Would this be a self-contained limited series, or could the story continue if ratings proved favorable? At a March 2013 appearance at WonderCon, Vaughan signaled the latter. "Vaughan said King gave them his blessing early on to expand the scope for the series," *Entertainment Weekly* reported. "'He told us, "Really use the book as a jumping off point. Use the characters, use the themes, but don't be afraid to go to new places."' said Vaughan . . . With a 13 episode order and a big story to tell, producers said they're, naturally, hoping for a long run. Whenever the end does come, however, 'we have a final episode in mind that's different from the book,' says Vaughan. 'There's a very cool, unexpected end to this dome, I think.'"

Filming began in a familiar place for a King production, Wilmington, North Carolina, on February 28, 2013. Niels Arden Oplev, who directed the

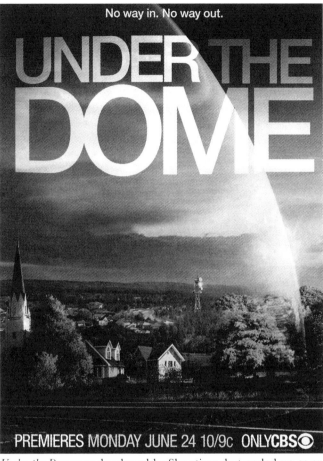

Under the Dome was developed by Showtime, but ended up as an unexpected summer hit on CBS.

Swedish version of *The Girl with the Dragon Tattoo*, was behind the camera, with a cast including Mike Vogel, Rachelle Lefevre, Colin Ford, and Dean Norris.

The premiere episode, airing June 24, 2013, suggests that Vaughn and company have done exactly as King advised in using his book as a jumping-off point while introducing some new wrinkles. As in the novel (and, as many wags have pointed out, as in the *Simpsons* movie), the town of Chester's Mill is inexplicably sealed off from the rest of the world by a transparent dome of unknown origin. How to visualize this threat that can't be seen? Oplev delivers an unforgettable image as a cow is sliced neatly in two, one half toppling over, the other sliding down the exterior of the dome, leaving a streak of blood behind. (A later CGI shot of a plane exploding against the side of the dome is somewhat less effective.)

The first hour effectively hopscotches around Chester's Mill, introducing us to the ensemble cast of characters: Dale "Barbie" Barbara (Vogel), an Army vet and drifter who was just passing through when the dome came down; Julia Shumway (Lefevre), the editor of the local paper, with whom Barbie develops an early flirtation; "Big Jim" Rennie (Norris), used car salesman and the true power in town; Rennie's son Junior, a spoiled, violent punk; and so on. The stage is set for a power struggle, as well as a battle for survival when the food and water supplies begin to run low.

With its lingering mysteries and group of disparate characters forced to find a way to coexist without outside help, the pilot inevitably recalls *Lost*. (The presence of Jeff Fahey, who played the pilot Frank Lapidus on that series, only draws attention to the resemblance.) Despite its strong start, both creatively and from a ratings standpoint (the premiere drew over 13 million viewers), the first season lost its way as it increasingly deviated from King's novel. The plot grew ever more convoluted and silly, and when CBS renewed the series for a second season, it became clear that no resolution was forthcoming anytime soon. With King himself tentatively set to pen the second-season premiere, it remains to be seen whether *Under the Dome* can recover from its early missteps.

Sometimes They Come Back

Sequels and Remakes

Sometimes Dead Is Better

A Return to Salem's Lot, Pet Sematary Two, and Other Needless Sequels

Creepshow 2 & 3

In the years before Stephen King had amassed the clout to dictate the terms of his movie contracts, sequel rights were often included in the deals he signed with producers and studios. In almost every case, King had nothing to do with the sequels that were made, no say over their creative content, and no interest in seeing them made at all. The one notable exception was *Creepshow 2,* which both King and George Romero had expressed interest in making even before the first movie reached theaters. When Romero left Laurel Entertainment in 1985 to pursue his own projects, it became clear that he would not be available to direct the sequel. King still wanted to keep the band together, though, so instead of scripting *Creepshow 2* himself, he wrote a detailed outline from which Romero wrote the screenplay.

"I sat down and did a sort of notebook," King told Paul Gagne. "I pretty much scripted the wraparound story, where this kid is chased by a bunch of juvenile delinquents, except they changed it from live action to animation." King sent his stories to Romero, who adapted them into the shooting script. "The notes I sent him were pretty detailed, and they even had some dialogue, but George really carried it off." One story about a dead bowling team, written in the style of EC's grisly baseball yarn "Foul Play," was cut before filming began. Another, "The Cat from Hell," was also cut, and later recycled for the *Tales from the Darkside* movie. That left three segments plus a wraparound story in search of a director.

Michael Gornick, a former Romero associate who had cut his teeth directing episodes of the *Tales from the Darkside* TV series, was handpicked to helm the sequel. Warner Bros., which had released the first *Creepshow,* passed on the second, so it was a much lower-budgeted horror anthology (roughly $3.5 million) that began production in Prescott, Arizona, in September 1986. Exteriors for two of the segments, "The Raft" and "Old Chief Wood'nhead," were shot in

Arizona. The third segment, "The Hitchhiker" (along with some "Wood'nhead" interiors), was shot in Maine, marking the first time any King adaptation had actually been filmed in his home state. (King contributed a much smaller cameo to "The Hitchhiker" than he had to the original *Creepshow*.)

Released by New World Pictures on May 1, 1987, *Creepshow 2* fizzled at the box office with a $3.5 million opening weekend. Given its low budget, its final haul of $14 million wasn't completely disastrous; creatively, however, the picture looks like leftovers. The first segment, "Old Chief Wood'nhead," features the biggest stars in the movie; given that they are George Kennedy and Dorothy Lamour, you can see why the youth market didn't exactly flock to *Creepshow 2*. This story of a cigar store Indian that comes to life in order to exact vengeance on behalf of its kindly owner sets a sluggish pace for the film: It's as predictable as it is interminable. The middle story, "The Raft," features an irritating crop of eighties teens being terrorized by what looks like a giant shredded Hefty bag. The only segment on par with the original *Creepshow* is the third, "The Hitch-Hiker," in which Lois Chiles is terrorized by the revenant of a hitcher she's hit with her car. The wraparound segment is mostly rendered in animation on par with Saturday morning cartoons of the time (which is to say it's terrible), and the first film's clever comic-book-come-to-life conceit hardly registers here.

Still, *Creepshow 2* is a masterpiece of modern horror when compared to *Creepshow 3* (or *III*, as it's sometimes listed). This 2006 direct-to-video disaster was made without the participation of any of the original *Creepshow* creators: None of its segments are based on Stephen King stories, nor did King, George Romero, or Richard Rubinstein have anything to do with its production. Instead, Taurus Entertainment acquired the rights to the title (along with *Day of the Dead*) in order to produce a dirt-cheap, in-name-only sequel for the home video market. The comic book conceit is gone; instead, the team of writers (including directors Ana Clavell and James Glenn Dudelson) have set the five interconnected tales in the same town. The segments range from the nonsensical ("Alice," in which a magical remote control causes a bratty teen to sprout unsightly blotches all over her face and body) to the truly moronic ("Haunted Dog," about a hot dog gone bad). Often found on the IMDb user's poll of the 100 worst movies ever made, *Creepshow 3* is a must-avoid for even the most ardent King completist.

A Return to Salem's Lot

In the mid-eighties, high-minded Hollywood executives figured out a new way to capitalize on the burgeoning home video market. In 1985, a no-budget slasher movie called *Blood Cult* was released on VHS, with a tagline on the box proclaiming, "The first movie made for the home video market. Might just scare you to DEATH!" The latter claim was dubious, but the implication of the former claim was clear: Why not bypass an expensive theatrical release altogether, particularly if the movie in question has easily exploitable elements . . . or better yet, a very familiar title?

That was the reasoning behind a deal Warner Bros. struck with cult film-maker Larry Cohen to direct two straight-to-video sequels to existing properties. After all, your average video store patron finding a sequel to *It's Alive!* in the horror section probably wouldn't know nor care whether the movie had ever received a proper theatrical release. One of the movies included in the deal was indeed *It's Alive III: Island of the Alive.* The other was a very tenuous sequel to *Salem's Lot.*

It's Alive III was at least a sequel to two movies Cohen had written and directed in the first place. But while Cohen had been one of the writers who attempted to adapt *Salem's Lot* when it was in development as a feature at Warner Bros., his script had been rejected long before the novel became a CBS mini-series. Now he would finally get a chance to put his own spin on the material with *A Return to Salem's Lot.* Although Cohen's movie would be credited as being "based on characters created by Stephen King," that wasn't the case at all. None of the characters from the original *Salem's Lot* return; only the name of the town and the vampire concept remain from King's work.

In Cohen's version, the vampires have actually been in Salem's Lot for hundreds of years, having fled from persecution and established their home base in the small Maine town. Anthropological filmmaker Joe Weber (Cohen's frequent star Michael Moriarty) stumbles upon the secret when he arrives at the cottage he inherited from his aunt with his bratty teenage son Jeremy in tow. The vampires, led by Judge Axel (Andrew Duggan), don't intend to feed on Joe; instead, they want him to write their "Bible," a true accounting of their history and behavior. (As opposed to those tall tales like, presumably, Stephen King's *'Salem's Lot.*) Joe is surprisingly amenable to this plan, but has a change of heart when his son starts spending his time in the company of the town's child vampires (particularly a little blonde girl played by a very young Tara Reid).

Cohen brings a few clever touches to his vampire mythology—for instance, the Salem's Lot elders are all rich, having spent the past several hundred years investing in real estate—but his usual wit and energy are in short supply here. The production values are shoddy, with frequently choppy editing and notice-able sound dropouts, and for the most part, the acting is terrible. Even Moriarty, who usually delivers weirdly memorable B-movie performances in Cohen works (most notably in *Q* and *The Stuff*), is off his game here. The movie only comes alive when legendary filmmaker Samuel Fuller shows up as a Nazi hunter. Fuller sinks his teeth into the material in a way no one else, not even Cohen, does: He chews down the scenery and leaves nothing standing.

Pet Sematary Two

The success of *Pet Sematary* in 1989 ensured a sequel was forthcoming, but by the time Paramount Pictures was ready to go forward, neither Stephen King nor Laurel Entertainment were involved. Instead, Ralph S. Singleton, who had served as an associate producer on the original movie, formed a new company called Columbus Circle to produce the film for Paramount on a lower budget. Mary Lambert agreed to return to direct the sequel with less time and less money, despite the fact that she was pregnant at the time shooting began.

"I give a lot of credit to the success of the first one and to Mary for saying, 'Sure, let's go and do it,'" Singleton told interviewer Patricia Ross. "Mary took 60 or 61 days to do the original film at about 10½ million dollars." By contrast, the follow-up was scheduled for a forty-day shoot (which it exceeded due to unforeseen circumstances) and an $8 million budget. Fortunately, Singleton didn't have to pay any returning cast members, as most of them had been killed off in the first movie. Instead, the script by Richard Outten focused on a teenage boy who is forced to relocate to Ludlow, Maine, with his father after his mother is killed in a freak accident.

Edward Furlong, the young star of *Terminator 2*, was cast as the boy, Jeff Matthews. The other recognizable faces in the film are Anthony Edwards, who plays Jeff's veterinarian father Chase, and Clancy Brown (*The Shawshank Redemption*) as Kennebago County Sheriff Gus Gilbert. This time around, Maine would not play itself in the film, forcing Singleton and Harron to find a match for the setting elsewhere. After searching Texas and North Carolina, they found their location. "Within two days in Georgia, we found 80% of the locations we needed. That was really kind of a phenomenon," Singleton told Ross. "I would say that probably here in Georgia, there was no increase in the cost of the crew, probably a little less, because there're more crew members available out of Atlanta than say Bangor, Maine." The Indian burial ground from the first movie was recreated on Mount Arabia, a preserve for endangered plants.

The shoot ran six days over schedule, which probably should have been expected given the old Hollywood adage about never working with children or animals; *Pet Sematary Two* had both. "We have two great animal trainers on this show, and two really great dogs," Lambert told Ross. "But, they're trained to do things that dogs normally do. It's really hard to train them to do things that zombie dogs would do." For certain scenes, such as close-ups of a dog attacking a human, a fully articulated puppet was used in place of the real animals.

Released on August 28, 1992, the sequel (also known as *Pet Sematary II*) didn't come close to matching the success of its predecessor. It opened in third place with a $4.8 million weekend and finished with a little over $17 million—not even one-third of the amount the first *Pet Sematary* earned. Reviews were dismal; *Toronto Star* critic Craig MacInnis wrote, "Some plots deserve to be buried in a plot, and this is one of them."

It's hard to dispute that point, but the sequel still might have been worth seeing had Harron and company gone completely over-the-top with the premise, pushing it into the realm of black comedy. The film makes a couple of nods in that direction—most notably through the casting of Clancy Brown, who plays up his already striking resemblance to Fred Gwynne by adopting the actor's *Pet Sematary* accent—but for the most part, Harron seems intent on sticking to the downbeat tone of the first movie. That makes for a rather dull rehash (particularly with Furlong's sullen performance front and center), with only a few glimpses of the wilder sequel that might have been.

Sometimes They Come Back . . . Again and . . . For More

The Dino De Laurentiis–produced television adaptation of *Sometimes They Come Back* didn't make much of a splash in the United States, but it performed well as a theatrical release internationally. Producer Michael Meltzer (along with Mark Amin and Barry Barnholtz) acquired the rights from De Laurentiis in order to produce a sequel, which would be billed in the credits as being "based on the characters created by Stephen King" in the short story "Sometimes They Come Back." That's not actually the case, as what came to be called *Sometimes They Come Back . . . Again* puts new characters through the same paces as its predecessor.

Meltzer and releasing company Trimark Pictures were impressed with a USC thesis film called *Trap Door,* directed by Adam Grossman. Grossman, a huge Stephen King fan, was hired to direct the film and rewrite the first-draft screenplay by Guy Riedel. Working on a $3 million budget and a thirty-day schedule, Grossman shot on location in the Los Angeles area, primarily at an old Victorian home in Pasadena. His cast included Michael Gross (best known as the father on *Family Ties*), Alexis Arquette, and a young Hilary Swank, several years before her breakthrough in *Boys Don't Cry.* Although Trimark had hoped to release the 1996 sequel theatrically, it ended up going straight to video in the United States.

Aside from its time-capsule value as evidence of Swank's short-lived career as a scream queen, *. . . Again* holds almost no interest. Gross delivers a listless, paycheck-cashing performance as a psychologist who returns to his hometown only to find himself haunted by his childhood tormentors. One of them is played by Arquette, who seems to be under the impression he's been cast as Batman's arch-nemesis, the Joker. Grossman adds a devil-worshipping cult to King's original concept, which adds little fear but plenty of unconvincing latex makeup to the proceedings.

Three years later, Grossman cowrote the third installment in the series, *Sometimes They Come Back . . . For More.* Directed by Daniel Zelik Berk, this unworkable blending of King's concept with a low-rent rip-off of John Carpenter's *The Thing* is also an unsuccessful attempt to turn chipmunk-voiced sitcom star Faith Ford into an action hero. Set at an Army outpost in Antarctica, *..For More* concerns a pair of military police officers investigating a massacre on the base, and their discovery of demonic activity, reanimated corpses, dogs and cats living together, and the most tenuous possible connection to the first two movies. Not that anyone cared at this point. Given the indifference that greeted this straight-to-video release, it seems Trimark finally got the message: Please don't come back . . . anymore.

The Rage: Carrie 2

Making a sequel to a movie in which the title character (and almost everyone else) died at the end might seem a daunting proposition, but if there's potential money to be made, Hollywood can always find a way. So it was with this much-belated follow-up to Brian De Palma's 1976 adaptation of Stephen King's first novel. By the late 1990s, teen horror movies were all the rage again, with films like *Scream* and *I Know What You Did Last Summer* topping the box office charts. It was inevitable that *Carrie* producer Paul Monash and United Artists, which had released the 1976 film, would finally exercise their sequel rights and unleash

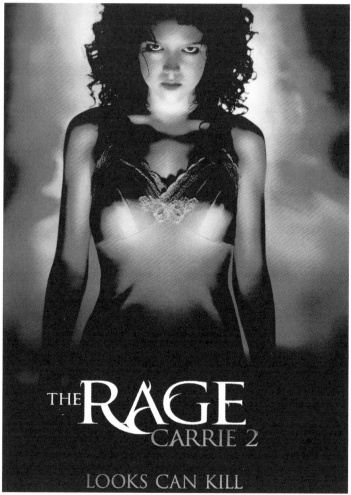

A sequel to a film in which the title character had died at the end didn't seem like a promising idea. *The Rage: Carrie 2* did nothing to dispel that impression.

another round of teleki-
netic mayhem.

It took a little longer
than expected. Originally
announced as *The Curse*
in 1996, the sequel went
through several titles,
including the less-than-
inspiring *Carrie 2: Say You're
Sorry*, before settling on *The
Rage: Carrie 2*. (King had
written a Bachman novel
called *The Rage*, which also
centered on high school
violence, but that's coincidental: The author had
no involvement with the
sequel and thought it was
a terrible idea.) Rafael
Moreau (*Hackers*) wrote
the script, but production
did not get underway until
1998. Original director
Roger Mandel left the project after a week of shooting
and was replaced by Katt
Shea (*Poison Ivy*).

The only cast member
of the original film to
return was Amy Irving,
reprising her role as Sue
Snell. According to the

Of the original cast of Brian De Palma's *Carrie*, only Amy Irving
returned for the woeful sequel.

movie's press kit, Irving only agreed to return after receiving De Palma's blessing. (Sissy Spacek does appear in flashbacks, but they are clips from the original
film, the use of which she had to approve.) Emily Bergl won the role of "the
new Carrie," Rachel Lang, a telekinetic teen who attends the high school built
to replace the one destroyed by Carrie in the first movie. Sue Snell is now the
guidance counselor at the school, and as one of the few survivors of Carrie's
rampage, she alone suspects Lang shares the same power.

Shot in the spring of 1998 in Charlotte, North Carolina, *The Rage: Carrie 2*
was released on March 12, 1999, earning $7 million in its opening weekend en
route to a disappointing total haul of $17.7 million. Teens chose to spend their
movie dollar on *Cruel Intentions* instead, and it's easy to see why when you notice
that *The Rage* only truly comes to life during the brief clips from De Palma's

Carrie. It was unwise of Shea to include these clips, as they only serve to make crystal clear what a shallow and unimaginative sequel she's directed.

Far from the tormented character played by Spacek, Bergl's Rachel is a generally well-adjusted, if slightly unpopular, teenager surrounded by stock types like the Jock, the Mean Girl, the Nerdy Friend, and every other one-dimensional high school caricature you can imagine. That includes the Understanding Adult, played by Irving as if she's counting the minutes until she's put out of her misery with a fireplace poker (which happens with little fanfare). As soon as these characters start talking about a party after the big football game, anyone with a passing familiarity with the original story will be able to predict how well that turns out.

Rachel's vengeance spree (spurred on, in a very nineties touch, by the public screening of a sex tape) features such graphic highlights as genital removal by speargun, but for the most part, *The Rage* is a tame, homogenized effort. Using the supernatural as a metaphor for the horrors of the high school years was a fresh conceit in 1976, but by 1999 it had already made its way to prime time in the form of *Buffy the Vampire Slayer*. *The Rage* unwittingly includes a perfect visual metaphor for itself when Sue Snell takes Rachel on a tour of the charred wreckage of the old Bates High School (for some reason still standing twenty years later): When you revisit the past, sometimes you find it's all used up.

The Mangler 2 and The Mangler Reborn

The Mangler 2 may well be the most shameless sequel-in-name-only in cinema history, but to be fair, how could its makers resist trying to cash in on a phenomenal success like the original *Mangler*? Actually, as you may recall from chapter 15, 1995's *The Mangler* was a staggering box office flop, but that didn't stop producer Glen Tedham and writer/director Michael Hamilton-Wright from acquiring the sequel rights on the cheap. Although the duo had wanted to adapt a Stephen King story, Hamilton-Wright's script, which he churned out in eight days, has absolutely nothing to do with either King's original short story or Tobe Hooper's movie. In fact, King's name appears nowhere in the credits.

Shot at a vacant military base in Chilliwack, British Columbia, in twenty days, *The Mangler 2* substitutes a posh boarding school for the original's industrial laundry. The "mangler" of the title is not a speed-ironing machine but a computer virus released into the school's high-tech security system. The Mangler 2.0 causes the central computer to go insane and begin killing people, but as far as personality is concerned, it's never going to give HAL 9000 a run for its money. (Visually, it's a dead ringer for the blobby CGI of *The Lawnmower Man*, another movie that bears no resemblance to the Stephen King story it's ostensibly based on.) Hamilton-Wright's murky, smeared images evoke more boredom than fear, and most of the killings happen offscreen, leaving us plenty of time to ogle scantily clad Daniella Evangelista and marvel at the "comedic" stylings of

Philippe Bergeron. If *The Mangler 2* proves anything, it's that there's no acting job Lance Henriksen won't take.

For reasons known only to him, the sequel's coproducer Barry Barnholtz decided to continue with the Mangler saga despite the lack of compelling evidence that audiences were even aware it existed. (Barnholtz also served as executive producer on *Sometimes They Come Back . . . Again*, so this is not the first time he made that mistake.) Barnholtz hired a couple of young former employees, Matt Cunningham and Erik Gardner, to write and direct the third installment. "To me the title *The Mangler Reborn* has more of a deeper meaning than just a title for a film," Cunningham told interviewer Herner Klenthur. "Is it more of a reflection of the 'rebirth' of the Mangler franchise? In a way yeah, we thought that since we are taking the machine aspect of it as King had in his original story and also having a rebirth in the movie—we figured it was the best title."

It's true that *Mangler Reborn* has more of a connection to King's story than the previous film had: The opening credits sequence is comprised of news clippings about the deaths at the Blue Ribbon Laundry, and the story (such as it is) concerns a washer/dryer repairman who buys pieces of the old mangler at auction and somehow becomes possessed by its spirit. But the movie's budgetary limitations (it was reportedly shot for $85,000) are all too apparent: Most of it was shot in the producer's garage and an empty L.A. house often used for porn shoots. For much of the running time we're watching a lumpy middle-aged man wander around with a mallet, occasionally whacking people in the head with it. When we finally see it, the reborn mangler is nifty: a Rube Goldberg-ian contraption made of whirring knives and saw blades. But its appearance is fleeting, and hardly worth justifying the eighty aimless minutes that precede it.

Firestarter 2: Rekindled

In the early 2000s, the Sci-Fi Channel (now known as SyFy) developed a couple of long-dormant properties owned by parent company Universal. One of these, a reimagined version of the short-lived seventies TV show *Battlestar Galactica*, went on to become one of the most acclaimed television series of the decade. The other, an update of Stephen King's *Firestarter*, did not.

Executive producer Tom Thayer had seen the potential for an ongoing series in the story of Charlene McGee, an adult version of the pyrokinetic young girl played by Drew Barrymore in the 1984 movie. "There is a lot to examine [in a series]," Thayer told the *Los Angeles Times* in March 2002. "There are certainly elements of *The Fugitive*, and you have elements of *The Incredible Hulk*." As with *Battlestar Galactica*, Sci-Fi gave the go-ahead to a two-night miniseries in order to test the waters. If successful, the miniseries would act as a backdoor pilot.

Marguerite Moreau (*Shameless*) was cast as the adult Charlie, still on the run from her old enemies from The Shop. (The script by Philip Eisner retroactively tweaks a few plot elements from the original: John Rainbird, burned to death by

Charlie in both book and movie, is here still alive, and Charlie's exposé to the *New York Times* is barely referenced, although clearly ineffective.) Danny Nucci costars as a hapless investigator who believes he's tracking down the survivors of the Lot-6 experiments in order to give them settlement checks. Dennis Hopper is another Lot-6 survivor, and the question "Who would make an even less convincing Cherokee Indian than George C. Scott?" is answered in the person of Malcolm McDowell, half his face covered in burn-victim makeup.

When filming of the miniseries got underway in Utah, the production did not get off to a smooth start. Moreau's mother suffered a brain aneurysm and nearly died on the first day of shooting, crew members quit without warning, and the pyrotechnic work was plagued with problems. "A bizarre set of circumstances during production forced us to bring in somebody at one point to 'cleanse' the set," Thayer told the *L.A. Times*. After receiving the psychic's blessing, the production carried on to completion, with the miniseries airing on the nights of March 10 and 11, 2002.

Rekindled isn't a travesty like most of the sequels discussed in this chapter, but even at its best, it feels unnecessary. Much of the first hour is taken up by flashback sequences that essentially constitute a remake of the 1984 movie. The present-day story line, in which Rainbird has assembled a small army of young boys with different paranormal abilities, plays like a mildly engaging *X-Men* knockoff. Moreau has a sexy swagger as the adult Charlie, and the best idea in the sequel is the notion that her sexuality is directly tied to her power, such that an orgasm causes her to unleash literal waves of heat. McDowell and Hopper make for an amusing pair of old hams, but the pyrotechnic finale is as underwhelming as it is inevitable.

In July 2002, Sci-Fi Channel president Bonnie Hammer announced at the annual Television Critics Association presentation that the miniseries had been so successful, it would be developed into an ongoing series. But unlike *Battlestar Galactica*, the weekly version of *Firestarter* never materialized. In December 2010, *Variety* reported that Universal planned to reboot *Firestarter* as a movie franchise, but so far that's nothing but smoke.

The Diary of Ellen Rimbauer

The history behind this 2003 ABC TV-movie is nearly as convoluted as that of the haunted house at its center. As part of the marketing campaign for Stephen King's 2002 miniseries *Rose Red*, the network aired a half-hour special called *Unlocking Rose Red: The Diary of Ellen Rimbauer*. Patterned after the very successful *Blair Witch Project* campaign, this mockumentary special used "found footage" and talking-head interviews as a conceit to suggest that the events depicted in *Rose Red* were based in fact.

At the same time, a book called *The Diary of Ellen Rimbauer: My Life at Rose Red* was published. Purporting to be Rimbauer's account of the building of Rose Red, as edited and annotated by Dr. Joyce Reardon (the character played by

Nancy Travis in the miniseries), the book became a surprise best seller, topping the *Publishers Weekly* fiction list. That's probably because it was widely speculated that the real author of *The Diary of Ellen Rimbauer* was Stephen King himself.

That was not the case. In fact, the novel was written by suspense-thriller author Ridley Pearson at King's request. The original plan was for an "architectural book that featured photos and drawings of the house with a ghost story subtly woven into the mix," according to a *Tacoma News Tribune* article by Ernest A. Jasmin. Pearson didn't think much of that idea, and instead seized on several mentions of a diary in the *Rose Red* screenplay. It was King's idea to keep the authorship of the book under wraps. "Part of Steve's idea was that no one would know who wrote it, rumors would circulate," Pearson told Jasmin. "And if his fan base jumped on it, we could have a real big book. And that's what happened."

After the miniseries aired, King admitted he was not the author and Pearson finally received credit for his work. He also received a phone call from King, who told him that ABC wanted to do a *Rose Red* prequel movie based on *Diary*, and that they wanted Pearson to write the script. Pearson agreed, and in January 2003 much of the *Rose Red* team, including director Craig Baxley, producer Mark Carliner, and production designer Craig Sterns, reassembled at Thornewood Castle in Tacoma, Washington, to shoot the TV-movie. (In his DVD commentary, Pearson reveals that King contributed to the screenplay as well, in the form of Ellen Rimbauer's voice-overs.) Julia Campbell, who had played Ellen Rimbauer in *Rose Red*'s flashback sequences, was replaced by Lisa Brenner. Steven Brand was cast as her husband, oil tycoon John Rimbauer, and Tsidii Leloka reprised her *Rose Red* role as Ellen's confidant Sukeena.

Baxley and company managed to recreate the lush look of the miniseries on a fraction of the budget and a much shorter shooting schedule (reportedly $6 million and thirty days, respectively). ABC aired the movie on May 12, 2003, once again hoping for big sweeps period ratings from a King project. The network's hopes were dashed when *Diary* scared up only 6.4 million viewers—a third as many as the original miniseries had drawn.

Although it's certainly far more watchable than the likes of *The Mangler Reborn* and *Sometimes They Come Back . . . Again*, *The Diary of Ellen Rimbauer* suffers from a severe case of prequel-itis. Because *Rose Red* was already so heavy with expository dialogue and flashback sequences, the backstory detailed in *Diary* is mostly familiar. We do learn more about the kinky sexual proclivities of John Rimbauer, but given that this is network television, the revelations are rather tame. *Diary* is well-made but superfluous and not particularly scary. Like the rest of the movies in this chapter, it's for King completists only.

All That You Love Will Be Carried Away

The Shining, *Carrie*, and Other Ill-Advised Remakes

The Shining: Another View of the Overlook

Stephen King had wanted to make his own version of *The Shining* practically from the moment the Stanley Kubrick version was released in 1980. In his 1983 *Playboy* interview, King said, "I'd like to remake *The Shining* someday, maybe even direct it myself if anybody will give me enough rope to hang myself with." After the success of *The Stand* on ABC, the opportunity finally arrived. When network executives asked the author what he'd like to do next, he told them he wanted to do *The Shining* and he wanted to do it his way.

It wasn't going to be quite that easy. Stanley Kubrick and Warner Bros. still held the rights to any remakes or sequels to the property, and King hadn't exactly endeared himself to Kubrick with his many derogatory comments about the movie version of *The Shining* over the years. But Kubrick decided to allow King to proceed after collecting a substantial fee and imposing a couple of conditions: King's version could not be released on home video (so as not to compete with Kubrick's), and King had to stop talking about Kubrick's film. (It appears that both of these conditions expired along with Stanley Kubrick himself in 1999: The miniseries was released on DVD in 2003, and King has long since gone back to talking about Kubrick and his film, albeit with a little more fondness these days.)

With a deal in place, King decided he didn't want quite enough rope to hang himself: He would write the television adaptation and serve as executive producer, but he wouldn't direct it himself. Having enjoyed his time working with Mick Garris on *The Stand*, King asked Garris if he'd be up for another ABC miniseries. Garris agreed, with the understanding that they were not so much remaking a Stanley Kubrick film as bringing King's book to the screen in the way the author intended. King scripted a three-night miniseries: six hours of airtime on ABC, which translated to four and a half hours of actual content, excluding commercials.

Casting the piece proved to be a huge problem, although it got off to a strong start. Rebecca De Mornay was someone King had in mind for a long time, and she agreed to play Wendy Torrance. Melvin van Peebles, legendary director of *Sweet Sweetback's Baadasssss Song*, took on the role of Dick Hallorann, while Elliott Gould signed on for a day of shooting as "officious prick" Stuart Ullman. Six-year-old Haley Joel Osment was considered for the part of Danny Torrance, but his father felt he was too young to participate in such a violent, disturbing show. Courtland Mead, who turned nine during the production, got the role instead.

Stephen King finally got to make *The Shining* his way, and even took on a cameo role as bandleader Gage Creed in the ABC miniseries.

The real issue was with Jack Torrance, and the reluctance of any actor to take on the role. "I had mentioned to Gary Sinise that we were doing it, and would it be something he'd be interested in," Garris told IGN.com. "He said, 'You know, I'd be very cautious about stepping into Nicholson's shoes.' And that should have been the clue. Everyone wanted to avoid that first line in the review, comparing them to Jack Nicholson." Tim Daly, then starring on *Wings* and later to headline King's *Storm of the Century*, expressed similar reservations. It was beginning to look like ABC would have to pull the plug on the entire production when Daly's *Wings* co-star Steven Weber came in to audition. Garris and King were both impressed, and Weber was hired three days before filming began.

The Shining returned to its point of origin when production of the miniseries got underway in February 1996. Stephen King had first gotten the idea for his book while wandering the corridors of the nearly deserted Stanley Hotel in Estes

Park, Colorado, and it was the Stanley itself that would serve as the location for much of *The Shining*. Sets were built in Denver for the Torrance apartment within the hotel, as well as a few corridors, the boiler room, and the crucial Room 217. The rest of the film, including the scenes in the ballroom and the kitchen, was shot in the hotel, where the production had rented all ninety-three rooms for the duration of the shoot. "I hadn't been inside the Stanley for 21 years," King told Steven Rosen of the *Denver Post*. "It was like walking inside my head."

The $21 million production was a testament to King's increased clout within the entertainment industry over a span of two decades. King had written a screenplay for the feature version of *The Shining* before Stanley Kubrick had taken on the project, but once the formidable auteur was aboard, King's script was discarded, and his involvement with the film essentially came to an end. By 1997, King was dictating his terms to ABC, and they were: take it or leave it. His script would be filmed as written, with all of its violence, domestic abuse, and childhood endangerment intact, or it wouldn't be filmed at all. Standards and Practices could complain all they wanted, but King simply went over their heads to the network executives. Since *The Stand* had performed so well, they had little incentive to tell King to tone it down.

So it was that Garris shot some of the most gruesome footage to air on network television to that point. His wife Cynthia played the woman in Room 217 as a ghastly, rotting corpse. Apparitions from the hotel's past appeared in varying states of decay. The final hour of the miniseries was particularly brutal, as Jack beat Wendy (and Halloran) with a croquet mallet, she responded by bloodying and battering his face with an oversized croquet ball, and young Danny faced peril at every turn. In the end, Standards and Practices got only the most token concessions from the creative team, such as reducing the number of on-screen mallet whacks by one.

Whether it was due to the violent content or a general feeling among the viewing audience that they'd already seen *The Shining* done as well as it could be, the ratings came as a stunning disappointment to the network, King, and Garris. On its opening night, Sunday, April 27, 1997, it finished behind a CBS TV-movie called *A Match Made in Heaven*, starring Olympia Dukakis. It was also beaten by an *X-Files* episode, and barely outpaced the network premiere of the theatrical movie *The River Wild* on NBC. *The Shining* won its time period on Monday night, albeit with fewer viewers than the premiere episode, and the final episode was clobbered by NBC's powerhouse Thursday night lineup, including *E/R*. Overall, *The Shining* was the lowest-rated Stephen King miniseries to that point.

Judged on its own merits, the miniseries isn't bad; in fact, it's probably the best work Garris has done, with or without King. In a way, it accomplishes what King set out to do, which was to recreate his book for the screen on his own terms. Iconic elements of the novel that never appeared in the Kubrick film, such as the overheating boiler, the croquet mallet, the hedge animals that come to life, the scrapbook recounting the past history of the Overlook, and the fact that Danny's imaginary friend "Tony" is actually his future self, are all present in the TV version.

Visually, the miniseries is a huge step up from *The Stand*, although it certainly benefits from being largely confined to a few locations. The manufactured foam snow works well enough, the makeup effects are top-notch, and the CGI is generally unobtrusive (although a few shots of the moving hedge animals, as well as the "floating" shots of Tony, are less than impressive). Weber's performance won't make anyone forget Nicholson, but he's closer to the "regular guy who goes crazy" King had in mind. Still, the transformation isn't as gradual and nuanced as it might have been. De Mornay offers a much different take on Wendy Torrance than did Shelley Duvall; she's certainly a stronger, less shrieky character. Mead is a bit too old for Danny, but he turns in a sensitive, if at times whiny, performance.

Thematically, too, the TV version hews closer to the novel than Kubrick's version did. King used the book to explore his own alcoholism and conflicted feeling about parenthood, and his fears about how that volatile mixture could lead down the road to domestic abuse. The central metaphorical image of the boiler that's about blow its top may be a bit too on-the-nose (certainly it was for Kubrick), but it works well enough in this context. Like most King miniseries, *The Shining* is too long, but it's not until the end that it goes off the rails, departing from King's text in a far more egregious way than Kubrick had ever done. In the novel, Jack has a brief moment of awareness near the end before he reverts to being the caretaker of the Overlook. Here, that moment is expanded to mawkish extremes. Instead of trying to prevent the boiler from blowing up, Jack fights his demons and causes the Overlook's destruction. In an epilogue set ten years later at Danny's high school graduation, Jack appears in ghostly form, and he and Danny exchange teary blown kisses. This forced happy ending, reeking of inappropriate sentimentality, nearly torpedoes the whole production.

At its best, the miniseries version of *The Shining* works as a live-action illustration of the novel: As Hallorann tells Danny (and Danny then repeats endlessly), it's just like pictures in a book. But the difference between it and the Kubrick film is encapsulated in the early scene between Jack and Ullman, the hotel manager. In the 1980 movie, their conversation is an exquisite passive-aggressive duet between Nicholson and Barry Nelson: Their dialogue is cordial enough, but their rapport is ambiguous and complicated by the uncomfortable presence of Bill Watson. Reading between the lines suggests that these two don't care for each other, but it's not that cut-and-dried. In the miniseries version of this scene, Jack and Ullman flat out state that they don't like each other. There's no mystery to it: The meaning is all on the surface. Kubrick's film retains its mystery, and its reputation has only improved through the years. The miniseries may have satisfied King's long-standing desire to see his novel filmed his way, but it's Stanley Kubrick's Overlook that will endure.

Used *Trucks*

So inconsequential it wouldn't even rate a mention if not for the completist nature of this book, the TV-movie *Trucks* seems to exist only to make *Maximum Overdrive* look like a masterpiece by comparison. Budgeted at a reported $3 million, all of which must have been spent on gasoline for the trucks and sandwiches for the crew, this 1997 TV-movie was shot in Manitoba, Canada, as a coproduction of Credo Entertainment and the USA Network.

The script by Brian Taggert (*Poltergeist III*) offers a new location and a different set of characters from King's only directorial effort but generally sticks to the same scenario. Here the truck stop besieged by sentient big rigs is located in Lunar, Nevada, the last stop before Area 51. The cause of the trucks coming to life isn't pinned down as it is in *Overdrive*, but several theories are offered, including a toxic cloud from a chemical spill, military experiments at Area 51, and a comet shower. Whatever the cause, a handful of people trapped in the truck stop diner must find a way to escape the killer vehicles.

Veteran TV-movie director Chris Thomson and his crew built the truck stop and a stretch of highway in a quarry between lakes Manitoba and Winnipeg. The mostly no-name cast was headlined by Timothy Busfield, a few years past his *thirtysomething* prime. Busfield expressed his ambivalence toward his motorized costars in an interview with Jay Bobbin of Tribune Media Services. "When there's a driver tucked down inside the cab and he's looking at you on a little black-and-white monitor, where your left is his right and vice versa—and he's driving straight at you at 40 mph—you're ready to say, 'Guys, could we increase my salary a little bit?'"

Trucks came and went without much notice when it aired on USA Network on October 29, 1997. Those who missed it didn't miss much: For the most part, the acting is godawful and the technical aspects, including muddy sound and cruddy visuals, are borderline inept. Some of the stuntwork is decent, but there are so many better options for viewing vehicular mayhem out there, it would take the most devoted enthusiast of trucks crashing into buildings to enjoy this one.

The two most bizarre scenes in the movie were added for the *Trucks* video release after its TV airing, and it's easy to tell which ones they are. None of the cast members from the rest of the film appear in them, and they contain the kind of gore and foul language that never would have made it onto the television broadcast. In the first, a Tonka truck attacks a mailman, repeatedly ramming into his skull and pounding it to a bloody pulp. In the second, members of a cleanup crew (presumably from Area 51) are bludgeoned to death with an axe by one of their own hazmat suits come to life. These scenes are ridiculous and completely disconnected from the rest of the movie, but they're also the only times *Trucks* exerts any kind of fascination.

Carrie On . . . and On . . .

By the late nineties, Stephen King's first novel had already spawned a movie, a sequel, and an ill-fated Broadway musical. Just about the only thing *Carrie* hadn't inspired, besides a Saturday morning cartoon show, was a TV remake that would also serve as a potential pilot for a weekly series. That changed in 2002, when NBC gave the green light to a prime-time update of Brian De Palma's horror classic. NBC Entertainment president Jeff Zucker made no bones about his reasons for wanting to remake a movie that hardly cried out for revision. "I think the thing that we're most excited about is that any time that there's a new or

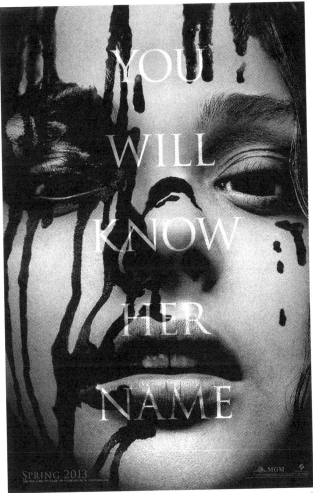

Third time's the charm? Kimberly Peirce, Chloe Moretz, and Julianne Moore had their fingers crossed when their remake of *Carrie* hit theaters in October 2013.

updated version of a Stephen King project, the audience loves it," Zucker said, according to the *San Antonio Express-News*. "You can't deny the fact that Stephen King properties (have) had great success, and we're just happy to be able to update the original."

Before moving forward, the network needed the cooperation of MGM, the studio that held the *Carrie* rights. According to Bryan Fuller, screenwriter of the TV version, MGM was less interested in a straightforward remake than a potentially more lucrative ongoing television series. As Fuller told Robert Taylor of *Comic Book Resources*, "that was another interesting negotiation between the network and the studio because the network wanted a movie-of-the-week and the studio needed more money so they said they wouldn't let them do a movie-of-the-week but they would let them do a backdoor pilot. And I don't think the network ever intended to do a series, they were just playing the studio."

Either way, Fuller (who has since pulled off the feat of turning Hannibal Lecter into a weekly TV hero) got the assignment to adapt King's novel for television. His script differs from the De Palma version in that he provides a framing device that works as a sort of equivalent to the "White Commission" sections of King's novel. In the TV version, a police detective (*Firestarter*'s David Keith) questions the survivors of Carrie's rampage, and the events leading up to and including prom night play out in flashback. Fuller's screenplay also included a "psychic investigator" looking into the prom night disaster, but although the character's scenes were shot with Jasmine Guy in the role, all of them were cut before the TV-movie aired.

The title role made famous by Sissy Spacek went to Angela Bettis, a relative unknown who had just finished filming a somewhat Carrie-like role in the independent horror film *May*. Kandyse McClure (who would later star in another King remake for television, *Children of the Corn*) took on Amy Irving's role (and, weirdly, Amy Irving's hairdo) as Sue Snell, future *Lost* star Emilie de Ravin filled Nancy Allen's short-shorts as Chris Hargensen, and Patricia Clarkson had the unenviable task of following Piper Laurie as Margaret White. With TV veteran David Carson directing, the telefilm was shot in British Columbia and scheduled for a November 4, 2002, broadcast.

Jeff Zucker may have been surprised when *Carrie* finished thirty-fifth for the week with only 12.2 million viewers, but he shouldn't have been. If a huge audience failed to materialize for a remake of *The Shining* with which Stephen King was heavily involved, why would they tune in for another remake he had nothing to do with at all? Both productions faced the same uphill battle: They were perceived as bloated, unoriginal, and unnecessary, as most viewers were happy with the existing film adaptations. That may have been a somewhat unfair perception where *The Shining* miniseries was concerned, but regarding the *Carrie* redo, it was right on the money.

At one point in the TV-movie, Sue Snell's boyfriend, Tommy, suggests that her plan to have him ask Carrie to the prom is like something out of a Freddie Prinze Jr. movie. And that's exactly how it plays out, at least up until the pig's blood is spilled. The young cast members all have a generic *90210* quality, especially compared to the vivid characterizations in De Palma's film. The exception is Bettis, who was actually pushing thirty at the time the TV-movie was shot. Her Carrie is very different from Spacek's, but in some ways just as impressive. She's smarter and stronger-willed but no less vulnerable, and frighteningly intense during the moments her powers are activated; she seems on the verge of vibrating right out of existence. (Clarkson, meanwhile, makes the wise decision to underplay Carrie's mother. There was certainly no point in trying to go even more over-the-top than Laurie in the original.)

Aside from the need to fill a three-hour network time slot, there's no reason such a familiar story should plod along as lethargically as this one does. The 2002 *Carrie* only comes to life once the title character is humiliated at the prom and lets her freak flag fly. Where De Palma was unable to convey the full scope of Carrie's vengeance spree due to budgetary constraints, the TV-movie uses digital effects to spectacular (albeit somewhat cheesy) effect in its extended climax. The impact is diluted by too many false endings, including a ludicrous turn of events that completely betrays King's book while opening the door to a potential series. Sue Snell finds Carrie in her bathtub, apparently drowned, but is able to resuscitate her. The two hit the road together, leaving the smoking remains of their town behind. Why Sue would team up with someone who is essentially a mass murderer responsible for the deaths of more than two hundred people (including all of Sue's friends) is a mystery that would never be solved.

Regarding the potential ongoing series, Bettis told *TV Guide*, "The ideas I've heard are Carrie and Sue Snell taking off for Florida like Thelma and Louise. I've heard something else about how the town reacts after this great catastrophe, like what happened after Columbine. Here's a girl dealing with her psychokinesis and the fact that she wiped out an entire town of people! So those are some ideas being bounced around, but who knows what would actually happen." Fuller knows at least a little, as he wrote an outline for the first episode of the series, but whether because the ratings were disappointing or because they'd never intended to pursue a series at all, NBC passed.

MGM didn't take the failure of the TV-movie to heart, as less than a decade later the studio was ready to remount yet another version of *Carrie*, this time for the big screen. Roberto Aguirre-Sacasa, a writer for Marvel Comics as well as the TV series *Big Love* and *Glee*, was hired to write what was once again billed as a more faithful adaptation of King's novel. As soon as the project was announced, speculation about the casting of the new Carrie began, and Stephen King himself was happy to participate. "Who knows if it will happen?" King told *Entertainment Weekly* in May 2011. "The real question is why, when the original was so good? . . . Although Lindsay Lohan as Carrie White . . . hmmm. It would certainly be fun to cast. I guess I could get behind it if they turned the project over to one of the Davids: Lynch or Cronenberg."

Instead of a David, Kimberly Peirce (*Boys Don't Cry*) got the nod to direct the Facebook generation update. "For me it's all about character," Peirce told fan site io9. "I read the novel and completely fell in love with just her. She's dynamic, she's interesting. You fall in love with her, you want to protect her." Lohan was never seriously considered for the role of Carrie, but some eyebrows were raised when Chloe Moretz (*Kick-Ass, Let Me In*) won the role. Fifteen years old at the time of shooting, Moretz was a far more age-appropriate choice than either Spacek or Bettis, but fans of the book grumbled that she was too beautiful to play the ultimate wallflower. Few complained about the casting of four-time Oscar nominee Julianne Moore as Margaret White.

Filming began in June 2012, with Toronto subbing for Chamberlain, Maine. *Carrie* was originally set for release on March 15, 2013, but was pushed back to October of that same year in order to take advantage of the Halloween box office.

'Salem's Lot Down Under

In 2001, Warner Bros. began kicking the tires on another attempt at bringing *'Salem's Lot* to the big screen, but when the project was officially announced in August of that year, it was a case of déjà vu all over again. King's vampire novel would become a two-night, four-hour miniseries, this time on the TNT network. "My sort of look at remakes is if you remember a film as being really good and then go back and look at it and it's not as good as you remembered it, that's a film you should remake," producer Mark Wolper told the *Boston Herald*. "The original *Salem's Lot*, I remember it as being horrifying. I watch it now and it's not as scary." Wolper hired screenwriter Peter Filardi (*Flatliners*) to pen a new adaptation of the book (and restore the apostrophe to the name of the town). Mikael Salomon (*Hard Rain*) took on directorial duties when the $23 million production got underway in April 2003 in Victoria, Australia.

The cast was impressive, particularly in comparison to the original 1979 miniseries. Rob Lowe, a self-proclaimed King fanatic who had previously starred in *The Stand*, took on the lead role of writer Ben Mears. The supporting cast included Donald Sutherland as Straker, Rutger Hauer as Barlow, James Cromwell as Father Callahan, Samantha Mathis as Susan Norton, and Andre Braugher as Ben's former teacher, Matt Burke. The little town of Creswick, Australia, won the title role. "We were looking for a town that could give us a certain look, and Creswick fitted the bill," location manager Alistair Reilly told *The Courier*. "We wanted a town with hills in the background where trees could be seen from the main street." American cars and artificial snow were imported to bolster the illusion.

Airing on June 20 and 21, 2004, the miniseries was a hit by TNT's standards, with its first part pulling in 5.9 million viewers to make it the most-watched basic cable movie of the year. (The second part dipped a bit to 5.3 million viewers.) Those numbers would have been unthinkably disastrous in the late seventies, when the original *Salem's Lot* aired on CBS, but there's no clearer object lesson in the huge aesthetic advances television has made in recent years than a side-by-side comparison between the 1979 and 2004 editions of the miniseries. The TNT version is slick with digital effects, sumptuous production values, high-definition visuals, and bursts of violence and gore than never would have made it past CBS Standards and Practices twenty-five years earlier. And although the original version did manage to land James Mason, the rest of its made-for-TV cast can't compare to the big names TNT landed for its production.

None of which is to say that the 2004 'Salem's Lot is without its own set of flaws. The Filardi script takes its fair share of liberties with King's story, few of them improvements. Ben Mears is now a nonfiction writer and a Pulitzer Prize winner for his book about being rescued from the Taliban in Afghanistan by soldiers who then killed ten innocent villagers. His voice-over narration is overtly cynical: "Beneath the postcard camouflage, there's little good in small towns. Mostly boredom,

Rob Lowe filled David Soul's shoes in the TNT remake of 'Salem's Lot, which strayed far afield of King's novel.

interspersed with a dull, mindless, moronic evil."

The miniseries seems to share his view. Where King's novel revealed the evil hidden beneath the town's Peyton Place veneer, the 2004 version does away with the veneer altogether. This 'Salem's Lot is a viper's nest of dark secrets—adultery, incest, drug-dealing, domestic abuse, murder—even before a wild-eyed, weird-bearded Donald Sutherland shows up with his partner in a coffin. The town hardly needs vampires to bring about its ruination: The whole mood is so rancid and most of the characters so unlikable (with Braugher being the one major exception), it doesn't feel like much is lost when Barlow's minions take over. Even the nerdy, sensitive Mark Petrie has been reimagined as a snotty juvenile delinquent; the father-son bond between Mears and Mark never develops here.

The 2004 version is more watchable than the original—better paced and acted, and far more visually appealing. Its interpretation of Barlow, as played by an impish Rutger Hauer, is much closer to King's creation than the blue Nosferatu of the 1979 version. Despite that, and a few in-jokes (a dog named Cujo, a karaoke singer performing "Stand by Me"), this 'Salem's Lot doesn't feel like part of Stephen King's world. Some King productions suffer from an overdose of sentiment, but this is one that could have used a little more heart.

Insomnia

The All-Night *Children of the Corn* Marathon

There may be a more inexplicable long-running movie franchise than the *Children of the Corn* series, but it's hard to imagine what it might be. The original 1984 version of *Children of the Corn* barely had enough story to sustain it for ninety minutes. How could such a movie spawn seven sequels and a remake? And more importantly, how could someone writing a book about the films of Stephen King be expected to sit through all of them? There are two schools of thought on this. One way to do it would be to space the viewings out over several months, allowing time for the painful memories of one sequel to subside before moving on to the next installment. The other way, and the one I ultimately decided on, is to rip the Band-Aid off in one fell swoop. So, with only my loyal but unwitting canine companion Maury by my side, it's time to embark upon a harrowing journey through the dregs of straight-to-video horror: The All-Night *Children of the Corn* Marathon. A running diary follows.

4:20 p.m.: *Children of the Corn II: The Final Sacrifice* (1992)

The most startling image in this belated sequel comes at the very beginning, when the Miramax logo appears on the screen. The indie studio best known for prestige fare like *The Crying Game* and *sex, lies, and videotape* had launched a subsidiary, horror-focused division called Dimension Films in 1992, and this *Children of the Corn* sequel was one of its earliest offerings (along with, naturally, *Hellraiser III*). One thing is immediately clear: Unless the rest of these sequels are about the perils of shucking, this is *not* going to be the final sacrifice.

Although it has been eight years since the release of the original *Children of the Corn* movie, the action in *The Final Sacrifice* picks up almost immediately after the events of that film. And unless everything we believe about children is a lie (which, according to these movies, is the case), that means none of the original corn kids are reprising their roles in the sequel. In the aftermath of a slaughter that has left fifty dead, one reporter has the courage to ask, "What is all this shit about the corn?" Another reporter, a disgraced yellow journalist who happens to be driving through town with his estranged son, sees the story of the mass slaughter as his ticket back to the big time.

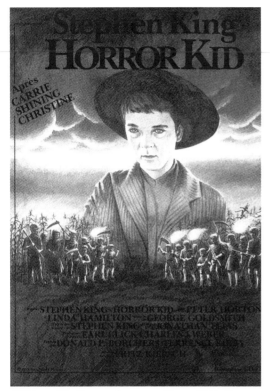

Children of the Corn was known as *Horror Kid* in France, but by any title it was one of the biggest misfires in the King catalogue. That didn't stop it from spawning countless sequels and a remake.

Micah, one of the corn children, gets sucked into some kind of digital cornfield wormhole (created with CGI that makes the effects in *Lawnmower Man* look like *Avatar*) and emerges possessed by a demon. He leads the kids on another killing spree, including a *Wizard of Oz* homage in which the corn children use hydraulic lifts to lower a house onto an old woman. (Later, another woman named "Miss West" accuses them of killing her sister. This is as clever as it gets.)

A wise old Indian named Redbear shows up to explain the concept of Koyaanisqatsi, or "life out of balance." As it turns out, this is an eco-horror story. A barn full of last year's corn, covered in toxic mold from pesticides, is causing madness and hallucinations—especially in children. So you see, there's a perfectly rational explanation for everything . . . except, in the end, He Who Walks Behind the Rows makes another appearance (once again via a special effect that resembles a giant gopher burrowing under a shag carpet). Micah is shredded by a harvester, and the demon abandons his body.

Unlike most of these sequels, *Children of the Corn II* was released in theaters, but even in the box office dead zone that is the month of January, it barely mustered an eighth-place finish. Is it even worse than its predecessor? It probably comes down to a coin flip.

Most creative kill: The corn children use a remote control on Miss West's motorized wheelchair, sending her into the street where a dumptruck hits her and knocks her through the window of a bingo hall.

5:55 p.m.: *Children of the Corn III: Urban Harvest* (1995)

If there are nine *Children of the Corn* movies, it only stands to reason that one of them is the very best *Children of the Corn* movie of all. *Urban Harvest* makes a compelling case for that title, although as honorifics go, this one is right up there with "best venereal disease." History has not recorded the name of the genius who proclaimed, "Let's make a *Children of the Corn* movie set in the city!" We can only hope it was Dimension Films overlord Bob Weinstein himself who was responsible for this brainstorm. Counterintuitive as it may seem, however, the "Children of the Corn meet the Boyz 'N the Hood" premise is far from the worst idea in franchise history.

Two surviving corn children, Eli and Joshua, are put into foster care in Chicago following the mysterious disappearance of their father. (It's not such an enigma to us, as we've seen the old man turned into a scarecrow by He Who Walks Behind the Rows.) In Chicago, the boys discover the wonders of pizza and ponder the mystery of backwards baseball caps. Eli has brought a suitcase full of corn with him, and he uses the seeds to plant his own cornfield in the courtyard of the abandoned factory next door.

It's not long before Eli's new foster parents begin to suspect he's a bad seed himself. While Joshua is assimilating into city life, Eli is still dressing like an eighteenth-century Amish farmer and serving his corn god. When his foster mother tries to cut down the corn, she ends up with her head impaled on a pipe, which doesn't prevent her grieving widower from pursuing the financial possibilities of such tasty corn. Eli has other plans for his field, however, as he is busy indoctrinating the neighborhood kids into the ways of He Who Walks Behind the Rows.

The mythology of this third installment doesn't quite square with the first two movies, but that will become a recurring feature of the series. Here we learn that Eli was present for the original slaying of the parents in Gatlin, Nebraska, which happened in 1964. (He's actually Joshua's adopted brother, having burned his real parents in their bed.) We also get our first full-on look at He Who Walks Behind the Rows, a regrettable decision on the part of director James D. R. Hickox (*Girls Gone Psycho*), as this fearsome demon looks like a half-melted wax figure of Godzilla. Still, this is easily the liveliest of the *Corn* movies, and Eli the most believably creepy corn child. The film also features the screen debut of Charlize Theron, although it's one she'd like to forget. She has no dialogue, only a scream . . . which was overdubbed by another actress.

(Incidentally, in an interview with *Fangoria* magazine, Stephen King mentioned that, while he'd missed most of the sequels, "There was one of those *Children of the Corn* movies, *Urban Harvest*, that I actually liked." So it's got that going for it, which is nice.)

Most creative kill: It's a toss-up between the social worker whose face is melted by the flame of her own lighter and Joshua's friend Malcolm, who has his head and entire spine yanked out of his body by sentient cornstalks.

7:35 p.m.: *Children of the Corn IV: The Gathering* (1996)

If the fourth installment in the series is remembered for anything—and really, there's no reason it should be—it's probably for one of the earliest screen performances by Naomi Watts. Watts stars as a medical student who returns to her hometown of Grand Island, Nebraska, to tend to her mother (Karen Black), who is apparently suffering from delusions. Her dreams of the town's children getting sick begin to come true after a farmer fishes the body of a boy preacher out of his well and the kid comes back to life.

The kids recover from their illnesses, but it soon becomes apparent that they are now possessed by dead children from the town's past, under the direction of boy preacher Josiah. Like Eli in the previous installment, Josiah never grew out of boyhood. (Otherwise, this sequel has little to do with the mythology established in the previous three movies; indeed, He Who Walks Behind the Rows is never mentioned.) Josiah had been burned by the townspeople and buried in the well, but now that he's escaped, he's seeking his vengeance.

If not the worst-made film in the series, *The Gathering* is easily the most boring. For the most part, it's as if the entire movie is in slow motion, only coming to life when one of Josiah's victims takes a scythe to the head or the groin. Director Greg Spence uses the "dream within a dream" gimmick so often, it starts to feel like the *Simpsons* episode with Sideshow Bob stepping on a rake over and over again. Spence clearly takes the material more seriously than his predecessors, but that doesn't prove to be a good thing.

Most creative kill: If you've seen one scythe attack, you've seen them all.

9:20 p.m. *Children of the Corn V: Fields of Terror* (1998)

This fifth installment is the closest the series comes to a "dead teenager" movie in the *Friday the 13th* mold (even featuring Kane Hodder, who played Jason Voorhees multiple times, in a small role). It also boasts the most eclectic cast in the series, including Eva Mendes, Fred Williamson, Ahmet Zappa, Alexis Arquette, and David Carradine. It's not as dull as its immediate predecessor, but five hours into this marathon, it's hard to work up much enthusiasm for more corn-related horror.

Fields of Terror centers on a different faction of the corn cult, this one occupying a farm in the town of Divinity Falls. They follow similar rules as the other disciples of He Who Walks Behind the Rows: Upon reaching the age of eighteen, adherents must sacrifice themselves to their god in the farm's corn silo. The one exception is their leader, Luke, played by Carradine with a minimum of effort. (The actor has two scenes in the movie, and spends most of his screen time sitting in a chair and uttering platitudes in a sleepy monotone.)

Enter a group of teenagers driving through town with the ashes of one of their fallen comrades (killed in a tragic bungee-jumping accident). When their car breaks down, those who aren't immediately scythed to death find themselves on Luke's farm, where Jacob, the brother of one of the traveling teens, happens to be a corn child. It is Jacob's time to sacrifice himself to He Who Walks Behind the Rows, but he's decided he doesn't like corn quite as much as he thought he did, and asks his sister and her friends to help him escape. Plenty of mayhem ensues, and the reasoning behind Carradine's somnambulant performance becomes clear as it is revealed that Luke has actually been dead for years. It's all mildly diverting, really dumb, and extremely forgettable.

Most creative kill: Carradine splits open, light pours out of him and shoots fire at Williamson's head, which explodes.

11:00 p.m.: *Children of the Corn 666: Isaac's Return* (1999)

Whatever happened to John Franklin, the kid who played Isaac in the original *Children of the Corn*? First of all, per the Internet Movie Database, he wasn't a kid at all when he originated the role. He was actually twenty-five years old in 1984, but due to a growth hormone deficiency, he appeared much younger. In the years between the first and sixth *Corn* movies, his most notable acting credits are the two *Addams Family* movies, in which he played Cousin Itt. Fifteen years after his first turn as Isaac, he returns (but you probably guessed that from the title), no longer looking like a little boy.

It seems Isaac wasn't killed off in the first movie after all; he's just been in a coma all this time. He awakens when Hannah (Natalie Ramsey), the first-born child of the original corn cult, returns to Gatlin in search of her real mother. (That her mother is played by Nancy Allen, a long way from her costarring role in the very first Stephen King movie, *Carrie*, is a little sad.) Still small and squeaky-voiced, but visibly aged, Isaac dons his familiar black preacher-boy hat and begins a new, somewhat more murky, reign of terror.

To her credit, director Kari Skogland manages to conjure up a creepier atmosphere than the earlier films possessed, particularly in the desolate hospital scenes, but Isaac isn't any scarier now than he was fifteen years earlier. Plot-wise, however, *Isaac's Return* is a particularly incoherent entry in the series (especially if you've already watched seven straight hours of this stuff). Somehow Isaac has a teenage son who is supposed to mate with Hannah before midnight in order to bring about the prophecy of He Who Walks Behind the Rows. Or something. Franklin cowrote the confusing screenplay, so perhaps it all makes sense to him.

Most creative kill: Stacy Keach, in a supporting role as Isaac's doctor, dies of shock when his patient electrifies the wet floor upon which he's standing.

12:45 a.m.: *Children of the Corn 7: Revelation* (2001)

There's a lot to criticize in the *Children of the Corn* series (as you may have noticed), but at least most of the movies clock in at eighty minutes or less. Even when they're terrible, as they usually are, at least they're not terrible for very long. Take *Revelations*, another *Corn* sequel that more or less ignores everything that has come before. He Who Walks Behind the Rows gets a mention or two, and as usual, there's a tiny kid in a big black hat causing trouble, but otherwise, there's no continuity with the other films.

This installment takes place in that noted hotbed of evil, Omaha, in and around a condemned apartment building. One of the residents, an older woman, has been having visions of a cornfield. When her granddaughter Jamie (Claudette Mink) arrives for a visit, the old woman has gone missing. Jamie meets some of the building's other residents, notably a pair of creepy, silent kids and the stoner superintendent. The latter meets his demise when the kids toss him off the roof, into the cornfield below.

A priest played by Michael Ironside arrives on the scene to give Jamie the backstory. Apparently her grandmother had been part of the corn cult as a child and was the only survivor of a fire that took place sixty years earlier on the very grounds where her apartment building now stands. A boy preacher named Abel had burned down his preachin' tent, with all of his followers still inside, but since grandma didn't die, He Who Walks Behind the Rows is now coming for Jamie. None of this adds much to our understanding of corn-based cultism, but since confusion has become one of the hallmarks of this franchise, it's best just to sit back and wait for the apartment building to blow up. Which it does. In addition to being one of the dopiest entries in the series, *Revelations* is also the cheapest-looking of the bunch. Dimension must have felt the franchise had finally run its course, as this would be the last sequel for a decade.

Most creative kill: Tiffany, a stripper who lives in the building, is strangled by cornstalks while taking a bath.

2:25 a.m. *Stephen King's Children of the Corn* (2009)

Donald Borchers, who produced the original *Children of the Corn* in 1984, finally decided he'd done it wrong. As discussed back in chapter 9, that first film took significant liberties with King's short story, changing the squabbling, doomed married couple to affectionate young lovers who survive their ordeal in the corn. As Borchers recalls in a "making of" documentary included on the DVD release of this movie, he became disenchanted with the changes he and his collabora-tors had made in the original adaptation, feeling they had "Hollywood-ized" King's story. Borchers decided to remake the film in a more faithful manner, going so far as to dig up the screenplay draft written by King twenty-five years earlier. Borchers polished the script and sent it on to the author, hoping to get his blessing, but he was told King wouldn't read it and wanted nothing to do with the remake.

It's certainly understandable that King was feeling *Corn*-ed out. (In fact, at this point in the all-night marathon, it's *very* understandable.) Borchers went ahead with his remake anyway, and the result premiered on the SyFy network in September 2009. Borchers certainly achieved his goal of making a more faith-ful adaptation, but his fidelity to the source material turns out to be a liability.

Specifically, the character of Vicky, as played here by Kandyse McClure in her second appearance in a King remake (following the *Carrie* TV-movie), is one of the most unpleasant, unbearable screen creations imaginable. There's no nuance to the presentation of this troubled marriage; Vicky is simply a shrieking, nagging shrew, and her husband Burt (David Anders) a long-suffering, stoic lug.

Otherwise, the first half of the movie plays out much as the original did, with the couple hitting a little boy with their car, discovering his throat has been slit, and bringing him into the town of Gatlin, where the corn children set upon them. But despite Borchers's stated intentions, he can't help but add his own spin on the material by making Burt into a Vietnam vet. (The film is set in 1975.) After Vicky is put out of our misery, Burt goes on a rampage against the corn children, having flashbacks to his time in the bush all the while. This plays more like a *Rambo* riff than anything King would have written, and even though the corn children are the villains, it's hard to root for a guy killing kids in cold blood.

Borchers also adds a bizarre scene in which Isaac orders two of the older corn children to disrobe and have sex on the church altar in front of the entire kiddie congregation. His ending is reasonably faithful to the original story, as both Burt and Vicky wind up as scarecrows in the cornfield, but that only serves as another reminder that had Borchers done it "right" in the first place, we would have been spared this remake altogether.

Most creative kill: It's not so creative, as we've seen it done multiple times in the series, but it's still gratifying to see Vicky crucified on cornstalks.

4:10 a.m.: *Children of the Corn: Genesis* (2011)

It's either very late or very early—either way, my loyal canine companion has long since abandoned me for the safety of his bed—but at last we've reached the final installment in the series, which will no doubt tie up all of the remaining loose ends and answer all the nagging questions.

Actually, there's no reason to believe *Genesis will* be the last *Children of the Corn* movie, but at least it's the last one available as of this writing. It's not a sequel to the remake, as that wasn't a Dimension release, but it's not really a sequel to any of the other movies, either. It almost seems to have been changed into a *Corn* movie in postproduction. In a familiar setup, a young couple suffers automotive failure on a desolate stretch of road. We're not in Nebraska or even Iowa this time, however, but somewhere in California. Our heroes knock on the wrong door: that of the grizzled Preacher (Billy Drago) and his mail-order Russian bride.

Preacher, we learn, grew up in Gatlin, Nebraska, and that fact (along with a handful of references to He Who Walks Behind the Rows) constitutes the only real connection to the previous films. Preacher allows the young couple to stay the night, but warns them not to go a-wanderin' around the premises. Of course they do so, discovering a child being held captive in the process. Is this tot the embodiment of evil or just a poor innocent? How many guesses would you like?

It didn't seem possible after *Revelation*, but a decade later, Dimension has managed to make an even cheaper-looking, less eventful sequel. Almost nothing happens until the young lovers make a break for freedom near the end, and the demon child uses telekinetic powers to knock cars off a carrier and into their escape route. (It may look like Dimension spent money on this scene, but much of it is comprised of stock footage from *Bad Boys II*.) The ending is a confused jumble, so at least that's in keeping with the spirit of the last few sequels. At this point, however, any ending at all is welcome.

Most creative kill: In the very last shot, long after we've forgotten he was in the movie, a policeman who had gone missing drops from the sky to his death.

Top Ten Lessons of the *Children of the Corn* Marathon

1. Radio stations in Nebraska exclusively broadcast fire-and-brimstone preachers.
2. Black Amish hats are always in fashion.
3. If you hear voices chanting in Latin or singing "Bringing in the Sheaves," something terrible is about to happen.
4. Any religion that requires its adherents to die at eighteen hasn't really thought through the fund-raising implications.
5. Scythes are underrated weapons of mass destruction.
6. Never take the "scenic route."
7. The cop is probably in on it. But if not, he'll be dead in five minutes.
8. There is no greater indignity than death by corncob. Particularly at the hands of an eight-year-old.
9. "Based on the story by Stephen King" is a phrase with no meaning.
10. Corn still isn't scary. Creamed corn, on the other hand . . .

Rock-Bottom Remainders

Oddities and Ephemera

Phantoms

Stephen King Movies That Never Were

In the course of this survey, we've encountered several films that spent many years in development hell before reaching the screen. Those were the lucky ones. This chapter concerns those projects that never escaped development hell at all . . . at least, not yet.

Night Shift (A.K.A. Daylight Dead)

The short story collection *Night Shift* has spawned several movies (including *Children of the Corn* and *Maximum Overdrive*), but all efforts at using the book as the basis of an anthology film have been thwarted. Producer Milton Subotsky, known for horror anthologies like *The House That Dripped Blood* and *Tales from the Crypt*, purchased the rights to six of the stories in hopes of making two movies. One, entitled *Night Shift*, would comprise three revenge-themed stories: "Quitters Inc.," "The Ledge," and "Sometimes They Come Back." The other would be called *The Machines* and include "Trucks," "The Lawnmower Man," and "The Mangler." Neither film materialized, and eventually a financially strapped Subotsky would be forced to sell off the rights to all the stories, mostly to Dino De Laurentiis. "Quitters Inc." and "The Ledge" both ended up in *Cat's Eye*, along with a new story. Subotsky got a producer credit on that film as well as *Maximum Overdrive*, although he was not directly involved in the making of either movie.

In the late 1970s, NBC commissioned a screenplay from King based on three of the *Night Shift* stories, with the intent of producing a prime-time horror anthology that would also serve as a backdoor pilot for a potential ongoing series. This project, at one point titled *Daylight Dead*, would include "Strawberry Spring," "I Know What You Need," and "Battleground." King wrote the script, which was promptly shot down by the network's Standards and Practices department. "It's not going to be done for TV because NBC nixed it . . . too gruesome, too violent, too intense," King told interviewer Bhob Stewart for *Heavy Metal* magazine.

King's *Night Shift* screenplay is on file with the Fogler Library's special collection at the University of Maine in Orono. The script opens on a country crossroads, with one sign pointing toward Jerusalem's Lot and the other toward Weathersfield. King introduces a narrator named Harold, who serves as a linking device for the three stories. Harold delivers a brief monologue on fear, paraphrased from King's foreword to the *Night Shift* collection. He talks about the boogeyman and the cold hand that grabs your foot when it's sticking out from under the covers.

The first segment is "Strawberry Spring," adapted from the story in which the first-person narrator gradually comes to realize he's responsible for a series of murders on a college campus. The screenplay version revolves around two journalism students, Lennie and Rich, covering the crimes for the school paper. Ten years later, Rich reads that Lennie has killed a coed and his wife. The second story, "I Know What You Need," is set at the same campus and sticks fairly closely to King's tale of an outcast who uses voodoo to woo the girl he's always loved. "Battleground," which would later be adapted for TNT's *Nightmares & Dreamscapes* series, finds a hit man battling an army of toy soldiers. (Unlike the TNT version, however, the segment is not completely silent.)

A reading of the script suggests that NBC's censors were overly squeamish. Even for the 1970s, it doesn't seem too violent for television. King agreed, telling Paul R. Gagne in a 1980 interview, "I thought it was pretty tame, but that's the way it goes."

The Shotgunners

An original screenplay that King later turned into *The Regulators*, a novel published under the Richard Bachman name, *The Shotgunners* attracted little notice except from one Hollywood legend: *Wild Bunch* director Sam Peckinpah. "Nobody liked it *except* Peckinpah," King told Gary Wood for *Cinefantastique*. "Peckinpah *loved* it."

The Shotgunners is also part of the Fogler Library special collection. The first page of the screenplay is a hand-drawn map of Maple Street, where all of the movie's action takes place. (As we later learn, this sketched map figures into the story.) The next page offers two definitions of the word "shotgun": the weapon and the verb meaning "to coerce." The movie proper opens with a hanging, followed by a shot of bodies covered with sheets. These are shotgunners—members of an offshoot of the Ku Klux Klan hunted down by Ohio vigilantes in 1874.

The action cuts to present-day Maple Street, where the normal suburban activities are disrupted by the arrival of several black Cadillacs, each carrying unseen passengers armed with shotguns. What follows is an incredibly violent sequence, variations of which repeat throughout the screenplay, as the shotgunners begin blowing holes in the Maple Street residents. It's a chaotic story that finds the residents unable to escape from the nightmare that has engulfed their street and the shotgunners revealing how thin the neighborly ties that bind really are.

The Shotgunners doesn't make for great reading, but it does provide an interesting window into King's creative process. Near the introduction of Mike,

Sam Peckinpah was intrigued by King's original screenplay *The Shotgunners*, but died before the project could gain much traction. The film was never made.

the ostensible hero of the piece, King has scribbled, "*not* Hollywood, *not* Richard Gere, *not* Robert Redford." Later he offers some visual advice, a hint that the seeds for his eventual directorial debut had already been planted: "The director may or may not want to cut a few 'tension-building' shots from Peter's POV ('disarming the bomb' shots John Huston used to call them)."

King met with Peckinpah to discuss the project and found the ailing film-maker in enthusiastic, feisty form. "We sat down, and he knew exactly what to do . . . He was a great guy, and he knew it would've been a great movie. But he died and it got nowhere *near* production." It never did. As of 1990, King still held out some hope that it would be made and become a "mega-hit. I'll look around at all the people who turned it down, the one piece of my work that I have liked the best that nobody has wanted anything to do with." It seems unlikely to happen now that King has turned it into *The Regulators*, which is actually quite a bit different than the original *Shotgunners* screenplay.

The Talisman

If any King work holds the record for serving the longest sentence in development hell, it's his 1984 collaboration with Peter Straub, *The Talisman*. An adaptation, either for the movies or for television, has been in the works for nearly three decades now, and seems no closer to reaching the screen than it did when the novel was published. At that time, King and Straub sold the movie rights to Universal on behalf of Steven Spielberg's Amblin Productions, with the understanding that it would only be made by Spielberg himself.

Some critics felt the book already read like a movie treatment, but condensing the six-hundred-page novel into a feature film that would meet Spielberg's exacting specifications proved easier said than done. Arlene Sarner and Jerry Leichtling, the screenwriting duo behind *Peggy Sue Got Married*, won the adaptation assignment. "It was a real interesting departure for us," Sarner told Jay Scott of *The Globe and Mail* in 1986. "You're working with Spielberg so you can let your imagination go wild and know they can do it, the resources are phenomenal. The first draft we handed in would have had a budget of about $50 million, so we had to temper our imaginations a little. Also, Steven really wanted a PG movie, and it's quite the violent book."

King met with Spielberg several times to discuss the project, but *The Talisman* was pushed to the back burner when the director moved on to other projects, including 1987's *Empire of the Sun*. In 1992, *The Fisher King* screenwriter Richard LaGravenese was brought in to take a crack at *The Talisman* script, but that version got no further than the earlier attempts. By 1999, Spielberg had abandoned the idea of a theatrical version, deciding instead to executive produce a four-hour miniseries for ABC. Predictably enough, Mick Garris was announced as the project's director in 2001. Garris planned to work with the LaGravenese script as the basis for an expanded screenplay, but in November of that year, ABC pulled out due to financial concerns.

The following year, Spielberg revived *The Talisman* as a feature film, hiring Ehren Kruger (*The Ring*) to adapt the novel for the big screen. By October 2003, this version seemed to be picking up steam, with *The Hollywood Reporter* noting that Spielberg would produce, with Vadim Perelman (*The House of Sand and Fog*) directing. Filming was set to get underway in August 2004 for a 2005 release, but in May, Perelman departed the production, to be replaced by Edward Zwick (*Courage Under Fire*). When script issues pushed the start date back to October, Zwick too dropped out and the project slipped back into limbo.

When it returned to active development in 2006, it was a miniseries again, this time a six-hour version for TNT. Kruger was still aboard as screenwriter, telling Edward Douglas of ComingSoon.net, "We're using some of the elements of the feature script and then, there's a lot to add and expand. The core structure of the feature was always that of the novel, but there was just no way we could include a lot of what's in the novel, so now we're able to go back and cherry-pick the best sequences and plotlines and subplots of the novel again."

TNT scheduled the miniseries for 2008, hinting that an ongoing *Talisman* series could follow in 2009.

In September 2007, the project was delayed yet again, for a familiar reason: budgetary issues. In 2008, producer Frank Marshall told IGN that *The Talisman* was back to being a movie. To this day, the Internet Movie Database lists the project as being in development, but that's only because the IMDb doesn't have a category for "development hell."

Miscellaneous

Other projects that never came to fruition include:

Insomnia—Before King came up with the idea for *Storm of the Century*, he and producer Mark Carliner kicked around some other possibilities for another ABC miniseries, one of which was an adaptation of this 1994 novel. Carliner commissioned a script, which King told *Fangoria* was "okay, but it didn't have any real pop to it." Years later, *Wrong Turn* director Rob Schmidt was rumored to be pursuing a big-screen adaptation of *Insomnia*, but no official confirmation was forthcoming, and the movie never got past the theoretical stage.

The Girl Who Loved Tom Gordon—Here's another entry for the film festival of Romero/King movies that never were. In 2000, Stephen King's official website announced that George Romero would direct an adaptation of this 1999 novel from a screenplay he'd already written. The project hit a snag over the casting of its young girl protagonist, but in 2004, Dakota Fanning was briefly attached to star. After signing with new management following the success of *Man on Fire*, however, Fanning departed the project. In 2005, the *Boston Herald* reported that *Tom Gordon* would film that summer in Boston, but that announcement proved premature.

From a Buick 8—King's 2002 novel was optioned by Chesapeake Films cofounders Johnathon Schaech and Richard Chizmar, who also penned a screenplay for the proposed film. In November 2005, Chesapeake signed—surprise, surprise—George Romero to direct. Two years later, however, *Variety* reported that Moonstone Entertainment had optioned the Schaech/Chizmar screenplay, and another King movie veteran, Tobe Hooper, was now in the *Buick* driver's seat. Hooper told the trade publication that *Buick* would not be "your stock horror film by any means. There's a really cool, layered quality to the story." As of 2009 Hooper was still attached, with Amicus Entertainment and Mick Garris aboard as producing partners, but this *Buick* has yet to get started.

Rose Madder—In 1996, HBO paid $1.5 million for the rights to this 1995 novel, one of King's less beloved efforts. Producer Rob Fried was attached to the project, which vanished from the radar until November 2011, when *Variety* reported that Palomar Pictures had partnered with Grosvenor Park to adapt it for the big screen. Naomi Sheridan (*In America*) penned the script, but although the report suggested *Rose Madder* would go into production within eighteen months, there hasn't been a peep since the initial announcement.

11/22/63—King's 2011 tale of a time-traveler attempting to stop the assassination of John F. Kennedy was widely acclaimed as one of his best novels ever, but even before its publication, there was reason to believe its film adaptation would be worth seeing. In August of that year, three months before the book was released, *Variety* reported that Jonathan Demme (*The Silence of the Lambs*) had acquired the rights and would write and direct the movie. The followed January, Demme told film blog *The Playlist* he was working on the script with King in hopes of getting the film into production by late 2012. "There's a dozen movies in *11/22/63*," Demme said. "We're finding the one that we think is kind of the best of all." As it turned out, that story wasn't so easy to find, and Demme exited the project in December 2012. "This is a big book, with lots in it," he told *Playlist*. "And I loved certain parts of the book for the film more than Stephen did. We're friends, and I had a lot of fun working on the script, but we were too apart on what we felt should be in and what should be out of the script."

I Am the Doorway

King's Influence on the Horror Genre (and Beyond)

The Post-King Horror Movie

While publicizing the CBS series *Under the Dome*, on which both Stephen King and Steven Spielberg serve as executive producers, writer Brian K. Vaughan compared the two men thusly: "Steven Spielberg sees the best in humanity and Stephen King is always seeing the worst . . . But there are similarities: they're both really aggressive humanists who love people so much and throwing them in extraordinary situations and seeing what happens."

Although it has taken more than three decades for them to finally collaborate, the careers of King and Spielberg have run parallel courses almost since the beginning. Both burst on the scene in the mid-seventies, King with *Carrie* and Spielberg with *Jaws*. Both possess a seemingly effortless "common touch" that has translated into worldwide success on an almost unprecedented scale, resulting in some of the most popular entertainment of our time. And both use the building blocks of everyday life as the jumping-off point for extraordinary narratives, often with the American family at the center and children as the viewpoint characters.

Their first near-miss of a collaboration should have been a seamless meshing of their sensibilities, but it was not to be. In 1980, Spielberg approached King with a treatment he'd written about a suburban family terrorized by ghosts. Spielberg offered King the job of turning what was then titled *Night Time* into a screenplay, and after a productive meeting, it seemed the collaboration was on course. "We wrote letters back and forth," King told interviewer Gary Wood. "We talked on the phone about it. I got ready to *do* it, went to England, and found out that Doubleday, who had been acting on my behalf, had asked for this *incredible* amount of money [for me] to do the screenplay. This is for somebody who had never *done* a screenplay that had been produced."

Instead of a King-scripted movie, *Poltergeist* would become among the first of the King-influenced movies. Its production is a source of controversy to this day. After hiring screenwriters Michael Grais and Mark Victor and then rewriting

Stephen King didn't end up writing *Poltergeist*, but his influence still shines through this suburban ghost story.

their draft, Spielberg passed the directing reins to Tobe Hooper. Officially, Spielberg was the film's producer, but over the years, many stories have surfaced suggesting that Hooper was the director in name only, and that it was Spielberg behind the camera for the bulk of the shooting. Spielberg himself fanned the flames with some comments published even before the film was released (telling the *L.A. Times*, "I thought I'd be able to turn *Poltergeist* over to a director and walk away. I was wrong."). For his part, Hooper insists he was the director, telling *The A.V. Club* in 2000 that Spielberg was picking up second-unit shots when the

L.A. Times reporter arrived on the set. "The moment they got there, Steven was shooting the shot of the little race cars, and from there the damn thing blossomed on its own and started becoming its own legend. Really, that is my knowledge of it, because I was making the movie and then I started hearing all this stuff after it was finished."

However the credit should be divided between Spielberg and Hooper, the finished film also reveals the influence of the man who never ended up writing it: Stephen King. As with many King works, *Poltergeist* establishes a relatable, recognizable contemporary setting, complete with minor domestic traumas (suburban mother JoBeth Williams caught in the act of flushing her little girl's dead parakeet), simmering neighborhood conflicts (her husband Craig T. Nelson feuding with the guy next door via remote control), and the detritus of contemporary culture (*Star Wars* bed sheets, Williams absently humming a beer jingle).

Once things start to go bump in the night, *Poltergeist* takes on a resemblance to a more specific King adaptation: *The Shining*. Both are haunted house movies with families at their center (although the Freelings are certainly more well adjusted than the Torrances). With her ability to commune with ghosts and her unnerving otherworldliness, young Heather O'Rourke is a sort of cross between Danny Torrance and the two creepy dead girls who torment him. And both films offer that old saw, the Indian burial ground, as a possible explanation for their supernatural shenanigans. (In his interview with Wood, King dismisses the Indian burial ground idea, saying "Maybe we could have done something more interesting," which is a little odd since he also uses the same device in *Pet Sematary*.)

The brand of suburban/small-town horror exemplified by *Poltergeist* and so many King works has become a staple of the genre. In 1984, Wes Craven directed *A Nightmare on Elm Street*, the very title of which could serve as a neat summation of the King aesthetic. Its small-town high school setting is straight out of *Carrie* or *Christine*, and the supernatural element, a serial killer who stalks teenagers in their dreams, is as ingenious in its simplicity as anything in the King oeuvre (although it grows less so through repetition in the countless sequels that followed). Future King collaborator Tom Holland made his directorial debut with 1985's *Fright Night*, in which a small-town teen discovers his neighbor is a vampire. The shadow of *Salem's Lot* looms over Holland's film, as well as Joel Schumacher's 1987 hit about a beach town infested with vampires, *The Lost Boys*.

The proliferation of supernatural tots and teens in pop culture over the past couple of decades, and the use of horror/fantasy elements as a metaphor for the real-life terrors of adolescence, also owes a debt to King. Some of the most popular franchises of our time have delved into the same territory King explored in *Carrie* (and to a lesser extent, *Firestarter*). In 1992's *Buffy the Vampire Slayer*, it is Los Angeles that's infested with vampires, and only a seemingly bubble-headed blonde cheerleader (who is in reality the chosen one known as The Slayer) can stop them. The movie tanked, but its screenwriter, Joss Whedon, was able to salvage the concept with the TV series of the same name. Relocating Buffy to the fictional suburbia of Sunnyvale, which happens to be built on a "Hellmouth," Whedon was able to make the demons of adolescence quite literal, with frequently engaging and occasionally quite spectacular results.

At around the same time *Buffy* premiered on television, the first book in what would become the most popular young-adult fantasy series of all time was published. J. K. Rowling would write a total of seven novels about Harry Potter, an orphan who learns he's a wizard, all of which went on to become blockbuster films. Rowling acknowledged reading King in her youth, and King, a fan of the Potter books, saw something of himself in her writing. "I think that has some kind of formative influence the same way reading Richard Matheson had an influence on me," King told *USA Weekend*. He was less willing to take any credit for Stephenie Meyer's *Twilight* series. "Both Rowling and Meyer, they're speaking directly to young people. . . . The real difference is that Jo Rowling is a terrific writer and Stephenie Meyer can't write worth a darn. She's not very good." King also perceived his influence in another popular young-adult series turned blockbuster movie franchise: Suzanne Collins's *The Hunger Games*, about a future dystopia in which teenagers chosen by lottery combat each other on a reality show until only one is left standing. Reviewing the first book for *Entertainment Weekly*, King wrote, "readers of *Battle Royale* (by Koushun Takami), *The Running Man*, or *The Long Walk* (those latter two by some guy named Bachman) will quickly realize they have visited these TV badlands before."

King's influence can also be seen in a pair of recent movies about youngsters with no special powers. Jacob Aaron Estes's *Mean Creek* (2008) plays as a sort of cross between *Stand by Me* and *Deliverance*, as middle schooler Rory Culkin and his friends invite the school bully on a boating trip in order to exact a humiliating revenge. Nothing goes quite as planned, and the young boaters are forced to contend with a series of moral dilemmas (and, as in *Stand by Me*, a dead body). J. J. Abrams's 2011 film *Super 8* genetically splices *Stand by Me* with the Spielberg of *E.T.* and *Poltergeist* to tell the story of a group of filmmaking tweens who stumble upon a government cover-up of an alien crash-landing. It was not the first or last time Abrams would pay homage to King.

Lost and Other Novelistic Television Series

In 2006, *Entertainment Weekly* staged a "summit" between Stephen King and *Lost* executive producers J. J. Abrams, Carlton Cuse, and Damon Lindelof. It was a mutual admiration society, with the *Lost* creators bringing treasured King books to be autographed and King proclaiming that he hands out DVDs of the ABC series to "everybody." The *Lost* brain trust had never been shy about the debt their series owed to King, and to *The Stand* in particular, and they couldn't wait to tell the author all about it.

"For us, *The Stand* has been a model," said Cuse. "*Lost* is about a bunch of people stranded on an island . . . But what sustains you are the characters. In *The*

Stand, I was completely gripped by everyone you introduced in that story—how they come together, what their individual stories are, how they face the premise." Lindelof added, "The thing about *The Stand* is that there are all the archetypes, and we embraced the same thing. The strong, silent, heroic type. The nerdy guy. The techie. The pregnant girl. All those characters exist in *The Stand,* too."

The overarching plot of *Lost* came to mimic *The Stand* as well, in ways that frustrated many longtime viewers as the series entered its endgame. Although the setting was not postapocalyptic, the fact that the survivors of a plane crash had to recreate society on their new island home leant itself to many of the tropes associated with postapocalyptic narrative and *The Stand* in particular. Ultimately the survivors would find themselves pitted against each other in a mythic battle of good vs. evil, with the late-added characters of Jacob and the Man in Black serving as the Mother Abigail and Randall Flagg surrogates in this scenario.

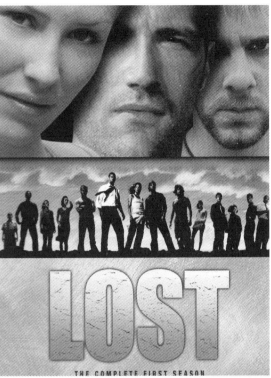

The creators of *Lost* often cited *The Stand* as one of their primary inspirations for the series.

The final episode, in which the on-island action ended with the forces of good victorious over the Man in Black while an alternate reality was revealed as a sort of purgatory reuniting the sprawling cast of characters, proved extremely divisive. Many fans despised it, and some continue to berate Lindelof in particular (via social media) to this day. It was an outcome King had predicted during their *Entertainment Weekly* summit. "However you end it, based on my experience with *The Dark Tower,* you will hear from thousands of people who fucking hate it."

Still, *Lost* had a six-season run that was groundbreaking for network television in a number of ways. In a sense, it pulled off what King himself had attempted but failed to do with *Golden Years* and *Kingdom Hospital.* (The first episode of *Lost* aired on ABC only two months after the last episode of *Kingdom Hospital,* and its ratings success must have come as a relief to network executives banking on another serialized drama with fantastical elements.) But while *Lost* may have been the most successful television series to be influenced by King, it was not the first nor the last.

In September 1995, CBS premiered *American Gothic*, an unlikely collaboration between creator Shaun Cassidy (yes, *that* Shaun Cassidy from *The Hardy Boys*) and executive producer Sam Raimi. The series about a small-town sheriff who may be the devil was dismissed by some at the time as a *Twin Peaks* knockoff, but Stephen King fans saw the author's influence all over it. While the show's fictional town of Trinity was set in South Carolina rather than Maine, it was the same sort of close-knit community beset by dark secrets found in many of King's works. Although Gary Cole received top billing for his mischievous turn as Sheriff Lucas Buck, the hero of the series was young Caleb Temple (Lucas Black), a boy who is able to communicate with his late sister (Sarah Paulson). With its supernatural elements, good vs. evil mythology, and series-long story arc, *American Gothic* might have thrived a decade later, but instead the series was subject to network mistreatment straight out of King's worst nightmares. The show was jerked around the schedule, episodes were shown out of order, and it was canceled with four hours left unaired. It has a loyal cult following, however, and is now available on DVD (with the episodes inexplicably *still* out of order).

The post-*Lost* environment was somewhat more welcoming for this type of programming, but failures still vastly outnumbered successes. In 2009, CBS premiered *Harper's Island*, a horror/mystery series unfolding against a backdrop producer Jon Turteltaub described to the *L.A. Times* as "so gothic and dramatic; it's sort of the West Coast equivalent to Stephen King's Maine." Shot on Bowen Island off the coast of Vancouver, the series concerned a group of people gathering for a wedding on an island where a series of murders took place years earlier. When the killing starts again, the cast begins to dwindle as those remaining alive (as well as the viewing audience) attempt to identify the killer. This time, however, the network was willing to make the deal King had wanted for *Golden Years*: *Harper's Island* would be a limited series, running only thirteen episodes, at the end of which the mystery would be resolved. The show even got King's seal of approval (he called it "cheesy but fun" in his *Entertainment Weekly* column), and one episode was directed by King's frequent collaborator Craig Baxley. Ratings plummeted when the network moved the show from Thursdays to Saturdays after the third episode, but CBS did allow the series to play out to its conclusion.

Two series premiering in fall 2012 self-consciously played upon their debt to King, with one proving more successful than the other. *666 Park Avenue* starred *Lost*'s Terry O'Quinn as the owner of a Manhattan apartment building beset by supernatural forces. Creator David Wilcox acknowledged the King connection when meeting with TV critics prior to the show's premiere. "It's absolutely Stephen King influenced," said Wilcox. "Who can't be influenced by Stephen King when working in this genre? . . . The building is like the Overlook Hotel from *The Shining*." The series would not have the staying power of the Overlook ghosts, however, as ABC canceled it after airing nine episodes, burning off the final four in the summer of 2013.

Faring somewhat better, at least from a ratings standpoint, was NBC's *Revolution*. Another J. J. Abrams production, this serialized drama is the latest prime-time variation on *The Stand*, set in a postapocalyptic America where all electrical power has been disabled by a mysterious force. Abrams and company play up the connection by salting the series with King references, from the character of "Randall Flynn" (a walkin' dude played by *Storm of the Century*'s Colm Feore) to the aliases used by two characters traveling incognito ("Stu Redman" and "Frannie"). Episode 11 of the series was even titled "The Stand," while the first-season finale, "The Dark Tower," clearly alluded to another corner of the Stephen King universe. *Revolution* was renewed for a second season, so look for episodes titled "Misery," "The Dead Zone," and "Stand by Me," no doubt coming soon to a television near you.

King as Character: The Horror Novelist in Film And Television

In 1984, Stephen King appeared in an American Express commercial, delivering the familiar line "Do you know me?" while carrying a candle through a Gothic set illuminated by flashes of lightning. The ad signaled a new level of celebrity for the author, cementing his reputation as America's favorite horror writer. And with this new level of fame, it was inevitable that Stephen King-esque characters would begin to filter into pop culture. That same year, a Canadian film called *Deadline* came and went without much notice. Its protagonist was a horror novelist and screenwriter named Steven Lessey who finds the line between his life and his work becoming blurred. Written and directed by Mario Azzopardi, the low-budget film has a few interesting ideas and disturbing moments (including some grisly images of sub-Cronenbergian body horror), but it can be hard to find them under all the bad writing and acting. In the end, Azzopardi tries to have to both ways, denouncing the genre even as he revels in its excesses.

More successful was 1986's *House*, starring William Katt as Roger Cobb, a Vietnam veteran turned horror novelist. When Cobb inherits a house from his aunt, he decides to hole up there to write his new book, a fact-based account of his war experiences. The house holds unpleasant memories for Cobb: His son Jimmy had disappeared there months earlier, and his wife subsequently left him. He soon discovers that the house is haunted and finds himself in a battle with the rubbery sort of monster that proliferated in eighties genre cinema. Directed by Steve Miner (veteran of several *Friday the 13th* installments), *House* eschews the predominant slasher aesthetic of its time in favor of slapstick-splatter humor. It works more often than not, but the movie is weighed down by Vietnam flashbacks straight out of a community theater play.

John Carpenter's 1995 film *In the Mouth of Madness* is largely a tribute to H. P. Lovecraft but also, at least in part, an homage to Stephen King. Written by Michael de Luca, who had penned a "Dollar Baby" adaptation of "The Lawnmower Man" while in film school, the movie concerns insurance investigator John Trent (Sam Neill), hired by a publishing house to investigate the disappearance of its most popular author, horror novelist Sutter Cane. Cane's name evokes King's, and his New England residence and the thick paperbacks attributed to him (with titles such as *The Thing in the Basement* and *The Feeding*) likewise recall the modern master of horror. Carpenter confronts the comparison head-on in a scene set at the publisher's office, when director Jackson Harglow (Charlton Heston) says, "You can forget about Stephen King. Cane outsells them all."

The Lovecraftian elements come to the fore when Trent travels to Hobb's End, a supposedly fictional New Hampshire town that serves as the setting for many of Cane's novels. The people and places in Hobb's End are straight of his books, as are the bizarre events that transpire once Trent and Cane's editor Linda (Julie Carmen) arrive. Cane eventually turns up (as played by Jurgen Prochnow, a German character actor who doesn't much resemble King in appearance or accent) and reveals that his writing has unleashed a number of ancient demons straight out of the Cthulhu mythos. Furthermore, Cane's writing has become reality, and Trent is just a character trapped in his latest novel, *In the Mouth of Madness*.

Or something like that. De Luca's script never really gels, and although Carpenter wrings enough eerie effects from it to keep the movie engaging for its first hour or so, *In the Mouth of Madness* eventually deteriorates into gratuitous weirdness.

By far the most entertaining pop culture depiction of a King-esque character is the 2004 limited series *Garth Marenghi's Darkplace*, which ran for six episodes on Britain's Channel 4. The title character, created by Matthew Holness and Richard Ayoade, originated on the stage at the Edinburgh Festival Fringe. As played by Holness, Marenghi is a horror writer with such novels as *Black Fang*, *The Ooze*, and *Juggers* to his credit. Unlike King, however, his massive ego far outstrips his actual accomplishments. He is also the creator and star of a long-forgotten, never-aired eighties TV series about a haunted hospital called *Darkplace*.

The Channel 4 series posits that Marenghi has recently rediscovered the original *Darkplace* episodes and is now presenting them for the first time, augmented with present-day commentary by himself and his publisher Dean Lerner (Ayoade). Marenghi's pomposity is undercut by the hilarious ineptitude of his creation, which is hampered by horrendous acting, choppy editing, awkward overdubbing, risible special effects, and plot holes big enough to drive a haunted semi through. An adroit, consistently funny and inventive spoof of lousy genre television, *Garth Marenghi's Darkplace* originally aired a few months before *Kingdom Hospital* debuted. The few who saw it at the time must have found it almost impossible to take the real thing seriously.

The Cannibals

Rip-offs, Parodies, and Homages

The Lawnmower Man Goes to Court

First published in *Cavalier* magazine in 1975, "The Lawnmower Man" was later collected in the *Night Shift* anthology. It was one of the stories from that book optioned by Milton Subotsky, who planned to include it in a three-part anthology film called *The Machines*. Subotsky would eventually sell off the rights to all the King stories he acquired, mostly to Dino De Laurentiis, but in the case of "The Lawnmower Man" to producers Steven Lane and Bob Pringle.

Lane and Pringle brought the project to Allied Vision, which jumped at the chance of producing its own Stephen King franchise. There was only one problem: King's seven-page story could hardly serve as the basis for a single feature film, let alone a series of movies. Allied brought the project to New Line Cinema, which held the rights to a spec script by Gimel Everett called *Cyber God*. A riff on the Daniel Keyes novel *Flowers for Algernon* by way of the then-cutting-edge technology of virtual reality, this screenplay had absolutely nothing to do with King's short story. Everett and her writing partner (and husband) Brett Leonard suggested incorporating elements of "The Lawnmower Man" into the *Cyber God* script, and New Line gave the project the green light.

"The screenplay is expanded from the short story," Leonard, who would also direct the film, told Gary L. Wood. "There is one scene in the film which is the short story . . . I'm a complete Stephen King fan, fanatic, and love all his work. What we tried to do is make this something that would fit into his style of work . . . My hope for this is that I get to meet Stephen King and he enjoys the film." Perhaps that would have happened had the finished film carried the same credit as the screenplay, which simply read, "Suggested by the short story by Stephen King." By the time *The Lawnmower Man* reached theaters, however, that would not be the case.

Budgeted at $10 million, *The Lawnmower Man* was shot in thirty-six days in the summer of 1991. Jeff Fahey starred as the titular lawnmower man, a mentally challenged landscaper named Jobe. Pierce Brosnan played Dr. Lawrence Angelo, a scientist who chooses Jobe as the subject of his virtual reality experiments. As Jobe grows smarter through Angelo's efforts, he also becomes vengeful toward those who mistreated him. This plot development leads to the only scene with

Although it was initially released as *Stephen King's The Lawnmower Man*, the author successfully sued to have his name removed from this 1992 cyber-thriller, which bore no resemblance to his short story of the same name.

any connection to King's story, as Jobe uses his new telekinetic powers to run down a former client with a lawnmower.

Though laughable now, the film's CGI effects were state-of-the-art at the time, and audiences responded, giving the movie a $10.3 million opening weekend en route to a total of $32 million. The fact that the film was released as *Stephen King's The Lawnmower Man* may have boosted its performance, although the author's name has certainly never been a guarantee of box office success. Still, King was miffed about the misleading credit, especially once he heard New Line was already exploring the possibility of a sequel. "The movie had nothing to do with what I wrote," King told Andy Marx of the *L.A. Times*. "It's like taking a Mercedes hood ornament and putting it on a Chevrolet and selling it as a Mercedes." Even though New Line had no plans to use King's name for the sequel, the author still fumed. "It doesn't matter if they're not using my name. Everybody is still going to associate my name with the sequel with or without my name on the credits."

King filed a lawsuit against Allied and New Line in an effort to have his name removed from future video releases and television airings of *The Lawnmower Man*. In July 1992, a judge ruled in his favor, awarding the author $3.4 million in damages. New Line retained the right to including a "Based on the short story by Stephen King" line in the credits, but per the ruling, King's name would have to be removed from the title. That should have been the end of it, but in 1993, King noticed that New Line had not complied with the ruling, and that video copies of *The Lawnmower Man* still carried his possessory credit. In 1994, New Line was found to be in contempt of court and ordered to pay King all profits derived from the home video since its release.

New Line went ahead with its plans for a sequel, releasing *Lawnmower Man 2: Beyond Cyberspace* in January 1996. Without King's name or a single member of the original cast, the movie flopped at the box office.

Sisters of Carrie

No King property has been ripped off quite as often as *Carrie*, probably because its simple, universal "revenge of the nerd" story line lends itself to low-budget productions intent on attracting the teen audience. The first such effort was a 1977 TV-movie called *The Spell*, written by Brian Taggart (who would later pen the screenplay for an official Stephen King TV production, *Trucks*) and directed by actor and longtime TV helmer Lee Philips. *The Spell*'s opening scenes skirt the boundaries of plagiarism so closely, they're almost truer to King's book than De Palma's movie had been. Rita (Susan Myers), the teenage wallflower taunted by her classmates, is overweight, just as Carrie was in the novel (but in none of its adaptations). During a P.E. exercise in rope-climbing, she uses her telekinetic abilities to cause her chief tormentor to fall and suffer an injury.

The Spell goes its own way when it comes to Rita's home life. Instead of sharing a dank, Gothic haunt with her fanatical mother, Rita lives in a luxurious, sprawling house with her parents, Glenn (James Olson) and Marilyn (Lee Grant), and kid sister Chris (a fourteen-year-old Helen Hunt). It's a beautiful life, except that everyone in her family is awful and they all seem to hate her. It doesn't take us long to figure out why: Rita is perhaps the most unlovable person on the planet. It's hard to feel any sympathy for her, or anyone else in the movie for that matter. As it turns out, Rita's powers derive from practicing witchcraft with her gym teacher, but even Rita is surprised to learn her mother is the real queen witch of the neighborhood. The kitchen showdown between mother and daughter kicks up more *Carrie* déjà vu, but the movie's only memorable moment comes when Marilyn uses her powers to make a nosy neighbor self-combust.

The following year, another movie-of-the-week, *The Initiation of Sarah*, trod similar ground. Here the title character is the supposedly mousy adopted sister of Patty Goodwin (Morgan Brittany), the popular new girl at college who is invited to join the exclusive, snobby sorority headed up by snooty Jennifer Lawrence (Morgan Fairchild). Sarah (Kay Lenz) is forced to settle for the outcast sorority, presumably because her hair is kind of flat and she tends to wear shapeless sweaters. When Patty is ordered by her new sisters to avoid her old one, Sarah takes it well right up until the moment she uses her telekinetic powers to drop a piano on Patty's head.

Sarah comes to her senses and knocks Patty out of danger's way just in time, but the precedent is set. Later she sends Jennifer flying into a fountain, but she doesn't really snap until Jennifer and friends pelt her with rotten vegetables in a low-rent variation on *Carrie*'s prom sequence. Sarah summons her mental powers and . . . creates a really strong wind, which somehow turns Jennifer old and craggy. But this lethargic thriller doesn't really cut loose until its final moments, when Sarah's house mother (Shelley Winters, in a loopy late-career turn) attempts to lead a ritual sacrifice of Sarah's friend Mouse. (The setting for this ceremony, a hedge maze, has to be coincidental, given that Kubrick was filming *The Shining* at the time the TV-movie first aired.) Sarah turns the ceremony into a conflagration, killing both herself and her house mother in the process.

The same year also saw the theatrical release of *Jennifer*, which finds another outcast at another snobby private school. The title character, played by Lisa Pelikan, is regarded as a yokel from the sticks by her fellow students, who push her too far one night, forcing her to rely on her power over snakes to exact a not-so-terrifying vengeance. By 1982, the formula had been played out to the point where it was ripe for parody, as well as a gender reversal. Enter director Robert J. Rosenthal and his cowriter Bruce Rubin, the brains behind the teen comedy *Zapped!* Scott Baio stars as nerdy Emerson High School science wonk Barney Springboro, imbued with telekinetic powers by a lab accident. Far from viewing his new abilities as a curse, Barney uses them to win prizes at the fair and fights with the school bullies (and, of course, to expose the breasts of his nubile classmates). That is, until his new girlfriend, Bernadette (Felice Schachter), disapproves of his selfish use of a scientific breakthrough. Lessons are learned all around but not before the obligatory prom scene in which Barney uses his powers to exact lukewarm vengeance on his nemeses. *Zapped!* is typical of its time in terms of its rather tame approach to titillation and double entendre, but its unsightly fashions and hairstyles and ghastly pop soundtrack make it a mildly amusing eighties relic for connoisseurs of the era.

Stephen King Goes Bollywood

Indian director Anurag Kashyap made a name for himself with 2004's *Black Friday*, a gritty, naturalistic crime drama based on a series of terrorist bombings in Mumbai in 1993. The film won critical acclaim internationally but was not released in Kashyap's home country for more than two years for fear that it would affect the trial of the accused bombers. Many were eager to see what Kashyap would do next, but few would have predicted an outlandish, surreal fable that also happened to be an unauthorized adaptation of a Stephen King story.

The protagonist of 2007's *No Smoking* is named K., a homage to another of the movie's literary forebears, Franz Kafka. As played by John Abraham, K. is a singularly unlikable individual: an arrogant chain-smoker of apparently unlimited wealth who treats friends, loved ones, and employees alike as doormats. Despite the pleas of those close to him, K. refuses to quit smoking, but when his wife leaves him, he finally agrees to undergo rehabilitation at a facility called "the Laboratory." He soon learns that the methods of Laboratory head Baba

Bangali (Paresh Rawal) are extremely unorthodox: The penalties for smoking even one cigarette range from the loss of a finger to the death of a loved one, and finally to the loss of the smoker's soul.

If all this sounds familiar, you probably remember Stephen King's story "Quitters Inc.," which was adapted into a segment of *Cat's Eye*, discussed earlier in this book. This is no coincidence, as Kashyap has admitted to lifting the entire premise from King's story. In a chat with Bollywood.com prior to the film's release, a fan asked Kashyap about his inspiration for *No Smoking*, to which the director replied, "A short story by Stephen King." But King receives no screen credit in *No Smoking*, and there's no evidence to suggest Kashyap ever secured permission to adapt the story.

To his credit, Kashyap takes the story in some bizarre directions undreamed of by King. His version of the Laboratory is a surreal totalitarian force, part religion, part government, but all-knowing. There's a magical element to the story not present in King: Those who have undergone the treatment and had fingers removed can grow them back if they find another candidate for rehabilitation. The line between reality and fantasy becomes increasingly blurred as Kashyap slathers his film with cartoon thought bubbles, sepia sitcom interludes, musical numbers, and other Bollywood excess until he loses sight of what made King's story work in the first place. His movie certainly isn't dull, but it never gives us much reason to care enough to parse its opaque narrative.

No Smoking was met with savage reviews and a hostile public response in Kashyap's home country. Those who had been moved by *Black Friday* couldn't understand why he would waste his time with such frantic and seemingly shallow nonsense. For his part, Kashyap stood by his work. "I was extremely angry and bitter after *No Smoking*," he told Sampurn of Bollywood Trade News Network. "People reviewed me rather than the movie. It was a new kind of film and while it was getting international recognition, in my own country it was being ripped apart. I learnt a lesson though and it was that if you have to do something new, you have to go step by step."

Miscellaneous Parodies and Homages

"The Shinning"—This "Treehouse of Terror" segment from *The Simpsons*' 1994 Halloween special is more a parody of Stanley Kubrick's film than of King's novel, but no less hilarious for that. Homer Simpson and his family are hired as the winter caretakers for Mr. Burns's remote mountain lodge, which has a colorful history: "It was built on an ancient Indian burial ground. It was the setting of Satanic rituals, witch burnings, and five John Denver Christmas specials." As the winter goes on, Homer begins to crack, finally realizing that "no beer and no TV make Homer go crazy." With the aid of a Moe the Bartender apparition, Homer sets after his family with an axe but is mollified just in time to save them by the discovery of a discarded portable television and its "warm, glowing, warming glow."

"Three Kings"—This seventh season episode of the Fox network's *other* eternal animated series, *The Family Guy*, parodies three different tales by "the greatest author of the last thousand years" (with King's permission, per the episode's DVD audio commentary). As narrated by Richard Dreyfuss, "Stand by Me" features Peter, Quagmire, Joe, and Cleveland as the four boys en route to see a dead body. "Misery" finds novelist Paul Sheldon (as played by Brian, the Griffin family dog) finishing off his "Snuggly Jeff" series, much to the dismay of number one fan Stewie. While driving through a snowy mountain pass, Sheldon accidentally runs over Stephen King (voiced by Danny Smith), who announces, "Hey! This would make a neat story!" in midair and finishes writing it before he hits the ground. And in "The Shawshank Redemption," Peter is Andy Dufresne and Cleveland is Red. As with most of Seth MacFarlane's work, the episode is hit-and-miss, overreliant on empty pop culture references and toilet humor. ("King" also appears in another episode, "A Picture's Worth a Thousand Bucks," in which he pitches a story about a "lamp-monster" to his editor.)

"The Sharktank Redemption"—This parody directed by Natalie van Doren combines elements of *The Shawshank Redemption* with 1994's black comedy about personal assistants to Hollywood agents, *Swimming with Sharks*. Alfonso Freeman, son of Morgan, narrates the film as Fred Redding, a CAA agent-in-training who sees his friend Randy escape the cubicle life for a better world. It's a gentle, mildly amusing spoof that caught *Shawshank* director Frank Darabont's attention: He included it as an extra on his film's special edition DVD release.

Monkeybone **(2001)**—There is a popular misconception that Stephen King appears as himself in this *Beetlejuice*-esque fantasy directed by Henry Selick, but that is not the case. *Monkeybone* stars Brendan Fraser as a cartoonist who refuses to sell out his creation, a crude, hyperactive monkey, to merchandising interests. After an accident, Fraser slips into a coma and enters a dreamworld populated by nightmare-makers from throughout history, including Lizzie Borden, Attila the Hun, Edgar Allan Poe (played by Poe's actual great-great-nephew, credited as Edgar Allan Poe IV), and Stephen King. According to Selick, King had planned to play himself until his near-fatal accident prevented his participation. Instead, the role went to actor Jon Bruno, who is credited as "Man in Dungeon" for legal reasons. That didn't prevent many reviewers from erroneously mentioning "Stephen King's cameo as himself." Visually, Bruno makes for a convincing King doppelganger, but his voice doesn't quite approximate the author's distinctive tones. The movie as a whole is visually appealing but something of a mess from a narrative standpoint.

You Can't Kill Stephen King **(2012)**—This independent comedy/horror film was cowritten and codirected by Monroe Mann, who grew up on the lake in Maine where Stephen King has a summer home. Mann was visiting the lake with his friend (and cowriter/codirector) Ronnie Khalil one rainy weekend when they decided to take a crack at writing a horror script. As Mann told *Fangoria*, "It's a campy horror film about six friends who visit a lake where Stephen King lives and start to get killed off one at a time. Oh wait, did I just give away our amazing plotline?" As of this writing, the movie has played some festivals and been released in several countries, but the U.S. is not yet among them. Stephen King is aware of the film's existence, though. "I ran into him twice during shooting at the local markets," said Mann. "This film is really a homage to his great work and how much he's influenced our generation."

King of All Media

Comics, Radio Dramas, and the Infamous *Carrie* Musical

The Dark Tower and Other Comic Books

Stephen King grew up on comics and has never made any secret of his affection for them. *Creepshow* was a loving homage to the EC horror comics of his childhood, but even as an adult, King continued to read such graphic novels as *The Preacher* and *Watchmen*. The medium seemed a natural fit for King material that had defied all attempts at being adapted for the screen, and his seven-volume magnum opus *The Dark Tower* was at the top of that list.

In 2005, Marvel Comics announced a new ongoing series that would both adapt and supplement the *Dark Tower* novels. Rather than starting with the first book in the series, the initial comic book arc, subtitled *The Gunslinger Born*, would tell a story of Roland Deschain's formative years, most of it lifted from an extended flashback in the fourth volume of King's saga, *Wizard and Glass*. King would be credited as Creative Director and Executive Director, but he would not actually write the series. Those duties fell to Robin Furth, author of the two-volume *Dark Tower Concordance*, who adapted the story lines, and longtime comic book writer Peter David, who wrote the scripts. Jae Lee, a comic book artist who had worked with Marvel on Spider-Man and Captain America, among others, provided the illustrations.

The Gunslinger Born arc ran for seven issues, later collected in a hardcover volume. Originally scheduled to debut in 2006, the first issue didn't arrive on shelves until February 2007. Although the series tells the story of Roland's youth chronologically rather than through flashbacks, it is largely faithful to the tale as told in King's novels. But as told by Furth and David, the story feels rushed and the characters far less defined than they are in the books. Lee's art offers photorealistic characters against hazy backgrounds, often comprised of little more than swirls of color. It lacks the definition that would bring this fantasy world to life and the kinetic quality that would help propel Roland's story in the page-turning manner associated with King.

Still, the first seven issues sold well enough for Marvel to continue the series. Roughly six months after the conclusion of *The Gunslinger Born*, a five-issue arc called *The Long Road Home* was launched with the same creative talent. This time, however, Furth and David concocted a new story of Roland and his original ka-tet, previously untold by King. Immediately following the events of *The Gunslinger Born*, *The Long Road Home* tells of the ka-tet's return to Gilead and the perils faced along the way. Unleashed from the burden of adapting hundreds of pages of text, the comics saga finds its own rhythm, resulting in a more satisfying read.

Furth, David, and Lee continued the story in the six-issue arc *Treachery*, after which Lee departed the series and was replaced by Richard Isanove, who had worked as the colorist on the first three arcs. The new team collaborated on the six-issue *The Fall of Gilead* before Lee returned for the following five-issue arc, *Battle of Jericho Hill*. Lee departed again, replaced by Sean Phillips for *The Journey Begins* and *The Little Sisters of Eluria*. After one more arc, *The Battle of Tull*, the comics finally catch up to the first volume of King's novel series with *The Way Station* and *The Man in Black*. No further adaptations are forthcoming, however: Marvel concluded the series with a one-shot, *So Fell Lord Perth*, in July 2013.

In an open letter included in the first *Dark Tower* trade paperback collection, Stephen King ponders other novels he might consider for comic book adaptation. "*Firestarter* would be a natural, but I don't know the rights situation." He also describes an idea for an original comic that would later become his time-travel novel about the Kennedy assassination, *11/22/63*. But his next project with Marvel turned out to be an adaptation of *The Stand*. Written by Roberto Aguirre-Sacasa (who would later go on to write the screenplay for the 2013 *Carrie* remake) and illustrated by Mike Perkins, the series debuted in September 2008 with a five-issue arc called *Captain Trips*. Covering the first part of King's book from the release of the plague to its widespread devastation of the United States, the comics delve

Following the success of its *Dark Tower* comics, Marvel adapted *The Stand* as a series of graphic novels.

deeper into the novel than the TV miniseries had, particularly in their depiction of the government cover-up of the superflu. The art is crisp and well detailed, and the pacing much more measured than in the early *Dark Tower* comics. *Captain Trips* was followed by five more arcs, all consisting of five issues except for the last one, *The Night Has Come*, which includes six. Together, the thirty-one issues tell the entire story of *The Stand*.

In 2009, a new comics imprint of Del Rey Books released a six-issue series called *The Talisman: The Road of Trials*, based on the first few chapters of King's collaboration with Peter Straub, *The Talisman*. The first issue, numbered zero, served as a prequel to the novel, telling of main character Jack Sawyer's father's adventures in the Territories, the story's fantasy realm. The next five issues follow the novel up to the point where Jack meets Wolf, his sidekick in the novel. Tony Shasteen's art, as colored by Nei Ruffino, nicely contrasts the dark tones of our world with the lighter, blue-sky fantasy world of the Territories, but Robin Furth's script is a stilted and dumbed-down take on the novel. Del Rey announced plans to follow up the first arc with *The Talisman: A Collision of Worlds*, but later decided not to proceed with the project.

Through all these comics, Stephen King himself never scripted an issue. That finally changed in 2010, although the venue for his comic book writing debut was not an adaptation of one of his own novels, but rather an original work by Scott Snyder. Fed up with "sparkly vampires" of the *Twilight* variety, Snyder created *American Vampire* in an effort to make the bloodsuckers scary again. Snyder approached King for a cover blurb and got more than he bargained for: King offered to write a couple of issues of the series. He ended up writing five 16-pages issues, which were then paired with the first five chapters of Snyder's ongoing arc to create five double-sized issues. *American Vampire* is published by DC Comics' Vertigo imprint and continues (without King) to this day.

The Mist and Other Audio Dramas

As mentioned in chapter 18, the first attempt at bringing *The Mist* to the screen took place in the early 1980s but fell apart over budgetary concerns. That version was scripted by Dennis Etchison, and although his screenplay wasn't used for the Frank Darabont movie, it did not go to waste. In 1984, ZBS Productions recorded an audio dramatization of King's novella, produced by Tom Lopez and largely based on Etchison's screenplay.

ZBS employed the Kunstkopf Binaural recording system to create 3D sound, essentially placing the listener in the center of the action. In this process, an artificial human head with two microphones implanted in the ears is used for recording. Depending on the placement and movement of the actors around the head, voices seem to get closer or farther away, or move from left to right. (The crew of *The Mist* audio drama nicknamed this head "Fritz.") Recording took place over three months, employing a cast of thirty-five including leading man William Sadler, who would go on to play a supporting role in Darabont's film. Sound effects for the creatures were created by digitally altering the growls of a common housecat. Tim Clark composed a throbbing, minimalist synthesizer score used to eerie effect throughout the production.

Originally released on audio cassette in 1986, *The Mist in 3D Sound!* is now available on CD and as a digital download, and well worth a listen, especially late at night while wearing headphones. Not all of the acting is first-rate—the child actor playing David Drayton's son has trouble with sentences of more than a few words—but the sound effects are first-rate, and for the most part the production achieves its goal of conjuring a creepy movie of the mind.

Beginning in the 1990s, BBC Radio produced and aired several radio dramas based on Stephen King novels. First up was a seven-part 1995 version of *Salem's Lot*, adapted by Gregory Evans. Evans had been writing radio and television dramas for the BBC since 1990, some original and some adapted from works by Graham Greene and Edgar Allan Poe, among others. Starring Stuart Milligan as Ben Mears, Theresa Gallagher as Susan Norton, and Doug Bradley (best known as Pinhead from the *Hellraiser* movies) as the vampire Barlow, the serial lacks *The Mist*'s impressive production values, but it effectively captures the spirit of old-timey radio, particularly if listened to with the lights off. Evans followed *Salem's Lot* with *Pet Sematary* in 1997 and *Secret Window, Secret Garden* in 1999.

Sing along with Carrie and the Ghost Brothers of Darkland County

Somehow the most misguided Stephen King adaptation of all, and one of the most notorious flops in Broadway history, found its way to a happy ending. It began when Lawrence Cohen, the screenwriter of Brian De Palma's 1976 film of *Carrie*, and his friend Michael Gore took in a performance of Alban Berg's opera *Lulu* in 1981. The pair had been looking for a subject for a potential Broadway musical for years, and after the performance, Gore had an idea. "If Alban Berg were alive today, the project he would be writing as an opera would be *Carrie*."

In a 1988 *New York Times* article, Cohen remembers calling Stephen King to run the idea past him and secure his permission. "When I'd finished, there was a such a long pause that I wondered if he had hung up on me. But then he said, 'Well, I guess if they can do a musical about a dictator in Argentina or a murderous barber on Fleet Street, *Carrie* as a musical makes enormous sense. Go ahead!'"

Carrie's journey to the Broadway stage was tumultuous, to say the least. Its premiere was originally planned for 1986, with Royal Shakespeare Company artistic director Terry Hands making his Broadway musical debut. After the original backers dropped out, however, the project floundered for a while until German producer Friedrich Kurz agreed to finance the production. Seventeen-year-old newcomer Linzi Hateley won the title role, and stage veteran Barbara Cook was cast as her mother, Margaret White. With book by Cohen, music by Gore, lyrics by Dean Pitchford (*Footloose*), and choreography by Debbie Allen,

One of the most notorious flops in Broadway history, the musical version of *Carrie* failed in England and on the Great White Way before its unlikely Off-Broadway revival in 2012.

the show was set to have its out-of-town tryout at the RSC theater in Stratford, England, in February 1988, before moving on to the Broadway stage in April.

After only four previews, *Carrie* debuted on the Stratford stage to a hail of technical problems, including collapsing sets and a microphone malfunction during the climactic scene in which Carrie is doused with pig's blood. Although Hateley received some praise for her turn as Carrie, British critics felt the show was a poor fit for a legendary theater. Nicholas De Jongh of *The Guardian* wrote that *Carrie* "turns out to be a resounding mistake. But to call it a catastrophe would be grossly to exaggerate its significance. Many shows as ridiculous and empty have proved themselves in the market place and the RSC is forced to go down there now."

A complete video of the opening night Stratford performance exists and can sometimes be found on YouTube. It's certainly not the ideal viewing situation— the video is taken from a distant stationary camera, and the quality is degraded— but it does give the impression of a rather chaotic production. It's certainly a product of its times: The music is often heavily synthesized and the regimented choreography is suggestive of vintage Janet Jackson videos. The poppier numbers clash with the more traditional musical balladry, the mix of British and American actors is chemically imbalanced, and Hands lacks De Palma's knack for integrating the campy moments with the operatic emotional undercurrents.

Cook departed the production following the Stratford run and was replaced by Betty Buckley, who had played the gym teacher Miss Collins in the Brian De Palma film. The show made its Broadway debut on April 28, 1988, at the Virginia Theater. In a featurette about the musical on the *Carrie* DVD, Buckley recalls the entire audience booing after the dramatic finale on opening night. But when Buckley and Hateley took their curtain call, the reaction turned on a dime. "The lights came back up, and as she and I are standing, the entire place, in a moment, turned into a full-house standing ovation . . . It was just insane."

If anything, the New York reviews were even more scathing than the British ones. Frank Rich of the *New York Times* called it a "typical musical-theater botch," while David Richards of the *Washington Post* wrote, "Like a reproduction of 'The Last Supper' made entirely out of broken bottles, it's hideous. But you can't help marveling at the lengths to which someone went to make it." Despite the fact that the show played to full houses for its sixteen previews and five performances, *Carrie*'s financial backers pulled the plug, closing the show on May 15. At a cost of $7 million, the production was considered the biggest flop in Broadway history.

That was not the end of the *Carrie* musical, however. More than two decades later, Cohen, Gore, and Pitchford launched an Off-Broadway revival of the show at the Lucille Lortel Theater. Several songs from the original production were dropped and replaced with new ones, and the revamped musical premiered in previews on January 31, 2012, directed by Stafford Arima, with Molly Ranson as Carrie and Marin Mazzie as Margaret White. Freed of its dated choreography and cheesy synthesizer score, the stripped-down Off-Broadway version still didn't attract universally ecstatic reviews, but it enjoyed a longer run than its predecessor—thirty-four previews and forty-six performances—and was nominated for five Drama Desk Awards. An original cast album was released on September 25, 2012, and new productions of the musical, including one in Los Angeles, continue to be mounted.

Stephen King decided to take his own stab at musical theater as far back as Halloween 2000. "Broadway is about to become the Great Fright Way, thanks to Stephen King, who's penning a new horror musical," Bill Hoffman wrote in the *New York Post*. "The best-selling author has joined forces with rock singer John Mellencamp to write a macabre rock opera that will feature a haunted house and rapping ghosts." Originally titled *Mississippi Ghost Brothers*, the idea was hatched by Mellencamp, who approached King with a story about two feuding brothers in a haunted cabin in the woods full of singing ghosts. As of October 2002, King had fleshed out Mellencamp's story, and the two were planning to get together in the spring to finish it off.

By April 2005, the project had a new title: *Ghost Brothers of Darkland County*. "'He's got a hundred pages of dialogue, and I've got 15 songs," Mellencamp told Jon Bream of the *Minneapolis Star-Tribune*. "Add all that up and, 'So far, Steve, we've got about five hours worth of play.' We have to figure how to cut it all down . . . If anyone's got the crazy idea that this is 'Jack and Diane' meets

Cujo, they're nuts." King and Mellencamp held a read-through that summer and expressed hopes to have the full production in out-of-town tryouts within a year. That didn't happen, and by February 2008, Mellencamp was telling *Rolling Stone* that the show would finally open the following spring in Atlanta.

The Alliance Theater in Atlanta scheduled the debut of *Ghost Brothers* for April 15, 2009, but quickly rescinded that date, postponing the production indefinitely. In late 2009, it was announced that *Ghost Brothers* would be released as a CD-and-book box set, with T-Bone Burnett producing, an all-star cast including Sheryl Crow, Elvis Costello, and Kris Kristofferson performing the songs, and actors such as Matthew McConaughey and Meg Ryan reading the dialogue. In 2011, the Alliance Theater once again announced plans to produce *Ghost Brothers* the following spring, under the direction of Susan V. Booth. This time, the production went forward, with a cast including Shuler Hensley, Emily Skinner, and *American Idol* finalist Justin Guarini. The show debuted in previews on April 4, 2012, with opening night following on April 11. Reviews were mixed: The *New York Times* wrote that *Ghost Brothers* "has an ungainliness that brings to mind the original *Spider-Man: Turn Off the Dark* . . . It has the feel of something devised over Skype," while the *Atlanta Journal-Constitution* raved, "All the advance hype surrounding *Ghost Brothers* has been somewhat scary . . . But never fear: Under the mesmerizing direction of Susan V. Booth, the Alliance production lives up to it."

The Alliance production ran through May 13, 2012. Over a year later, on June 4, 2013, the CD version of *Ghost Brothers* was finally released. Even largely divorced from its dramatic context, the album works surprisingly well as a collection of rootsy rock, blues, and folk tunes, with standout tracks including "So Goddam Smart" (which reunites real-life feuding brothers Dave and Phil Alvin of the Blasters), Taj Mahal's "Tear This Cabin Down," and Kris Kristofferson's "What Kind of Man Am I?" A touring version of the show, reconfigured as a concert rather than a full stage production, was launched in October 2013 in Mellencamp's hometown of Bloomington, Indiana.

Other theatrical ventures based on King's work include a nonmusical stage play based on *Misery*, penned by the film's screenwriter William Goldman and starring Johanna Day as Annie Wilkes, which had a brief run at Pennsylvania's Bucks County Playhouse in November 2012. (An earlier theatrical adaptation by Simon Moore debuted in London and has been performed throughout the United States.) *The Shawshank Redemption* was also adapted for the London stage in 2009 by Owen O'Neill and Dave Johns. An opera based on *Dolores Claiborne*, composed by Tobias Picker with a libretto by J. D. McClatchy, was slated to premiere at the San Francisco Opera in September 2013.

The Rock Bottom Remainders

Stephen King's musical side manifested in another way beginning in 1992 with the first performance by the Rock Bottom Remainders. Kathi Kamen Goldman, a musician with a day job escorting authors to their media appearances, came up with the idea after meeting more than a few writers who were frustrated musicians at heart. The initial plan was to put together a benefit concert at the American Booksellers Convention in Anaheim, California. Goldman sent a fax around to the authors she'd met, hoping a few would sign up. Those who took her up on the offer included Dave Barry, Ridley Pearson, Amy Tan, Barbara Kingsolver, and Stephen King.

The band's first performance was taped and released on VHS in 1993. The set list was comprised of golden oldies like "Money," "Louie Louie," and "Gloria," leavened with ample doses of self-deprecating humor. ("We play music about as well as Metallica writes novels.") The humor is much needed, as the musicianship can most charitably be described as enthusiastic but sloppy. King takes the lead vocals on two numbers, crooning "Sea of Love" and unveiling an impressive early nineties mullet for a campy, melodramatic reading of "Teen Angel." It's amusing but definitely a "don't quit your day job" scenario.

In later years, the band's revolving lineup included sports columnist Mitch Albom, Scott Turow, and James McBride. The group also brought in actual working musicians for some gigs, with the likes of Warren Zevon, Roger McGuinn, and even Bruce Springsteen sitting in over the years. In 1994, the group published a book called *Mid-Life Confidential*, a scrapbook of their nine-city tour in 1993, including essays from the band members and photos by Tabitha King.

Twenty years after their debut, the Remainders held a farewell gig at the same Anaheim convention. Goldman had passed away on May 24, 2012, and the band members decided that this show would be an appropriate send-off for the group

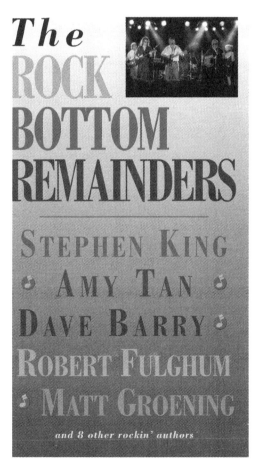

King and some of his fellow authors (including Dave Barry, Robert Fulghum, and Amy Tan) formed the Rock Bottom Remainders, a garage band comprised of "musicians" who knew better than to quit their day jobs.

and tribute to its founder. The final performance on June 23 featured Stephen King's breathless rendition of the Trashmen classic "Surfin' Bird." To the end, the Remainders lived up to the words of the Boss as recounted by King: "A few years ago, Bruce Springsteen told us we weren't bad, but not to try to get any better otherwise we'd just be another lousy band. After 20 years, we still meet his stringent requirements."

A Hell of a Band

The Ultimate Stephen King Movie Soundtrack

R ock and roll has always been very important to Stephen King and to his writing. He describes his process thusly in *On Writing*: "I work to loud music—hard rock stuff like AC/DC, Guns 'N Roses, and Metallica have always been particular favorites." In 1983, he purchased AM radio station WLBZ and rechristened it WZON—The Zone. The format was, of course, the same brand of hard rock King favors while writing. Rock lyrics feature prominently in many of his books; every chapter in *Christine* starts with a quote from a different classic rock song. So it's a no-brainer that the movies made from his works tend to feature King's favorite rock tunes.

What follows is not intended to be any sort of comprehensive account of music used in Stephen King movies. It's a playlist, or what we over-forty types used to call a mix tape; a soundtrack you can listen to while you read this book or do your time on the treadmill. You can find it on Spotify here: *http://open.spotify. com/user/scottvond/playlist/7HfQvJybwIIxsXZ6wa7mnI*. (Bear in mind, though, that not everything is available on Spotify: For instance, the AC/DC song is performed by a soundalike band.) Crank it up and enjoy!

1. "Bad to the Bone," George Thorogood and the Destroyers—What better way to kick off this set than with one of the most overused songs in motion picture history? "Bad to the Bone" has long since become a comedic cue in pop culture, but you can't blame King or director John Carpenter for that. *Christine* marked its first ever appearance in a movie, and its down-and-dirty guitar riff set the perfect menacing tone for that film's brilliant opening sequence.

2. "Sleep Walk," Santo and Johnny—This dreamy instrumental from 1959 has found its way into two King movies: *Sleepwalkers* (of course) and *Hearts in Atlantis*, as well as the premiere episode of the *Dead Zone* TV series. Its steel guitar lead is one of the most evocative sounds in all of rock music, immediately transporting the listener to a blissful world of exotica. It hit the top spot on the pop charts in 1959.

3. "Lollipop," the Chordettes—This doo-wop classic from 1958 set the nostalgic tone for Rob Reiner's *Stand by Me*. Originally written by Julius Dixson and Beverly Ross for recording duo Ronald and Ruby, the song reached #2 on

This EP from Austin root-rock band the Gourds includes their cover of "Gin and Juice," which was featured in the series premiere of *Kingdom Hospital*.

the *Billboard* pop charts for the Chordettes. In addition to *Stand by Me*, it has appeared in the movies *Crazy Mama*, *Chicken Little*, and *Whip It*, among others.

4. "Time Has Come Today," the Chambers Brothers—Another two-timer, this psychedelic artifact was used in both *Riding the Bullet* and the final episode of *Kingdom Hospital*. It's also found its way into more than a dozen other movies, and with good reason. Released on the 1967 album *The Time Has Come* as an eleven-minute epic and reaching #11 on the *Billboard* singles chart in the fall of 1968 in a more radio-friendly three-minute edit, the song's ominous tick-tock opening, surging guitar and vocals, and end-times lyrics add up to the perfect cinematic shorthand to indicate things are about to get crazy.

5. "Who Made Who," AC/DC—Perhaps the best decision Stephen King made when it came to his directorial debut (and, so far, swan song) *Maximum Overdrive* was hiring AC/DC to perform the soundtrack. In his memoir,

Rockers and Rollers, lead singer Brian Johnson recalls, "We flew to the Bahamas to record it as Compass Point Studio, where we'd done *Back in Black*. And there to meet us was Stephen King himself, who both wrote and directed the film, and Dino De Laurentiis, the producer. We saw the rushes and came up with the song 'Who Made Who,' which still rocks. Stephen liked it, but Dino couldn't stand it, which was just as well, because we couldn't stand him." The only real shame is that Johnson and company didn't actually write a song called "Maximum Overdrive," which still sounds like an AC/DC title waiting to happen.

6. "Pet Sematary," the Ramones—Another song written specifically for a Stephen King movie, this morbid ditty was commissioned by *Pet Sematary* director Mary Lambert, a good friend of Dee Dee Ramone. King's novel had specifically included a Ramones song in the scene in which the truck driver runs over Gage Creed, so it wasn't much of a leap to have the band record the title track. While it certainly doesn't rank with the band's classic work, the line "I don't want to live my life again" has a certain chilly resonance.

7. "(Don't Fear) the Reaper," Blue Öyster Cult—The highlight of ABC's eight-hour miniseries adaptation of *The Stand* comes early, with a montage of devastation scored to this 1976 death anthem. It was an obvious choice, given that King had extensively quoted the lyrics to the song at the beginning of his novel, but that doesn't mean it was the wrong choice. These days the song is probably best known for the *SNL* sketch in which Christopher Walken as producer Bruce Dickinson keeps demanding "more cowbell!"

8. "Shotgun," Jr. Walker and the All-Stars—Another sixties nugget, this Top 5 Motown hit was featured in *Misery* (and a number of other films, such as *Malcolm X* and Martin Scorsese's debut, *Who's That Knocking at My Door*). There's not much to analyze here lyrically, but Walker and his band (including Willie Woods on guitar and Victor Thomas on organ) lay down an irresistible groove.

9. "Golden Years," David Bowie—CBS may not have allocated the biggest budget in the world for King's limited summer series, but at least the network shelled out for the original version of the title track. Released as a single in 1975 and included on Bowie's 1976 album *Station to Station*, the upbeat funk-inflected tune, with its "stick with you, baby, for a thousand years" refrain, makes for a rather ironic theme song for a series about a man aging in reverse and leaving his "golden years" (and in the process, his elderly wife) behind.

10. "Worry About You," Ivy—Here's the theme song to King's other limited series, *Kingdom Hospital*. Pop trio Ivy is comprised of two American musicians and French singer Dominique Durand, and this song is taken from their third album, 2001's *Long Distance*. From a deceptively simple, almost nursery-rhyme opening, "Worry About You" blossoms into a lush, moody ballad with sinister undercurrents—an ideal tone-setter for a show about the evil that lurks beneath surface normality.

11. "Red Dragon Tattoo," Fountains of Wayne—Featured heavily throughout the *Kingdom Hospital* premiere, and recurring later in the series, this is a ridiculously catchy pop tune from a ridiculously catchy pop band. (Oddly enough, Fountains of Wayne shares songwriter and bass player Adam Schlesinger with the above band Ivy.) Included on the 1999 album *Utopia Parkway*, the song is playing on Peter Rickman's iPod when he is hit by the van and subsequently haunts him throughout his coma, as any good earworm should.

12. "Gin and Juice," the Gourds—Also featured in the *Kingdom Hospital* premiere, this cover of the Snoop Doggy Dogg song by a rollicking rootsy band from Austin had to be heavily censored for its network broadcast. The Gourds' version was a viral sensation in the Wild West days of Napster, although at the time it was often misattributed to Phish. What could have been little more than an amusing novelty proves to be an irresistible roll-the-top-down anthem.

13. "New Year's Prayer," Jeff Buckley—Released posthumously on the album *Sketches for My Sweetheart, the Drunk* after Buckley drowned in 1997, this moody mid-tempo number served as the opening credits song for the first three seasons of *The Dead Zone*. (As of the fourth season, it was replaced by an instrumental called "Dead Zone Epic" by Blues Saraceno.)

14. "Twilight Time," the Platters—The title alone should qualify this dreamy 1958 chart-topper for inclusion: Twilight time is Stephen King time, after all. But the song, originally an instrumental by the Three Suns before Buck Ram added lyrics in 1944, also gave King the title for his story "Heavenly Shades of Night Are Falling" in *Hearts in Atlantis*. The Platters' version appears in the movie *Hearts in Atlantis*.

15. "Stand by Me," Ben E. King—No King playlist would be complete without the song that gave Rob Reiner's film of "The Body" its new title. Regarded as a timeless classic now, "Stand by Me" was originally written for Ben E. King's former band the Drifters, who rejected it. King recorded it himself and saw it go to the top ten of the pop charts twice: in 1961 and again in 1986, when it was rereleased on the *Stand by Me* soundtrack. The song has been recorded countless times over the years, including a version by Warren Zevon and Stephen King, released on the charity compilation *Stranger than Fiction*.

16. "The Host of Seraphim," Dead Can Dance—Frank Darabont didn't choose the subtlest possible music cue for the controversial climax of *The Mist*, but then again, it wasn't the subtlest possible scene. Australian band Dead Can Dance recorded "The Host of Seraphim" for their 1988 album *The Serpent's Egg*, and the music certainly suggests the celestial beings of the title. A percussive track featuring a church-like organ and nearly supernatural vocalizations by singer Lisa Gerrard, the track makes for an evocative capper on a chilling scene.

17. "The End of the World," Skeeter Davis—This mournful country-pop tune was a #2 hit in 1962, and an appropriate choice for the first season of *Under the Dome*. Music supervisor Ann Kline told Radio.com that executive producer

Neal Baer "brought up the song in a music meeting and everyone in the room thought it would be a cool song for the show." Written by Arthur Kent and Sylvia Dee, "The End of the World" is more about the emotional apocalypse of lost love than a literal one, but it captures the right mood of desperation nonetheless.

18. "Midnight, the Stars and You," Al Bowlly—The name Al Bowlly may not ring a bell, but he was a fascinating figure in early twentieth-century music. He's considered to be the first crooner as well as the first vocalist to be credited on recordings (which had previously been credited to bandleaders); he recorded more than one thousand songs but lost his voice in the 1930s and was forced to have throat surgery; and he was killed by a bomb blast from a Luftwaffe parachute mine in London in 1941. This popular tune from 1934 is the song that haunts the halls of the Overlook Hotel in the closing minutes of *The Shining*.

Bonus Tracks

- "In," Premiere Cast, *Carrie: The Musical*—The opening number from the ill-fated musical (here performed by the cast of the much-better-received revival) promises a good time that the rest of the show (at least in its initial incarnation) couldn't deliver. The rousing number sets the stage for Carrie's first humiliation, as her classmates obsess over the importance of fitting in with the crowd.

- "Tear This Cabin Down," Taj Mahal—You don't have to know a thing about the story of *Ghost Brothers of Darkland County* to enjoy this barn-burner from the soundtrack. Legendary bluesman Taj Mahal performs the stomping tune with an appropriate backwoods growl and howling harmonica riffs.

- "Dirty Water," the Rock Bottom Remainders—A rarity from the all-author band featuring Stephen King on lead vocals, this ode to Boston was originally performed by the Standells, and must surely be near and dear to King's heart, as it is played after every Red Sox victory at Fenway Park. As for the Remainders version, which can be found on YouTube as of this writing . . . well, it's got a lot of spunk. Let's just leave it at that.

Keys to the Kingdom

Cameos, Guest Shots, Awards, and Quotable Quotes

Cameos

Stephen King fans, like those of Alfred Hitchcock before him, have come to expect the author's appearance in films based on his work. King has described himself as a "frustrated actor," but he's realistic about his limitations. To hear him tell it, his range runs the gamut from "total scuzzo" to "just your basic country asshole." Here's a complete guide to King's gallery of cameos.

Creepshow (**Jordy Verrill**)—King's first appearance in one of his own works was actually more than a cameo: The author played a leading role in the segment "The Lonesome Death of Jordy Verrill." Encouraged by director George Romero, King delivered the broadest possible interpretation of the backwoods farmer who discovers a meteor in his yard and begins to sprout green moss from every orifice. **Key dialogue:** "It's . . . meteorshit!"

Maximum Overdrive (**Man at ATM**)—King not only directed this 1986 flop, he contributed an appearance early in the movie as a customer insulted by his bank's automatic teller. **Key dialogue:** "Honey? Come on over here, Sugar Buns. This machine just called me an asshole!"

Creepshow 2 (**Truck Driver**)—King took on a smaller role in the follow-up to *Creepshow* but played the same sort of low-wattage working stiff. In the segment "The Hitchhiker," King is a truck driver who happens upon the scene of an accident. **Key dialogue (while eyeing mangled corpse):** "He's a black guy, huh?"

Pet Sematary (**Minister**)—In a change of pace, King plays a respectable role as a priest presiding over the funeral of young Gage Creed. **Key dialogue:** "May the Lord bless you and keep you."

Golden Years (**Bus Driver**)—King reverted to form in the fifth episode of his short-lived TV series, playing an impatient bus driver who unwittingly aids the escape of two characters from their shadowy government pursuers.

Sleepwalkers (**Cemetery Caretaker**)—The author met his frequent collaborator Mick Garris for the first time on the set of this film. King shared his scene with director John Landis (as Lab Assistant) and Clive Barker (as Forensic Tech). **Key dialogue:** "It's not my fault if every horny kid and weirdo pervert comes in here. I lock this place up. I don't need this action!"

***The Stand* (Teddy Weizak)**—In his biggest role since *Creepshow*, King appears in several scenes throughout the miniseries. Teddy gives Nadine a lift to Mother Abigail's home, helps clean out a church piled with dead bodies, and welcomes Stu and Tom Cullen back while serving guard duty. **Key dialogue:** "It's the baby. It's come early . . . and it's got the flu."

***The Langoliers* (Tom Holby)**—With this miniseries practically being shot in King's backyard in Bangor, Maine, the author could hardly resist contributing a cameo. He plays the boss of Bronson Pinchot's character . . . or more accurately, a hallucination of Pinchot's boss, leading a board meeting on the tarmac at Bangor International Airport.

***Thinner* (Dr. Bangor)**—Even the name of King's character is an inside joke here. The author plays a pharmacist who fills a prescription for Tadzu immediately before the old Gypsy woman is hit by a car. He later testifies at the inquest, claiming that the Gypsies were stealing.

***The Shining* (Gage Creed)**—In the TV remake scripted by King, the author takes on an appropriate role: Leader of the band. King plays the Overlook Hotel ballroom's undead orchestra conductor, who happens to share the same name as the dead little boy from *Pet Sematary*. An extended scene of Creed's flesh melting was cut from the miniseries but appears as an extra on the DVD.

***Storm of the Century* (Lawyer in Ad)**—King appears as a sleazy personal injury lawyer, seen only in a commercial playing on a broken television in the home of Andre Linoge's first victim, Martha Clarendon. **Key dialogue:** "Stick it to them before they stick it to you."

***Rose Red* (Pizza Delivery Guy)**—Another self-explanatory role: King shows up at the door of the titular mansion with an armful of pizzas just as a dance party breaks out among the paranormal investigators. **Key dialogue:** "Hey, this is some place, huh? Is it haunted?"

***Kingdom Hospital* (Johnny B. Goode)**—A running joke throughout the series has the easily exasperated Dr. Stegman continually foiled in his attempts at meeting with the hospital's head of maintenance, Johnny B. Goode. He is informed by a string of replacements (played in a series of celebrity cameos by the likes of Charles Martin Smith, Wayne Newton, and Dick Smothers) that Mr. Goode is out of the office for, variously, a dental appointment, vacation, and jury duty. Finally, in the last episode, Stegman comes face-to-face with Goode, who is, of course, played by Stephen King. King pulls double-duty in the scene, as Goode's television is playing the same lawyer commercial seen in *Storm of the Century*.

***Gotham Cafe* (Mr. Ring)**—This 2005 Dollar Baby short attracted more big-name talent than most. Steve Wozniak, one of the cofounders of Apple, contributed a cameo, as did Mick Garris. The big get, however, was King himself, who agreed to a voice-only appearance as main character Steve's lawyer.

Guest Shots

Not all of King's acting work has been done in service of his own material. He's also helped out a few friends along the way by doing bit roles, and like any self-respecting celebrity, he's played himself for laughs a time or two as well.

Knightriders (**Hoagie Man**)—King's first screen appearance came not in a movie based on one of his own works but in this 1981 George Romero film about modern-day knights jousting on motorcycles. King and his wife, Tabitha, played a couple of spectators at the event, with the author establishing his rube bona fides in a paisley shirt and trucker hat, a Budweiser near at hand as he tears into a sandwich in the most slovenly possible fashion. **Key dialogue:** "You know, I don't have the balls to wear anything like that." (Although Tabitha King steals the shows from him with her reading of the rejoinder, "Don't I wish. Gimme a beer!")

Frasier (**Brian**)—The long-running *Cheers* spin-off, in which Kelsey Grammer's psychiatrist Frasier Crane relocates to Seattle and becomes a talk radio host, attracted a plethora of voice-only cameos from celebrities acting as Frasier's callers, among them Rob Reiner, Ron Howard, John Cusack, and Stephen King. In the 2000 episode "Mary Christmas," King plays Brian, whose call Frasier picks up after another caller balks at squeezing in his problem in the minute before the show goes to commercial break. **Key dialogue:** "For what? 30 seconds? I'll wait, too."

The Simpsons (**Himself**)—As we've already seen, King's work has been parodied on *The Simpsons*, but the author himself finally appeared in the 2000 episode "Insane Clown Posse." Marge approaches King at a book-signing to ask what tale of horror he's currently working on, and is disappointed to hear he's busy writing a biography of Benjamin Franklin. **Key dialogue:** "And that key he tied to the end of a kite? It opened the gates of Hell!"

Diary of the Dead (**Radio Preacher**)—King makes his third appearance in a George Romero film (following *Knightriders* and *Creepshow*), albeit uncredited and voice-only. Along with Guillermo del Toro, Simon Pegg, and others, King literally phoned in his performance, in which he emulates the old-time cadences of a fire-and-brimstone preacher.

Fever Pitch (**Himself**)—On September 4, 2004, Stephen King threw the first pitch at Fenway Park. The Red Sox lost the game against the Texas Rangers that day, but King had the last laugh when the Sox won the World Series that year: He and Stuart O'Nan published a running diary of the season called *Faithful* that became a best seller. King's first pitch is immortalized in this Farrelly Brothers film about an obsessive Red Sox fan.

***Sons of Anarchy* (Bachman)**—After hearing King was a fan of his pulpy biker soap, *Sons* creator Kurt Sutter reached out to the author and offered him a small role in the third-season episode "Caregiver." King plays a "cleaner" named Bachman (a hat tip, of course, to his Richard Bachman pen name) called in by the Sons to dispose of a body. It's probably King's best performance (although, granted, there isn't much competition), simultaneously creepy and funny. **Key dialogue:** "How's the drain in that slop sink?"

***Stuck in Love* (Himself)**—King plays the world's best-selling horror novelist in this 2013 film about a somewhat less successful writer (Greg Kinnear) obsessing over his ex (Jennifer Connelly) and encouraging his daughter (Lily Collins) to follow in his footsteps.

Stephen King (seen here on the set of *The Night Flier*) has never been shy about appearing in adaptations of his work.

Awards

King would be the first to admit that the vast majority of movies adapted from his work aren't Academy Award material. But over the course of nearly four decades, the various awards guilds are bound to take notice now and then. Here's a complete list of Oscars, Emmies, and Golden Globes for which King-related works have been nominated (and in some cases won).

Academy Awards

1976
Best Actress (nominated): Sissy Spacek, *Carrie*
Best Supporting Actress (nominated): Piper Laurie, *Carrie*

1987
Best Adapted Screenplay (nominated): Raynold Gideon and Bruce A. Evans, *Stand by Me*

1990
Best Actress (won): Kathy Bates, *Misery*

1994
Best Picture (nominated): *The Shawshank Redemption*
Best Actor (nominated): Morgan Freeman, *The Shawshank Redemption*
Best Adapted Screenplay (nominated): Frank Darabont, *The Shawshank Redemption*
Best Cinematography (nominated): Roger Deakins, *The Shawshank Redemption*
Best Film Editing (nominated): Richard Francis-Bruce, *The Shawshank Redemption*
Best Original Score (nominated): Thomas Newman, *The Shawshank Redemption*
Best Sound (nominated): Robert J. Litt, et al, *The Shawshank Redemption*

1999
Best Picture (nominated): *The Green Mile*
Best Supporting Actor (nominated): Michael Clarke Duncan, *The Green Mile*
Best Adapted Screenplay (nominated): Frank Darabont, *The Green Mile*
Best Sound (nominated): Robert J. Litt, et al., *The Green Mile*

Emmy Awards

1979
Makeup (nominated): Ben Lane and Jack H. Young, *Salem's Lot*
Graphic Design and Title Sequence (nominated): Gene Craft, *Salem's Lot*
Music Composition for Limited Series or Special (nominated): Harry Sukman, *Salem's Lot*

1990
Editing for a Miniseries or Special—Single Camera (nominated): Robert F. Shugrue and David Blangsted, *It*
Music Composition for Miniseries or Special (won): Richard Bellis, *It*

1993
Sound Editing for Miniseries or Special (nominated): Richard Taylor, et al., *The Tommyknockers*

1994
Outstanding Miniseries (nominated): *The Stand*
Cinematography for Miniseries or Special (nominated): Edward J. Pei, *The Stand*
Art Direction for Miniseries or Special (nominated): Nelson Coates, et al., *The Stand*
Music Composition for Miniseries or Special (nominated): W. G. Snuffy Walden, *The Stand*
Makeup for Miniseries or Special (won): Steve Johnson, et al., *The Stand*
Sound Mixing for Drama Miniseries or Special (won): Grant Maxwell, et al., *The Stand*

1995

Sound Mixing for Drama Miniseries or Special (nominated): Jay Meagher and Grant Maxwell, *The Langoliers*

1997

Outstanding Miniseries (nominated): *The Shining*

Makeup for Miniseries or Special (won): Bill Corso, et al., *The Shining*

Sound Editing for Miniseries or Special (won): James Hebenstreit et al., *The Shining*

Music Composition for Miniseries or Special (nominated): Mark Mothersbaugh, *Quicksilver Highway*

1999

Special Visual Effects for Miniseries or Movie (nominated): Boyd Shermis, et al., *Storm of the Century*

Sound Editing for Miniseries, Movie, or Special (won): Richard Taylor, et al., *Storm of the Century*

2002

Art Direction for Miniseries, Movie, or Special (nominated): Craig Stearns, et al., *Rose Red*

2004

Music Composition for Miniseries, Movie, or Special (nominated): Lisa Gerrard and Christopher Gordon, *'Salem's Lot*

Main Title Design (nominated): Paul Matthaeus, et al., *Kingdom Hospital*

Special Visual Effects for Series (nominated): James Tichenor, et al., *Kingdom Hospital*

2006

Art Direction for Miniseries or Movie (nominated): Phil Dagort, et al., *Desperation*

Sound Editing for Miniseries, Movie, or Special (nominated): Richard Taylor, et al., *Desperation*

Lead Actor in Miniseries or Movie (nominated): William H. Macy, *Nightmares & Dreamscapes*

Makeup for Miniseries, Movie, or Special, Non-Prosthetic (nominated): Angela Conte and Kate Birch, *Nightmares & Dreamscapes*

Special Visual Effects for Miniseries, Movie, or Special (nominated): David Vana, et al., *Nightmares & Dreamscapes* ("The End of the Whole Mess")

Special Visual Effects for Miniseries, Movie, or Special (won): Sam Nicholson, et al., *Nightmares & Dreamscapes* ("Battleground")

Music Composition for Miniseries, Movie, or Special (won): Jeff Beal, *Nightmares & Dreamscapes*

Golden Globe Awards

1976
Best Supporting Actress (nominated): Piper Laurie, *Carrie*

1986
Best Motion Picture, Drama (nominated): *Stand by Me*
Best Director, Motion Picture (nominated): Rob Reiner, *Stand by Me*

1990
Best Actress in a Motion Picture, Drama (won): Kathy Bates, *Misery*

1994
Best Actor in a Motion Picture, Drama (nominated): Morgan Freeman, *The Shawshank Redemption*
Best Screenplay, Motion Picture (nominated): Frank Darabont, *The Shawshank Redemption*

1999
Best Supporting Actor in a Motion Picture, Drama (nominated): Michael Clarke Duncan, *The Green Mile*

Quotable Quotes

"Most of [my novels] have been plain fiction for plain folks, the literary equivalent of a Big Mac and a large fries from McDonald's."
—*Different Seasons* afterword

"I have grown into a Bestsellasaurus Rex—a big, stumbling book-beast that is loved when it shits money and hated when it tramples houses."
— *"The Politics of Limited Editions,"* Castle Rock *newsletter, June/July 1985*

"Good books don't give up all their secrets at once."
—*Hearts in Atlantis*

"The thing under my bed waiting to grab my ankle isn't real. I know that, and I also know that if I'm careful to keep my foot under the covers, it will never be able to grab my ankle."
—*Night Shift*

"I recognize terror as the finest emotion and so I will try to terrorize the reader. But if I find that I cannot terrify, I will try to horrify, and if I find that I cannot horrify, I'll go for the gross-out. I'm not proud."

—*Danse Macabre*

"I guess when you turn off the main road, you have to be prepared to see some funny houses."

—*The Bachman Books*

"Nobody loves a clown at midnight."

—*Lisey's Story*

"Speaking personally, you can have my gun, but you'll take my book when you pry my cold, dead fingers off of the binding."

—*Time,* June 2000

"Americans are apocalyptic by nature. The reason why is that we've always had so much, so we live in deadly fear that people are going to take it away from us."

—*Salon,* October 2008

"Life isn't a support system for art. It's the other way around."

—*On Writing*

Everything's Eventual

The Dark Tower and Beyond

T he release of this book comes at a particularly fertile time for Stephen King adaptations. After a lull of sorts in the past decade or so, Hollywood has returned to the work of "America's best-loved bogeyman" with a vengeance. In addition to the 2013 summer series *Under the Dome* and the Kimberly Peirce remake of *Carrie* (both discussed in earlier chapters), a number of other King projects are in various stages of production or development as of this writing

Mercy

King's short story "Gramma" has already been adapted once, as an episode of the 1980s *Twilight Zone* revival scripted by Harlan Ellison. In October 2012, *Variety* announced that Blumhouse Productions, the company behind such horror hits as *Insidious* and the *Paranormal Activity* movies, would team with Universal for a big-screen version of "Gramma" to be titled *Mercy*. Matt Greenberg, cowriter of *1408*, penned the screenplay, and Peter Cornell (*The Haunting in Connecticut*) got the nod to direct the feature.

Frances O'Connor (*A.I.*) was the first announced member of the cast, set to play the mother of two young boys who are forced to take care of their ailing grandmother. Dylan McDermott and Mark Duplass later joined the project, along with Chandler Riggs (*The Walking Dead*) and Joel Courtney (*Super 8*) as the two boys. Per the official plot description released by Universal, "Once George (Riggs) and Buddy McCoy (Courtney) arrive at their Gramma Mercy's (Shirley Knight), what they find inside her 150-year-old home is nothing short of terrifying. As the brothers experience deeply disturbing phenomena they believe to be the work of an ancient witch, they must fight for their lives and overcome the evil forces threatening their family."

Production on the film got underway in January 2013. Universal is eyeing a 2014 theatrical release.

The Ten O'Clock People

A short story from the *Nightmares & Dreamscapes* collection, "The Ten O'Clock People" concerns a man who discovers while trying to quit smoking that his reduced nicotine intake allows him to see people in positions of power for what they really are: bat-faced monsters. It's a premise reminiscent of John Carpenter's great paranoid sci-fi thriller *They Live*, and it will be brought to the big screen by King-movie veteran Tom Holland, who directed *The Langoliers* and *Thinner*. Holland had discussed the project with King as far back as 1994, when *The Langoliers* was in production. "This was Stephen trying to deal with his cigarette jones and the fairly new no-smoking laws back in the '90s," Holland told *Deadline Hollywood*. "This film will be a modernization of the original short story, a paranoid suspense piece."

Holland disclosed more about his plans for the film to Jonathan James of the horror site *Daily Dead*. "It seemed to me that the themes that were in *The Ten O'Clock People* went further than just having a cigarette. I thought it was an interesting platform to make a metaphor of what could happen if things went wrong. What I've done is added a drug element. It's about people who have taken a stop smoking drug and went back to smoking. Then they start seeing things that they shouldn't be seeing."

Since the project was announced in the summer of 2012, several production start dates have come and gone. The film is tentatively scheduled for a 2014 release, but at this writing, the cast is not yet set. James Franco is "rumored" to star, according to the IMDb, but Justin Long and Chris Evans have also been reported to be in talks for the role, with Maine-born actress Rachel Nichols also attached.

Cell

King's 2006 novel *Cell* appears to have emerged from a long stint in development hell. The story revolves around a signal called "The Pulse" that is transmitted by cellular phones, turning those who hear it into zombies—which explains why King dedicated the book to both Richard Matheson and George Romero. Given the vast number of King projects to which Romero's name has been attached over the years, the father of the living dead would seem like the logical choice to direct the film adaptation of *Cell*. But when the rights to the novel were snapped up by Dimension Films only a few weeks after its publication, Eli Roth (*Cabin Fever*) was tapped to direct the film.

As the director explained it in an interview with *Now Playing* magazine, several producers tried to land the *Cell* rights, but King decided to go with Roth's producer Mike Fleiss because he'd enjoyed Roth's earlier horror movie *Hostel*. Roth was committed to making a sequel to *Hostel* and planned to make *Cell* as his follow-up. "I love zombie movies and I love horror movies that have some level of social commentary in them," Roth told *TV Guide*. "When you read that book, you feel that Stephen King has been driven crazy by people on cell phones. I think it's such a smart contemporary idea to have everyone on cell phones turn into psychotic serial killers."

Scott Alexander and Larry Karaszewski, the screenwriting duo behind *Ed Wood* and cowriters of *1408* with Matt Greenberg, were hired to adapt the novel. Roth planned to shoot the film in 2007 but later announced it would probably be late 2008 before production began. By 2009, Roth had dropped out of the project. The script still wasn't to his liking, and he had major disagreements with Dimension honchos Bob and Harvey Weinstein over the creative direction of the project.

In July 2009, *Fangoria* reported that *Tales from the Darkside* director John Harrison was writing *Cell* as a four-hour miniseries for the Weinstein Company. Nothing ever came of that incarnation of the project either, and *Cell* dropped back into limbo. Answering an audience question at a Wal-Mart book signing in November 2009, Stephen King announced that he'd just finished writing a screenplay for *Cell*. "I got so many complaints about the end of the book that I changed everything," he quipped.

Finally, in October 2012, former Dimension executive Richard Saperstein announced that he would produce a big-screen version of *Cell* with John Cusack attached to star. In February 2013, *Screen Daily* announced that Tod Williams (*Paranormal Activity 2*) had been hired to direct the film from a screenplay by King and Adam Alleca (*Last House on the Left*). However, during a Reddit AMA ("ask me anything") chat on February 27, Cusack said, "Stephen King is a great writer to work with. Doing a version of *Cell* with *War, Inc.* writer Mark Leyner. It should be another mind bender!" Filming was set to get underway in September 2013, with a release date yet to be determined.

It and the Stand

Both of these massive King novels became ABC miniseries in the early 1990s, and both are on track for big-screen remakes. As far back as 2009, Warner Bros. had been eyeing a feature film version of *It*, with *Variety* reporting that Dan Lin, Roy Lee, and Doug Davison would produce the film, to be scripted by David Kajganich (*Blood Creek*). In an interview with horror site Dread Central, Kajganich promised to deliver the goods. "I think the real twist here is that my pitch to WB—which they've assured me they're on board for—is that this will not be PG-13. This will be R. Which means we can really honor the book and engage with the traumas (both the paranormal ones and those they deal with at home and school) that these characters endure . . . I plan to be very protective of the book. The reality, though, is that WB wants to do this as a single film, so I will have to kill a few darlings to make that happen."

That version never got off the ground, but by June 2012 Warner Bros. was ready to revive the big-screen version of *It*, this time as two films. According to

Ben Affleck, seen here directing *The Town*, signed on to direct a big-screen adaptation of *The Stand*. Like many before him, he could not solve the narrative challenges posed by the book, and eventually left the project.

the *Hollywood Reporter*, Chase Palmer, who had penned an unproduced adaptation of Frank Herbert's *Dune* for Paramount, would script the movies, with Cary Fukunaga (*Jane Eyre*) directing. As of this writing, no casting or projected release date has been announced.

In January 2011, Warner Bros. announced it would also produce a feature film version of *The Stand*, in partnership with CBS Films. Warners had, of course, been involved with the first attempt at bringing King's massive novel to the big screen in the 1980s. In February, King told *Entertainment Weekly* "10 things I know about the remake of *The Stand*," including "I didn't know anything about the remake until I read about it on the Internet" and "You absolutely can't make it as a two-hour movie. If it was a trilogy of films . . . maybe."

In August of that year, Drew McWeeny of the entertainment site HitFix made the "exclusive" announcement that "Warner Bros. is in the process of finalizing the deals for David Yates and Steve Kloves to reteam for a multimovie version of Stephen King's epic *The Stand*." (Yates and Kloves had previously worked together on four of the Harry Potter movies.) In November, however, Yates told the fan site Collider, "I was offered *The Stand*. I love *The Stand*, I read it when I was a kid, it was one of my favorite books when I was growing up . . . My issues though were about the adaptation . . . I could see making a miniseries from it, a really interesting, intricate, layered, enjoyable long-burn of a miniseries, I could see that, but what was missing for me were the big movie moments in the material, the big set pieces."

Of course, *The Stand* already was a miniseries, and Warners wasn't interested in going that route again. By then, however, the studio had already found a new director for the project: Ben Affleck. Although his acting career had fallen on hard times, Affleck had remade himself as an acclaimed filmmaker with two Boston crime pictures, *Gone Baby Gone* and *The Town*, and has since gone on to direct the Best Picture–winning *Argo*. But *The Stand* would be a much larger-scale project than anything he'd tackled before.

By January 2012, the movie(s) had a writer: the ever-popular David Kajganich, who had already penned unproduced remakes of *It* and *Pet Sematary*. But by November of that year, it seemed history was repeating itself, as Affleck struggled with the same problems that had doomed the George Romero adaptation in the 1980s. A *GQ* article proclaiming Affleck the filmmaker of the year revealed, "Affleck is also working on an adaptation of Stephen King's *The Stand*, struggling to condense its epic nature into a manageable form. "Right now we're having a very hard time," he says. "But I like the idea—it's like *The Lord of the Rings* in America. And it's about how we would reinvent ourselves as a society. If we started all over again, what would we do?"

It's still unclear whether *The Stand* will be produced as one, two, or even three films should it actually make it to the screen this time. The revival took another blow when Affleck was cast as Batman in the *Man of Steel* sequel, forcing him to bow out. Scott Cooper, director of *Crazy Heart*, has been tapped to replace him. It's possible that *The Stand* will slip back into the depths of development hell, but King has made it clear that this time, he won't be dragged down with it.

The Dark Tower

In 2012, King added an eighth volume to what was already his most sprawling opus, the *Dark Tower* series. King had started writing the first story in 1970, but after typing up about ten pages, he set it aside. He picked it up again later in the decade, writing five short stories that were published in the *Magazine of Fantasy and Science Fiction* between 1978 and 1981 and later collected in a limited edition called *The Dark Tower: The Gunslinger*. This became the first chapter in the epic tale of Roland Deschain and his quest for the dark tower. King published three more installments before his 1999 car accident, then a final three volumes in the early twenty-first century. The *Dark Tower* mythology weaved through many of his other works, and elements from familiar King tales like *Salem's Lot* and *The Stand* found their way into Roland's quest. Even the author himself played a pivotal role in the story line. It was a hugely ambitious undertaking that developed a large, loyal following, but the prospect of adapting for the screen made the tortuous development of *The Stand* look like a walk in the park.

So it came as some surprise when King took the stage at New York's Comic-Con in February 2007 to announce that an adaptation of *The Dark Tower* was in the works. "I know J. J. Abrams' work and Damon Lindelof, who is his collabora-tor on *Lost*. Damon is just a total comic-book freak, and he loves the *Dark Tower* books. I trust those guys, and they have a lot on the ball. When they said they wanted to talk about doing this, I said, 'You know what? Why don't you buy the option on this and see what you can come up with.' They asked, 'How much do you want for an option?' I said, '$19.' . . . And that's what they paid me, and that's where it is."

The big question remained: What form would this adaptation take? A series of movies? A television series? By September 2008, Lindelof still didn't know. "*The Dark Tower* is to me every bit as daunting an adaptation as the *Lord of the Rings* trilogy must have been for Peter Jackson, except we've got seven books we're looking at," Lindelof told AMC. "There are always *Dark Tower* conversa-tions, but the figuring out of what this will look like as a movie has not begun." Abrams and Lindelof never did it figure out. "After working six years on *Lost*, the last thing I want to do is spend the next seven years adapting one of my favorite books of all time," Lindelof told *USA Today* in November 2009. "I'm such a mas-sive Stephen King fan that I'm terrified of screwing it up."

Only a few months later, in April 2010, the project was reborn with a new creative team: director Ron Howard, producer Brian Grazer, and writer Akiva Goldsman. Their plan for the material entailed an ambitious and expensive mul-timedia adaptation: a film trilogy as well as a television series. More details fol-lowed in September, when Universal Pictures signed on to the project: Howard would direct the first film, as well as the first season of the subsequent NBC television series. The series would serve as a bridge to the second film, which would in turn be followed by another season of the series, leading into the con-cluding feature. "The worlds of Stephen King's *The Dark Tower* series are richly detailed, inter-locking and deeply connected," Goldsman said in a press release. "By telling this story across media platforms and over multiple hours—and with a view to telling it completely—we have our best chance of translating Roland's quest to reach *The Dark Tower* onto screen."

Javier Bardem agreed to take on the role of the gunslinger Roland, but by mid-2011, Universal was beginning to get cold feet about the project. According to *Variety*, "Universal's unprecedented *Dark Tower* movie trilogy and interlock-ing TV series, seen as a hugely ambitious project from the start, may wind up being too big for the studio's appetite." In July, Universal announced that it was backing out of the project, leaving Ron Howard and Imagine scrambling to find another home for *The Dark Tower*. In October, Grazer told MTV News that HBO was onboard to do the television series, although no studio had yet signed on to finance the movies. Throughout 2012, Warner Bros. flirted with the project, but by August, they too had passed on it. On August 21, Deadline Hollywood reported that a new financier, Media Rights Capital, was in "serious negotiations" to take on *The Dark Tower*. As of mid-2013, Ron Howard had not given up on the project (both Netflix and a "mysterious Silicon Valley investor" were rumored to be showing interest), but it's starting to look like it may take as long for King's opus to reach the screen as it took him to write it in the first place.

Miscellaneous

The Breathing Method—The only one of the four novellas included in *Different Seasons* that has not previously been adapted for the screen is finally in the works. *Sinister* director Scott Derrickson is set to direct from a screenplay by Scott Teems. Jason Blum, whose company Blumhouse is behind *Mercy*, will produce.

Eyes of the Dragon—In April 2012, *Entertainment Weekly* reported that King's 1987 fantasy novel was being developed by SyFy, the network home of the *Haven* TV series. Michael Taylor (*Battlestar Galactica*) and Jeff Vintar (*I, Robot*) were hired to adapt the project, which could end up as either a TV-movie or a miniseries.

A Good Marriage—In September 2012, *The Hollywood Reporter* broke the news that this short story from *Full Dark, No Stars* was heading to the big screen. Peter Askin, who had directed the stage production of *Ghost Brothers of Darkland County*, would direct from a script written by King himself. Joan Allen signed on to play Darcy Anderson, a Maine woman who discovers her husband of nearly three decades is living a grisly double life.

Pet Sematary—A remake of the 1989 horror hit has been in the works at Paramount for some time. The first crack at the screenplay was given to David Kajganich, who had also worked on the *It* remake. When Paramount decided to go in a different, youth-oriented direction with the movie, *1408* screenwriter Matt Greenberg turned in a new draft. In August 2011, Twitchfilm reported that Paramount was trying to land Alexandre Aja (*High Tension*) to direct, but the project hasn't made much headway since then.

The Overlook Hotel—In June 2012, the *L.A. Times* reported that Warner Bros. was "quietly exploring the possibility of a prequel to *The Shining.*" The studio solicited *Shutter Island* screenwriter Laeta Kalogridis to develop a story that would explore the history of the Overlook Hotel before the events depicted in the Kubrick film. As of April 2013, Glen Mazzara, former showrunner of *The Walking Dead*, was in talks to write the screenplay.

Between the time I write these words and the time you hold this book in your hands, some of these projects may have come to fruition, others may have been abandoned, and undoubtedly at least a half-dozen more King-related films and television shows will have been announced. Some long-dormant projects, like *The Talisman* and *11/22/63*, may even have come back to life. And of course, as long as Stephen King keeps up his prolific pace, there will be new grist for the Hollywood mill. Two new King novels appeared in 2013, the crime thriller *Joyland* (already optioned by Tate Taylor, writer and director of *The Help*) and the much-anticipated sequel to *The Shining*, *Doctor Sleep*. Somewhere in the future, their movie adaptations no doubt await.

Bibliography

Baxter, John, *Stanley Kubrick: A Biography* (HarperCollins, 1997)

Bjorkman, Stig, *Trier on von Trier* (Faber & Faber, 2003)

Bliss, Michael, *Brian De Palma* (Scarecrow Press, 1983)

Boulenger, Gilles, *John Carpenter: The Prince of Darkness* (Silman-James Press, 2003)

Bouzereau, Laurent, *The De Palma Cut* (Dembner Books, 1988)

Conner, Jeff, *Stephen King Goes to Hollywood* (Plume, 1987)

Cronin, Paul, *Herzog on Herzog* (Faber & Faber, 2003)

Darabont, Frank, *Shawshank Redemption: The Shooting Script* (Newmarket, 2004)

Frank, Alan, *The Films of Roger Corman* (B. T. Batsford, 1998)

Goldman, William, *Which Lie Did I Tell?* (Knopf Doubleday, 2000)

Howard, James, *Stanley Kubrick Companion* (B.T. Batsford, 1999)

Jones, Stephen, *Creepshows: The Illustrated Stephen King Movie Guide* (Crown, 2002)

King, Stephen, *Storm of the Century: An Original Screenplay* (Pocket, 1999)

Knapp, Laurence F., *Brian De Palma: Interviews* (University Press of Mississippi, 2003)

Lloyd, Ann, *The Films of Stephen King* (St. Martin's, 1994)

Magistrale, Tony, *Hollywood's Stephen King* (Palgrave MacMillan, 2003)

Muir, John Kenneth, *Eaten Alive at a Chainsaw Massacre* (McFarland, 2002)

Muir, John Kenneth, *The Films of John Carpenter* (McFarland, 2001)

Muir, John Kenneth, *Horror Films of the 1980s* (McFarland, 2007)

Naha, Ed, *The Films of Roger Corman: Brilliance on a Budget* (Arco, 1982)

Prawer, S. S., *Caligari's Children: The Film as Tale of Terror* (Da Capo Press, 1989)

Rhodes, Gary, ed., *Horror at the Drive-In: Essays in Popular Americana* (McFarland, 2008)

Rodley, Chris, ed. *Cronenberg on Cronenberg* (Faber & Faber, 1997)

Skal, David J., *The Monster Show: A Cultural History of Horror* (W. W. Norton, 1993)

Spadoni, Robert, *Uncanny Bodies: The Coming of Sound Film and the Origins of the Horror Genre* (Berkeley: University of California Press, 2007)

Underwood, Tim and Miller, Chuck, *Bare Bones: Conversations on Terror with Stephen King* (McGraw-Hill, 1988)

Index

THE FAQ SERIES